Kotlin In-Depth

2nd Edition

A Guide to a Multipurpose Programming Language for Server-Side, Front-End, Android, and Multiplatform Mobile

Aleksei Sedunov

www.bpbonline.com

FIRST EDITION 2020

SECOND EDITION 2022

Copyright © BPB Publications, India

ISBN: 978-93-91030-63-6

Distributors:

BPB PUBLICATIONS
20, Ansari Road, Darya Ganj
New Delhi-110002
Ph: 23254990/23254991

DECCAN AGENCIES
4-3-329, Bank Street,
Hyderabad-500195
Ph: 24756967/24756400

MICRO MEDIA
Shop No. 5, Mahendra Chambers,
150 DN Rd. Next to Capital Cinema,
V.T. (C.S.T.) Station, MUMBAI-400 001
Ph: 22078296/22078297

BPB BOOK CENTRE
376 Old Lajpat Rai Market,
Delhi-110006
Ph: 23861747

To View Complete
BPB Publications Catalogue
Scan the QR Code:

Published by Manish Jain for BPB Publications, 20 Ansari Road, Darya Ganj, New Delhi-110002 and Printed by him at Repro India Ltd, Mumbai

www.bpbonline.com

Dedicated to

Tatiana,
my guiding light
and the incessant source of inspiration

About the Author

Aleksei Sedunov has been working as a Java developer since 2008. After joining JetBrains in 2012, he's been actively participating in the Kotlin language development focusing on IDE tooling for the IntelliJ platform. Currently, he's working in a DataGrip team, a JetBrains Database IDE, carrying on with using Kotlin as the main development tool.

About the Reviewers

Sanjay Kakadiya is currently working as a Sr Software developer of the e-commerce Android app. He completed his Bachelor of Engineering in IT from Gujarat University in 2012 and has more than 9 years of experience in mobile application development using Java, React Native, and Kotlin. He has been a co-organizer of the Ahmedabad Web and Mobile Developers Meetup group since 2015. He is a Kotlin and Java addict. He is obsessed with the elegant and functional style code. He mainly focuses on the mobile apps architecture.

Sanjay has created and improvised dozens of successful applications for clients in areas of social networking, education, video streaming, entertainment, self-help, fitness, lifestyle, and commerce.

Touhidul Islam is currently working as a mobile engineer at Toptal. He has a good grasp at data structure and algorithms and an eye for better architecture. Although, he has professional software experience in both cross-platform mobile and back-end technologies, he shines on native Android development. He has hands-on experience working at startups from his early career and one of the software developed by him earns about 40% of the revenue for that company. He later joined a big tech company developing pixel-perfect customer-facing mobile software and led the development there. He is currently working with Australia's one of the leading service provider companies to revolutionize how people interact with service providers.

Acknowledgments

Above all others, I would like to give my gratitude to the entire Kotlin team at JetBrains which has created such a beautiful language and continues to relentlessly work on its improvement – especially Andrey Breslav who's been leading the language design from the very first day.

I'm really grateful to everyone at BPB Publications for giving me this splendid opportunity for writing this book and lending a tremendous support in improving the text before it gets to the readers. Many thanks to Sanjay Kakadiya and Touhidul Islam for their great help as technical reviewers for the second edition.

Last but not least, I'd like to thank my beloved family for their support throughout the work on the book.

Preface

Since its first release in 2016 (and even long before that), Kotlin has been gaining popularity as a powerful and flexible tool in a multitude of development tasks being equally well-equipped for dealing with mobile, desktop, and server-side applications and finally, getting its official acknowledgment from Google in 2017 and 2018 as a primary language for Android development. This popularity is well-justified since language pragmatism, the tendency to choose the best practice among known solutions was one of the guiding principles of its design.

With the book you're holding in your hands, I'd like to invite you to the beautiful world of Kotlin programming where you can see its benefits for yourself. After completing this book, you'll have all the necessary knowledge to write in Kotlin on your own.

The first volume deals with the fundamentals of Kotlin language such as its basic syntax, procedural, object-oriented, and functional programming aspects as well as the Kotlin Standard Library. The book is divided into 9 chapters as follows:

Chapter 1 explains key ideas behind the language design, gives an overview of the Kotlin ecosystem and tooling, and guides the reader through the first steps required to set up a Kotlin project in various environments.

Chapter 2 introduces the reader to the Kotlin syntax, explains how to use variables, and describes simple data types such as integers or Boolean values as well as their built-in operations. It also addresses the basics of more complex data structures such as strings and arrays.

Chapter 3 discusses the syntax of Kotlin functions and explains the uses of various control structures supported by Kotlin such as binary/multiple choice, iteration, and error handling. Additionally, it addresses the matter of using packages for code structuring.

Chapter 4 introduces the reader to the basic aspects of object-oriented programming in Kotlin. It explains how to create and initialize a class instance and how to control member access, describe the use of object declarations and non-trivial kinds of properties, and brings up the concept of type nullability.

Chapter 5 explains the functional aspects of Kotlin and introduces the reader to the idea of higher-order and anonymous functions, addresses the uses of inline functions, and explains how one can add features to existing types using extension functions and properties.

Chapter 6 explains the use of special kinds of classes tailored at specific programming tasks: data classes for simple data holders, enumerations for representing a fixed set of instances, and inline classes for creating lightweight wrappers.

Chapter 7 explores object-oriented features introduced in Chapters 4 and 6 focusing on the idea of a class hierarchy. It explains how to define subclasses, how to use abstract classes and interfaces, and how to restrict hierarchies using sealed classes.

Chapter 8 describes a major part of the Kotlin standard library which is concerned with various collection types and their operations as well as utilities simplifying file access and stream-based I/O.

Chapter 9 introduces the idea of generic declarations and explains how to define and use generic classes, functions, and properties in Kotlin. It also explains the notion of variance and how it can be used to improve flexibility of your generic code.

The second volume introduces you to the more advanced Kotlin features such as reflection, domain-specific languages and coroutines, discusses Java/Kotlin interoperability issues, and explains how Kotlin can be used in various development areas, including testing, Android applications, and Web. It's divided into the following 8 chapters:

Chapter 10 addresses the use of annotations which allow you to accompany the Kotlin code with various metadata and explains the basics of Reflection API which provides access to runtime representation of Kotlin declarations.

Chapter 11 describes some advanced features which help developer in composing flexible APIs in the form of the domain-specific languages: operator overloading, delegated properties, and builder-style DSLs based on the higher-order functions.

Chapter 12 discusses common issues of combining Java and Kotlin code within the same codebase and explains the specifics of using Java declarations in Kotlin code and vice versa.

Chapter 13 introduces the reader to the Kotlin coroutines library which introduces a set of building blocks for programming asynchronous computations. Additionally, it describes some utilities simplifying the use of Java concurrency API in Kotlin code.

Chapter 14 discusses the KotlinTest, a popular testing framework aimed specifically at the Kotlin developers. It describes various specification styles, explains the use of assertion API, and addresses more advanced issues like using fixtures and test configurations.

Chapter 15 serves as an introduction to using Kotlin for development on the Android platform. It guides the reader through setting up an Android Studio project and explains basic aspects of Android development using an example of a simple calculator application.

Chapter 16 explains the basic features of the Ktor framework aimed at development of connected applications which make heavy use of Kotlin features and asynchronous computations.

Chapter 17 describes how to build a microservice application using Spring Boot and Ktor frameworks.

Code Bundle and Coloured Images

Please follow the link to download the
Code Bundle and the *Coloured Images* of the book:

https://rebrand.ly/04dc29

The code bundle for the book is also hosted on GitHub at **https://github.com/bpbpublications/Kotlin-In-Depth**. In case there's an update to the code, it will be updated on the existing GitHub repository.

We have code bundles from our rich catalogue of books and videos available at **https://github.com/bpbpublications**. Check them out!

Errata

We take immense pride in our work at BPB Publications and follow best practices to ensure the accuracy of our content to provide with an indulging reading experience to our subscribers. Our readers are our mirrors, and we use their inputs to reflect and improve upon human errors, if any, that may have occurred during the publishing processes involved. To let us maintain the quality and help us reach out to any readers who might be having difficulties due to any unforeseen errors, please write to us at :

errata@bpbonline.com

Your support, suggestions and feedbacks are highly appreciated by the BPB Publications' Family.

Did you know that BPB offers eBook versions of every book published, with PDF and ePub files available? You can upgrade to the eBook version at www.bpbonline.com and as a print book customer, you are entitled to a discount on the eBook copy. Get in touch with us at :

business@bpbonline.com for more details.

At **www.bpbonline.com**, you can also read a collection of free technical articles, sign up for a range of free newsletters, and receive exclusive discounts and offers on BPB books and eBooks.

Piracy

If you come across any illegal copies of our works in any form on the internet, we would be grateful if you would provide us with the location address or website name. Please contact us at **business@bpbonline.com** with a link to the material.

If you are interested in becoming an author

If there is a topic that you have expertise in, and you are interested in either writing or contributing to a book, please visit **www.bpbonline.com**. We have worked with thousands of developers and tech professionals, just like you, to help them share their insights with the global tech community. You can make a general application, apply for a specific hot topic that we are recruiting an author for, or submit your own idea.

Reviews

Please leave a review. Once you have read and used this book, why not leave a review on the site that you purchased it from? Potential readers can then see and use your unbiased opinion to make purchase decisions. We at BPB can understand what you think about our products, and our authors can see your feedback on their book. Thank you!

For more information about BPB, please visit **www.bpbonline.com**.

Table of Contents

CHAPTER 1
Kotlin - Powerful and Pragmatic

This chapter is meant to explain the major features which make Kotlin an excellent and efficient language for modern application development and the reasons why you might want to learn it. We'll learn the basic ideas which stand behind the Kotlin design and get an overview of Kotlin libraries and frameworks for different application areas such as Android applications, concurrency, testing and web development. In conclusion, we'll guide you through the steps required to set up a Kotlin project in two popular development environments, IntelliJ IDEA and Eclipse, and introduce you to the interactive Kotlin shell.

Structure

We will cover the following topics:

- What is Kotlin?
- Major components of the Kotlin ecosystem
- Setting up a Kotlin project in IDE and online editors

Objectives

At the end of the chapter, you'll get an understanding of the basic Kotlin principles and the Kotlin ecosystem as well as what simple a Kotlin program looks like and you will be able to set up a project in common IDEs.

What is Kotlin?

Kotlin is a multiplatform and multiparadigm programming language emphasizing safety, conciseness, and interoperability. Conceived in late 2010, it had reached its first release in February 2016 and has been steadily becoming an increasingly popular and promising tool in many development areas such as Android development, desktop applications, or server-side solutions. The company which stands behind the language and has been investing in its development ever since is JetBrains which is famous for its excellent software engineering tools such as IntelliJ IDEA. By August 2020, Kotlin had reached version 1.4, acquiring massive community, well-developed ecosystems, and extensive tooling. Having overgrown an original intent of creating a better Java alternative, it now embraces multiple platforms, including Java Virtual Machine, Android, JavaScript, and native applications. In 2017, Google announced Kotlin an officially supported language of the Android platform which gave a tremendous boost to the language popularity. Nowadays, a lot of companies – among them Google, Amazon, Netflix, Pinterest, Uber, and many others – are using Koltin for production development, and the number of open positions for Kotlin developers is growing steadfast.

It all became possible thanks to the efforts devoted to the careful language design and putting into action the primary traits which make Kotlin such an excellent development tool. The language philosophy has mainly arisen based on the problems it was intended to solve back in 2010. By that time, JetBrains had already accumulated an extensive Java code base for products centered around its IntelliJ platform which was arguably the most known IntelliJ IDEA, had also included a set of minor IDEs dedicated to different technologies such as WebStorm, PhpStorm, RubyMine, etc. The maintenance and growth of such codebase, however, was being hampered by Java itself due to its slow evolution and lack of many useful features which at that moment had already been available in such languages as Scala and C#. Having researched the JVM languages available at that moment, the company concluded that no existing language proved satisfiable for their needs and decided to invest resources into implementation of their own language. The new language was eventually named Kotlin as a tribute to an island near Saint-Peteresburg, Russia where most of its development team was located.

So what are those traits which have been shaping the language from the very beginning? In fact, we've already given the answer in its definition. The reason behind Kotlin is a need for a *multiparadigm* language emphasizing *safety, conciseness,* and *interoperability*. Let's look at these traits in more detail.

Safe

For a programming language, being *safe* means being able to prevent a programmer's errors. In practice, designing the language with respect to safety is a matter of tradeoff since error prevention typically comes at a cost. You give the compiler more detailed information about your program or allow it to spend more time reasoning about it correctness (probably both). One of Kotlin design goals was to find a sort of golden mean; contriving a language with more stronger safety guarantees than Java, but not so strong to frustrate a developer's productivity. And although the Kotlin solution is by no means absolute, it has repeatedly proved to be an efficient choice in practice.

We'll discuss various aspects of Kotlin safety as we go through the book. Here, we'd like to point out some major features:

- Type inference which allows the developer to omit explicit declaration types in most cases (Java 10 introduced this for local variables)
- Nullable types regulate the usage of null and help to prevent infamous NullPointerException
- Smart casts which simplify type casting reducing the chance of casting errors at runtime

Multiparadigm

Initially, the meaning behind Kotlin multiparadigmality implied the support of *functional* programming in addition to the conventional *object-oriented* paradigm typical for many mainstream programming languages such as Java. The functional programming is based around the idea of using functions as values: passing them as parameters or returning from other functions, declaring locally, storing in variables, etc. Another aspect of the functional paradigm is an idea of immutability which means that objects you manipulate can't change their state once created and functions can't produce side effects.

The major benefit of this approach is improved programming flexibility. Being able to create a new kind of abstraction, you can write more expressive and concise code, thus increasing your productivity. Note that although functional programming principles can be employed in many languages (Java's anonymous classes, for example, were an obvious choice before introduction of lambdas), not every language has necessary syntactic facilities encouraging the writing of such code. Kotlin, on the contrary, included necessary features right from the start. They include, in particular, functional types smoothly integrating functions into the language type systems and lambda expressions meant to create functionally-typed values from code blocks. The standard library as well as external frameworks provides an extensive API facilitating the functional style. Nowadays, many of that also apply to Java which had introduced functional programming support starting with Java 8. But its expressiveness still somewhat falls behind Kotlin's.

We'll cover the basics of functional programming in *Chapter 5, Leveraging Advanced Functions and Functional Programming*, but its applications and examples will accompany us throughout the book.

Over its growth, the language also began to exhibit two more programming paradigms. Thanks to the ability to design APIs in the form of domain-specific languages (DSLs) Kotlin can be used in a *declarative* style. In fact, many Kotlin frameworks provide their own DSLs for specific tasks with no need to sacrifice type-safety or expressive power of the general-purpose programming language. For example, the exposed framework includes a DSL for defining database schema and manipulating its data, whereas kotlinx.html gives a concise and type-safe alternative to HTML template languages. In *Chapter 11, Domain-Specific Languages,* we'll discuss these examples in more detail as well as learn how to create our own DSLs.

One more paradigm, namely, *concurrent programming*, entered the language with the introduction of coroutines. Although, concurrency support by itself is present in many languages, including Java, the Kotlin features a rich set of programming patterns which enable a new programming approach. We'll cover the basics of this approach in *Chapter 13, Concurrency*.

All in all, the presence of multiple paradigms greatly increases the language's expressive power, making it a more flexible and multi-purposed tool.

Concise and expressive

Developer productivity is largely tied with the ability to quickly read and understand the code, be it some other developer's work or maybe your own after a significant time has passed. In order to understand what a specific piece of code does, you need to also understand how it's related to other parts of your program. That's why reading the existing code generally takes more time than writing a new one and that's why language conciseness and the ability to clearly express a programmer's intents without much information noise is a crucial aspect of language efficiency as a development tool.

The designers of Kotlin did their best to make language as concise as possible, eliminating a lot of notorious Java boilerplate such as field getters and setters, anonymous classes, explicit delegation, and so on. On the other hand, they made sure the conciseness is not overtly abused – unlike Scala; for example, Kotlin doesn't allow the programmer to define custom operators, but only redefine existing ones since the former tends to obfuscate the operation meaning. In the course of the book, we'll see numerous implications of this decision and how useful it turned to be.

Another aspect of Kotlin's conciseness is tightly related to the DSLs (see *Chapter 11, Domain-Specific Languages* which greatly simplify the description of specific programming domains with a minimum of syntactic noise.

Interoperable

Java interoperability was a major point in Kotlin design since the Kotlin code wasn't mean to exist in isolation, but to cooperate as smoothly as possible with the existing codebase. That's why Kotlin designers made sure that not only the existing Java code can be used from Kotlin, but that Kotlin code can also be used from Java with little to no effort. The language also includes a set features specifically meant to tune interoperability between Java and Kotlin.

As the language overgrew, the JVM and spread to other platforms, interoperability guarantees were extended as well to cover interaction with JavaScript code for the JS platform and C/C++/Objective C/Swift code for native applications.

We'll devote *Chapter 12, Java Interoperability,* to discuss the Java interoperability issues and how Kotlin and Java can be mixed together in the same project.

Multiplatform

Multiplatformity wasn't an original intent of Kotlin designers, but rather manifested itself as a result of language evolution and adaptation to the needs of the development community. While JVM and Android remain a primary target of Kotlin development, nowadays the supported platforms also cover the following:

- JavaScript, including browser and Node.js applications as well as JavaScript libraries
- Native applications and libraries for macOS, Linux and Windows

Since 1.3 Kotlin supports multiplatform development with major uses cases being sharing the code between Android and iOS applications and creating multiplatform libraries for JVM/JS/Native world.

Kotlin ecosystem

Throughout its evolution, Kotlin has given rise to a rich set of libraries and frameworks covering most of software development aspects. Here, we will try to give you an overview of available tools which hopefully will serve as a guide in this ocean of possibilities. Note, however, that as the ecosystem is continuously growing, the state-of-the-art presented in this book at the moment that is being written will inevitably fall out of date, so don't hesitate looking for it by yourself. A good starting point is a community-updated list of libraries and frameworks available on the *Awesome Kotlin* website at https://interlink.

It's also worth noting that thanks to well-conceived Java interoperability Kotlin applications may benefit from a whole lot of existing Java libraries. In some cases, they have specific Kotlin extensions allowing one to write more idiomatic code.

Coroutines

Thanks to the concept of suspendable computations, Kotlin is able to support concurrency-related programming patterns such as aync/await, futures, promises, and actors. The Coroutines framework provide a powerful, elegant, and easily scalable solution to concurrency problems in the Kotlin application whether it is a server-side, mobile, or desktop one. The major features of the coroutines include, among others:

- A lightweight alternative to threads
- Flexible thread dispatching mechanism
- Suspendable sequences an iterators
- Sharing memory via channels
- Using actors to share mutable state via message sending

We'll cover the basics of the coroutine API in *Chapter 13, Concurrency,* which deals with concurrency issues in Kotlin.

Testing frameworks

Apart from familiar Java testing frameworks such as JUnit, TestNG, and Mockito which can be with little effort employed in a Kotlin application, the developers can enjoy the power of Kotlin-tailored frameworks providing useful DSLs for testing purposes; be it test definitions or mocking your objects. In particular, we'd like to point out the following:

- *Mockito-Kotlin*, an extension for the popular Mockito framework simplifying object mocking in Kotlin.

- *Spek*, a behavior-driven testing framework supporting Jasmine- and Gherkin-styled definition of test cases.

- *KotlinTest*, a ScalaTest-inspired framework which supports flexible test definitions and assertions.

In *Chapter 14, Testing with Kotlin,* we'll pay more attention to the features provided by Spek and Mockito and consider how to use them in your projects.

Android development

Android is one of the major and most actively growing application areas of Kotlin. This has become especially relevant after Google's announced the Kotlin a first-class Android language implying, in particular, that Android tooling is now being designed and developed with due regard to the Kotlin features as well. Apart from the excellent programming experience brought by the Android Studio plugin, Android developers can benefit from the smooth interoperability with many popular frameworks such as Dagger, ButterKnife, and DBFlow. Among Kotlin-specific Android tools, we'd like to pay attention to Anko and Kotlin Android Extensions:

- *Kotlin Android Extensions* is a compiler plugin whose main feature is data-binding which allows you to use XML-defined views as if they're implicitly defined in your code, thus avoiding the infamous findViewById() calls. It supports view caching and the ability to automatically generate Parcelable implementations for user-defined classes. Thanks to this there is no need to employ external frameworks like ButterKnife in pure Kotlin projects.

- *Anko* is a Kotlin library which simplifies the development of Android applications. In addition to numerous helpers, it includes a domain-specific language (*Anko Layouts*) for composing dynamical layouts accompanied by the UI preview plugin for Android Studio as well database query DSL based around Android SQLite.

We'll cover some of these features in *Chapter 15, Android Applications,* which introduces the reader to Kotlin-powered Android development.

Web development

Web/Enterprise application developers can also benefit from using Kotlin. Popular frameworks such as Spring 5.0 and Vert.x 3.0 include Kotlin-specific extensions which allow you to use their functionality in more Kotlin-idiomatic way. You can employ pure Kotlin solutions using a variety of frameworks:

- *Ktor* a JetBrains framework for creating an asynchronous server and client applications.
- *kotlinx.html* a domain-specific language for building HTML documents.
- *Kodein* a dependency injection framework.

We'll discuss specifics of building web applications and microservices using Ktor and Spring in *Chapter 16, Web Development with Ktor* and *Chapter 17, Building Microservices,* respectively.

Desktop applications

Developers of desktop applications for the JVM platform can employ *TornadoFX,* a JavaFX-based framework. It provides helpful domain-specific languages for building GUI and style description via CSS, support FXML markup, and MVC/ MVP architecture. It also comes with an IntelliJ plugin simplifying the generation of TornadoFX projects, views, and other components.

Getting started with Kotlin

Now, you should have an idea of the Kotlin ecosystem, and the only thing we need to discuss before we can start exploring the language is how to set up a working environment.

Setting up an IntelliJ project

Although Kotlin by itself, like most programming languages, is not tied to a particular IDE or text editor, the choice of development tools has a great impact on the developer's productivity. As of now, the JetBrains IntelliJ platform provides the most powerful and comprehensive support of the Kotlin development lifecycle. Right from the start, Kotlin IDE has been developed in tight integration with the language itself which helps it to stay up-to-date with Kotlin changes. For these reasons, we recommend using it for your own projects and employ it for the examples in the book.

Since IntelliJ IDEA 15 Kotlin support is bundled into the IDE distribution, you won't need to install any external plugins to facilitate Kotlin development. For this book, we've been using IntelliJ IDEA 2020.3 released in the late December, 2020.

If you don't have an IDEA installed, you can download the latest version from www.jetbrains.com/idea/download and follow the installation instructions from https://www.jetbrains.com/help/idea/install-and-set-up-product.html. IDEA comes in two editions: Community which is free and open-source and Ultimate which is a commercial product. The major difference is that the Ultimate edition includes a set of features related to the development of web and enterprise applications as well as database tools. You can find a more detailed list of changes at the download page. For this book, we won't need the Ultimate features, so IDEA Community is more than enough.

If you haven't opened a project in IntelliJ before, you'll see a welcome screen on startup where you can click on the *Create New Project* option to go directly to the project wizard dialog box. Otherwise, IntelliJ opens the recently edited project(s); in this case, choose **File** | **New** | **Project** in the application menu.

Project types are grouped into categories you can see in the left pane. The exact set of categories and projects depends on the plugin installed, but for now, we're interested in the *Kotlin* category which is available out-of-the box thanks to the bundled Kotlin plugin. When you click on it, you'll see the list of available project templates (*Figure 1.1*):

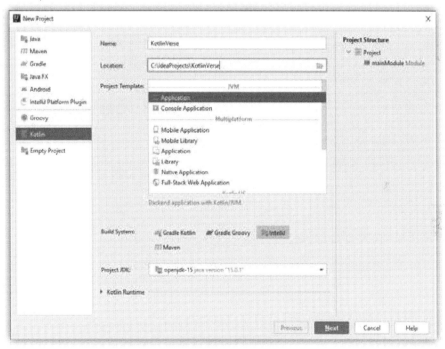

Figure 1.1: *New project wizard (step 1)*

As of version 1.4.21 (which we've used when writing this book), the Kotlin plugin supports creating of projects targeting JVM, JavaScript, native applications as well several cases of multiplatform projects such as mobile applications targeting both Android and iOS. The platform determines both the type of compiler artifacts (bytecode for the JVM, .js files for JavaScript, and platform-specific executables for Kotlin/Native) and a set of available dependencies your project can use; a project targeting JavaScript, for example, can't access classes from the Java class library. As we go ahead, our primary interest will be the JVM applications, so for this example, we'll choose the corresponding option in the *JVM* group.

The wizard also allows you to choose a particular build system for automating common tasks related to the project lifecycle: compilation, testing, packaging, publication, and so on. Detailed treatment of a particular build system specifics goes beyond the scope of the book and has little effect on our code examples apart from the project file structure. So in this tutorial, we'll just choose *IntelliJ* as the default option before proceeding with project creation.

Besides that, you'll need to provide the project name and location which is a root directory for the project-related content, including its source files. Note that IntelliJ suggests the location automatically based on the project name you've typed, but you can change it if necessary.

Since our project targets the JVM platform, we also have to specify a default JDK to use for the project compilation. That would allow our project to use classes from the Java standard library as well as compile Java sources in mixed-language projects. In *Chapter 12, Java Interoperability*, we'll cover such projects in more detail and also discuss how to introduce Kotlin support to the existing Java projects.

We recommend using JDK 8 or higher. For this example, we've chosen the latest (as of the book's writing) release version of Oracle OpenJDK 15. Usually, IntelliJ auto-detects the JDK installed on your machine, but if that doesn't happen or none of preconfigured JDKs in the Project SDK list suit your purposes, you can add a new one by choosing **Add JDK** options specifying the path to some preinstalled JDK instance, or **Download JDK** to have IDE download one of the popular JDK implementations (such as OpenJDK or Corretto) for you.

One more thing worth mentioning is a Kotlin runtime library the IntelliJ has preconfigured for our project. By default, the project will reference a library in the IDE plugin directory which means it's upgraded automatically whenever you update the plugin itself. If you, however, want your project to depend on a particular version of Kotlin runtime, only updating it manually out of necessity, you may change that behavior. To do that, expand the **Kotlin Runtime** group, click on the **Create** button and choose the **Copy to** option specifying the directory name where the library needs to be kept.

Clicking on the **Next** button will bring the second step of the project wizard where you can specify additional options such as minimum JVM version on which your application is supposed to run, a test framework, and a predefined template the IDE will use to generate the initial project structure (for example; a console or Ktor-based web application). The example of step 2 is shown in *Figure 1.2*:

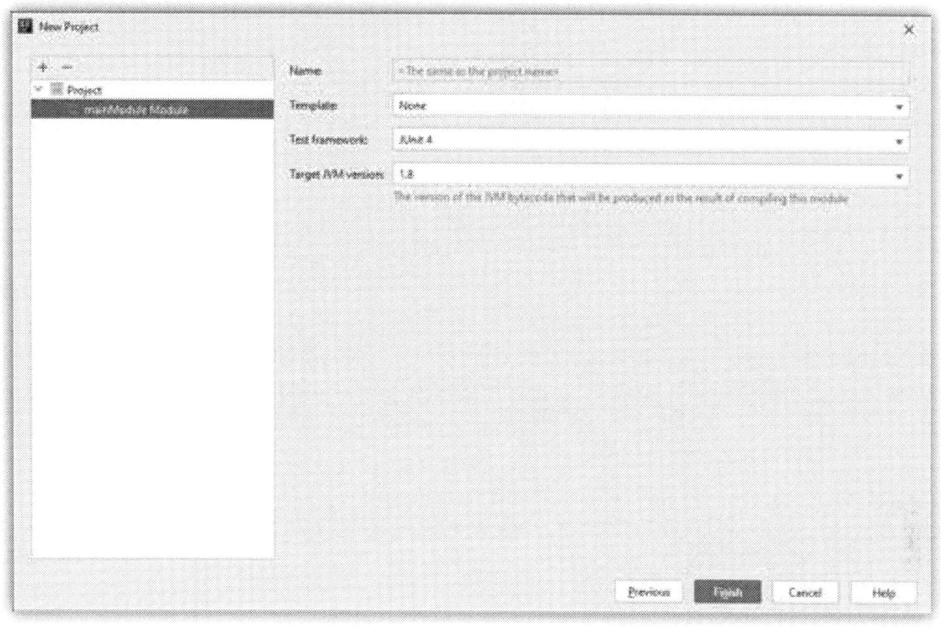

Figure 1.2: *New project wizard (step 2)*

In the final step, click on the **Finish** button and you will get IntelliJ to generate and open an empty project. By default, IntelliJ presents it in a two-panel view: Project tool window on the left and the editor area occupying most of the remaining area. The editor is initially empty since we haven't opened a single file yet, so we'll first focus on the Project window and use it to create a new Kotlin file.

If the Project tool window is absent, you can bring it by clicking on the **Project** button (usually, it's on the left-hand side of the window border) or using the shortcut *Alt+1* (Meta+1).

The **Project** window shows the hierarchical structure of your project. Let's expand the root nodes and see what it contains (*Figure 1.3*). Currently, we're mostly interested in the following three items:

- **src** directory which serves as a **content root** containing project source files.
- **out** directory where the compiler puts the generated bytecode (absent initially but created automatically on project compilation).
- External Libraries which list all libraries the project depends on.

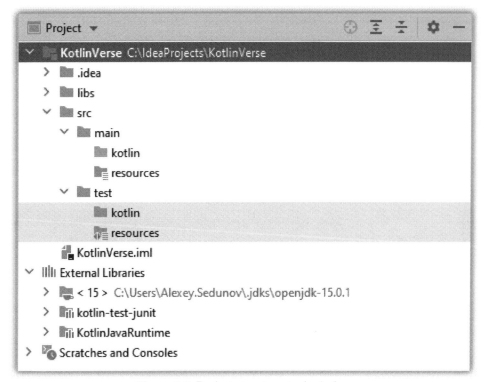

***Figure 1.3:** Project structure tool window*

Now, right-click on the **src/main/kotlin** directory and select the **New | Kotlin File/Class** command. In the dialog box that follows, type a file name **main.kt.** Make sure that the **Kind** field is set to **File** and click on **OK**. You'll see the **Project** window updated to show a new file which is at the same time opened in the editor. Note that Kotlin source files must have the **.kt** extension.

At last, we're ready to write an actual code. Let's type the following in the editor window (*Figure 1.3*):

```
fun main() {

    println("Hello, KotlinVerse!")

}
```

The preceding code defines the **main** function which serves as an entry-point for the Kotlin application. The function body consists of a single statement, a call to the standard library function **println()** writing its argument to the program's standard output with a new line added at the end.

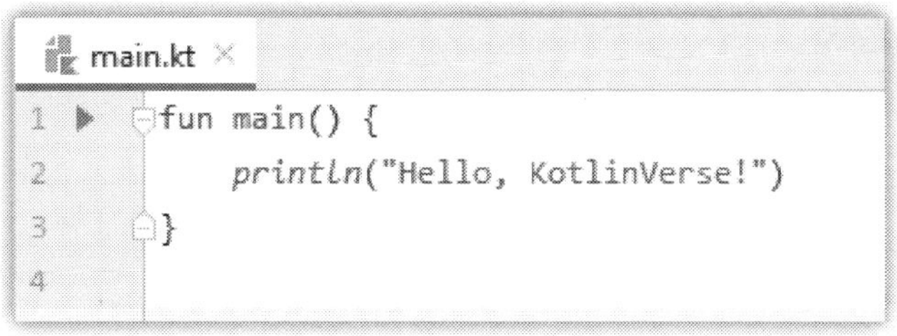

```
main.kt ×
1  ▶  ⊟fun main() {
2           println("Hello, KotlinVerse!")
3       ⊟}
4
```

Figure 1.4: *"Hello, World" program*

Java developers will surely recognize a similarity between this code and the following Java program:

```
public class Main {

  public static void main(String[] args) {

    System.out.println("Hello, World!")

  }

}
```

In fact, JVM's version of the Kotlin **println()** function is just a call to **System.out. println()**. Since the JVM entry-point must be a static class method, you might be wondering how the Kotlin application is started without defining a single class. The answer is that although we haven't defined a class *explicitly*, the Kotlin compiler will create one behind the scenes, putting there the JVM's entry-point which in turn would call our **main()** function. We'll get back to these so called *facade classes* in *Chapter 12, Java Interoperability* because they constitute a major aspect of Kotlin/Java interoperability.

Also, note that unlike the JVM entry-point which is supposed to take an array of command-line arguments as its parameter, our **main()** function has no parameters at all. This comes in handy for the cases when command-line arguments are not used. If necessary, however, you can still define the entry-point taking these arguments:

```
fun main(args: Array<String>) {

    println(args)

}
```

Parameterless **main()** is in fact a comparatively recent feature introduced in Kotlin 1.3. In earlier language versions, the only acceptable entry point was the one taking the **String<Array>** argument just like its Java counterpart.

This feature took further development in Kotlin 1.4 where the compiler produces a warning if the **main()** parameter is not really used in the function's body (see *Figure 1.5*):

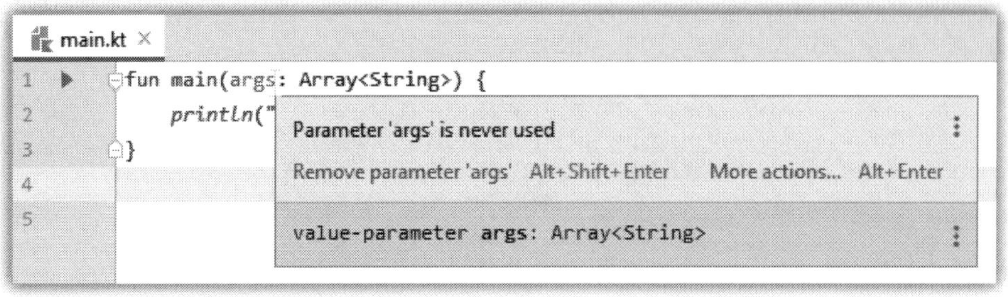

Figure 1.5: Unused parameter in the main() function

You might've noticed a small green triangle on the left-hand side of the **main()** definition. This *line marker* indicates that function **main()**, being an entry-point, is executable. Clicking on that marker brings up a menu which allows you to run or debug its code. Let's choose the **Run MainKt** option and see what happens (*Figure 1.6*).

MainKt, by the way, is the name of the compiler-generated facade class we mentioned earlier. On choosing the Run command, IntelliJ compiles our code and executes the program. The Run tool window which is opened on program startup gets automatically linked to its standard I/O streams serving as a built-in console. If you've done everything correctly, the program will print **Hello, KotlinVerse** to the console and terminate successfully.

Figure 1.6: Running a program

If you look inside the out directory, you will see the .class files generated by the Kotlin compiler from our source program.

Congratulations! You now have an understanding of how to set up and run a Kotlin project in the IntelliJ IDEA environment, and you are ready to delve into the language fundamentals. KotlinVerse, here we go!

Using REPL

Kotlin plugin for IntelliJ provides an interactive shell which allows you to evaluate program instructions on-the-fly. This can be used for quick testing of your code or experimenting with library functions. It is also quite handy for those who are just learning the Kotlin language. This feature is called REPL. The meaning behind this name is "Read/Evaluate/Print Loop" because that's what the shell does. The reading code the user has typed, evaluates it, prints the result (if any), and loops the whole thing over. In order to access the REPL, select **Tools** | **Kotlin** | **Kotlin REPL**.

You can type the Kotlin code in the REPL window just like you do it in the editor. The major difference is that each piece of code is compiled and executed right after you enter it. Once the code is typed, you need to press *Ctrl + Enter* (Command + Return) telling the IDE to process your input. Let's try it out with:

println("Hello from REPL")

As far as you can see, IntelliJ responds with printing "Hello from REPL" to the console which in this case is shared with the REPL window.

The printing of the preceding string is in fact a side effect of the **println()** function which by itself doesn't return any result to the calling program. If we, however, attempt to evaluate some expression which *does* have some meaningful result, the output is slightly different. Let's try entering 1+2*3 (*Figure 1.7*):

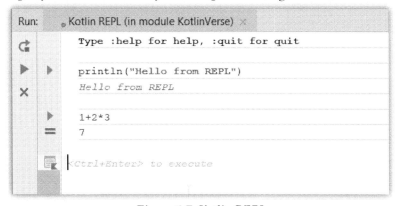

Figure 1.7: Kotlin REPL

The REPL gives us the expression result which is 7. Note the difference in font and = icon as opposed to the **println()** example. This is to signify that 7 is an actual result of the code you've typed. To sum it up, we advise you to get acquainted with this tool and use it throughout the book (and beyond) to experiment with any features you feel necessary.

Interactive editors

Apart from the REPL shell available in IntelliJ, it's worth mentioning a similar, but more powerful online tool which lies somewhere in between a REPL and a full-fledged IDE. The tool in question is the Kotlin Playground. To give it a try open https://play.kotlinlang.org in your browser (*Figure 1.8*).

The Kotlin Playground is basically an online environment which allows you to explore the language with no need for an actual IDE yet having some of its intelligent features at your disposal, including code editor, syntax and error highlighting, code completion, and console program runner.

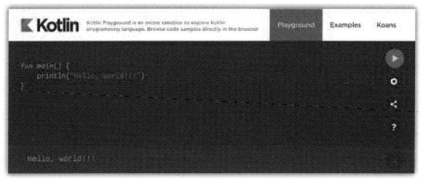

Figure 1.8: The Kotlin Playground

The Playground site also includes a bunch of examples and exercises to familiarize the developer with major Kotlin features. The exercises, also known as Kotlin *koans*, take a form of failing test cases which must be fixed in order to pass (*Figure 1.9*):

Figure 1.9: Kotlin Koans

We strongly recommend going through these examples as a valuable complement to the book itself.

Kotlin support is also available in popular data science notebooks such as Jupyter and Apache Zeppelin. These notebooks provide an interactive code editor where you can execute commands on the fly and see their results. They come very handy in data science and machine learning applications, especially in the context of visualization and exploratory research.

Apache Zeppelin, in particular, comes with a bundled Kotlin plugin starting from 0.9.0.

Jupyter plugin, on the hand, must be installed manually (as explained in https://github.com/Kotlin/kotlin-jupyter ReadMe).

Setting up an Eclipse project

Kotlin tooling is not limited to IntelliJ. Thanks to the Eclipse plugin, the developers who prefer that IDE can use Kotlin as well. Although language support in Eclipse is not as extensive as IntelliJ's, it still provides a lot of code assistance features for the developer's benefit such as code highlighting, completion, program execution and debugging, basic refactorings, and more.

If you don't have Eclipse, it can be freely downloaded at www.eclipse.org/downloads. After running the installer, choose "**Eclipse IDE for Java Developers** (or "Enterprise Java Developers") and follow the instructions. For that tutorial, we've used Eclipse 4.18 released in December of 2020.

Unlike IntelliJ IDEA, Eclipse doesn't come with bundled Kotlin support meaning that the plugin must be installed from the Eclipse Marketplace before we can get to writing the code. To do that, select **Help | Eclipse Marketplace** and search for the Kotlin plugin (*Figure 1.10*).

After you click on the **Install** button, the IDE will download and install the plugin. Make sure to accept license agreements and restart Eclipse in order to complete the installation.

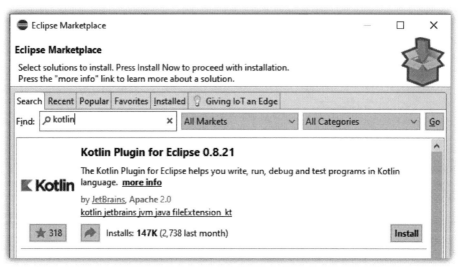

Figure 1.10: Installing Kotlin plugin from Eclipse Marketplace

Now, we can get to setting up a project. First, we switch IDE to Kotlin perspective using the **Window | Perspective | Open Perspective | Other** command and choose Kotlin in the dialog box that follows. Apart from the layout change, this perspective makes some Kotlin actions accessible directly from the application menu. So in order to create a project, we need to choose **File | New | Kotlin Project** to specify a new project name and click on **Finish** (*Figure 1.11*).

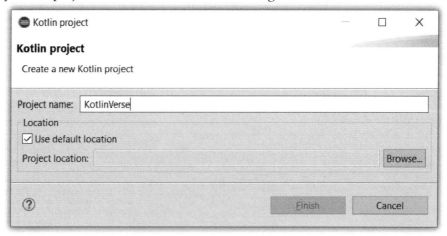

Figure 1.11: Creating Koltin project

We're almost there! By expanding the KotlinVerse node in the Package Explorer view, you can see the components of our newly created project. The Java Runtime Environment (JRE) library, the Kotlin Standard Library and, as of yet empty, the **src** directory where the source files are kept. Now, let's create our first Kotlin file. Right-click on the **src** directory and choose **New | Kotlin File**. Type the file name and click on **Finish** (*Figure 1.12*):

Figure 1.12: Creating Kotlin file

Eclipse automatically opens a new file in the editor window. Let's type **"Hello, World"** program you can recognize from our earlier example (*Figure 1.13*):

Figure 1.13: "Hello, World" in Eclipse

That's it! To run the program, you may use the **Run | Run** command: Eclipse will compile your file to the JVM bytecode, start resulting program and redirect its output to the Console view.

Conclusion

In this chapter, we learned the major aspects of Kotlin language such as safety, conciseness, and support of functional and object-oriented programming paradigms. Together with support of multiple development platforms such as JVM, Android, JavaScript, and native applications, well-designed interoperability with Java or other platform-specific code, extensive ecosystem of tools, libraries and frameworks and fast-growing community makes Kotlin an excellent language definitely worth learning.

We also looked at common tools you can use for getting started with Kotlin programming, including IntelliJ IDEA, Eclipse IDE, and Kotlin Playground. Now, we are ready to move ahead. In the next chapter, we'll focus on the anatomy of some basic syntactic structures like variables and expressions as well as get acquainted with basic Kotlin types.

Points to remember

- Kotlin is a multiparadigm and multiplatform language with a focus on safety, conciseness, and interoperability.
- Kotlin has an extensive IDE support (mainly provided by the IntelliJ plugin).
- Kotlin has a large ecosystem covering virtually all aspects of development process.

Questions

1. Explain the meaning of the basic principles underlying the design of Kotlin language.
2. List Kotlin project setup steps for IntelliJ IDEA and Eclipse IDEs.
3. What interactive editors are available for working with Kotlin code?
4. Describe major libraries and frameworks comprising the Kotlin ecosystem.

CHAPTER 2

Language Fundamentals

In this chapter, you'll learn the basic syntactic elements of the Kotlin program and how to define and use variables. You'll get an understanding of Kotlin types which are used to represent numeric, character, and boolean values as well as their built-in operations and get acquainted with more complex structures such as strings and arrays. Along the way, we'll also point out major differences from the Java syntax and type system which should ease the migration to Kotlin.

Structure

- Basic syntax
- Primitive types
- Strings
- Arrays

Objectives

Introduce the reader to the fundamentals of the Kotlin syntax such as variables and expressions as well as built-in data structures represented by strings and array types.

Basic syntax

We'll start by explaining basic aspects of the Kotlin syntax such as rules governing placement of comments, identifiers, and simple variable definitions as well as building complex expressions from simple ones.

Comments

Like Java, Kotlin supports three varieties of comments that you can use to document your code:

- Single-line comments which start with **//** and continue till the end of line.
- Multi-line comments delimited by **/*** and ***/.**
- KDoc multi-line comments delimited by **/**** and ***/.**

KDoc comments are used to generate rich text documentation similar to Javadoc:

```
/*

  multi-line comment

  /* nested comment */

 */
```

```
println("Hello") // single-line comment
```

Java vs. Kotlin: Unlike Java, multi-line comments in Kotlin can be nested.

Defining a variable

The simplest form of a variable definition in Kotlin takes the following form:

```
val timeInSeconds = 15
```

Let's consider the elements which make it up:

- The **val** keyword (from *value*)
- The variable *identifier* which is a name you give to a new variable and use it to refer to it later in the code
- An expression which defines the variable's *initial value* and follows after the = sign

Java vs. Kotlin: You might've noticed that we didn't put a semicolon (;) at the end of the variable definition. This is not a mistake. In Kotlin, you can omit the semicolon at the end of the line. In fact, this is a recommended code style; putting one statement per line, you'll virtually never need to use semicolons in your code.

IDE Tips: IntelliJ enforces this code style by showing a warning for each unnecessary semicolon.

Suppose we want to write a program which asks the user for two integer numbers and outputs their sum. Here is how it might look like in Kotlin:

```kotlin
fun main() {
    val a = readLine()!!.toInt()
    val b = readLine()!!.toInt()
    println(a + b)
}
```

Let's look more closely at what it does:

1. `readLine()` is a *call expression* which tells the program to execute the `readLine`, a standard Kotlin function which reads a single line from the standard input and returns it as a character string.

2. `!!` is a *not-null assertion operator* which throws an exception if the `readLine()` result is null. Unlike Java, Kotlin tracks if a type can contain nulls and will not allow us to call the `toInt()` function unless we make sure that nulls are ruled out. For now, we can simply ignore it since `readLine()` never returns null when reading from the console. In the next chapter, we'll discuss the issue of the type nullability in more detail.

3. We then call the `toInt()` function on the result of the `readLine()` call. `toInt` is a method defined in the Kotlin's `String` class which converts the character string on which it's called into the integer value. If the string in question does not correspond to a valid integer, `toInt()` fails with a runtime error which in this case just terminates our program. For now, we won't worry about that assuming that all user inputs are valid and postpone the issue of error handling till the next chapter.

4. The result of the `toInt()` call is assigned to the variable a we define in the same line.

5. Similarly, we define the second variable b which is assigned an integer entered on the second line.

6. Finally, we compute the sum of two integers, `a + b`, and pass the result to the `println()` function call which prints it to the standard output.

The preceding variables that we have introduced are called *local* since they're defined in the body of a function (in our case, it's **main()**). Apart from that, Kotlin allows definition of properties which are similar to variables, but in general, we can perform some computations on reading or writing. For example, as we'll see later, all strings in Kotlin have the property **length** which contains the number of characters.

If you're familiar with Java, you've probably noticed that we didn't specify the type of our variables, and yet the program successfully compiles and runs (*Figure 2.1*). The reason is a so called *type inference*; a language feature which in most cases allows the compiler to deduce type information from the context. In this case, the compiler already knows that the **toInt()** function returns a value of the type **Int**, and since we assign the **toInt()** result to our variable, it assumes that the variable must also be of type Int. Thanks to the type inference, Kotlin remains a strongly-typed language, yet saving the developer from cluttering the code with unnecessary type annotations. Throughout the book, we'll see various examples of how the type inference can simplify programming in Kotlin.

Java vs. Kotlin: Java 10 has introduced a similar feature for local variables in version 10. Now, you can write, say:

var text = "Hello"; // *String is inferred automatically*

In Kotlin, however, the type inference is not limited to local variables and has much wider applications that we'll see in the upcoming chapters.

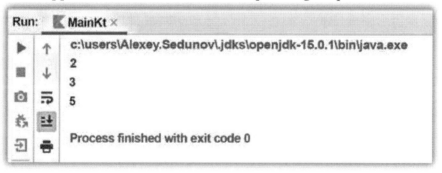

Figure 2.1: Running summation program in IntelliJ

You can also specify the type explicitly when necessary. To do that, you need to put the type specification after the variable identifier separating them with a colon (**:**):

val n: Int = 100

val text: String = "Hello!"

Note that in this case, the initial value must belong to the variable type. The following code will produce the compilation error:

`val n: Int = "Hello!"` `//` Error: assigning String value to Int variable

IDE Tips: IntelliJ allows you to see the compiler-inferred type for any expression or variable. To do it, select the expression of interest in editor or simply put the caret at the variable identifier and press *Ctrl + Shift + P* (Command + Shift+ P):

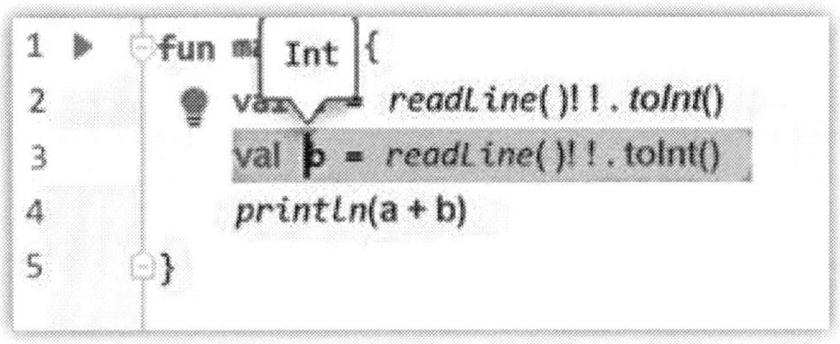

Figure 2.2: *Running summation program in IntelliJ*

On top of this, you can add or remove explicit types using simple actions. Just place the editor caret at the variable identifier, press *Alt + Enter,* and choose **Specify type explicitly** or **Remove explicit type specification,** respectively (the latter also works on the type specification itself).

It's possible to omit an initial value and initialize a variable later, in a separate statement. This could be helpful if computing an initial value can't be put into a single expression. In this case, you'll have to specify the variable type explicitly:

`val text: String`

`text = "Hello!"`

Note that a variable must be initialized before you can read its value. If the compiler can't guarantee that a variable is definitely initialized before use, it will report an error:

`val n: Int`

`println(n + 1) // Error: variable n is not initialized`

Identifiers

Identifiers are names you give to the entities defined in the program, like variables or functions. Kotlin identifiers come in two flavors. The first one is quite similar to a Java identifier and can be an arbitrary string of characters conforming to the following rules:

- It may only contain letters, digits, underscore characters (_), and may not start with a digit.

- It may not consist entirely of underscores: names like `_`, `__`, `___`, and so on are reserved and can't be used as identifiers.

- It may not coincide with a hard keyword.

Hard keywords (like **val** or **fun**) are considered keywords regardless of where they are put in the code. *Soft* keywords (like **import**), on the other hand, are parsed as keywords only in the specific context, outside which they can be used as normal identifiers. You can find the complete list of hard and soft keywords at kotlinlang.org/docs/reference/keyword-reference.html.

Letters and digits, like in Java, are not limited to ASCII, but include national alphanumeric characters as well. It is, however, considered a good practice to use names based on the English words.

Java vs. Kotlin: Note that unlike Java, dollar signs ($) are not allowed in Kotlin identifiers.

The second form, a *quoted* identifier, is an arbitrary non-empty character string enclosed inside backquotes (`):

```
val `fun` = 1
```

```
val `name with spaces` = 2
```

Quoted identifiers may not contain new lines and backquotes themselves. On top of that, they must satisfy platform-specific requirements. In the Kotlin/JVM code, for example, such identifiers may not contain any of the following characters since they are reserved by the JVM itself: `. ; [ ] / < > : \`.

For better readability, this feature shouldn't be abused, though. It primarily exists for Java interoperability because Java declaration names might coincide with Kotlin keywords (**fun**, for example, is a keyword in Kotlin, but not in Java) and the Kotlin code should be able to use them if necessary. One more use case is naming of test case methods which we'll see in *Chapter 14, Testing with Kotlin*.

Mutable variables

The variables we've considered so far are in fact *immutable*; in other words, you can't reassign their value once they're initialized. In this regard they resemble final variables in Java. You should aim at declaring all variables immutable as much as practical since using immutable variables and avoiding functions with side effects facilitates the functional style and simplifies the reasoning about your code.

If necessary, however, you can still define a mutable variable by using the **var** keyword (from *variable*) instead of **val**. The basic syntax remains the same, but now we can change the variable's value as many times as we like. The operation (=) we use to change the variable's value is called the *assignment*. We've already seen its use for initialization of immutable variables:

```
var sum = 1

sum = sum + 2

sum = sum + 3
```

Note that the variable type specified or inferred at its declaration stays the same whether it's mutable or not. Assigning the value of a wrong type is a compile-time error:

```
var sum = 1

sum = "Hello" // Error: assigning String value to Int variable
```

Additionally, Kotlin supports so called *augmented assignments* which combine changing the variable's value with one of the binary operators: **+, -, *, /, %**. For example:

```
val result = 3

result *= 10 // result = result * 10

result += 6  // result = result + 6
```

Such assignments are available whenever the corresponding binary operators make sense for a given variable.

Java vs. Kotlin: As opposed to Java, Kotlin assignments are statements, rather than expressions and do not return any value. This, in turn, means that in Kotlin, you can't form an assignment chain similar to Java's **a = b = c**. Such assignments are forbidden in Kotlin because they are considered error-prone and are rarely useful. This includes augmented assignments as well.

There are two more operations concerned with changing a variable's value: increment (**++**) and decrement (**--**). Their most obvious usage is increasing or decreasing a numeric variable by 1. Like in Java, these operations come in the prefix and postfix form:

```
var a = 1

println(a++) // a is 2, 1 is printed

println(++a) // a is 3, 3 is printed
```

```
println(--a) // a is 2, 2 is printed
```

```
println(a--) // a is 1, 2 is printed
```

These examples demonstrate that while both the prefix and the postfix operations modify the variable, the former's result is a new value, while the latter returns the variable's value before changing it.

Expressions and operators

Kotlin expressions we've used in the preceding examples can be divided into the following categories:

- *Literals* representing specific values of particular types (like 12 or 3.56)
- *Variable/property references* and *function calls* (a, readLine(), "abc".length, "12".toInt())
- Prefix and postfix *unary operations* (-a, ++b, c--)
- *Binary operations* (a + b, 2 * 3, x < 1)

Every expression has a definite *type* which describes a possible range of values and allowed operations. For example, literal 1 has a type **Int**, while the **readLine()!!** call is of the type String.

Also, note that variable references and function calls may have a dot-separated *receiver expression*, like in **readLine()!!.toInt().** This means that we are using the **toInt()** function defined for the type String (which is of the type **readLine()!!**) in the context of **readLine()!!.**

Unary and binary operations have different precedence which determines the order of evaluation; for example, in 2 + 3*4 expression, we first evaluate 3*4 and then add the result to 2, thus getting 14. The order can be changed with parentheses, so (2 + 3)*4 will be equal to 5*4 or 20 instead. The precedence of operators we will consider in this chapter can be summarized in the following table:

Category	Operations	Examples	
Postfix	++ -- .	a*b++	// a*(b++)
		++b--	// ++(b--)
		a*b.foo()	// a*(b.foo())
Prefix	+ - ++ -- !	+a*b	// (+a)*b
		++a*b	// (++a)*b
		!a || b	// (!a) || b

Multiplicative	* / %	a*b + c	// (a*b) + c
		a – b%c	// a - (b*c)
Additive	+ -	a + b and c	// (a + b) and c
Infix	Named operators	a < b or b < c	// (a < (b or b)) < c
		a == b and b == c	// (a == b) and (b == c)
Comparison	< > <= >=	a < b == b < c	// (a < b) == (b < c)
		a < b && b < c	// (a < b) && (b < c)
Equality	== !=	a == b || b != c	// (a == b) || (b != c)
Conjunction	&&	a || b && c	// a || (b && c)
Disjunction	||	a && b || c	// (a && b) || c
Assignment	= += -= *= /= %=	a = b*c	// a = (b*c)
		a *= a + b	// a *= (a + b)

Table 2.1: Operation precedence

Binary operators with the same priority are evaluated from left to right. For example:

```
a.foo().bar()                   // (a.foo()).bar()

a*b%c                           // (a*b)%c

(a == 1) or (b < 1) and (c > 1) // ((a == 1) or (b < 1)) and (c > 1)
```

Over the course of the book, we'll introduce additional operations refining this table.

Primitive types

In this section, we'll consider Kotlin types which describe simple values like numbers, characters, and booleans. If you're familiar with Java, you can think of them as counterparts of Java primitive types, but the analogy is not perfect. In Java, you have a clear distinction between primitive types like **int** whose values are stored directly in the preallocated memory of the method and class-based reference types like String whose values are just references to dynamically allocated data of the corresponding class. In Kotlin, the distinction is somewhat blurred since the same type say, Int – can be represented as either primitive or reference one depending on the context. Java includes special boxing classes which can be used to wrap primitive values, but Kotlin performs boxing implicitly when necessary.

Java vs. Kotlin: As opposed to Java, *all* Kotlin types are ultimately based on some class definition. This, in particular, means that even primitive-like types, such as Int, have some member functions and/or properties. You can, for example, write

1.5.toInt() to call the **toInt()** operation on 1.5, a value of the type Double, which converts it to an integer number.

Types can form hierarchies based on a notion of *subtyping*; in essence, when we say that type A is a subtype of B, we mean that any value of A can be used in any context which requires a value of B. For example, all Kotlin types that disallow null values are direct or indirect subtypes of a built-in type **Any**, so the following code is correct although it forces a value of 1 to become boxed:

```
val n: Any = 1 // Ok: Int is a subtype of Any
```

Integer types

There are four basic Kotlin types that represent integer numbers (Table 2.2):

Type	Size (in bytes)	Range	Java Counterpart
Byte	1	$-128 .. 127$	byte
Short	2	$-32768 .. 32767$	short
Int	4	$-2^{31} .. 2^{31} - 1$	int
Long	8	$-2^{63} .. 2^{63} - 1$	long

Table 2.2: Integer types

The simplest form of a literal expressing some value of an integer type is just a decimal number:

```
val n = 12345
```

Since Kotlin 1.1 you can, like in Java 7+, put underscores inside numeric literals for better readability. This comes in handy when literals are rather big:

```
val n = 34_721_189
```

A literal itself has either type **Int** or **Long** depending on its size. You can, however, assign literals to variables of smaller types as well, provided they fit into the expected range:

```
val one: Byte = 1                                  // OK
val tooBigForShort: Short = 100_000                 // Error: too big for Short
val million = 1_000_000                             // OK: Int is inferred
val tooBigForInt: Int = 10_000_000_000              // Error: too big for Int
val tenBillions = 10_000_000_000                    // OK: Long is inferred
val tooBigForLong = 10_000_000_000_000_000_000 // Error: too big for Long
```

Adding the L suffix forces the literal type to become **Long:**

```
val hundredLong = 100L     // OK: Long is inferred

val hundredInt: Int = 100L // Error: assigning Long to Int
```

You can also specify literals in the binary or hexadecimal numeral system prefixing them with **0b** and **0x,** respectively:

```
val bin = 0b10101 // 21

val hex = 0xF9     // 249
```

Note that the numeric literal may not start with zero unless it is **0** itself. Some programming languages (including Java) use zero-prefixed literals to denote octal numbers which are not supported in Kotlin as it is rarely useful and often a misleading feature. For this reason, zero-prefixed numbers are forbidden so that developers accustomed to the octal notation are not confused:

```
val zero = 0      // OK

val zeroOne = 01 // Error
```

Negative numbers like **-10** are not technically literals, but are unary-minus expressions applied to literals:

```
val neg = -10

val negHex = -0xFF
```

Each integer type defines a pair of constants that contains its minimum (**MIN_VALUE**) and maximum (**MAX_VALUE**) values. To use them, just qualify the constant with the type name:

```
Short.MIN_VALUE    // -32768

Short.MAX_VALUE    // 32767

Int.MAX_VALUE + 1 // -2147483648 (integer overflow)
```

Floating-point types

Like Java, Kotlin provides support for IEEE 754 floating-point numbers with types Float and Double. Their Java counterparts, as you might've guessed, are **float** and **double,** respectively.

The simplest form of a floating-point literal is a decimal number which consists of integer and fractional parts separated by a dot:

```
val pi = 3.14

val one = 1.0
```

The integer part may be empty in which case it's assumed to be zero. The fractional part, however, is mandatory:

```
val quarter = .25 // 0.25

val one = 1.      // Error

val two = 2       // No error, but that's integer literal
```

Kotlin also supports scientific notation where you can follow a decimal number with an exponent part signifying the power of ten:

```
val pi = 0.314E1             // 3.14 = 0.314*10

val hundredPpi = 0.314E3     // 314.0 = 0.314*1000

val piOver100 = 3.14E-2      // 0.0314 = 3.14/100

val thousand = 1E3           // 1000.0 = 1*1000
```

Note that in scientific notation, the fractional part is optional.

Java vs. Kotlin: Unlike Java 6+, Kotlin doesn't support hexadecimal literals for Float and Double types.

By default, literals have the Double type. Tagging them with **f** or **F** forces the type to Float: (in this case, the fractional part is also optional):

```
val pi = 3.14f

val one = 1f
```

Java vs. Kotlin: In Java you can tag a literal with d or D forcing its type to be Double (like **1.25d**). Kotlin, however, has no such suffix: **Double** type is only assigned by default.

Note that Float literals are not automatically converted to **Double** types. The following code will lead to a compile-time error:

```
val pi: Double = 3.14f // Error
```

Float and Double define a set constants that represent some special values of the following types:

- **MIN_VALUE**, **MAX_VALUE**: The smallest/the largest positive finite value representable by the type.

- **NEGATIVE_INFINITY**, **POSITIVE_INFINITY**: The negative/positive infinite value, which is respectively the smallest/the largest value of the type.
- **NaN**: "Not a number" value for uncertainties like 0/0.

```
println(Float.MIN_VALUE)              // 1.4E-45

println(Double.MAX_VALUE)             // 1.7976931348623157E308

println(Double.POSITIVE_INFINITY)     // Infinity

println(1.0/Double.NEGATIVE_INFINITY) // -0.0

println(2 - Double.POSITIVE_INFINITY) // -Infinity

println(3 * Float.NaN)                // NaN
```

Arithmetic operations

All numeric types support basic arithmetic operations:

Operation	Meaning	Example	Result
+ (unary)	the same value	+2	2
− (unary)	opposite value	-2	-2
+	addition	2 + 32.5 + 3.2	5 5.7
−	subtraction	1 − 33.4 − 1.8	-2 1.6
*	multiplication	3 * 4 3.5 * 1.5	12 5.25
/	division	7/4 -7/4 7/(-4) (-7)/(-4) 6.5/2.5 -6.5/2.5 6.5/(-2.5) (-6.5)/(-2.5)	1 -1 -1 1 2.6 -2.6 -2.6 2.6

%	remainder	7%4	3
		-7%4	-3
		7%(-4)	3
		(-7)%(-4)	-3
		6.5%2.5	1.5
		-6.5%2.5	-1.5
		6.5%(-2.5)	1.5
		(-6.5)%(-2.5)	-1.5

Table 2.3: Arithmetic operations

The behavior of arithmetic operations is consistent with Java. Note that integer division operations give a result rounded to zero, while the remainder has the same sign as the numerator. Floating-point operations are carried out according to the IEEE 754 specification.

Numeric types support ++/−− operations which amount to increasing/decreasing the value by 1.

The result of unary +/− operations has the same type as their argument with an exception for Byte and Short where it results in an **Int**:

```
val byte: Byte = 1

val int = 1

val long = 1L

val float = 1.5f

val double = 1.5


-byte    // -1: Int

-int     // -1: Int

-long    // -1: Long

-float   // -1.5: Float

-double // -1.5: Double
```

Each of the binary arithmetic operation comes in multiple variants covering all possible combinations of numeric types. Since there are 6 numeric types, it means 6*6 = 36 versions for each operation. It allows you to combine different numeric types in arithmetic expressions without an explicit conversion. The result of such an operation is taken to be a "bigger" one between its arguments where "bigger" means the following:

```
Double > Float > Long > Int > Short > Byte
```

For most types, it essentially means a larger set of values, but that's not always the case: the obvious example is conversion from **Long** to **Float** which can lead to loss of precision. Note that the result type is never smaller than Int even when arguments have the **Byte** or **Short** type.

Going ahead with our previous example, we get:

```
byte + byte     // 2: Byte

int + byte      // 2: Int

int + int       // 2: Int

int + long      // 2: Long

long + double   // 2.5: Double

float + double  // 3.0: Double

float + int     // 2.5: Float

long + double   // 2.5: Double
```

Bitwise operations

Int and Long support a range of bit-level operations:

Operation	Meaning	Examples	Java Counterpart
shl	shift left	*// 13: 0...00001101* 13 shl 2 *// = 52: 0...00110100* *// -13: 1...11110011* (-13) shl 2 *// = -52: 1...11001100*	<<

shr	shift right	`// 13: 0...00001101`
		`13 shr 2 // = 3: 0...00000011`
		`// -13: 1...11110011`
		`(-13) shr 2 // = -4: 1...11111100`
			>>

ushr	shift right unsigned	`// 13: 0...00001101`
		`13 ushr 2 // = 3: 0...00000011`
		`// -13: 1...11110011`
		`(-13) ushr 2`
		`// = 1073741820: 001...111100`
			>>>

and	bitwise AND	`// 13: 0...00001101`
		`// 19: 0...00010011`
		`13 and 19 // = 1: 0...00000001`
		`// -13: 1...11110011`
		`// 19: 0...00010011`
		`-13 and 19 // = 19: 0...00010011`
			&

or	bitwise OR	`// 13: 0...00001101`
		`// 19: 0...00010011`
		`13 or 19 // = 31: 0...00011111`
		`// -13: 1...11110011`
		`// 19: 0...00010011`
		`-13 and 19 // = -13: 1...11110011`
			|

xor	bitwise XOR	`// 13: 0...00001101`
		`// 19: 0...00010011`
		`13 xor 19 // = 30: 0...00011110`
		`// -13: 1...11110011`
		`// 19: 0...00010011`
		`-13 xor 19 // = -32: 1...11100000`
			^

inv	b i t w i s e inversion	// 13: 0...00001101
		
		13.inv() // = -14: 1...11110010
		
		// -13: 1...11110011
		
		(-13).inv() // = 12: 0...00001100
			~

Table 2.4: Bitwise operations

Note that **inv** is not a binary operation, but a simple method which is invoked using the dot notation.

Since Kotlin 1.1, **and**, **or**, **xor**, and **inv** are also available on **Byte** and **Short**.

Java vs. Kotlin: If you're familiar with Java, you might know about the bitwise operators: **&, |, ^, ~, <<, >>** and **>>>**. These operators are not currently supported in Kotlin; you have to use **and, or, xor, inv, shl, shr,** and **ushr,** respectively which have exactly the same semantics on JVM.

Char type

The **Char** type represents a single 16-bit Unicode character. A literal of this type is just a character itself surrounded by single quotes:

```
val z = 'z'
```

```
val alpha = 'α'
```

For special characters like newlines, Kotlin provides a set of escape sequences: **\t** (tab), **\b** (backspace), **\n** (newline), **\r** (carriage return), **\'** (single quote), **\"** (double quote), **** (backslash), **\$** (dollar sign):

```
val quote = '\''
```

```
val newLine = '\n'
```

You can also put arbitrary Unicode characters into the literal using the **\u** sequence followed by the 4-digit hexadecimal character code:

```
val pi = '\u03C0' // π
```

Although internally the **Char** value is just a character code, the **Char** itself is not considered a numeric type in Kotlin. It does, however, support a limited set of arithmetic operations concerned with moving around the Unicode character set. This is what you can do with characters:

- Add/remove an integer with +/− operators which give a character shifted by the corresponding number of steps.

- Subtract two characters by getting a number of steps between them.

- Increment/decrement a character with ++/−− operators.

Let's consider some examples:

```
var a = 'a'
var h = 'h'
/* 5th character after 'a' */       println(a + 5) // f
/* 5th character before 'a' */      println(a - 5) // \
/* distance between 'a' and 'h' */  println(h - a) // 7
/* get character preceding 'h' */   println(--h)   // g
/* get character following 'a' */   println(++a)   // b
```

Java vs. Kotlin: Note that while in Java, results of all arithmetic operations on characters are implicitly converted to **int**, **Char** operations in Kotlin (except the difference of two characters) give Char as their result.

Numeric conversions

Each numeric type defines a set of operations to convert its value to any other numeric types as well as Char. Operations have self-explanatory names corresponding to the target type: **toByte()**, **toShort()**, **toInt()**, **toLong()**, **toFloat()**, **toDouble()**, and **toChar()**. The same set of operations is available for **Char** values.

Java vs. Kotlin: Unlike Java, values of smaller-range types cannot be used in the context where the larger type is expected; you can't, for example, assign an **Int** values to the **Long** variable. The following code will produce a compilation error:

```
val n = 100     // Int

val l: Long = n // Error: can't assign Int to Long
```

The reason behind this is implicit boxing we've mentioned earlier. Since in general, values of **Int** (or any other numeric type) are not necessarily represented as primitives, such *widening* conversions could potentially amount to producing a value of different boxing type, thus violating equality and leading to subtle errors. If the preceding code was considered correct, the following instruction

```
println(l == n)
```

would print **false** which is rather an unexpected result. In Java, there is a similar issue related to boxing types:

```
Integer n = 100;

Long l = n;       // Error: can't assign Integer to Long
```

Conversion between integer types is lossless when the target type has a larger range. Otherwise, it basically truncates extra most significant bits and reinterprets the remainder as a target type. The same also goes for a conversion to/from the Char type:

```
val n = 945

println(n.toByte())  // -79

println(n.toShort()) // 945

println(n.toChar())  // α

println(n.toLong())  // 945
```

Conversions involving floating-point types can, in general, lead to precision loss regardless of the target type: say, converting a very big **Long** value to **Float** can zero some lower digits. Converting floating-point numbers to integers is basically the same as rounding to zero:

```
println(2.5.toInt())                                  // 2

println((-2.5).toInt())                               // -2

println(1_000_000_000_000.toFloat().toLong()) // 999999995904
```

Starting from Kotlin 1.4, **toByte()** and **toShort()** conversions are considered deprecated for floating-point types because their usage often leads to unpredictable results due to small range of target values. Now, such calls produce a compiler warning:

```
println(2.5.toByte()) // use of deprecated toByte()
```

Note that indirect conversion via other types is considered acceptable:

```
println(2.5.toInt().toByte())
```

Boolean type and logical operations

Kotlin has a Boolean type representing a logical operation which can be either true or false:

```
val hasErrors = false;

val testPassed = true;
```

Like in Java, Kotlin's `Boolean` is distinct from numeric types and can't be converted to numbers (and vice versa) neither implicitly, nor with some kind of built-in operations like **toInt()**. The developer is supposed to use comparison operations and conditionals (see below) to build **Boolean** values from non-**Boolean** ones.

Operations supported by **Boolean** include:

- `!` – Inversion
- **or, and, xor:** Eager disjunction/conjunction and exclusive disjunction
- **||, &&:** Lazy disjunction/conjunction

Lazy operations have essentially the same semantics as their Java counterparts. Operation || does not evaluate its right argument if the first one is true. Similarly, the operation && doesn't evaluate its right arguments if the first one is false. This can be useful if evaluating the right argument entails some side effects.

Java vs. Kotlin: Unlike Java, Kotlin doesn't have **&** and **|** operators. Their role is performed by **and** / **or,** respectively.

Let's consider some examples using equality/inequality operations == and != (more on them in the next section):

```
println((x == 1) or (y == 1))        // true

println((x == 0) || (y == 0))        // false

println((x == 1) and (y != 1))       // true

println((x == 1) and (y == 1))       // false

println((x == 1) xor (y == 1))       // true

println((x == 1) xor (y != 1))       // false

println(x == 1 || y/(x - 1) != 1)    // true

println(x != 1 && y/(x - 1) != 1)    // false
```

In the previous two examples, using lazy operations is essential since an attempt to evaluate the right argument when **x == 1** will result in a runtime error due to division by zero.

Note the precedence difference between eager/lazy conjunction and disjunction. Eager operations **and, or, xor** are named infix operators and thus have the same precedence and dominate the **&&** operation which, in turn, dominates **||**. For example, the following expression:

```
a || b and c or d && e
```

is evaluated as:

```
a || (((b and c) or d) && e)
```

In doubtful cases, we suggest using parentheses to clarify the meaning behind your code.

Comparison and equality

All types we've considered so far support the standard set of comparison operations: **==** (equals), **!=** (not equals), **<** (less than), **<=** (less than or equals), **>** (greater than), **>=** (greater than or equals):

```
val a = 1

val b = 2

println(a == 1 || b != 1) // true

println(a >= 1 && b < 3)  // true

println(a < 1 || b < 1)   // false

println(a > b)            // false
```

In general, equality operations **==** and **!=** are applicable to values of any type. There is, however, an exception for numeric types, `Char` and `Boolean`. Consider the following code:

```
val a = 1              // Int

val b = 2L             // Long

println(a == b)        // Error: comparing Int and Long

println(a.toLong() == b) // Ok: both types are Long
```

Basically, for such types, Kotlin only permits **==** and **!=** when both arguments are of the same type; you can't, for example, apply **==** when one argument is `Int` while another is **Long**. This is explained by the same reasoning we've seen for assignments; the equality check would produce different results depending on whether values are boxed, and since boxing in Kotlin is implicit, it could lead to confusion if permitted for any pair of types.

Operations **<, <=, >, >=,** however, allow you to compare any numeric types; just like arithmetic operations, they are overloaded to cover all possible cases. So you can write, for example:

```
1 <= 2L || 3 > 4.5
```

Note that **Char** and **Boolean** values also support comparison operations, but they can be compared only with a value of the same type:

```
false == true // false

false < true  // true

false > 1       // Error: comparing Boolean and Int

'a' < 'b'      // true

'a' > 0        // Error: comparing Int and Char
```

Note that **false** is assumed to be less than **true**, and **Char** values are ordered by their character code.

Java vs. Kotlin: Unlike Kotlin, in Java where boxed and unboxed values are represented by different types (such as **long** vs. **Long**), primitive numeric types (including char) can be freely compared with each other using ==/!= as well as </<=/>/>= operators. Boolean values in Java, however, are not ordered and can only be checked for equality.

In the context of floating-point types, comparison operations follow the IEEE 754 standard. This, in particular, assumes a specific treatment of NaN values:

```
println(Double.NaN == Double.NaN)            // false

println(Double.NaN != Double.NaN)            // true

println(Double.NaN <= Double.NaN)            // false

println(Double.NaN < Double.POSITIVE_INFINITY) // false

println(Double.NaN > Double.NEGATIVE_INFINITY) // false
```

Basically, NaN is not equal to anything, including itself is neither considered lesser nor greater than any other value, including infinities.

These rules, however, are only put in action when the compiler knows statically that the value of interest has a floating-point type. In more generic cases, which involve, for example, storing numbers in a collection, the compiler falls back to using equality and comparison rules imposed by the boxed type. On JVM, this is equivalent to comparing instances of Double/Float wrapper types:

```
val set = sortedSetOf(Double.NaN, Double.NaN,

                      Double.POSITIVE_INFINITY, Double.NEGATIVE_INFINITY,

                      0.0)
println(set) // [-Infinity, 0.0, Infinity, NaN]
```

The preceding code creates a tree sorted internally by natural ordering of the element type (on JVM, this is basically a **TreeSet**) and prints its items. The output shows that in this case:

- NaN is equals to itself, since only one such value was added to the set
- NaN is considered the largest value of Double (even greater than positive infinity)

In the upcoming chapters, we'll discuss the concepts of equality and ordering in more detail.

Strings

The **String** type represents strings of characters. Like in Java, Kotlin strings are immutable; in other words, you can't change characters once a **String** object is created, you can only read them or create new strings based on the existing one. In this section, we'll consider how to construct new strings and perform some basic manipulations with them.

String templates

The simplest way to define a string literal, as we've already seen in this chapter, is to enclose its content in double quotes just like in Java:

```
val hello = "Hello, world!"
```

If the string needs to contain some special symbols like newline characters, you need to use one of the escape sequences (see the section):

```
val text = "Hello, world!\nThis is \"multiline\" string"

println("\u03C0 \u2248 3.14") // π ≈ 3.14
```

These literals are basically the same as in Java. In addition to them, Kotlin provides a much more powerful way to define a string which comes in useful when you want to compose it from various expressions. Suppose, for example, we want to welcome the user with a message saying hello and print the current date and time:

```kotlin
import java.util.Date

fun main() {

    val name = readLine()

    println("Hello, $name!\n Today is ${Date()}")

}
```

Basically, you can replace any part of the string with a valid Kotlin expression by putting it inside **${ }**. If the expression is a simple variable reference, like the name in our example, you may just prefix it with a dollar sign. Such a literal is called a *string template*.

Note that expressions in string templates may take any values; they are automatically converted to strings using the **toString()** method available for any Kotlin type.

If you run the program and enter some name (say, John), you'll see something like this:

Hello, John!

Today is Sat Dec 28 14:44:42 MSK 2019

The result may vary depending on your locale.

The *import directive* we've used in the first line allows us to refer to the JDK class **Date** by its simple name instead of **java.util.Date**. In the next chapter, we'll discuss the issue of imports and packages in more detail.

One more variety of string literals is called a *raw string*. It allows you to write strings without escape sequences. Such a literal is enclosed by triple quotes and may contain arbitrary characters, including newlines:

```kotlin
val message = """
    Hello, $name!

    Today is ${Date()}
""".trimIndent()
```

The **trimIndent()** is a standard Kotlin function which removes the common minimal indent.

In rare cases, when you still want to put some special character sequence into a raw string (like triple quotes), you have to embed them into **${ }**:

```
val message = """
```

```
    This is triple quote:'${"\"\"\""}'
```

```
""".trimIndent()
```

In JVM-targeted applications, strings are represented by instances of the JVM String class.

Basic string operations

Every **String** instance has the **length** and **lastIndex** properties which contain the number of characters and the last character index, respectively:

```
"Hello!".length    // 6
```

```
"Hello!".lastIndex // 5 since indices start from zero
```

You can also access individual characters using the **indexing** operator with the zero-based index inside brackets. On JVM, the passing invalid index will produce **StringIndexOutOfBoundsException** similar to Java:

```
val s = "Hello!"
```

```
println(s[0])  // H
```

```
println(s[1])  // e
```

```
println(s[5])  // !
```

```
println(s[10]) // invalid index
```

You can concatenate strings using the operator +. The second argument may in fact be any value which is automatically converted to a string by calling its **toString()** function. In most cases, though, we suggest using string templates instead as they usually are more concise:

```
val s = "The sum is: " + sum // can be replaced by "The sum is $sum"
```

Strings can be compared for equality with operators == and !=. These operators compare the string content, so even two different instances are considered equal if they contain the same sequence of characters:

```
val s1 = "Hello!"
```

```
val s2 = "Hel" + "lo!"
```

```
println(s1 == s2) // true
```

Java vs. Kotlin: In Java, == and != operators check the referential equality, so you have to use the **equals()** method to compare the actual string content. In Kotlin, == is basically a more convenient synonym for **equals()** so usually there is no need to call **equals()** directly. Keeping null-checking aside, the preceding code is equivalent to Java's **s1.equals(s2)**. What about referential equality in Kotlin? For that, you can use === and !== operators.

Strings are lexicographically ordered, so you can compare them using operators <, >, <=, and >=:

```
println("abc" < "cba") // true

println("123" > "34")  // false
```

String also supports conversion functions for numeric types and **Boolean: toByte(), toShort(), toInt(), toLong(), toFloat(), toDouble(), toBoolean().** Note that numeric conversions will produce a run-time error if the string doesn't contain a well-formed number.

Here is a list of some additional useful functions String is able to offer:

isEmpty
isNotEmpty
	Check if string is empty	"Hello".isEmpty() // false
		"".isEmpty() // true
		"Hello".isNotEmpty() // true

substring	Extract substring	"Hello".substring(2) // "llo" "Hello".substring(1, 3) // "el"
startsWith endsWith	Check prefix/suffix	"Hello".startsWith("Hel") // true "Hello".endsWith("lo") // true

indexOf()	Get first occurrence index of character or substring	// search from start
		"abcabc".indexOf('b') // 1
		"abcabc".indexOf("ca") // 2
		"abcabc".indexOf("cd") // -1
		// search from given index
		"abcabc".indexOf('b', 2) // 4
		"abcabc".indexOf("ab", 2) // 3

Table 2.5: Useful string functions

Throughout the book (*Chapter 7*, *Exploring Collections and I/O* in particular), we'll see more examples of the Kotlin String API. For more information, we advise you to visit the documentation page at <u>kotlinlang.org/api/latest/jvm/stdlib/kotlin/-string/index.html</u>.

Arrays

An array is a built-in Kotlin data structure which allows you to store a fixed number of same-typed values and refer to them by an index. They are conceptually similar to arrays in Java which are in fact used as their representation in Kotlin/JVM applications. In this section, we'll consider how to define an array and access its data.

Constructing an array

The most general Kotlin type implementing an array structure is **Array<T>** where **T** is a common type of its elements. In *Chapter 1*, *Kotlin - Powerful and Pragmatic*, we've already see an example of the **main()** function accepting a parameter of type **Array<String>** which holds command-line arguments passed to the program. If the number of elements is known in advance, we can create an array using one of the standard functions:

```
val a = emptyArray<String>()      // Array<String> (zero elements)

val b = arrayOf("hello", "world") // Array<string> (2 elements)

val c = arrayOf(1, 4, 9)          // Array<Integer> (3 elements)
```

These functions are *generic* which means they refer to unknown element types which must be specified in the call. Thanks to type inference, however, the compiler can figure out the unknown type in the second and third calls using arguments we pass. If we, for example, create an array from a series of integer numbers, it obviously has the **Array<Integer>** type. In the first call, however, the compiler has no such information, so we have do specify the element type in angular brackets of the call expression. For now, we'll just take this syntax for granted and postpone the detailed discussion of generic types and functions till *Chapter 9*, *Generics*.

There is a more flexible way to create an array by describing how to compute an element with a given index. The following code generates an array containing squares of integers from 1 to whatever the user has entered:

```
val size = readLine()!!.toInt()

val squares = Array(size) { (it + 1)*(it + 1) }
```

The construct inside braces, also called *lambda,* defines an expression to compute an element value based on its index which is represented by an automatically declared variable it. Since array indices range from 0 to size - 1, its elements will take form 1, 4, 9, and so on. For now, we'll just use this syntax as is and come back to lambdas in Chapter 5, *Leveraging Advanced Functions and Functional Programming.*

Using **Array<Int>** is working, but it is an impractical solution since it will force the boxing of numbers. For this reason, Kotlin provides a more efficient storage with specialized array types such as **ByteArray, ShortArray, IntArray, LongArray, FloatArray, DoubleArray, CharArray,** and **BooleanArray**. On JVM, these types are represented by Java primitive arrays such as **int[]** or **boolean[]**. Each of them is accompanied by functions similar to **arrayOf()** and **Array()**:

```
val operations = charArrayOf('+', '-', '*', '/', '%')
```

```
val squares = IntArray(10) { (it + 1)*(it + 1) }
```

Java vs. Kotlin: Unlike Java, Kotlin doesn't have a **new** operator, so a construction of the Array instance looks like an ordinary function call. Also, note that in Kotlin, you have to explicitly initialize array elements on its creation.

Using arrays

Array types are quite similar to Strings. In particular, they have the size (analogous to String's length) and **lastIndex** properties and their elements can be accessed by the indexing operator. Using an invalid index will produce **IndexOutOfBoundsException** at runtime:

```
val squares = arrayOf(1, 4, 9, 16)

squares.size        // 4

squares.lastIndex // 3

squares[3]          // 16

squares[1]          // 4
```

Unlike string characters, though, array elements can be changed:

```
squares[2] = 100 // squares: 1, 4, 100, 16

squares[3] += 9  // squares: 1, 4, 100, 25

squares[0]--     // squares: 0, 4, 100, 25
```

Note that like in Java, an array variable itself stores a *reference* to actual data. For this reason, assigning array variables basically shares the same set of data between variables:

```
val numbers = squares

numbers[0] = 1000    // mutates data shared between squares and numbers

println(squares[0]) // prints 1000
```

If you want to create a separate array, use the **copyOf()** function which can also produce an array of different sizes if necessary:

```
val numbers = squares.copyOf()

numbers[0] = 1000 // squares is not affected

squares.copyOf(2) // truncated: 1, 4

squares.copyOf(5) // padded with zeros: 1, 4, 9, 16, 0
```

Note that arrays with different types can't be assigned to each other. The following code will fail with a compilation error:

```
var a = arrayOf(1, 4, 9, 16)

a = arrayOf("one", "two")    // Error: can't assign Array<String> to
                                                        Array<Int>
```

Java vs. Kotlin: In Java, you can assign an array of a subtype to an array of its super type. Since arrays are mutable, this can lead to problems at runtime:

```
Object[] objects = new String[] { "one", "two", "three" };

objects[0] = new Object(); // fails with ArrayStoreException
```

For this reason, the Kotlin array type is not considered a subtype of any other array type (apart of itself) and such assignments are prohibited. So even though **String** is a subtype of **Any**, **Array<String>** is *not* a subtype of **Array<Any>**:

```
val strings = arrayOf("one", "two", "three")

val objects: Array<Any> = strings // Error
```

In fact, that's a specific case of a powerful *variance* concept which we'll cover in *Chapter 9, Generics*.

Although the array length can't change after it's created, you can produce a new array by adding extra elements with the **+** operation:

```
val b = intArrayOf(1, 2, 3) + 4    // add single element: 1, 2, 3, 4

val c = intArrayOf(1, 2, 3) + intArrayOf(5, 6)         // add another
                                                  array: 1, 2, 3, 5, 6
```

Unlike strings, == and != operators on arrays compare references rather than elements themselves:

```
intArrayOf(1, 2, 3) == intArrayOf(1, 2, 3) // false
```

If you want to compare array content, you should use the **contentEquals()** function:

```
intArrayOf(1, 2, 3).contentEquals(intArrayOf(1, 2, 3)) // true
```

IDE Tips: IntelliJ issues a warning when you try to compare arrays using == or != and suggests to replace it with the **contentEquals()** call instead.

Some standard functions which may be helpful when using arrays are given in *Table 2.6*:

isEmpty isNotEmpty	Check if array is empty	`intArrayOf(1, 2).isEmpty()    // false` `intArrayOf(1, 2).isNotEmpty() // true`
indexOf	Get first index of an array item	`intArrayOf(1, 2, 3).indexOf(2) // 1` `intArrayOf(1, 2, 3).indexOf(4) // -1`

Table 2.6: Useful array functions

In the upcoming chapter, we'll consider additional array functions. They will mostly be introduced in *Chapter 7, Exploring Collections and I/O*, which deals with the Kotlin collections API.

Conclusion

In this chapter, we got a first taste of Kotlin. We learned about variables and type inference and acquired an understanding of basic types as well as fundamental operations on numbers, characters, and booleans as well as constructing and manipulating more complex data in the form of strings and arrays. We also saw examples of how the Kotlin design helps to avoid common programming mistakes known in the Java world. Having built this foundation, we're ready to make the next step. In the next chapter, we'll learn Kotlin control structures and how to structure your code with functions and packages.

Points to remember

1. Kotlin identifiers may contain arbitrary characters when enclosed in backquotes.

2. Kotlin comments may be nested into each other.

3. Variables in Kotlin can be declared as either mutable or immutable.

4. Kotlin primitive types are pretty much similar to their Java counterparts although specifics of supported operations may vary.

5. Unlike Java, char values are not considered numbers but support some numeric operations.

6. Strings, like arrays, support indexing operators.

7. String literals can contain embedded expressions and support both single- and multi-line form.

8. Kotlin has special types for arrays of primitive elements (e.g. IntArray).

Multiple choice questions

1. Choose all options which represent a valid Kotlin identifier.

   A. foo

   B. `123`

   C. 1foo

   D. fOo!

2. What does the following program print?

```
fun main() {
    val a = 1
    val b = "2"
    val c = 3
    println("$a, ${b + c}, $b + $c")
}
```

   A. 1, 23, 5

   B. 1, 5, 5

   C. 1, 23, 2 + 3

   D. 1, 5, 2 + 3

3. Which of these are Kotlin integer types?

   A. Long

   B. Double

C. Char

D. Byte

4. Which keyword marks the variable as final?

   A. var

   B. let

   C. final

   D. val

5. Choose all expressions which evaluate to true.

   A. "234" < "768"

   B. "hello"[2] == 'e'

   C. "test" == "te" + "st"

   D. "147392".substring(2, 5).toInt() < 500

6. Which of the following expressions can be used to create an array of integer squares from 1 to 49?

   A. `intArrayOf(1, 4, 9, 16, 25, 36, 49)`

   B. `Array<Int>(7) { (it + 1)*(it + 1) }`

   C. `byteArrayOf(1, 4, 9, 16, 25, 36, 49)`

   D. IntArray(7) { (it + 1)*(it + 1) }

7. What operation can be used to compare arrays for equality element-wise?

   A. deepEquals

   B. `==`

   C. `===`

   D. `contentEquals`

Answers

1. A, B
2. C
3. A, D
4. D
5. A, C
6. A, B, C, D
7. D

Questions

1. Explain differences between quoted and non-quoted identifiers.

2. How do you define mutable and immutable variables?

3. What kinds of expressions are supported in Kotlin?

4. Describe Kotlin numeric types and their operations.

5 What operations are supported for Boolean values?

6. Which primitive values can be compared with each other? What are restrictions of equality operators?

7. Describe string template syntax. What are the differences between single-line and multi-line string templates?

8. Describe different ways to create arrays in Kotlin.

9. What operations are available on values of array types?

CHAPTER 3
Defining Functions

The central topic of this chapter is the concept of a `function. We'll learn the basic function anatomy and address some important issues such as using named arguments, default values, and vararg-style functions. We'll also introduce you to the imperative control structure of the Kotlin language. We'll discuss how to implement binary and multiple choice with if and when statements, discuss various forms of iteration, and error handling. We'll see that many of these constructs are very similar to the ones employed by Java (and, in fact, many other programming languages supporting an imperative paradigm) and learn the major differences which will ease migration to Kotlin for developers with Java experience. One more topic of interest is the structuring of your program with packages which group related declarations and using import directives for cross-package references.

Structure

In this chapter, we'll cover the following topics:

- Function definitions
- Packages and imports
- Conditionals

- Loops
- Exception handling

Objective

Our aim for this chapter is to get you acquainted with the fundamentals of imperative programming in Kotlin using conditional, iterative, and error-handling control structures as well as the means to structure your code using functions and packages.

Functions

Similar to Java's methods, a Kotlin **function** is a reusable block of code which accepts some input data (called parameters) and may return an output value to its calling code. In this section, we'll see how to define functions and take a look at their anatomy.

Function anatomy

Let's start with a simple example and define a function which computes an area of a circle with a given radius:

```kotlin
import kotlin.math.PI


fun circleArea(radius: Double): Double {

    return PI*radius*radius

}


fun main() {

    print("Enter radius: ")

    val radius = readLine()!!.toDouble()

    println("Circle area: ${circleArea(radius)}")

}
```

Note that we've used a standard constant **PI** which denotes an approximate value of π. The import directive at the start allows us to refer to **PI** by its simple name.

Now, let's look more closely at what makes up the **circleArea** definition:

- The **fun** keyword (from *function*) tells a compiler that what follows is a function definition.

- The function *name*, **circleArea**, which is like a variable name, can be an arbitrary identifier.

- The comma-separated *parameter list* enclosed in parentheses tells a compiler which data can be passed to our function upon its call.

The *return type*, **Double**, is a type of value returned to the function caller.

The *function body* is enclosed in a **block {}** and describes the implementation of our function.

Note that parentheses in a function definition and its call are mandatory even if the function has no parameters:

```kotlin
fun readInt(): Int {
    return readLine()!!.toInt()
}


fun main() {
    println(readInt())
}
```

Similar to Java, the function result is specified by the **return** statement which also terminates its execution by passing the control back to the caller. Any code placed after the return statement is effectively "dead", that is, never gets executed.

Java vs. Kotlin: As opposed to Java, the unreachable code in Kotlin is not a compile-time error. The compiler will, however, report a warning, and the IDE provides highlighting which clearly marks which portion of your code is "dead" (Figure 3.1):

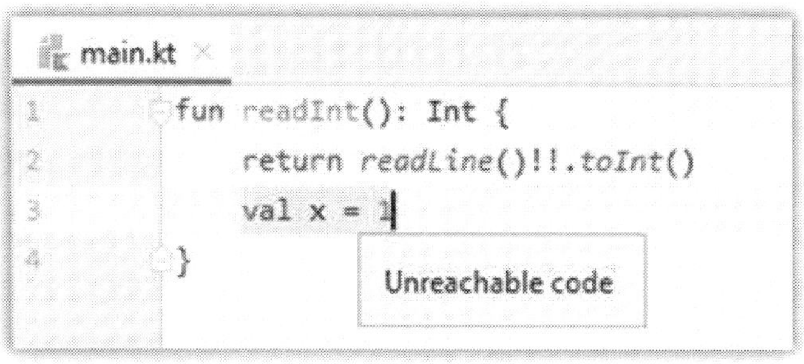

Figure 3.1: *Unreachable code highlighting*

In Kotlin, similar to Java, you have a block statement which is basically a group of statements enclosed in **{}**. Statements are separated by either a new line (which is the preferred style) or semicolons and are executed sequentially.

We've already employed blocks when writing a body of the function, but in fact, they're used whenever you need to perform multiple statements in a context which syntactically requires just one – like a body of a loop or a branch of some conditional statement. Blocks are also used to improve code readability; for example, a loop body is often enclosed in a block even when it consists of a single statement.

A block can contain definitions of local variables and functions: the scope of such declarations is limited to the block itself.

Parameter definition is basically an implicit local variable which is automatically initialized to the value passed in its call before executing the body.

Java vs. Kotlin: Unlike Java's method parameters which are mutable by default and must be marked with the final modifier to forbid further changes in the method body, Kotlin parameters are *immutable*. In other words, changing the parameter value inside a function body is a compilation error:

```
fun increment(n: Int): Int {

    return n++ // Error: can't change immutable variable

}
```

Note also that marking the parameter with the **val** or **var** keyword is forbidden. The reason behind this is that parameter assignments is considered error-prone while using parameters as immutable values lead to more clean and understandable code.

Kotlin follows "call by value" semantics which means that parameter values are copied from the respective call arguments. In particular, it means that changes to some variables passed as call arguments, like radius in the main function above), passed after the method call, do not affect the value of the parameter inside the called function. However, when the parameter is a reference – for example, has an array type – what gets copied is only the reference itself while the data behind it becomes shared between the function and its caller. So even though parameters themselves can't change inside the function, the data they reference in general may be mutable. For example:

```
fun increment(a: IntArray): Int {
    return ++a[0]

}
```

```
fun main() {

    val a = intArrayOf(1, 2, 3)

    println(increment(a))      // 2

    printl(a.contentToString) // [2, 2, 3]

}
```

Note that unlike variables parameters always have explicit types since a compiler can't infer it from the function definition.

The return type, on the contrary, *can* be inferred given types of function parameters but still must be specified explicitly. The rationale behind this decision is that functions often have more than one exit point where their result is determined and it may be difficult for a programmer to understand what kind of value is returned just by looking at the function definition. In this sense, explicit return types serve as a kind of documentation which immediately tells you about values the function can produce.

This rule, however, has two exceptions which allow you to omit the return type in some cases. The first one is a function of the so called Unit type which is a Kotlin counterpart for Java's **void** and basically signifies a function which doesn't need a meaningful return value. The actual return value of such a function is a constant Unit which is also the single value of the built-in Unit type. If you skip the return type in your function definition, the Kotlin compiler automatically assumes that you're declaring a Unit function. In other words, the following definitions are equivalent:

```
fun prompt(name: String) {

    println("***** Hello, $name! *****")

}
```

and

```
fun prompt(name: String): Unit {

    println("***** Hello, $name! *****")

}
```

We've already seen such functions through the example of **main()**. Note that **Unit** functions do not need the **return** statement to specify their result, since it's always the same. You can, however, use the **return** statement to terminate the function execution before it reaches the end of its body (**return Unit** is valid, but redundant in this case).

Another exception is so called *expression-body* functions. If the function can be implemented by a single expression, we can drop the return keyword and braces and write it in the following form:

```
fun circleArea(radius: Double): Double = PI*radius*radius
```

This syntax is similar to the one of variable definitions where you specify the initializing expression after the = symbol. Like variables, expression-body functions allow you to omit the result type:

```
fun circleArea(radius: Double) = PI*radius*radius // Double is inferred
```

Expression-body functions are considered simple enough to spare the explicit type specification. But this feature should be used with care: complex expressions are often worth to be written in a usual block form for better readability.

Note that if you try placing `{}` the block after the = sign to define a block-body function, you'll get a not quite expected result since the block in such a position is interpreted as a lambda (basically, a simplified syntax for anonymous function). In particular, the following definition:

```
fun circleArea(radius: Double) = { PI*radius*radius }
```

corresponds to a function which *returns another function* computing the circle area for a fixed value of radius, while the definition

```
fun circleArea(radius: Double) = {

    return PI*radius*radius // expected function, but returning Double

}
```

will produce a compile-time error due to the type mismatch and the fact that **return**, as we'll see in *Chapter 5, Leveraging Advanced Functions and Functional Programming*, is by default forbidden in lambdas.

Trailing commas

Since Kotlin 1.4, it's possible to leave trailing commas when listing elements such as arguments in a function call or parameters in a function header:

```
fun volume(length: Int, width: Int, height: Int, ) = length*width*height

val numbers = intArrayOf(1, 2, 3, 4, 5,)
```

The main rationale behind this feature revolves around a multi-line syntax for expression/declaration lists. For example, in the case of a call such as:

```
val numbers = intArrayOf(

    1,

    2,

    3,

    4,

    5,

)
```

The presence of a trailing comma simplifies swapping individual lines since you don't have add/remove commas by hand.

Note that the trailing comma is considered incorrect if it's not preceded by a list element. This is demonstrated by the following example:

```
val names = arrayOf<String>(,) // error
```

```
val numbers = intArrayOf(1, 2, 3, ,) // error
```

This syntax is in fact supported for any list of comma-separated syntactic elements such as parameters of a class constructor, variables inside a destructuring declarations, or enum entries. We'll cover them in the upcoming chapters.

Positional vs named arguments

By default, call arguments are mapped to parameters by their position. The first argument corresponds to the first parameter, the second to the second, and so on. In Kotlin, such arguments are called positional:

```
fun rectangleArea(width: Double, height: Double): Double {
    return width*height
}


fun main() {
    val w = readLine()!!.toDouble()
    val h = readLine()!!.toDouble()
    println("Rectangle area: ${rectangleArea(w, h)}")

}
```

Apart from positional arguments known in Java and many other languages, Kotlin supports the so called *named* arguments which are mapped to parameters by explicit names rather than positions. For example, we could have written the call to **rectangleArea()** as follows:

```
rectangleArea(width = w, height = h)
```

or even like this:

```
rectangleArea(height = h, width = w)
```

With the named argument, the style actual argument order is irrelevant, so both calls have exactly the same semantics as **rectangleArea(w, h)**.

You can also mix positional and named arguments in the same call. In Kotlin 1.3 and earlier versions, such a mix was a subject to the following rule; once you've used a named argument in a call, all subsequent arguments in the same call must also be named. Consider, for example, a function which swaps two characters in a string (the original string is, of course, unaffected since the **String** values are immutable):

```kotlin
fun swap(s: String, from: Int, to: Int): String {
    val chars = s.toCharArray() // convert to array
    // Swap array elements:
    val tmp = chars[from]
    chars[from] = chars[to]
    chars[to] = tmp
    return chars.toString() // Convert back to
}
fun main() {
    println(swap("Hello", 1, 2))              // Hlelo
    println(swap("Hello", from = 1, to = 2))      // Hlelo
    println(swap("Hello", to = 3, from = 0))      // lelHo
    println(swap("Hello", 1, to = 3))             // Hlleo
    println(swap(from = 1, s = "Hello", to = 2)) // Hlelo
    // Incorrect mixing of positional and named arguments
```

```
    println(swap(s = "Hello", 1, 2))              // Compilation error

    println(swap(s = "Hello", 1, to = 2))         // Compilation error

}
```

Starting from Kotlin 1.4, this limitation is relaxed. Now, you can mix both argument kinds in any possible way provided all positional arguments are placed in the correct order with respect to each other as well as named arguments. As a result, both of the lines:

```
    println(swap(s = "Hello", 1, 2))

    println(swap(s = "Hello", 1, to = 2))
```

from our earlier example are considered valid in Kotlin 1.4 while the following calls:

```
    println(swap(1, s = "Hello", 2))

    println(swap(1, "Hello", to = 2))
```

produce a compilation error due to violation of the order between **s** and **from**.

This improvement becomes quite handy when a call contains multiple literals so that you can't immediately guess which parameter they correspond to just by looking at the call text. Consider the following example:

```
fun format(num: Int, radix: Int, pad: Int, prefix: String): String {
    var s = num.toString(radix)
    if (pad > 0 && s.length < pad) {
        s = "0".repeat(pad - s.length) + s
    }
    return prefix + s
}


fun main() {
    println(format(255, 16, 8, "0x"))
    println(format(13, 2, 8, "0b"))
}
```

The **format()** function takes four arguments; three of which are integers. If you look at a particular call the **main()** body, you'll likely guess that the first argument is a number to be formatted while the last one is a prefix but still might mistake radix for **pad** and vice versa. Using 1.4 argument mixing, you can accompany them with explicit names thus improving your code readability:

```kotlin
fun main() {

    println(format(255, radix = 16, pad = 8, "0x"))

    println(format(13, radix = 2, pad = 8, "0b"))

}
```

IDE Tips: Even when a call argument is written in a positional form, you can still see the name of a corresponding parameter using the so called *inlay hint*. This IntelliJ IDEA feature is automatically enabled for Java and Kotlin files (although you can switch it off if needed) as shown in *Figure 3.2*:

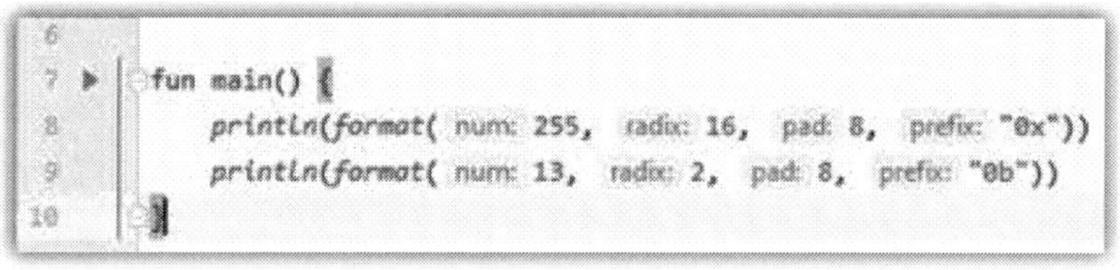

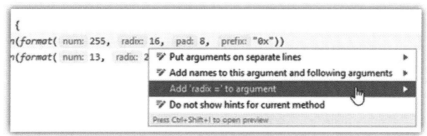

Figure 3.2: Inlay hints inside function call

IDE Tips: There is a special intention action that allows you to convert the positional argument into a named form. To use it, you just need to press *Alt + Enter* on the argument of interest and choose **"Add '…=' to argument"** (see *Figure 3.3* for example):

```
{
n(format( num: 255,   radix: 16,    pad: 8,   prefix: "0x"))
n(format( num: 13,   radix: 2    ⚡ Put arguments on separate lines                    ▶
                                 ⚡ Add names to this argument and following arguments  ▶
                                    Add 'radix =' to argument                          ▶
                                 ⚡ Do not show hints for current method
                                 Press Ctrl+Shift+I to open preview
```

Figure 3.3: Adding argument names

Overloading and default values

Kotlin functions, like Java methods, can be *overloaded*. In other words, you can define multiple functions sharing the same name. The overloaded function must have different parameter types so that the compiler can distinguish them while analyzing a call. For example, the following definitions comprise a valid overloading:

```
fun readInt() = readLine()!!.toInt()

fun readInt(radix: Int) = readLine()!!.toInt(radix)
```

while the following do not since they only differ in return types:

```
fun plus(a: String, b: String) = a + b

fun plus(a: String, b: String) = a.toInt() + b.toInt()
```

When choosing the function for a given Kotlin compiler, it follows an algorithm which is quite similar to the Java overload resolution:

1. Collect all functions which *can* be called with given arguments according to the parameter count and types.
2. Remove all less specific functions. A function is less specific if all its parameter types are supertypes of the corresponding parameters of some other function in the candidate list. This step is repeated until no less specific functions remain.
3. If the candidate list is reduced to a single function, it's considered the call target, otherwise the compiler reports an error.

Consider the following function definitions:

```
fun mul(a: Int, b: Int) = a*b              // 1
fun mul(a: Int, b: Int, c: Int) = a*b*c    // 2
fun mul(s: String, n: Int) = s.repeat(n)   // 3
fun mul(o: Any, n: Int) = Array(n) { o }   // 4
```

and the results of the overload resolution for some calls:

```
mul(1, 2)    // Choosing 1 between 1 and 4 since Int is a subtype of Any

mul(1, 2L)   // Error: no overload accepts (Int, Long)

mul(1L, 2)   // Choosing 4 as it's the only acceptable overload

mul("0", 3) // Choosing 3 between 3 and 4 since String is a subtype of Any
```

If you want to call an overload which is otherwise considered less specific, you can explicitly cast some argument(s) to their supertypes using the **as** operation:

```
mul("0" as Any, 3) // Choosing 4 as it's the only acceptable overload
```

We'll come back to the **as** operation in *Chapter 8, Understanding Class Hierarchies* where we'll take a closer look at subtyping and inheritance in Kotlin.

In Java, overloaded methods often perform the same operation and differ only in the set of their parameters that allows the user to omit one or more arguments in a function call assuming that they take some default values. Looking at the pair of the **readInt()** functions defined at the beginning of this section, we see that both of them parse the input **String** into an integer number with the second one being more general and allowing you to parse numbers in some range of numeral systems, while the first parses only decimals. In fact, we could have rewritten the first function in terms of the second one as follows:

```kotlin
fun readInt() = readInt(10)
```

In Kotlin, you don't need to use overloaded functions in such cases. Thanks to the more elegant solution; you just need to specify default values for parameters of interest in a similar way to how you specify a variable initializer:

```kotlin
fun readInt(radix: Int = 10) = readLine()!!.toInt(radix)
```

Now, you can call this function with either zero or one argument:

```kotlin
val decimalInt = readInt()
```

```kotlin
val decimalInt2 = readInt(10)
```

```kotlin
val hexInt = readInt(16)
```

Note that if some non-default parameters come after default ones, the only way to call such functions with default parameter(s) omitted is to use named arguments:

```kotlin
fun restrictToRange(
    from: Int = Int.MIN_VALUE,
    to: Int = Int.MAX_VALUE,
    what: Int
): Int = Math.max(from, Math.min(to, what))


fun main() {
    println(restrictToRange(10, what = 1))
}
```

It is, however, considered a good style to put parameters with default values at the end of the parameter list.

Default values somewhat complicate the overloading resolution since some functions may be called with different number of arguments. Consider the definitions:

```
fun mul(a: Int, b: Int = 1) = a*b          // 1

fun mul(a: Int, b: Long = 1L) = a*b        // 2

fun mul(a: Int, b: Int, c: Int = 1) = a*b*c // 3
```

and the corresponding calls:

```
mul(10)           // Error: can't choose between 1 and 2

mul(10, 20)       // Choosing 1 between 1 and 3 as having fewer parameters

mul(10, 20, 30) // Choosing 3 as the only acceptable candidate
```

You can see that function 3 is considered less specific than 2 for the two-argument call, **mul(10, 20)** since it basically extends the second signature by adding a third parameter **c**. If we, however, change, the first definition to:

```
fun mul(a: Number, b: Int = 1) = a*b
```

mul(10, 20) will resolve to the third function while the second one will be considered less specific due to Number being a supertype of Int.

Varargs

We've already seen several examples of functions like **arrayOf()** which accept a variable number of arguments. This feature is also available for functions you define in your own code. All you need to use it is place the **vararg** modifier before the parameter definition:

```
fun printSorted(vararg items: Int) {

    items.sort()

    println(items.contentToString())

}

fun main() {

    printSorted(6, 2, 10, 1) // [1, 2, 6, 10]

}
```

Inside the function itself such a parameter is available as an appropriate array type; for example, in case of our **printSorted()** it's **IntArray**.

You can also pass an actual array instance instead of the variable argument list prefixing it with a **spread** operator *:

```kotlin
val numbers = intArrayOf(6, 2, 10, 1)

printSorted(*numbers)

printSorted(numbers) // Error: passing IntArray instead of Int
```

Note that spread creates an array copy so changes to elements of items parameter do not affect values of the numbers elements:

```kotlin
fun main() {
    val numbers = intArrayOf(6, 2, 10, 1)

    printSorted(*numbers)        // [1, 2, 6, 10]

    println(a.contentToString()) // [6, 2, 10, 1]
}
```

The copying, however, is shallow. If array elements are themselves references, copying those references lead to sharing the data between the function and its caller:

```kotlin
fun change(vararg items: IntArray) {
    items[0][0] = 100
}

fun main() {
    val a = intArrayOf(1, 2, 3)

    val b = intArrayOf(4, 5, 6)

    change(a, b)

    println(a.contentToString()) // [100, 2, 3]

    println(b.contentToString()) // [4, 5, 6]
}
```

Declaring more than one parameter as **vararg** is forbidden. Such a parameter, however, can accept any mix of command-separated ordinary parameters and spreads; on the call, they are merged into a single array preserving the original order:

```kotlin
printSorted(6, 1, *intArrayOf(3, 8), 2) // [1, 2, 3, 6, 8]
```

If the **vararg** parameter is not the last one, values for parameters coming after it can only be passed with the named arguments notation. Similar to default values, it's considered a good style to place the **vararg** parameter at the end of the parameter list. **vararg** itself can't be passed as a named argument unless you're using the spread operator:

```
printSorted(items = *intArrayOf(1, 2, 3))
```

```
printSorted(items = 1, 2, 3) // Error
```

Note that parameters having default values do not mix very well with **vararg.** Placing defaults before **vararg** will force first values of the **vararg** argument to be interpreted as values of preceding defaults unless you pass **vararg** in a named form which defeats the purpose of using **vararg** in the first place:

```
fun printSorted(prefix: String = "", vararg items: Int) { }
```

```
fun main() {

    printSorted(6, 2, 10, 1) // Error: 6 is taken as value of prefix

    printSorted(items = *intArrayOf(6, 2, 10, 1)) // Correct

}
```

Placing defaults after the **vararg** parameter, on the other hand, will require you to use the named form for the defaults:

```
fun printSorted(vararg items: Int, prefix: String = "") { }
```

```
fun main() {

    printSorted(6, 2, 10, 1, "!") // Error: "" is taken as part of vararg

    printSorted(6, 2, 10, 1, prefix = "!") // Correct

}
```

varargs also affect overload resolution in a sense that function with vararg parameter, all other things being equal, is considered less specific than a function having a fixed number of parameters of the same type:

```
fun printSorted(vararg items: Int) { }        // 1
```

```
fun printSorted(a: Int, b: Int, c: Int) { } // 2
```

```
fun main() {
```

```
printSorted(1, 2, 3)      // Choosing 2 between 1 and 2 as non-
                                                vararg function

printSorted(1, 2)// Choosing 1 as the only acceptable candidate
}
```

Function scope and visibility

Kotlin functions can be broken down into three categories depending on where they're defined:

- *top-level* functions are declared directly in a file.
- *member* functions are declared in some type.
- *local* functions are declared inside another function.

In this chapter, we'll focus on top-level and local functions while the member functions are postponed till *Chapter 4, Working with Classes and Objects* where we'll deal with the concept of a Kotlin class.

So far, we've only defined top-level functions like **main()**. By default, these functions are considered *public*; in other words, they can be used anywhere in the project and not just in their enclosing file. Let's, for example, create two Kotlin files, **main.kt** and **util.kt** in the same directory. We can see that the **main()** function defined in the **main.kt** file calls the **readInt()** function defined in **util.kt** (*Figure 3.2*):

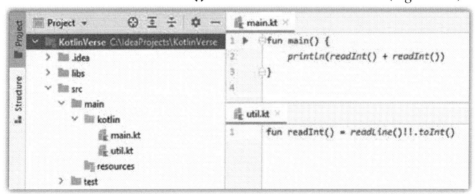

Figure 3.2: Calling public function from another file

In some cases, you might want to hide implementation details from other parts of your project, thus narrowing the function *scope*, or the set of places in code where it can be used. To do that, you may prefix the top-level function definition with either of the keywords **private** or **internal** which are called *visibility modifiers*.

Marking a function as **private** makes it accessible only in the containing file. For example, if we make **readInt()** private, we can still use it inside **util.kt**, but not from **main.kt** (*Figure 3.3*):

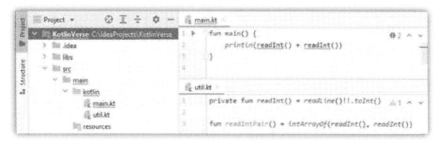

Figure 3.3: *Calling private function from another file*

Using the **internal** modifier allows you to restrict function usages to its containing module. A Kotlin *module* is basically a group of files which are compiled together. Its specific meaning depends on the build system you use to assemble your project, but in case of IntelliJ IDEA, it corresponds to a single IDE module. So making a function internal allows you to use from any other file in the same module, but not from other modules of your project.

You can also use the **public** modifier, but that's considered redundant since top-level functions are public by default.

A local function, like a local variable, is declared inside another function. The scope of such a function is limited to the enclosing code block:

```kotlin
fun main() {
    fun readInt() = readLine()!!.toInt()


    println(readInt() + readInt())
}


fun readIntPair() = intArrayOf(readInt(), readInt()) // Error
```

Local functions are able to access declarations available in enclosing functions, including their parameters:

```kotlin
fun main(args: Array<String>) {
    fun swap(i: Int, j: Int): String {
```

```
        val chars = args[0].toCharArray()

        val tmp = chars[i]

        chars[i] = chars[j]

        chars[j] = tmp

        return chars.toString()

    }



    println(swap(0, chars.lastIndex))

}
```

Note that local functions and variables may not have any visibility modifiers.

Java vs Kotlin: Java language and JVM in general require all methods to be members of some class. So, you're probably wondering how Kotlin top-level and local functions can be compiled on the JVM platform. In *Chapter 1, Kotlin - Powerful and Pragmatic,* we've already seen that from the JVM view-point, the top-level **main()** function is in fact a static member of a special facade class generated per Kotlin file. For the local functions, the Kotlin compiler performs a similar trick which involves a declaration of a special class (you can compare it with a local class in Java) which contains the local function as its member and captures its context-like variables and parameters of the enclosing function. Note that this implies some performance overhead as your program may need to create a new instance of such a class on every call of the local function. We'll come back to this issue in *Chapter 5, Leveraging Advanced Functions and Functional Programming* while discussing lambdas.

Packages and imports

A Kotlin package is a way to group-related declaration. Any package has a name and may be nested into some other package. This concept is very similar to its Java counterpart, but has its own specifics which we'll highlight in the upcoming sections.

Packages and directory structure

Similar to Java, you can specify the package name at the start of a Kotlin file making the compiler to put all top-level declarations listed in the file into the corresponding package. If package is not specified, the compiler assumes that your file belongs to the default *root* package which has an empty name.

Package directive starts with a package keyword and contains a dot-separated list of identifiers comprising *qualified name* of the package which is basically a path to the current package in the project's package hierarchy starting from the root. For example, the following file:

```
package foo.bar.util
```

```
fun readInt() = readLine()!!.toInt()
```

belongs to the package util which is contained in the package bar which, in turn, is contained in the package **foo**, while the file:

```
package numberUtil
```

```
fun readDouble() = readLine()!!.toDouble()
```

is put into the package **numberUtil** which is contained just in the package hierarchy root.

Multiple files share the same package if they have the same package directives; in this case, the package will include all contents of these files combined.

Top-level declarations which comprise a package include types, functions, and properties. We've already acquainted ourselves with a top-level function definition and will see how to define types and properties in the upcoming chapter. Within the same package, you can refer to its declarations using their simple names. This is what we've been doing so far in our examples since all our files were implicitly put into the same root package. *Figure 3.4* shows you a similar example with the non-default package name:

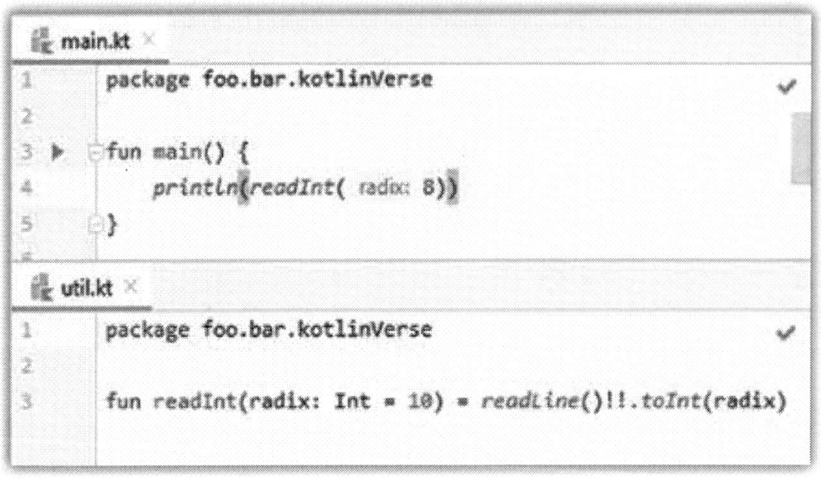

Figure 3.4: *Calling a function from the same package*

What if a declaration you want to use belongs to a different package? In this case, you can still refer to it using its qualified name which is basically a simple name prefixed with a qualified name of the enclosing package (*Figure 3.5*):

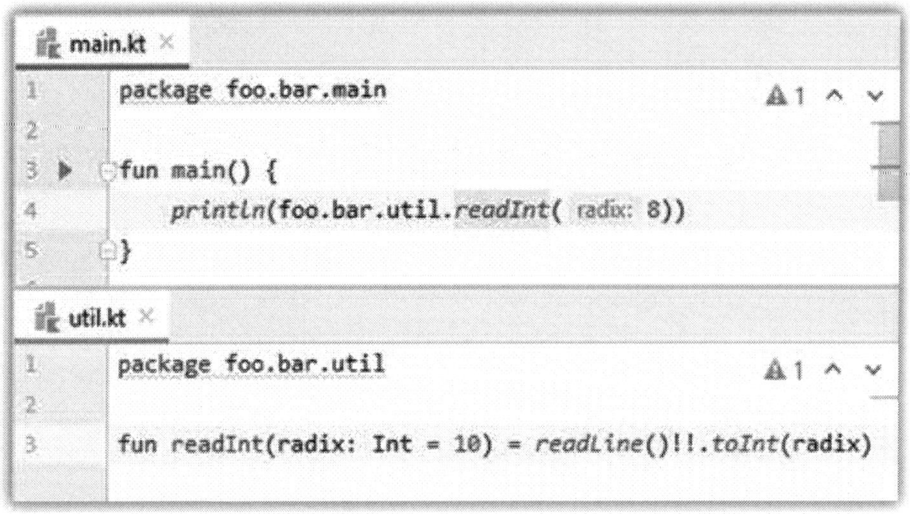

Figure 3.5: *Using a qualified name to call a function from a different package*

In general, this approach is not practical because it produces hard-to-read code with excessively long names. For that reason, Kotlin provides an import mechanism. By placing an *import directive* with a qualified declaration name once at the beginning of your file, you can refer to it using a simple name (*Figure 3.6*).

IDE Tips: The IntelliJ plugin takes care of many tedious operations with imports.

In particular, if you try to use some declaration which is located in another package but refer to it with a simple name only, IDE will automatically bring up a popup suggesting to import it from relevant packages. It also highlights unused imports and allows you to optimize the entire import list by removing unused ones and sorting remaining directives with an Optimize Imports command available by the *Ctrl + Alt + O* (Command + Alt + O) shortcut.

Note that the package hierarchy is a separate structure inferred purely from the package directives in the source files. It may coincide with a directory structure of the source file tree, but that's not necessary. For example, source files may reside in the same directory but belong to different packages and vice versa.

Java vs Kotlin: In Java, on the contrary, the package structure must be a direct reflection of the source tree directories in the compilation root. Any mismatch is treated as a compilation error.

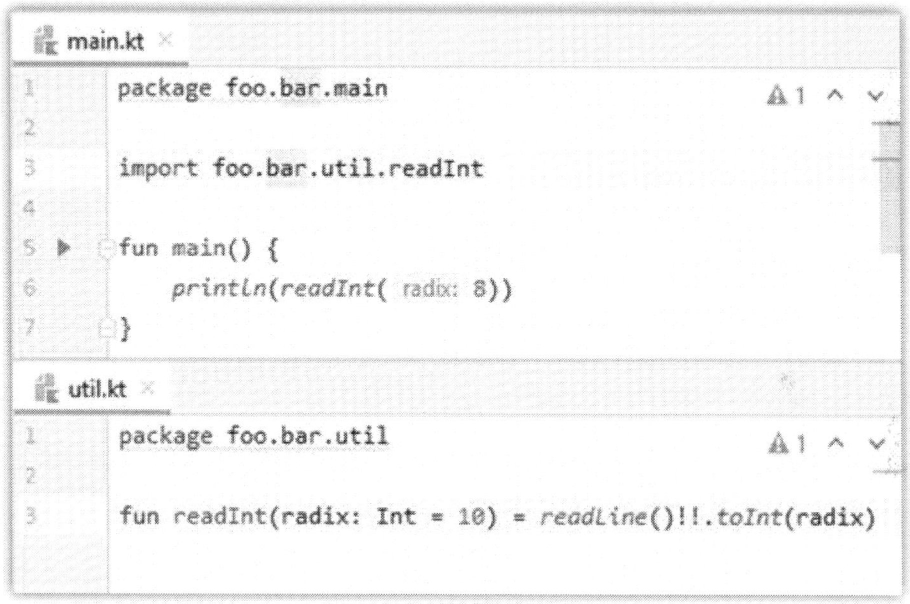

```kotlin
main.kt ×
1    package foo.bar.main
2
3    import foo.bar.util.readInt
4
5 ▶  fun main() {
6        println(readInt( radix: 8))
7    }
```

```kotlin
util.kt ×
1    package foo.bar.util
2
3    fun readInt(radix: Int = 10) = readLine()!!.toInt(radix)
```

Figure 3.6: *Using import directive*

It is, however, recommended to keep the directory and package structure matched as it simplifies the navigation between different parts of your project.

IDE Tips: By default, the IntelliJ plugin enforces the package/directory matching and displays a warning whenever it's violated. You've probably noticed that package directives in *Figure 3.6* are highlighted. That's because the package directives we've put do not match the directory paths. By pressing *Alt + Enter* within the highlighted area, you can either change the directive itself, or move the containing file into the corresponding directory.

Using import directives

We've already seen how import directives allow you to avoid using qualified names and simplify your code. In this section, we'll look more closely at what kinds of import directives are available in Kotlin and how they differ from their Java counterparts.

The simplest form that we've already seen in the earlier examples allows you to import some specific declaration by specifying its qualified name:

```
import java.lang.Math       // JDK class

import foo.bar.util.readInt // top-level function
```

The import directive is not limited to top-level declarations such as classes or functions. It can also be used to import various member declarations such as nested classes or enum constants. In *Chapter 4, Working with Classes and Objects,* and *Chapter 6, Using Special-Case Classes*, we'll address this issue in more detail.

```
import kotlin.Int.Companion.MIN_VALUE

fun fromMin(steps: Int) = MIN_VALUE + n // refer to MIN_VALUE by simple name
```

Java vs Kotlin: Unlike Java, Kotlin doesn't have a separate construct which imports type members similar to Java's "import static". All declarations in Kotlin are imported using the general import directive syntax.

In some declarations residing in different packages, may have the same name. What if you need to use them in a single file? Suppose we have two **readInt()** functions in packages **app.util.foo** and **app.util.bar,** respectively. Trying to import them both won't solve the problem:

```
import app.util.foo.readInt

import app.util.bar.readInt

fun main() {
    val n = readInt()   // Error: can't choose between two variants
                                              of readInt()
}
```

You can always use the qualified name to distinguish between the too, but Kotlin gives you a better solution which is called an *import alias*. This feature allows you to introduce a new name for an imported declaration which has an effect in the scope of the entire file:

```kotlin
import foo.readInt as fooReadInt

import bar.readInt as barReadInt


fun main() {

    val n = fooReadInt()

    val m = barReadInt()
}
```

Another form of an import directive allows you to import all declarations from a given scope:

```kotlin
import kotlin.math.* // import all declarations from kotlin.math.package
```

Note that such "on-demand" import has a lower priority than an import directive referring to some specific declarations. If we consider our example with two **readInt()** functions but change one of the import directives to on-demand, the specific one takes over:

```kotlin
import app.util.foo.readInt

import app.util.bar.*


fun main() {
    val n = readInt()    // No ambiguity: resolves to app.util.foo.
                                                           readInt

}
```

Conditionals

Conditional statements allow you to choose one of the two or more actions depending on the value of some condition. In Kotlin, they are represented by **if** and **when** statements which can be roughly compared to Java's **if** and **switch**.

Making decisions with if statements

Using the **if** statement, you can select between two alternatives depending on the value of some boolean expression. It has the same syntax as a similar statement in Java:

```kotlin
fun max(a: Int, b: Int): Int {
    if (a > b) return a
    else return b
}
```

Basically, it performs the first statement when the condition in parentheses is true and the second one (else-branch) otherwise. Else-branch may be absent in which case the statement does nothing if the condition is false. Each of the two branches may be a block statement which allows you to execute multiple statements within the same alternative:

```kotlin
fun main(args: Array<String>) {
    if (args.isNotEmpty()) {
        val message = "Hello, ${args[0]}"
        println(message)
    } else {
        println()
    }
}
```

Note that the condition must be an expression of the **Boolean** type.

The key difference from the if statement in Java is that Kotlin's **if** statement can also be used as an expression. For example, we could have written our max function in a simpler form as follows:

```kotlin
fun max(a: Int, b: Int) = if (a > b) a else b
```

This is also true when one or both of the branches are blocks; in which case the value of the entire conditional statement coincides with the last expression in the corresponding block:

```kotlin
fun main() {
    val s = readLine()!!
    val i = s.indexOf("/")
    // Split line like 10/3 into 10 and 3 and perform the division
```

```
    val result = if (i >= 0) {

        val a = s.substring(0, i).toInt()

        val b = s.substring(i + 1).toInt()

        (a/b).toString()

    } else ""

    println(result)

}
```

Note that when **if** is used as an expression both branches must be present. The following code won't compile since it misses an else-branch:

```
val max = if (a > b) a
```

Java vs Kotlin: Kotlin doesn't have the conditional ? operator, which you might've used in Java. This is, however, mostly mitigated by the fact that **if** can be used as both a statement and an expression.

Sometimes, it can be helpful to use **return** in an **if** expression. The **return** statement can be used as an expression of a special type Nothing which denotes a non-existing value. Basically, if some expression has the Nothing type, it indicates some break in the sequential control-flow of the program since such an expression never reaches any definite value. In case of return, it means termination of the enclosing function. One useful aspect of the Nothing type is that it's considered a subtype of every Kotlin type and thus its expressions may be used in any context where an expression is expected. Suppose we're given a qualified package name and want to know how it would look like if its simple name was changed:

```
fun renamePackage(fullName: String, newName: String): String {

    val i = fullName.indexOf('.')

    val prefix = if (i >= 0) fullName.substring(0, i + 1) else return
    newName

    return prefix + newName

}


fun main() {
```

```
    println(renamePackage("foo.bar.old", "new")) // foo.bar.new
}
```

Note that the value of **newName** in **return newName** is not the value of the return expression, but rather a resulting value of the enclosing function. The **return** expression itself has no value just like any expression of the type **Nothing**. Keep in mind the difference between Unit and Nothing: as opposed to **Nothing, Unit** has a *single* instance which is generally used to denote the absence of any *useful* value, rather than an absence of any value at all.

Ranges, progressions, and in operation

Kotlin includes several built-in types which represent some interval of ordered values. They are particularly useful for iteration over numeric ranges using the **for** loop. In Kotlin, these types are collectively known as *ranges*.

The simplest way to construct a range is to use .. operation on numeric values:

```
val chars = 'a'..'h'    // all characters from 'a' to 'h'

val twoDigits = 10..99  // all two-digit integers from 10 to 99

val zero2One = 0.0..1.0 // all floating-point numbers in the range
    from 0 to 1
```

Using the **in** operation, you can check whether a given value fits into the range. This is basically equivalent to a pair of comparison:

```
val num = readLine()!!.toInt()

println(num in 10..99) // num >= 10 && num <= 99
```

There is also an opposite operation **!in** which allows you to write expressions like **!(a in b)** in a simplified form:

```
println(num !in 10..99) // !(num in 10.99)
```

In fact, the .. operation is available for all comparable types, including numeric, **Char, Boolean,** and **String**. Basically, whenever you can use **<=** or **>=,** you can also use .. to construct a range:

```
println("def" in "abc".."xyz") // true

println("zzz" in "abc".."xyz") // false
```

Ranges produced by the .. operation are *closed* which means they include both start and end points. There is another operation which allows you to create semi-closed ranges with excluded end points. This operation is only available for integer types and basically produces a range with a smaller end point:

```
val twoDigits = 10 until 100  // same as 10..99, 100 is excluded
```

Note that built-in ranges are empty if if their end point is strictly less than the start one.

```
println(5 in 5..5)      // true
```

```
println(5 in 5 until 5) // false
```

```
println(5 in 10..1)     // false
```

In general, that's not true if the comparison on a given type is ill-behaved. In particular, if it's not transitive, there is a possibility that **x** in **a..b** might be true even when **a > b**.

There is also a related concept of *progression* which is an ordered sequence of integer or Char values separated by some fixed step. Every range over these types is an ascending progression with step 1, but progressions in general give you additional options. For example, you can define the descending progression using the **downTo** operation:

```
println(5 in 10 downTo 1) // true
```

```
println(5 in 1 downTo 10) // false: progression is empty
```

You can also specify a custom progression step:

```
1..10 step 3      // 1, 4, 7, 10
15 down 9 step 2 // 15, 13, 11, 9
```

The progression step must be positive, so if you want to construct a descending sequence, you should use **step** together with the **downTo** operation as seen in the preceding example.

Progression elements are generated by successively adding steps to its starting point, so if the end point does not actually correspond to one of the progression values, it's automatically adjusted to the nearest progression element:

```
1..12 step 3      // 1, 4, 7, 10: the same as 1..10 step 3
15 down 8 step 2 // 15, 13, 11, 9: the same as 15 downTo 9 step 2
```

Using ranges, you can extract a portion of a string or an array. Mind the difference between the **substring()** function taking a closed integer range and the one taking a pair of indices where the end-point is excluded:

```
"Hello, World".substring(1..4)               // ello
```

```
"Hello, World".substring(1 until 4)        // ell
"Hello, World".substring(1, 4)             // ell: like substring(1
                                           until 4)

IntArray(10) { it*it }.sliceArray(2..5)        // 4, 9, 16, 25
IntArray(10) { it*it }.sliceArray(2 until 5)   // 4, 9, 16
```

Range and progression types are defined in the Kotlin standard library as a set of classes like **IntRange**, **FloatRange**, **CharProgression**, **IntProgression,** and so on. You can find an exhaustive list of the classes together with their functions and properties on the documentation page for the **kotlin.ranges** package at kotlinlang.org/api/latest/jvm/stdlib/kotlin.ranges/. In general, using ranges instead of comparisons involve a slight overhead since ranges are dynamically allocated objects. The compiler, however, tries to avoid creating actual objects when possible. For example, in the following program, no IntRange instance is created; instead, it just compares 5 with entered values:

```
fun main() {

    val a = readLine()!!.toInt()

    val b = readLine()!!.toInt()

    println(5 in a..b)

}
```

So in terms of performance, it's equivalent to a pair of comparisons: a <= 5 && 5 <= b. Another major use case of range/progression optimization is a **for** loop.

IDE Tips: The IntelliJ plugin includes a JVM bytecode viewer which can be useful to explore a low-level semantics of the Kotlin code. To open it, choose **Tools |** **Kotlin | Show Kotlin Bytecode** in the IDE menu. The viewer updates to reflect the bytecode of the current Kotlin file in the editor and automatically preselects the portion of bytecode corresponding to the caret position in the source code.

If you're not particularly familiar with the JVM bytecode, you can click on the **Decompile** button transforming it into a Java code. Note that due to specifics of bytecode generated by the Kotlin compiler, such a decompiled code can be formally incorrect, but it still can give you a good understanding of the original Kotlin code's inner workings.

Ranges are not the only types supporting the **in/!in** operation. You can use for other types describing some kind of container such as strings or arrays:

```
val numbers = intArrayOf(3, 7, 2, 1)
```

```
val text = "Hello!"

println(2 in numbers)  // true

println(9 !in numbers) // true

println(4 in numbers)  // false

println('a' in text)   // false

println('H' in text)   // true

println('h' !in text)  // true
```

In terms of precedence, the range operation **..** fits between additive and infix ones while **in/!in** are placed between infix and comparisons. In other words, the relevant portion of the table from *Chapter 2, Language Fundamentals*, will now look like this:

Additive	+ -	a + b..c - d	// (a + b)..(c - d)
Range	..	a..b step c	// (a..b) step c
		a in b..c	// a in (b..c)
Infix	Named operators	a < b or b < c	// (a < (b or b)) < c
		a == b and b == c c	// (a == b) and (b == c)
		a in b or a in c c	// (a in (b or a)) in c
Named check	**in !in**	a < b in c	// a < (b in c)
		a !in b > c	// (a !in b) > c
Comparison	< > <= >=	a < b == b < c	// (a < b) == (b < c)
		a < b && b < c	// (a < b) && (b < c)

Operations **until**, **downTo,** and **step** have the same precedence as any other named infix operation (**and**, **or**, **xor**, and so on).

when statements and multiple choice

Since **if** statements can choose between two options, one way to implement a multiple choice is combining several **if** statements into a cascade-like structure which sequentially checks all conditions of interest. Suppose we want to convert a decimal number between 0 and to the corresponding hexadecimal digit:

```
fun hexDigit(n: Int): Char {
```

```
    if (n in 0..9) return '0' + n

    else if (n in 10..15) return 'A' + n - 10

    else return '?'

}
```

Kotlin, though, provides you a more concise construct to select among multiple alternatives which is called a **when** statement. Using this construct, you can rewrite the preceding function in the following form:

```
fun hexDigit(n: Int): Char {

    when {

        n in 0..9 -> return '0' + n

        n in 10..15 -> return 'A' + n - 10

        else -> return '?'

    }

}
```

Basically, the **when** statement is a block which is preceded by the when keyword and consists of zero or more branches of the general form **condition -> statement** as well as an optional else-branch. The statement execution proceeds according to the following rule. The program subsequently evaluates conditions in the order they're written until it finds the one which evaluates to true. If such a condition is found, the program executes the statement-part of the corresponding branch. If all conditions evaluate to false, the program executes the else-branch (if there is one).

IDE Tips: The IntelliJ plugin provides an intention action for automatic conversion between nested **if**s and **when**. To access it, press *Alt + Enter* with the caret placed in the **if/when** keyword and choose "Replace 'if' with 'when'" or "Replace 'when' with 'if'" action, respectively.

Similar to **if**, a **when** statement can be used as an expression. In this case, else-branch is mandatory since **when** should be able to provide some definite value for each possible case:

```
fun hexDigit(n: Int) = when {

    n in 0..9 -> '0' + n

    n in 10..15 -> 'A' + n - 10
```

```
        else -> '?'
}
```

Java vs Kotlin: Kotlin's **when** is similar to Java's **switch** statement which can also select multiple options. The crucial difference, however, is that **when** allows you to check arbitrary conditions while **switch** can only choose among values of a given expression. Besides this, the **switch** statement in Java follows the so called fall-through semantics. When some condition is matched, the program executes its statements as well as statements in subsequent branches unless the execution is explicitly stopped by the **break** statement. Kotlin's **when** executes only statements in the matched branch and never "falls through" the entire **when** block.

The when statement has another form which is suitable for multiple checks that involve equality and **in** operations. Consider the following function:

```
fun numberDescription(n: Int): String = when {
        n == 0 -> "Zero"
        n == 1 || n == 2 || n == 3 -> "Small"
        n in 4..9 -> "Medium"
        n in 10..100 -> "Large"
        n !in Int.MIN_VALUE until 0 -> "Negative"
        else -> "Huge"
}
```

Since all conditions of the expression above are either equality, **in** or **!in** operation with the same left operand, **n**, we can express the same logic by making n the *subject expression* of when and rewriting it in the following form:

```
fun numberDescription(n: Int, maxLarge: Int = 100): String = when
(n) {
        0 -> "Zero"
        1, 2, 3 -> "Small"
        in 4..9 -> "Medium"
        in 10..max -> "Large"
        !in Int.MIN_VALUE until 0 -> "Negative"
```

```
        else -> "Huge"

}
```

IDE Tips: The IntelliJ plugin can transform one form of the **when** expression into another by eliminating and introducing subject expressions when necessary. You can access these actions by placing the caret on the **when** keyword and pressing *Alt + Enter*; you can then choose a command depending on the statement form; either "Introduce ... as subject of 'when'", or "Eliminate argument of 'when'".

This form of the **when** statement is distinguished by a subject expression which is written in parentheses after the **when** keyword. A branch of such a statement can start with either **in/!in**, an arbitrary expression or the **else** keyword (there is also **is/!is** branch which we'll refer to *Chapter 8, Understanding Class Hierarchies*). The execution is similar to the first form of **when**:

1. First, the subject expression is evaluated; suppose its value is **subj**.
2. The program successively evaluates conditions of branches until it finds the one which is true. The **in/!in** branch is treated as the **in/!in** expression with **subj** as its left operand, while the free-form expression **e** is interpreted as the equality operation **subj == e**.
3. If such a condition is found, the program executes the corresponding statement, the else-statement is executed if it's present.

The subject form allows you to write multiple conditions in a single branch, separating them by commas (**1, 2, 3 -> "Small"** branch in the preceding example). During condition evaluations, these commas are effectively treated as logical OR (**||**).

Note that expressions in the branches of the subject when are not necessarily boolean; they may have an arbitrary type as long as the corresponding operations (**== or in/!in**) are applicable.

Java vs Kotlin: Since Java 12, **switch** has acquired an expression form which is very similar to the subject form of Kotlin's **when**. It, however, has some limitations. In particular, **switch** doesn't support range checks (unlike **in/!in** operation in Kotlin) and can be applied only to limited set of types: integers, enums, and strings. Note also that **when** branches can use arbitrary expressions and are not limited to constants.

Since Kotlin 1.3, **when** statements allow you to bind the subject expression to a variable using the following syntax:

```
fun readHexDigit() = when(val n = readLine()!!.toInt()) { // define n

    n in 0..9 -> '0' + n
```

```
    n in 10..15 -> 'A' + n - 10

    else -> '?'

}
```

Such a variable can only be used inside the when block and can not be declared as **var**.

Loops

Kotlin supports three control structures which repeat the same sequence of instructions for a given set of data or till some condition is satisfied. **while** and **do-while** loops have the same structure corresponding to Java statements, and the **for** loop is very similar to Java's **for-each**. All loops in Kotlin are statements rather than expressions and so do not have any value as such, only side effects.

while/do-while loop

Suppose we want to compute a sum of integers entered by a user. Let's agree that zero will serve as a stop-value after which we cease reading the input and report the result:

```
fun main() {

    var sum = 0

    var num = 0

    do {

        num = readLine()!!.toInt()

        sum += num

    } while (num != 0)

    println("Sum: $sum")
```

The **do-while** loop is evaluated according to the following rules:

1. Execute the *loop body* between do and while keywords.
2. Evaluate the *condition* coming after the while keyword and if it's true, go back to step 1; otherwise proceed to the statement after loop.

Note that the loop body is always executed at least once since the condition is checked afterwards.

There is another form of loop which also executes its body while the condition holds true, but checks whether the condition before running instructions in the body. It means that if the condition is false on entering the loop, its body will never execute.

Suppose we want to write the program that generates some number and then asks the user to guess it giving hints if the guess was wrong (like: "too small" or "too big") and stop when the guess is right:

```kotlin
import kotlin.random.*


fun main() {

    val num = Random.nextInt(1, 101)

    var guess = 0

    while (guess != num) {

        guess = readLine()!!.toInt()

        if (guess < num) println("Too small")

        else if (guess > num) println("Too big")

    }

    println("Right: it's $num")

}
```

The number is generated using the **Random.nextInt()** function from the standard library.

These examples clearly demonstrate that the **while/do-while** statements in Kotlin are essentially the same as in Java.

Iterables and for loop

Kotlin **for** loop allows you to iterate over collection-like values which can contain or produce multiple elements. We can, for example, use a for loop to sum array elements:

```kotlin
fun main() {

    val a = IntArray(10) { it*it } // 0, 1, 4, 9, 16, …

    var sum = 0
```

```
    for (x in a) {

        sum += x

    }

    println("Sum: $sum") // Sum: 285

}
```

The loop consists of the following three parts:

- iteration variable definition (x)

- a container expression (a) which produces values to iterate over

- a loop body statement ({sum += x}) which is executed on each iteration

The iteration variable is accessible only inside the loop body and is automatically assigned a new value at the start of each iteration. Note that a loop variable is not marked with the **val** or **var** keywords like you do with an ordinary variable and is implicitly immutable. In other words, you can't change its value inside the loop body. In the simplest case, the loop variable definition is a simple identifier. You can specify its type, though, but that's rarely needed in practice:

```
for (x: Int in a) {

    sum += x

}
```

Java vs Kotlin: The Kotlin **for** loop is quite similar to Java's **for-each** loop which gives you a simple syntax for iteration over any Iterable instance; be it an array, list, set, or a user-defined type. Kotlin, however, doesn't have a counterpart for the ordinary Java **for** loop which requires you to explicitly declare, initialize, check, and update an iteration variable. In Kotlin, such iterations are just special cases of the **for** loop statement you've seen earlier.

You can use a **for** loop to iterate over string characters. Let's, for example, write our own function which parses a binary string representation of a positive number to Int:

```
fun parseIntNumber(s: String, fallback: Int = -1): Int {

    var num = 0

    if (s.length !in 1..31) return fallback

    for (c in s) {
```

```kotlin
    if (c !in '0'..'1') return fallback

    num = num*2 + (c - '0')

  }

  return num

}
```

When a string in question doesn't represent a valid number or doesn't fit into, the function returns some fallback value.

Java vs Kotlin: In Java, direct iteration on `string` is not possible, so you have to use some workaround like iterating over its indices or converting the string to character array first.

What about ordinary iteration over numeric intervals? For that purpose, you use a progression we've introduced in the previous section. Suppose we want to double all array elements with even indices:

```kotlin
val a = IntArray(10) { it*it } // 0, 1, 4, 9, 16, ...

for (i in 0..a.lastIndex) {     // 0, 1, 2, 3, ...

    if (i % 2 == 0) {           // 0, 2, 4, 6, ...

        a[i] *= 2

    }

}
```

We can simplify this loop even further using the progression with the custom step:

```kotlin
for (i in 0..a.lastIndex step 2) { // 0, 2, 4, 6, ...

    a[i] *= 2

}
```

Strings and arrays have the **indices** property which contains a range of character or item indices:

```kotlin
val a = IntArray(10) { it*it } // 0, 1, 4, 9, 16, ...

for (i in a.indices step 2) {  // 0, 2, 4, 6, ...

    a[i] *= 2

}
```

The real beauty of the **for** loop comes from the fact that the compiler doesn't just support some limited set of disparate use cases like numeric ranges or collections, etc., but provides a unified mechanism which allows you to iterate over all kinds of values. The only thing required of the container expression is the `iterator()` function which returns an `Iterator` object capable of extracting element values. We'll postpone detailed discussions of iterators till *Chapter 7, Exploring Collections and I/O*, but for now, it suffices to know that many standard Kotlin types already have built-in iterators. That's why **for** loops work just as well for progressions, arrays, and strings. As we'll see further, using an *extension* mechanism allows you to attach an iterator to any type you like, thus extending the range of possible expressions to iterate.

Java vs Kotlin: Java **for-each** loop is similar in a sense that it can be applied to any subtype of `Iterable`. Kotlin **for** loop convention is more flexible, though, as it doesn't require a container to be of any particular type; all a **for** loop needs is the presence of the `iterator()` function.

Changing loop control-flow: break and continue

Sometimes, it's convenient to alter an ordinary control-flow of the loop; for example, it may be convenient to check an exit condition not at the start or end of a loop iteration, but somewhere in the middle. For that purpose, Kotlin includes a pair of expressions:

- **break** which immediately terminates iterating, forcing the execution to continue from the next statement after the loop.
- **continue** which stops the current iteration and jumps to the condition check.

In other words, these statements have the same semantics as their Java counterparts. Consider, for example, our "Guess the number" program. We could have used a break statement to write it like this:

import kotlin.random.*


```kotlin
fun main() {
    val num = Random.nextInt(1, 101)
    while (true) {
        val guess = readLine()!!.toInt()
        if (guess < num) println("Too small")
```

```kotlin
        else if (guess > num) println("Too big")

        else break

    }

    println("Right: it's $num")

}
```

Note that the loop condition became unnecessary since all exit checks now happen in its body. Thanks to that we can also move the **guess** variable into the loop.

Java vs Kotlin: Like **return, break,** and **continue** statements in Kotlin can be used as expressions of the type **Nothing**. We could, for example, have rewritten the preceding program to calculate the message text before printing:

```kotlin
import kotlin.random.*


fun main() {
    val num = Random.nextInt(1, 101)
    while (true) {
        val guess = readLine()!!.toInt()
        val message =
            if (guess < num) "Too small"
            else if (guess > num) "Too big"
            else break
        println(message)
    }
    println("Right: it's $num")
}
```

This feature shouldn't be abused, though, as in more complex expressions, it might in fact hinder the understanding of your code.

Suppose that we want to count a number of times each English letter occurs in a given string. In the following example, we use a **continue** expression to stop the current iteration when a character is not a letter before trying to access an array:

```kotlin
fun countLetters(text: String): IntArray {

    val counts = IntArray('z' - 'a' + 1)

    for (char in text) {

        val charLower = char.toLowerCase()

        if (charLower !in 'a'..'z') continue

        counts[charLower - 'a']++

    }

    return counts

}
```

Java vs Kotlin: In Java, a **break** is also used to stop the execution of the remaining branches in a **switch** statement. Since **when** expressions don't follow a fall-through semantics, **break** statements do not serve the same purpose in Kotlin.

In the pre-1.4 Kotlin version, using simple **break** or **continue** expressions inside **when** was prohibited; the intention being to protect developers from potentially confusing code, especially when migrating to Kotlin from a Java codebase. On top of that **continue** was reserved for an optional fallback semantics to be implemented in some further language version. If would have replaced the **if** cascade from our "Guess the number" game with a single **when** expression, the compiler would have reported an error:

```kotlin
val message = when {

    guess < num -> "Too small"

    guess > num -> "Too big"

    else -> break // Error

}
```

The workaround was to employ a labeled **break/continue** which is generally used with nested loop statements that we'll cover in the next section.

Since 1.4, this restriction has been lifted and now both **break** and **continue** can be used freely inside **when** expressions as shown in *Figure 3.7*:

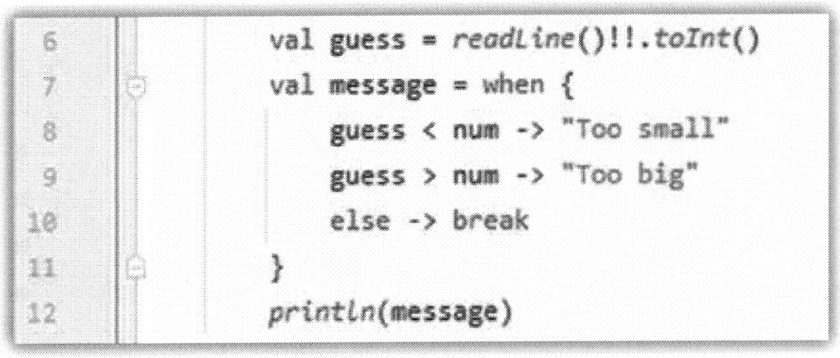

```
 6          val guess = readLine()!!.toInt()
 7          val message = when {
 8              guess < num -> "Too small"
 9              guess > num -> "Too big"
10              else -> break
11          }
12          println(message)
```

*Figure 3.7: Using **break** inside **when**-expression*

The fallback semantics mirroring that of Java **switch** statement currently remains a matter of further language design.

Nested loops and labels

When using nested loop statements, simple **break**/**continue** expressions that we've seen in the previous section are always applied to the nearest enclosing loop. In some cases, you might want them to affect the control-flow of the outer loop. To do that, Kotlin provides a statement labeling which is similar to Java's albeit with a slightly different syntax.

Suppose we want to write a function which searches a given subarray in an array of integer similar to how **indexOf()** does for strings:

```
fun indexOf(subarray: IntArray, array: IntArray): Int {
    outerLoop@ for (i in array.indices) {
        for (j in subarray.indices) {
            if (subarray[j] != array[i + j]) continue@outerLoop
        }
        return i
    }
    return -1
}
```

Here, we attach the label to the outer loop and use **continue@outerLoop** to terminate the current iteration of the outer loop which looks for subarray offset as soon we see the first mismatch between **subarray** and **array** elements. At this point, we know that it makes no sense to check the remaining **subarray** items and the search must continue starting from the next offset.

In Kotlin, you can attach the label to any statement, but **break** and **continue** specifically require those labels to be attached to the loop. If it's not the case, the compiler reports an error. The label name as that of the variable or function can be an arbitrary identifier.

Java vs Kotlin: Note the syntactic difference between the label definition and usage in Kotlin and Java:

```
loop@ while(true) break@loop // Kotlin

loop: while(true) break loop // Java
```

Labeling, among others, allows you to use **break/continue** inside **when** expressions which are in turn nested into a loop body. Thanks to that we can write the "Guess the number" program from the previous section as follows:

```
import kotlin.random.*
fun main() {
    val num = Random.nextInt(1, 101)
    loop@ while (true) {
        val guess = readLine()!!.toInt()
        val message = when {
            guess < num -> "Too small"
            guess > num -> "Too big"
            else -> break@loop // Correct
        }
        println(message)
    }
    println("Right: it's $num")
}
```

Tail-recursive functions

Kotlin supports an optimized compilation for the so-called *tail-recursive* functions. Suppose we want to write a function that implements a binary search in an integer array. Assuming that the array is pre-sorted in the ascending order, let's write this search in a recursive form:

```
tailrec fun binIndexOf(
    x: Int,
```

```kotlin
    array: IntArray,
    from: Int = 0,
    to: Int = array.size
): Int {
    if (from == to) return -1
    val midIndex = (from + to - 1) / 2
    val mid = array[midIndex]
    return when {
        mid < x -> binIndexOf(x, array, midIndex + 1, to)
        mid > x -> binIndexOf(x, array, from, midIndex)
        else -> midIndex
    }
}
```

This definition concisely expresses an algorithm idea, but in general has a performance overhead and risks stack overflow compared to the more cumbersome non-recursive version. In Kotlin, however, you can tell a compiler to automatically translate a tail-recursive function into non-recursive code by adding the **tailrec** modifier. As a result, you get the best of both worlds: a concise recursive function with no extra performance penalties. The preceding function, in particular, would be equivalent to the code:

```kotlin
fun binIndexOf(
    x: Int,
    array: IntArray,
    from: Int = 0,
    to: Int = array.size
): Int {
    var fromIndex = from
    var toIndex = to
    while (true) {
        if (fromIndex == toIndex) return -1
        val midIndex = (fromIndex + toIndex - 1) / 2
        val mid = array[midIndex]
        when {
```

```
            mid < x -> fromIndex = midIndex + 1
            mid > x -> toIndex = midIndex
            else -> return midIndex
        }
    }
}
```

To be eligible for such a transformation, the function must not perform any action after a recursive call. That's the meaning behind *tail-recursive*. If this requirement is not satisfied but the function is still marked as **tailrec**, the compiler will issue a warning and the function will be compiled as a recursive one. For example, the following summation function is not tail-recursive because the **sum(array, from + 1, to)** call is followed by addition:

```
tailrec fun sum(array: IntArray, from: Int = 0,  to: Int = array.size): Int {

    // Warning: not a tail-recursive call

    return if (from < to) return array[from] + sum(array, from + 1, to) else 0

}
```

The compiler will also report a warning if the function is marked as **tailrec** but contains no recursive calls:

```
tailrec fun sum(a: Int, b: Int): Int {

    return a + b // Warning: no tail-recursive calls

}
```

Exception handling

Exception handling in Kotlin is very similar to Java's approach. A function may terminate either normally which means that it returns some value – possibly a trivial one of type Unit – or abnormally by throwing an *exception* object when some error occurs. In the latter case, an exception can be either caught and handled by its caller or propagated further up the call stack. Let's now consider exception-related control structures.

Throwing an exception

To signal an error condition, you can use a throw expression with an exception object just like in Java. Let's revise our earlier **parseIntNumber()** function to throw an exception when its input is ill-formed rather than return some fallback value:

```kotlin
fun parseIntNumber(s: String): Int {
  var num = 0
  if (s.length !in 1..31) throw NumberFormatException("Not a number: $s")
  for (c in s) {
    if (c !in '0'..'1') throw NumberFormatException("Not a number: $s")
    num = num*2 + (c - '0')
  }
  return num
}
```

Java vs Kotlin: Unlike Java, creating a class instance (in this case, it's an exception) doesn't require any special keywords like Java's **new**. In Kotlin, a constructor invocation **NumberFormatException("Not a number: $s")** looks like an ordinary function call.

When an exception is thrown, the following actions are taken:

1. The program looks for an exception handler which can *catch* a given exception. If such a handler is found, it gains a control.

2. Is no handler is found in the current function, its execution is terminated, the function is popped out the stack, and the whole search is repeated in the context of its caller (if any). We can say that exception is *propagated* to the caller.

3. If the exception propagates uncaught to the entry point, the current thread gets terminated.

You can see that exception handling steps in Kotlin are basically the same as in Java.

Java vs Kotlin: In Kotlin, **throw** is an expression of type Nothing like **break** and **continue** we've seen in one of the earlier sections. For example:

```kotlin
fun sayHello(name: String) {
    val message =
        if (name.isNotEmpty()) "Hello, $name"
```

```
        else throw IllegalArgumentException("Empty name")

    println(message)

}
```

Handling errors with try statements

To handle an exception in Kotlin, you can use a **try** statement which has essentially the same syntax as in Java. Consider the following function which returns some default value when it can't parse an input string to a number:

```
import java.lang.NumberFormatException


fun readInt(default: Int): Int {
    try {
        return readLine()!!.toInt()
    } catch (e: NumberFormatException) {
        return default
    }
}
```

The code which may throw an exception (in our case, it's **toInt()** call) is wrapped in the **try** block. The first form of the **try** statement also includes at least one **catch** block which handles an exception of the appropriate type (for example, **NumberFormatException**). The exception to handle is represented by the exception parameter which you can use anywhere inside the **catch** block. When the code inside the **try** block throws some exception, its execution terminates and the program chooses the first **catch** block which is able to handle it; if no such block is found, the exception propagates.

Java vs Kotlin: In Java 7 or later, a single **catch** block can handle multiple exceptions using the syntax of the sort: **catch (FooException | BarException e) {}**. In Kotlin, such handlers are not supported yet.

Since **catch** blocks are checked in order of their declaration, placing a block which can handle some exception type before a block which can handle one of its supertype is useless since any exception of that subtype will be caught by the preceding block.

For example, since **NumberFormatException** is a subtype of Exception, the second **catch** block in the following function is effectively "dead":

```kotlin
import java.lang.NumberFormatException


fun readInt(default: Int): Int {
    try {
        return readLine()!!.toInt()
    } catch (e: Exception) {
        return 0
    } catch (e: NumberFormatException) {
        return default // dead code
    }
}
```

Java vs Kotlin: Note that in Java, a similar statement will produce a compile-time error since Java explicitly forbids such kind of unreachable code.

The major difference between **try** statements in Java and Kotlin is that Kotlin's **try** can be used as an expression. The value of such an expression is either the value of the **try** block (if no exceptions are thrown), or the value of a **catch** block which manages to handle an exception:

```kotlin
import java.lang.NumberFormatException


fun readInt(default: Int) = try {
    readLine()!!.toInt()
} catch (e: NumberFormatException) {
    default
}
```

Java vs Kotlin: Unlike Java, Kotlin doesn't distinguish between checked and unchecked exceptions. The rationale is that in large projects that require explicit specification of possible exceptions in fact decrease the productivity and produce excessive boilerplate code.

Another form of the **try** statement uses the **finally** block which allows you to perform some actions just before the program leaves the **try** block:

```
import java.lang.NumberFormatException


fun readInt(default: Int) = try {

    readLine()!!.toInt()

} finally {

    println("Error")

}
```

This block is useful to clean up some resources which might have been allocated before/in the **try** block; for example, to close a file or network connection. You may also use the **catch** and **finally** blocks within a single **try** statement.

Note that the value of the **finally** block doesn't affect the value of the entire **try** statement when it's used as an expression.

Java vs Kotlin: You're probably familiar with a try-with-resources statement which is introduced in Java 7 and allows you to perform automatic cleanup of resources like file streams and network connections. Although Kotlin doesn't have a special construct for that purpose, it does provide the library function **use()** which solves the same task. We'll look at it more closely in *Chapter 7, Exploring Collections and I/O*.

Conclusion

Let us summarize what we've done in this chapter. We acquired the knowledge of fundamental control structures which constitute the algorithmic basis of imperative programming. We learned how to define and use functions facilitating the reuse of common pieces of program code. Finally, we discussed how to structure your program by grouping related functions into packages. Now, you have all the necessary knowledge for exploiting imperative and procedural paradigms within the Kotlin language.

In the next chapter, we will move towards object-oriented programming. We'll look at how to define classes and objects, get an understanding of class initialization, and learn to declare and use properties.

Points to remember

1. When calling a function, you can choose between positional and named

arguments or combine them.

2. Function parameters may have default values that you can omit in calls.

3. Functions with variable number of arguments can be introduced with the **vararg** modifier.

4. Kotlin functions may be local.

5. Kotlin has a built-in support for tail-recursive functions.

6. Package hierarchy in Kotlin is independent from the directory structure.

7. Most control flow statements (except loops) can be used as expressions.

Multiple choice questions

1. Given the function definition below, choose correct ways to call it in Kotlincode:

```
fun foo(a: Int, b: Int, c: Int = 1) {}
```

A. `foo(1, 2)`

B. `foo(b = 1, 2, 3)`

C. `foo(a = 1, c = 2, 3)`

D. `foo(a = 1, 2)`

2. Which of the following is a/are valid function definition(s)?

A. `fun foo(vararg n: Int) {}`

B. `fun foo(a: Int, vararg n: Int) {}`

C. `fun foo(vararg n: Int, a: Int) {}`

D. `fun foo(vararg a: Int, vararg n: Int) {}`

3. Choose valid statements about relations between ranges and progressions.

A. Every range is a progression

B. Progressions are supported only for integers and chars

C. Ranges always include both endpoints

D. Progressions always include both endpoints

4. Which statement can be used to prematurely exit from a when-branch?

A. break

B. continue

C. return

D. throw

5. Which operations can be used in a when-statement with subject expression?

    A. equality

    B. inequality (!=)

    C. comparisons (<, >, <=, >=)

    D. `in/!in`

6. Which of the following can be iterated over using the for-loop?

    A. Arrays

    B. Strings

    C. Ranges

    D. Progressions

7. Which exceptions are considered unchecked in Kotlin?

    A. Only descendants of RuntimeException or Error

    B. Only descendants of RuntimeException

    C. All descendants of Exception

    D. All descendants of Throwable

Answers

1. A, D
2. A, B, C
3. A, C
4. C, D
5. A, D
6. A, B, C, D
7. D

Questions

1. Explain the difference between positional and named arguments.

2. Describe the semantics of default values in function arguments.

3. How do you define a function with a variable number of arguments? What vararg restrictions are imposed by Kotlin?

4. What is package hierarchy? Explain how one can refer to declarations from another package.

5. What are import aliases? Give an example of how they can be used to resolve ambiguities.

6. Explain difference between ranges and progressions.

7. Describe the syntax of when-expressions. What is a subject expression?

8. Compare various kinds of loop statements in Kotlin.

9. Explain the behavior of break/continue.

10. What's the purpose of the **tailrec** modifier?

11. Explain the basics of exception handling. Does Kotlin have checked exceptions?

Key terms

1. Positional argument: An argument identified by its index in a call argument list.

2. Named argument: An argument identified by its explicit name in an argument list.

3. Default value: An expression whose value is passed to the function when the corresponding argument is omitted in a call.

4. Vararg-function: A function with a parameter that can take an arbitrary number of arguments.

5. Local function: A function defined inside another function body.

6. Import alias: An optional part of the import directive that allows you to refer to imported declaration using specified, rather than its own, name.

7. Range: An object representing a closed interval of numeric/char values.

8. Progression: An object representing a sequence of evenly spaced integer/char values.

CHAPTER 4
Working with Classes and Objects

In this chapter, we will get a taste of object-oriented programming in Kotlin and see how to define our own types using classes. We'll address major topics such as initialization of class instances, using visibility for hiding implementation details, implementing singletons with object declarations, and utilizing different kinds of properties for various effects beyond a simple storage of data: lazy computations, deferred initialization, custom read/write behavior, etc. In this chapter, you'll also get to know a concept of a nullable type that allows the Kotlin compiler to distinguish between values which can be null and those which cannot.

Structure

In this chapter, we will cover the following topics:

- Defining a class
- Nullability
- Properties: beyond simple variables
- Objects and companions

Objectives

By the end of the chapter, the reader will be introduced to the basics of object-oriented programming in Kotlin using classes and objects, handle nullable values, and get an understanding of how to use different varieties of properties.

Defining a class

A class declaration introduces a new type with a custom set of operations. The readers familiar with Java or some other object-oriented programming language such as C++ will surely find class declaration familiar. In this section, we will discuss a basic class structure, initialization of newly allocated instances, the issue of visibility, and special kinds of classes declared inside other classes or function bodies.

By default, a class declaration defines a referential type: in other words, the values of such type are references pointing to actual data of a particular class *instance*. Similarly, Java instances themselves are created explicitly with a special *constructor call* and freed automatically by a garbage collector after the program loses all references to them. Kotlin 1.3 had introduced a concept of an inline class which allows you to define non-referential types as well. We will address this topic in *Chapter 6, Using Special-Case Classes*.

A class anatomy

Similarly to Java, a class is defined using a **class** keyword with a name followed by a class body which is a block containing definitions of members. Let's define a class which holds some information about a person:

```
class Person {
    var firstName: String = ""
    var familyName: String = ""
    var age: Int = 0

    fun fullName() = "$firstName $familyName"

    fun showMe() {
        println("${fullName()}: $age")
    }
}
```

This definition tells us that every instance of the `Person` class will have *properties* **firstName, familyName, age,** and two functions **fullName()** and **showMe().** The simplest property variety is basically a variable associated with a particular class instance. You can compare it with a class field in Java. In more general cases, a property may involve arbitrary computations. Their values may be generated on-the-fly rather than stored in a class instance, or computed lazily, taken from a map, and so on. The common feature of all properties is a reference syntax which allows us to use them like a variable:

```
fun showAge(p: Person) = println(p.age) // reading from a property

fun readAge(p: Person) {

    p.age = readLine()!!.toInt() // assignment to a property

}
```

Note that since the property is associated with a particular class instance, we have to qualify it with an expression (like p in the preceding code). It's called a *receiver* and signifies an instance which you can use to access a property. The same also goes for member functions which are often called *methods*:

```
fun showFullName(p: Person) = println(p.fullname()) // calling a method
```

The receiver can be thought of as an additional variable available for all class members. Inside a class, you can refer to it using the **this** expression. In most cases, it's assumed by default, so you don't have to write it explicitly to access members of the same class. For example, our first example could have been written as follows:

```
class Person {
    var firstName: String = ""
    var familyName: String = ""
    var age: Int = 0

    fun fullName() = "${this.firstName} ${this.familyName}"

    fun showMe() {
        println("${this.fullName()}: ${this.age}")
    }
}
```

Sometimes, though, this is necessary; for example, you can use to distinguish between a class property and a methods parameter with the same name:

```kotlin
class Person {
    var firstName: String = ""
    var familyName: String = ""

    fun setName(firstName: String, familyName: String) {
        this.firstName = firstName
        this.familyName = familyName
    }
}
```

Java vs. Kotlin: Unlike Java's fields, Kotlin properties do not violate encapsulation since you're free to change their implementation; for example, add a custom getter or setter – without the need to change the client code. In other words, the **firstName** reference remains valid regardless of how the property is implemented. In the following section, we'll see how such custom properties are defined.

Note that the underlying field used by the property is always encapsulated and can't be accessed outside the class definition and in fact, outside the property definition itself.

A class instance must be explicitly created before you can access its method. This is accomplished by a constructor call which has a form of an ordinary function call. The difference is that you can use a class name instead of a function's:

```kotlin
fun main() {
    val person = Person() // Create a Person instance
    person.firstName = "John"
    person.familyName = "Doe"
    person.age = 25
    person.showMe() // John Doe: 25
}
```

When you use a constructor call, the program first allocates a heap memory for a new instance and then executes a constructor code which initializes an instance state. In the preceding example, we were relying on a default constructor which doesn't take any parameters; hence, no arguments in a constructor call. In the next section, we'll see how to define custom constructors which allows running your own initialization code.

Kotlin classes are public by default which means they can be used in any part of your code. Similar to top-level functions, you may also mark top-level classes as private or internal limiting their visibility scope to the containing file or compilation module, respectively.

Java vs. Kotlin: In Java, on the contrary, class visibility is by default limited to the containing package. You have to mark its definition with the explicit **public** modifier to make it visible everywhere.

Note also that in Kotlin, you don't need to name your source file exactly as a public class it contains. You may also define multiple public classes in a single file. If a file contains exactly one class, though, the file and the class usually *do* have the same name, but in Kotlin, it's more like a matter of code style than a strict requirement (as opposed to Java).

Class properties may be immutable just like local variables. In such cases, however, we need a way to provide some actual values for them during initialization lest all instances get stuck with the same values, as shown in the following code:

```kotlin
class Person {
    // all instances will have the same value of firstName
    val firstName = "John"
}
```

This may be accomplished by using a custom constructor which brings us to the next topic.

Constructors

A **constructor** is a special function which initializes a class instance and is invoked upon its creation. Consider the following class:

```kotlin
class Person(firstName: String, familyName: String) {
    val fullName = "$firstName $familyName"
}
```

Note the parameter list we've added after the class keyword. These parameters are passed to the class when the program creates its instance and can be used to initialize properties and perform some other work:

```kotlin
fun main() {
    val person = Person("John", "Doe") // Create new Person instance
    println(person.fullName)           // John Doe
}
```

Java vs. Kotlin: Note that Kotlin doesn't use a special keyword (like Java's new) to denote a constructor call.

The parameter list in the class header is called a *primary constructor declaration*. The primary constructor doesn't have a single body like a function; instead, its body consists of property initializers as well as initialization blocks taken in the order they appear in the class body. The *initialization block* is a block statement prefixed with the **init** keyword. Such blocks can be used for non-trivial initialization logic which you need on class instantiation. For example, the following class will print a message each time its primary constructor is called:

```kotlin
class Person(firstName: String, familyName: String) {
    val fullName = "$firstName $familyName"


    init {
        println("Created new Person instance: $fullName")
    }
}
```

A class may contain multiple **init** blocks. In that case, they are executed sequentially together with property initializers.

Note that the initialization block may not contain the **return** statements:

```kotlin
class Person(firstName: String, familyName: String) {
    val fullName = "$firstName $familyName"


    init {
        if (firstName.isEmpty() && familyName.isEmpty()) return // Error
        println("Created new Person instance: $fullName")
    }
}
```

So far we've always specified a property initial value in its initializer. In some cases, though, you may need more complex initialization logic which can't be fit into a single expression. For that reason, Kotlin permits to initialize properties inside the **init** blocks:

```kotlin
class Person(fullName: String) {
    val firstName: String
    val familyName: String

    init {
        val names = fullName.split(" ")
        if (names.size != 2) {
            throw IllegalArgumentException("Invalid name: $fullName")
        }
        firstName = names[0]
        familyName = names[1]
    }
}
fun main() {
    val person = Person("John Doe")
    println(person.firstName) // John
}
```

In the preceding example, the **init** block splits **fullName** into an array of space-separated substrings and then uses them to initialize the **firstName** and **familyName** properties.

The compiler ensures that every property is definitely initialized. If it can't guarantee that every execution path in the primary constructor either entails initialization of all member properties or throws an exception, you get a compilation error:

```kotlin
class Person(fullName: String) {
    // Error: properties may be uninitialized
    val firstName: String
    val familyName: String

    init {
        val names = fullName.split(" ")
        if (names.size == 2) {
```

```
                    firstName = names[0]

                    familyName = names[1]

            }

        }

}
```

Primary constructor parameters may not be used outside property initializers and **init** blocks. For example, the following code is wrong since **firstName** is not available inside the member function:

```
class Person(firstName: String, familyName: String) {

    val fullName = "$firstName $familyName"


    fun printFirstName() {

        println(firstName) // Error: first name is not available here

    }

}
```

A possible solution would be to add member properties holding values of constructor parameters:

```
class Person(firstName: String, familyName: String) {

    val firstName = firstName // firstName refers to constructor parameter

    val fullName = "$firstName $familyName"


    fun printFirstName() {

      println(firstName) // Ok: firstName refers to member property here

    }

}
```

Kotlin, however, provides out-of-the-box solution which allows you to combine the property and constructor parameter in a single definition:

```
class Person(val firstName: String, familyName: String) {

    val fullName = "$firstName $familyName" // firstName refers to parameter

    fun printFirstName() {

        println(firstName) // firstName refers to member property
```

```
        }
}


fun main() {
    val person = Person("John", "Doe")
    println(person.firstName) // firstName refers to property
}
```

Basically, when you mark the primary constructor parameter with the **val** or **var** keyword, you also define a property which is automatically initialized with a parameter value. When you refer to such a definition in a property initializer or the **init** block, it means the constructor parameter; in any other context, it's a property.

IDE Tips: The IntelliJ plugin can detect the code when you initialize the member property by the value of the constructor parameter and convert it to the **val/var** parameter (as shown in *Figure 4.1*):

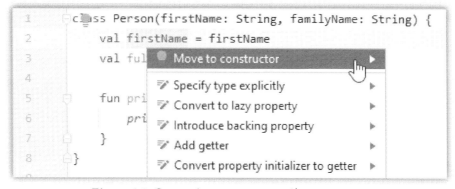

Figure 4.1: *Converting property to val/var parameter*

Note that using the **val/var** parameters, you can define a class which possesses non-trivial members but has an empty body:

```
class Person(val firstName: String, val familyName: String = "") {

}
```

In such cases, Kotlin allows you to omit the body entirely. In fact, that's a recommended code style enforced by the IntelliJ plugin:

```
class Person(val firstName: String, val familyName: String = "")
```

Similar to functions, you can use default values and **vararg** for constructor parameters:

```kotlin
class Person(val firstName: String, val familyName: String = "") {
    fun fullName() = "$firstName $familyName"
}


class Room(vararg val persons: Person) {
    fun showNames() {
        for (person in persons) println(person.fullName())
    }
}


fun main() {
    val room = Room(
        Person("John"),
        Person("Jane", "Smith")
    )
    room.showNames()
}
```

In some cases, you need to provide multiple constructors which initialize a class instance in different ways. Many of them are covered by a single primary constructor with default parameters, but sometimes, that's not enough. In Kotlin, this problem can be solved by *secondary constructors*. The secondary constructor syntax is similar to that of a function definition with the **constructor** keyword in place of a function name:

```kotlin
class Person {
    val firstName: String
    val familyName: String

    constructor(firstName: String, familyName: String) {
        this.firstName = firstName
        this.familyName = familyName
    }

    constructor(fullName: String) {
```

```
        val names = fullName.split(" ")
        if (names.size != 2) {
            throw IllegalArgumentException("Invalid name: $fullName")
        }
        firstName = names[0]
        familyName = names[1]
    }
}
```

Although a secondary constructor can't be given a return type, it has a form of an effectively `Unit`-typed function. In particular, you can use return statements inside its body (as opposed to the **init** blocks).

If the class doesn't have a primary constructor, then every secondary constructor invokes the property initializers and **init** blocks before executing its own body. This ensures that the common initialization code runs exactly once on class instantiation regardless of which secondary constructor is called.

An alternative option is to make a secondary constructor call another secondary constructor using a *constructor delegation call*:

```
class Person {
    val fullName: String

    constructor(firstName: String, familyName: String):
        this("$firstName $familyName")

    constructor(fullName: String) {
        this.fullName = fullName
    }
}
```

A constructor delegation call is written after the colon (:) separating it from the constructor parameter list and looks like an ordinary call with the keyword this in place of the function name.

When a class has a primary constructor, all secondary constructors (if any) must delegate either to it, or to some other secondary constructor. We can, for example, turn one secondary constructor from our example to a primary one:

```kotlin
class Person(val fullName: String) {

    constructor(firstName: String, familyName: String):

        this("$firstName $familyName")

}
```

Note that secondary constructors may not declare property-parameters using the **val/var** keywords:

```kotlin
class Person {

    constructor(val fullName: String) // Error

}
```

There is also a separate issue of using secondary constructors in combination with the class inheritance to call superclass constructors. We'll deal with it in *Chapter 8, Understanding Class Hierarchies.*

Member visibility

Class members may have different visibility which determines their usage scope. This is a major part of class definition since visibilities allow you to enforce encapsulation of implementation-specific details effectively hiding them from the outside code. In Kotlin, a class member visibility is represented by one of the following modifier keywords:

- **public**: A member may be used anywhere; this is assumed by default, so usually there is no need to use the **public** keyword explicitly.
- **internal**: A member is accessible only within the compilation module containing its class.
- **protected**: A member is accessible within the containing class and all of its subclasses; we'll postpone the detailed discussion of this case till *Chapter 8, Understanding Class Hierarchies* which deals with class inheritance;
- **private**: A member is accessible only within the containing class body.

The meaning of these modifiers is in fact quite similar to the ones we've seen for top-level functions and properties.

Java vs. Kotlin: In Java, the default visibility is package-private which means that a member is accessible anywhere within the containing package. If you want a member to be public, you have to explicitly mark it with the **public** modifier. In Kotlin, on the other hand, class members (and, in fact, all non-local declarations) are public by default. Note also that currently Kotlin doesn't have a direct counterpart for Java's package-private visibility.

In the preceding code, the properties **firstName** and **familyName** are declared as private and thus inaccessible to the **main()** function. The **fullName()** function, on the other hand, is public:

```kotlin
class Person(private val firstName: String, private val familyName: String)
{
    fun fullName() = "$firstName $familyName"

}
fun main() {
    val person = Person("John", "Doe")
    println(person.firstName)  // Error: firstName is not accessible here
    println(person.fullName()) // Ok

}
```

The visibility modifiers are supported for functions, properties – both declared in the class body and as primary constructor parameters – as well as primary and secondary constructors. If you want to specify visibility for a primary constructor, you have to also add the explicit **constructor** keyword:

```kotlin
class Empty private constructor() {
    fun showMe() = println("Empty")

}


fun main() {
    Empty().showMe() // Error: can't invoke private constructor

}
```

Note that the class **Empty** can't be instantiated since its only constructor is private and so it is not available outside the class body. In the 'Objects' section, we'll see how constructor hiding can be used together with so called companion objects to create factory methods.

Nested classes

Apart from functions, properties, and constructors, Kotlin classes may include other classes as its members. Such classes are called *nested*. Let's consider the following example:

```kotlin
class Person (val id: Id, val age: Int) {
    class Id(val firstName: String, val familyName: String)


    fun showMe() = println("${id.firstName} ${id.familyName}, $age")
}


fun main() {
    val id = Person.Id("John", "Doe")
    val person = Person(id, 25)
    person.showMe()
}
```

Note that outside the containing class body, references to nested classes must be prefixed with the outer class name, like **Person.Id** in the preceding code.

Like other members, nested classes may have different visibilities. Being members of their containing class, they may also access its private declarations:

```kotlin
class Person (private val id: Id, private val age: Int) {
    class Id(private val firstName: String, private val familyName: String)
    {

        fun nameSake(person: Person) = person.id.firstName == firstName

    }


    fun showMe() = println("${id.firstName} ${id.familyName}, $age")
}
```

Java vs. Kotlin: Unlike Java, the outer class may not access private members of its nested classes.

The nested class may be marked as **inner** to be able to access the current instance of its outer class:

```kotlin
class Person(val firstName: String, val familyName: String) {
    inner class Possession(val description: String) {
        fun showOwner() = println(fullName())
    }
```

```
    fun fullName() = "$firstName $familyName"
}


fun main() {
    val person = Person("John", "Doe")
    val wallet = person.Possession("Wallet") // Possession constructor call
    wallet.showOwner() // John Doe
}
```

Note how the call of the inner class constructor is qualified with an outer class instance: **person.Possession("Wallet")**. Similar to other member references, qualification may be omitted if the instance in question is **this**:

```
class Person(val firstName: String, val familyName: String) {
    inner class Possession(val description: String) {
        fun showOwner() = println(fullName())
    }


    val myWallet = Posession("Wallet")
                                // the same this.Possession("Wallet")
}
```

In general, **this** always means the innermost class instance, so inside an inner class body it refers to the current instance of an inner class itself. When you need to reference the outer instance from an inner class body, you may use a qualified form of **this** expression:

```
class Person(val firstName: String, val familyName: String) {
    inner class Possession(val description: String) {
        fun getOwner() = this@Person
    }
}
```

The identifier coming after the @ symbol is a name of the outer class.

Java vs. Kotlin: Nested classes in Kotlin and Java are very similar. The major difference is a default behavior in the absence of additional modifiers. While Java classes are inner by default and must be explicitly marked as **static** if you do not want their objects to be associated with instances of the outer class. Kotlin classes are not. In other words, take a look at the following Kotlin code:

```kotlin
class Outer {
    inner class Inner
    class Nested
}
```

is basically equivalent to the Java declaration:

```java
public class Outer {
    public class Inner {
    }

    public static class Nested {
    }
}
```

Local classes

Similarly to Java, Kotlin classes can be declared inside the function body. Such *local classes* can only be used inside the enclosing code block:

```kotlin
fun main() {
    class Point(val x: Int, val y: Int) {
        fun shift(dx: Int, dy: Int): Point = Point(x + dx, y + dy)
        override fun toString() = "($x, $y)"
    }
    val p = Point(10, 10)
    println(p.shift(-1, 3)) // (9, 13)
}

fun foo() {
    println(Point(0, 0)) // Error: can't resolve Point
}
```

Similarly to the local function, Kotlin local classes can access declarations from the enclosing code. In particular, they capture local variables which can be accessed and even modified inside the local class body:

```kotlin
fun main() {
    var x = 1
    class Counter {
        fun increment() {
            x++
        }
    }
    Counter().increment()
    println(x) // 2
}
```

Java vs. Kotlin: Unlike Kotlin, Java doesn't allow modification of captured variables. Moreover, all such variables must be explicitly marked as **final** when used inside the anonymous class. Note, however, that the ability to change captured variables in Kotlin comes with a certain price. In order to share variables between the anonymous object and its enclosing code, the Kotlin compiler boxes their values inside special wrapper objects. The Java's equivalent of the preceding Counter example would look as follows:

```java
import kotlin.jvm.internal.Ref.IntRef;

class MainKt {
    public static void main(String[] args) {
        final IntRef x = new IntRef(); // create wrapper
        x.element = 1;

        final class Counter {
            public final void increment() {
                x.element++;                    // modify shared data
            }
        }

        (new Counter()).increment();
        System.out.println(x.element); // read shared data
    }
}
```

Note that immutable variables have no such overhead since they do not require any wrappers.

Unlike nested classes, local classes can't have visibility modifiers. Their scope is always limited by the enclosing block.

Local classes may contain all the members permitted in any other classes such as functions, properties, constructors, or nested classes. Note, however, that their nested classes must always be marked as **inner**:

```kotlin
fun main(args: Array<String>) {
    class Foo {
        val length = args.length
        inner class Bar {
            val firstArg = args.firstOrNull()
        }
    }
}
```

Allowing non-inner classes would lead to somewhat counterintuitive behavior where the outer class can access the local state (such as the preceding **args** variable) while its nested class, being non-inner, can not.

Nullability

Similar to Java, referential values in Kotlin include the special constant **null** which represents a *null reference*, that is, a reference which doesn't correspond to any allocated object. Null doesn't behave like any other reference. In Java, you can assign the null to a variable of any referential type, but can't use any methods or properties defined for the corresponding type as any attempt to access null members results in NullPointerException (NPE for short). The worst part is that such errors only reveal themselves at runtime as the compiler can't detect them using the static type information.

A significant advantage of the Kotlin type system is its ability to make clear distinction between referential types which allow null values and those which do not. This feature shifts the problem to compilation time and helps you to mostly avoid the notorious NullPointerException.

In this section, we'll discuss types which are used to represent nullable values and basic operations you can use to deal with nulls. In *Chapter 12, Java Interoperability,* we'll also address nullability issues related to Java-Kotlin interoperability.

Nullable types

One of the major features of the Kotlin type system is its ability to distinguish between types which *do* include null values and those which do not. In Java, all reference types are assumed to be nullable. In other words, the compiler can't guarantee that a particular variable of a reference type can't hold null.

In Kotlin, however, all references types are non-nullable by themselves, so you can't store a null in a variable of, say, the String type. Consider the following function which checks whether a given string contains only letter characters:

```kotlin
fun isLetterString(s: String): Boolean {
    if (s.isEmpty()) return false
    for (ch in s) {
        if (!ch.isLetter()) return false
    }
    return true
}
```

If we try to pass null for the s parameter, we'll get a compilation error:

```kotlin
fun main() {
    println(isLetterString("abc")) // Ok
    println(isLetterString(null))  // Error
}
```

The reason is that the argument in the second call has a nullable type, but String doesn't accept nulls, so the call is forbidden. You don't need to write any additional checks in the **isLetterString()** itself to ensure that no null is passed or worry that it may throw NPE on trying to dereference its parameter. The Kotlin compiler prevents such errors at compilation time.

Java vs. Kotlin: In Java, on the other hand, passing null into the following function is completely acceptable from the compiler's point of view, but produces a **NullPointerException** at runtime:

```java
class Test {
    static boolean isLetterString(String s) {
        for (int i = 0; i < s.length; i++) {
            if (!Character.isLetter(s.charAt(i))) return false;
```

```
        }
        return true;
    }


    public static void main(String[] args) {
                    // Compiles but throw an exception at runtime
        System.out.println(isEmpty(null))
    }
}
```

What if you need to write a function which *may* accept the null value? In this case, you mark the parameter type as nullable by placing the ? sign after it:

```
fun isBooleanString(s: String?) = s == "false" || s == "true"
```

Types like **String?** are called *nullable* types in Kotlin. In terms of the type system, every nullable type is a supertype of its base type which enlarges its original set of values by including null. That, in particular, means that the nullable variable can be always assigned a value of the corresponding non-nullable type, but the opposite is, of course, false:

```
fun main() {
    println(isBooleanString(null)) // Correct
    val s: String? = "abc"          // Correct
    val ss: String = s              // Error
}
```

Note that the last assignment in the preceding example is incorrect. Even though the variable s doesn't hold the null value at runtime, the compiler has to be conservative since it can only use a static type information which tells it that the variable s is nullable because we've explicitly marked it as such.

At runtime, non-nullable values do not actually differ from the nullable ones. The distinction exists on the compilation level only. The Kotlin compiler doesn't use any wrappers (such as the Optional class introduced in Java 8) to represent non-nullable values so no additional runtime overheads are involved.

Primitive types like Int or Boolean also have nullable versions. Bear in mind, though, that such types always represent *boxed* values:

```kotlin
fun main() {
    val n: Int = 1   // primitive value
    val x: Int? = 1 // reference to a boxed value
}
```

The smallest nullable type is Nothing? which doesn't contain any other value apart from the null constant. This is a type of the null itself and a subtype of any other nullable type. The largest nullable type **Any?** is also the largest type in the whole Kotlin type system and is considered a supertype of any other type, nullable or not.

Nullable types don't retain methods and properties available for their base types. The reason is that usual operations such as calling a member function or reading a property don't make sense for the null value. If we change the **isLetterString()** function by replacing its parameter type with String? but leave everything else untouched, we'll get a compilation error as now all usages of s in the function body becomes incorrect:

```kotlin
fun isLetterString(s: String?): Boolean {
    // Error: isEmpty() is not available on String?
    if (s.isEmpty()) return false
    // Error: iterator() is not available on String?
    for (ch in s) {
        if (!ch.isLetter()) return false
    }
    return true
}
```

Note that you can't use the for loop to iterate over the nullable **String** since **String?** doesn't have an **iterator()** method.

In fact, nullable types *may* have their own methods and properties thanks to the Kotlin extension mechanism. In *Chapter 5, Leveraging Advanced Functions and Functional Programming,* we'll address this issue in more detail. One example is a string concatenation which also works for values of **String?** type:

```kotlin
fun exclaim(s: String?) {
    println(s + "!")
}
```

```kotlin
fun main() {
```

```
    exclaim(null) // null!
}
```

So how do we fix the code like the **isLetterString()** function to correctly process nullable values? To do the job, Kotlin suggests several options which we'll cover in the following sections.

Nullability and smart casts

The most straightforward way to process a nullable value is to compare it with null using some kind of a conditional statement:

```
fun isLetterString(s: String?): Boolean {
    if (s == null) return false
    // s is non-nullable here
    if (s.isEmpty()) return false
    for (ch in s) {
        if (!ch.isLetter()) return false
    }
    return true
}
```

Although we haven't changed the type of s itself, adding the check against null somehow makes the code compileable. This is possible thanks to a helpful Kotlin feature which is called a *smart cast*. Basically, whenever you make an equality check against null, the compiler knows that in one control-flow branch the value of interest is exactly null, while in another it's definitely not null. It then uses this information to refine the value type, implicitly casting it from nullable to non-nullable, hence the name 'smart cast'. In the preceding example, the compiler understands that since the branch corresponding to **s == null** being true ends with a return statement, the code coming after **if (s == null) return false** never executes when s is null. As a result, the variable s is assumed to have the non-nullable type String in the remaining piece of the function body.

Smart casts are not limited to nullability. In *Chapter 8, Understanding Class Hierarchies*, we'll see how they enable safe type casting in the context of class hierarchies.

IDE Tips: The IntelliJ plugin has a special highlighting for variable references affected by smart casts. Thanks to it, you can easily distinguish such variables just by looking at your code. It also shows the refined type in the reference tooltip (see *Figure 4.2 for an example*):

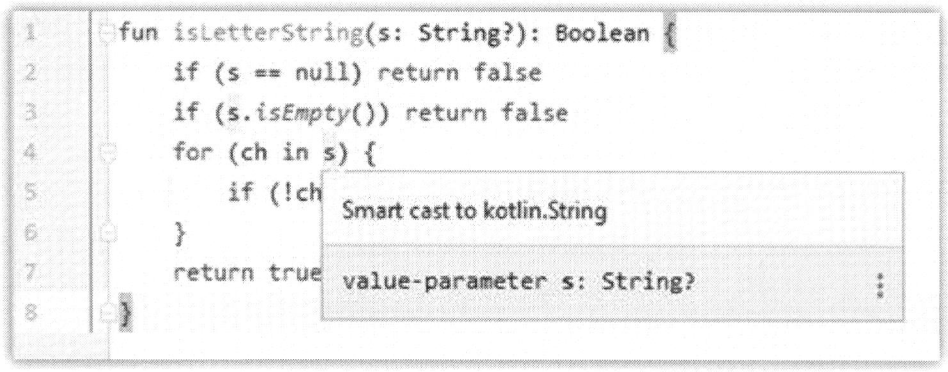

```
1   fun isLetterString(s: String?): Boolean {
2       if (s == null) return false
3       if (s.isEmpty()) return false
4       for (ch in s) {
5           if (!ch
6       }                  Smart cast to kotlin.String
7       return true   value-parameter s: String?                    ⋮
8   }
```

Figure 4.2: *Smart cast highlighting*

Smart casts also work inside other statements or expressions concerned with condition checking such as **when** expressions and loops:

```
fun describeNumber(n: Int?) = when (n) {
    null -> "null"
    // n is non-nullable in the following branches
    in 0..10 -> "small"
    in 11..100 -> "large"
    else -> "out of range"
}
```

or right-hand sides of **||** and **&&** operations:

```
fun isSingleChar(s: String?) = s != null && s.length == 1
```

Note that in order to perform, a smart cast compiler has to ensure that the variable in question doesn't change its value between the check and the usage. In particular, immutable local variables we've seen so far permit smart casts without limitations since they can't change the value after initialization. Mutable variables, however, may prevent smart casts when modified between the null check and the usage:

```
var s = readLine() // String?
if (s != null) {
    s = readLine()
    // No smart cast below as variable has changed its value
    println(s.length) // Error
}
```

Mutable properties never permit smart casts since in general they may be changed by other code at any time. In *Chapter 8, Understanding Class Hierarchies*, we'll discuss these rules and their exceptions in more detail.

Not-null assertion operator

We've already come across the !! operator in our earlier examples involving the **readLine()** function. !!, also called a *not-null assertion*, is a postfix operator which throws a **KotlinNullPointerException** (on JVM, it's a subclass of the well-known **NullPointerException**) when its argument is null and return it unchanged when it's not. The resulting type is a non-nullable version of the original type. Basically, it reproduces the behavior of the Java program which throws an exception on attempt to dereference the null value:

```
val n = readLine()!!.toInt()
```

In general, this operation should be avoided because null values usually require some reasonable response instead of simply throwing an exception. Sometimes, though, its usage is justified. Consider, for example, the following program:

```
fun main() {
    var name: String? = null

    fun initialize() {
        name = "John"
    }

    fun sayHello() {
        println(name!!.toUpperCase())
    }

    initialize()
    sayHello()
}
```

In this case, not-null assertion is an appropriate solution since we know that the **sayHello()** function is called after the name is assigned a non-nullable value. The compiler, however, can't recognize that such usage is safe and won't refine the variable type to **String** inside **sayHello()**, so one solution is to ignore its alerts and use non-null assertion. Note, however, that even in cases like this it often makes sense to use less blunt tools for dealing with nulls or even rewriting the control-flow of your code in such a way that the compiler can employ smart casts.

Using not-null assertion on a non-nullable receiver is not considered an error. Such code, though, is redundant and should be avoided.

IDE Tips: The IntelliJ plugin comes with an inspection which highlights and suggests to remove redundant usages of the !! operator.

Like any other postfix operator, not-null assertion has the highest possible precedence.

Safe call operator

We've already mentioned that values of the nullable types do not allow you to call methods available for the corresponding non-nullable type. There is, however, a special *safe-call* operation which allows you to circumvent this restriction. Let's consider one of our earlier examples:

```kotlin
fun readInt() = readLine()!!.toInt()
```

This function works fine as long as your program uses the console as its standard I/O. If, however, we've started the program piping some file as the standard input, it could've failed with **KotlinNullPointerException** if the file in question was empty. Using the safe call operator, we can rewrite it into the following form:

```kotlin
fun readInt() = readLine()?.toInt()
```

which is basically equivalent to the code:

```kotlin
fun readInt(): Int? {
    val tmp = readLine()
    return if (tmp != null) tmp.toInt() else null
}
```

In other words, the safe call operator behaves like an ordinary call when its receiver (left-hand operand) is not null. When its receiver *is* null, however, it doesn't perform any calls and simply returns null. Similar to || and && operations, safe calls follow a lazy semantics. They do not evaluate call arguments if the receiver is null. In terms of precedence, **?** takes the same level as an ordinary call operator (**.**).

The pattern 'do something meaningful when the receiver is not null or return the null otherwise' happens quite often in practice, so safe calls can greatly simplify your code by relieving you from unnecessary **if** expressions and temporary variable declarations. One useful idiom is to chain safe calls into something like this:

```
println(readLine()?.toInt()?.toString(16))
```

Note that since the safe call operator may return null, its type is always the nullable version of the corresponding non-safe call. We have to take this into account on the call site of our new **readInt()** function:

```
fun readInt() = readLine()?.toInt()
```

```
fun main() {
    val n = readInt() // Int?
    if (n != null) {
        println(n + 1)
    } else {
        println("No value")
    }
}
```

Like not-null assertions, safe calls can be applied to non-nullable receivers. Such code, however, is completely redundant as it behaves exactly like a simple dot-call (**.**).

IDE Tips: The IntelliJ plugin automatically highlights redundant usages of the **?** operator and suggests to replace them with ordinary calls.

Elvis operator

One more useful tool for dealing with nullable values is a null coalescing operator **?:** which allows you to provide some default value in place of null. It's usually called the *Elvis operator* due to its resemblance to an emoticon of Elvis Presley. Let's consider the following example:

```
fun sayHello(name: String?) {
    println("Hello, " + (name ?: "Unknown"))
}
```

```
fun main() {
    sayHello("John") // Hello, John
```

```
    sayHello(null)    // Hello, Unknown
}
```

In other words, the result of this operator is the left argument when it's not null and the right one otherwise. Basically, the preceding **sayHello()** function is equivalent to the code:

```
fun sayHello(name: String?) {
    println("Hello, " + (if (name != null) name else "Unknown"))
}
```

The Elvis operator is useful in combination with safe calls to substitute a default value when the receiver is null. In the following code, we substitute a zero when the program's standard input is empty:

```
val n = readLine()?.toInt() ?: 0
```

One more handy pattern is to use the control-flow breaking statement like **return** or **throw** as a right argument of Elvis. This serves as an abbreviation of the corresponding **if** expression:

```
class Name(val firstName: String, val familyName: String?)
class Person(val name: Name?) {
    fun describe(): String {
        val currentName = name ?: return "Unknown"
        return "${currentName.firstName} ${currentName.familyName}"
    }
}
fun main() {
    println(Person(Name("John", "Doe")).describe()) // John Doe
    println(Person(null).describe())                // Unknown
}
```

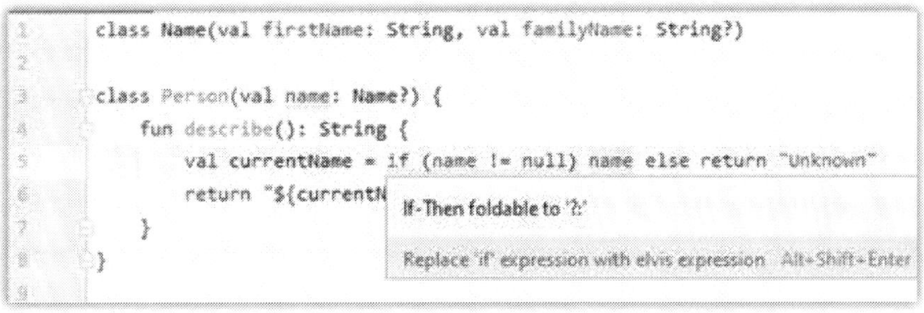

Figure 4.3: Replacing if *expression with Elvis operator*

IDE Tips: The IntelliJ plugin has a special inspection which detects null-checking **if** expressions that can be replaced with the Elvis operator (*Figure 4.3*).

In terms of precedence, the Elvis operator occupies an intermediate place between infix operations like **or** and **in/!in** operators yielding, in particular, to comparison/ equality operators, **||**, **&&** and assignments.

Properties: Beyond simple variables

In the first section, we've introduced you to an idea of property as a variable bound to a particular class instance or file facade similar to the Java field. In general, however, Kotlin properties possess far richer capabilities which go beyond simple variables offering you the means to control how the property value is read or written. In this section, we will have a closer look at non-trivial property semantics.

Top-level properties

Similar to classes or functions, properties may be declared at the top-level. In this case, they serve as a sort of global variables or constants:

```kotlin
val prefix = "Hello, " // top-level immutable property


fun main() {
    val name = readLine() ?: return
    println("$prefix$name")
}
```

Such properties may have one of top-level visibilities (public/internal/private). They also may be used in import directives:

```kotlin
// util.kt
package util


val prefix = "Hello, "


// main.kt


package main


import util.prefix
```

```kotlin
fun main() {
    val name = readLine() ?: return
    println("$prefix$name")
}
```

Late initialization

Sometimes, the requirement to initialize class properties on its instantiation may be unnecessarily strict. Some properties can only be initialized later, after the class instance is already created, but before its actual use. They might be, for example, specified in some initialization method like unit test setup or assigned via dependency injection. One solution would be to assign some default value (e.g. null) which basically means 'uninitialized state' in the constructor and provide an actual value when necessary. Consider, for example, the following code:

```kotlin
import java.io.File


class Content {
    var text: String? = null


    fun loadFile(file: File) {
        text = file.readText()
    }
}

fun getContentSize(content: Content) = content.text?.length ?: 0
```

We assume that **loadFile()** is called elsewhere to load the string content from some file. The drawback of this example is that we have to deal with the nullable type while the actual value is supposed to be always initialized before access and thus non-null. Kotlin provides a built-in support for this kind of pattern via the **lateinit** keyword. Let's apply it to our example:

```kotlin
import java.io.File


class Content {
    lateinit var text: String
```

```
fun loadFile(file: File) {
    text = file.readText()
}
}
```

```
fun getContentSize(content: Content) = content.text.length
```

The property with a **lateinit** marker works just like an ordinary property short of a single difference. On attempt to read its value the program will check whether the property is initialized and throw **UninitializedPropertyAccessException** if it's not. This behavior is somewhat similar to an implicit **!!** operator.

There are some requirements a property must satisfy in order to be eligible for late initialization. First, it must be declared as mutable (**var**) since its value may be changed in different parts of your code. Second, it must have a non-nullable type and may not represent a primitive value like **Int** or **Boolean**. The reason is that internally the **lateinit** property is represented as a nullable variable with null reserved to mean 'uninitialized'. Finally, the **lateinit** property may not have an initializer since such a construct would have defeated the purpose of declaring it **lateinit** in the first place.

Kotlin 1.2 has introduced a couple of **lateinit**-related improvements. In particular, it's now possible to use late initialization for top-level properties and local variables:

```
lateinit var text: String
```

```
fun readText() {
    text = readLine()!!
}
```

```
fun main() {
    readText()
    println(text)
}
```

Another improvement is an ability to check whether a **lateinit** property is initialized before trying to access its value. We'll discuss how to do it in *Chapter 10, Annotations and Reflection* which deals with the Kotlin reflection API.

Using custom accessors

The properties we've seen so far had essentially behaved like ordinary variables stored either in an instance of some Kotlin class, or in the context of a file (which on JVM is also represented as an instance of a special *facade* class). The real power of Kotlin properties, however, comes from their ability to combine a variable- and a function-like behavior in a single declaration. This is to be achieved with *custom accessors* which are special functions invoked when the property value is accessed for reading or writing.

In the following example, we define custom *getter*, i.e., an accessor which is used to *read* a property value:

```kotlin
class Person(val firstName: String, val familyName: String) {
    val fullName: String
        get(): String {
            return "$firstName $familyName"
        }
}
```

The getter is placed at the end of the property definition and basically looks like a function albeit with a keyword **get** instead of a name. Whenever such a property is read, the program automatically invokes its getter:

```kotlin
fun main() {
    val person = Person("John", "Doe")
    println(person.fullName) // John Doe
}
```

Similar to functions, accessors support an expression-body form:

```kotlin
val fullName: String
    get() = "$firstName $familyName"
```

Note that the getter may not have any parameters while its return type, if present, must be *the same* as the type of the property itself:

```kotlin
val fullName: Any
    get(): String { // Error
        return "$firstName $familyName"
```

```
}
```

Since Kotlin 1.1, you can just omit the explicit property type and rely on the type inference instead:

```
val fullName
    get() = "$firstName $familyName" // String is inferred
```

The value of the **fullName** property we've introduced earlier is computed on each access. Unlike **firstName** and **familyName,** it doesn't have a backing field and thus doesn't occupy memory in a class instance. In other words, it's basically a function which simply has a property form. In Java, we'd usually introduce a method like **getFullName()** for the same purpose. The rule regarding backing fields is as follows: the backing field is generated when a property has at least one default accessor or a custom accessor which explicitly mentions the field. Since immutable properties have only one accessor, a getter, and in our example, it doesn't reference the backing field directly, the **fullName** property will have no backing field.

What about the direct field reference? It's useful when you want your property to be based on some stored value, but still needs to customize access. For example, we could use it to log property reads:

```
class Person(val firstName: String, val familyName: String, age: Int) {
  val age: Int = age
    get(): Int {
      println("Accessing age")
      return field
    }
}
```

The backing field reference is represented by the **field** keyword and is valid only inside an accessor's body.

When a property doesn't use a backing field, it can't have an initializer because the initializer is basically a value assigned directly to the backing field on initialization of a class instance. That's why we didn't add the initializer for the **fullName** definition above: being a computed property it doesn't need one.

Since the property with a customer getter behaves like a parameterless function albeit with a slightly different syntax, this poses a question how you should choose between both constructs in a particular case. The official Kotlin coding conventions recommend using a property instead of a function when the computation doesn't result in throwing an exception, the value is cheap enough or cached, and different invocations produce the same result unless the state of the containing class instance is not changed.

Mutable properties defined with the **var** keyword have two accessors: a getter for reading and a *setter* for writing. Let's consider the following example:

```
class Person(val firstName: String, val familyName: String) {
  var age: Int? = null
    set(value) {
        if (value != null && value <= 0) {
            throw IllegalArgumentException("Invalid age: $value")
        }
        field = value
    }
}


fun main() {
    val person = Person("John", "Doe")
    person.age = 20      // calls custom setter
    println(person.age) // 20, uses default getter
}
```

A property setter must have a single parameter of the same type as the property itself. The parameter type is usually omitted since it's always known in advance. The convention parameter name is called value, but it's possible to choose a different one if you like.

Note that the property initializer does not trigger a setter call since the initializer value is assigned to the backing field directly.

Since mutable properties have two accessors, they always possess a backing field unless both accessors are custom and do not reference it via the **field** keyword. For example, the **age** property has a backing field due to the default getter and direct mention in the setter, while the following property does not:

```
class Person(var firstName: String, var familyName: String) {
  var fullName: String
    get(): String = "$firstName $familyName"
```

```kotlin
set(value) {
 val names = value.split(" ") // Split string space-separated words
  if (names.size != 2) {
      throw IllegalArgumentException("Invalid full name: '$value'")
  }
  firstName = names[0]
  familyName = names[1]
 }
}
```

Property accessors may have their own visibility modifiers. They can be useful if you, say, want to forbid changing your property outside their containing class, thus making it effectively immutable for the outside world. If you don't need a non-trivial implementation of an accessor, you can abbreviate it by a single **get/set** keyword:

```kotlin
import java.util.Date

class Person(name: String) {
    var lastChanged: Date?
        private set // can't be changed outside Person class

    var name: String = name
        set(value) {
            lastChanged = Date()
            field = value
        }
}
```

Java vs. Kotlin: From the JVM point of view, a Kotlin property in general corresponds to one or two accessor methods (like **getFullName()** and **setFullName()**) possibly backed by a private field. Although the method itself is not available in the Kotlin code, it can be called from the Java classes and comprise a major point in Java/Kotlin interoperability. In *Chapter 12, Java Interoperability*, we'll discuss this issue in more detail. Private properties, on the other hand, by default have no accessor methods generated since they can't be used outside the containing class or file. Access to such properties is optimized to refer to their backing fields directly.

Custom accessors are not allowed for the **lateinit** properties since their accessors are always generated automatically. They are also not supported for properties declared as primary constructor parameters, but that can be solved by using the ordinary non-property parameter and assigning its value to a property in the class body just like we did with the **val age** earlier.

Lazy properties and delegates

In a previous section, we've seen how to implement late initialization using the **lateinit** modifier. In many cases, though, we'd like to defer the value computation until its first access. In Kotlin, this can be achieved with **lazy** properties. Let's consider the following example:

```kotlin
import java.io.File


val text by lazy {
    File("data.txt").readText()
}


fun main() {
    while (true) {
        when (val command = readLine() ?: return) {
            "print data" -> println(text)
            "exit" -> return
        }
    }
}
```

The **text** property mentioned earlier is defined as lazy. We specify how it's initialized in the block coming after the **by lazy** clause The value itself is not computed until we first access it in the **main()** function when the user types an appropriate command. After initialization, the property value is stored in a field and all successive attempts to access it will just read the stored value. If we have, for example, define a property with a simple initializer:

```kotlin
val text = File("data.txt").readText()
```

The file would be read right at the program start while the property with a getter like this:

```kotlin
val text get() = File("data.txt").readText()
```

Would reread the file every time the program tries to access the property value.

You can also specify the property type explicitly, if necessary:

```kotlin
val text: String by lazy { File("data.txt").readText() }
```

This syntax is in fact a special case of the so called *delegated property* which allows you to implement a property via a special *delegate* object which handles reading/writing and keeps all related data if necessary. The delegate is placed after the **by** keyword and can be an arbitrary expression which returns the object conforming to specific convention. In our example, **lazy {}** is not a built-in language construct, but rather just a call to a standard library function with a lambda supplied (we've already seen a similar example in *Chapter 2, Language Fundamentals* while discussing the creation of array instances).

Kotlin provides some delegate implementations out of the box. Apart from enabling lazy computations, standard delegates allow you to create observable properties which notify a listener before/after every change of their value and to back properties by a map instead of storing them in separate fields. In this section, we'll give you a basic taste of delegates in the context of lazy properties and defer their comprehensive treatment till *Chapter 7, Exploring Collections and I/O* and *Chapter 11, Domain-Specific Languages* where we'll consider standard delegates available in the Kotlin library and the means to design your own delegates, respectively.

Note that unlike **lateinit** properties, lazy properties may not be mutable. They don't change the value once initialized:

```kotlin
var text by lazy { "Hello" } // Error
```

By default, lazy properties are thread-safe. In a multi-threaded environment, the value is computed by a single thread and all threads trying to access a property will ultimately get the same result.

Since Kotlin 1.1, you can use delegates for local variables. This, in particular, allows you to define a lazy variable in a function body:

```kotlin
fun longComputation(): Int {...}


fun main(args: Array<String>) {
    val data by lazy { longComputation() } // lazy local variable
    val name = args.firstOrNull() ?: return
```

```
        println("$name: $data") // data is only accessed when name is not null
}
```

Note that delegated properties currently do not support smart casts. Since delegates may have an arbitrary implementation, they are treated similarly to properties with custom accessors. It also means that you can use smart casts with local delegated variables:

```
fun main() {
    val data by lazy { readLine() }
    if (data != null) {
        // Error: no smart cast, data is nullable here
        println("Length: ${data.length}")
    }
}
```

Lazy properties/local variables are not an exception. Currently, you can't apply smart casts to them even though their values do not actually change after initialization.

Objects and companions

In this section, we will discuss the concept of object declarations. An object declaration in Kotlin is a kind of mix between a class and a constant which allows you to create singletons – classes which have exactly one instance. We'll also look at object expressions which play a role similar to Java's anonymous classes.

Object declarations

Kotlin has a built-in support of the Singleton pattern which basically ensures that some class can only have a single instance. In Kotlin, you declare a singleton similar to a class, but using the **object** keyword instead:

```
object Application {
    val name = "My Application"

    override fun toString() = name

    fun exit() { }
}
```

Such *object declaration* can be used as both a class and a value representing its instance. For example:

```kotlin
fun describe(app: Application) = app.name // Application as a type
fun main() {
    println(Application)                    // Application as a value
}
```

Note that using an object as a type is usually meaningless since such a type has exactly one instance so you can just as well refer to that instance itself.

Object definitions are thread-safe. The compiler ensures that even if you concurrently access the singleton from different execution threads, there is still exactly one shared instance and initialization code is run only once.

The initialization itself happens lazily on the loading of the singleton class which usually happens when the program first refers to the object instance.

Java vs. Kotlin: In Java, singletons have to be emulated using ordinary class declarations which are usually achieved using a combination of private constructors and some static states. Such 'object declarations' can have different features depending on the implementation details; the most common being lazy vs. eager and thread-safe vs. non-thread-safe singletons. Looking at the JVM bytecode of Application object, we see that it basically amounts to the following Java class:

```java
public final class Application {
    private static final String name = "My Application";

    public static final Application INSTANCE;

    private Application() { }

    public final String getName() {
        return name;
    }

    public final void exit() { }

    static {
```

```
        INSTANCE = new Application();
        name = "My Application";
    }
}
```

Note that the **INSTANCE** variable is not accessible in the Kotlin code itself, but can be used in Java classes referring to the Kotlin's singleton. In *Chapter 12, Java Interoperability*, we'll consider this issue in more detail.

Similar to classes, object declarations can include member functions and properties as well as initializer blocks, but may not have primary or secondary constructors. An object instance is always created implicitly so constructor calls make no sense for objects.

Classes in the object body can't be marked as **inner**. Instances of inner classes are always associated with the corresponding instance of their enclosing class, but object declarations have only one instance which makes the inner modifier effectively redundant. That's the reason why it is forbidden.

Object members can be imported and later referred by their simple names similar to top-level declarations. Suppose, for example, that the Application object is defined in a separate file:

```
import Application.exit


fun main() {
    println(Application.name) // using qualified reference
    exit()                    // using simple name
}
```

You may not, however, import all the object members at once using an on-demand import:

```
import Application.* // Error
```

The reason behind such a restriction is that object definitions, like any other classes, include common methods such as **toString()** or **equals()** which can be imported too if on-demand was allowed.

Like classes, objects can be nested into other classes or even into other objects. Such declarations are also singletons which have exactly one instance per entire application. If you need a separate instance per enclosing class, you should use an *inner class* instead. You can't, however, put objects inside functions as well as local or inner classes because such definitions in general would depend on some enclosing context and thus couldn't be singletons. Locally-scoped objects can be created using an *object expression* which we'll consider later in this chapter.

Java vs. Kotlin: In the Java world, you can often come across a so called *utility class*. It's essentially a class which doesn't have instances (usually by means of a private constructor) and instead serves as a kind of grouping for related methods. This pattern proves to be useful in Java, but it's generally discouraged in Kotlin, although you can certainly declare utility-style classes if that's what you want. The reason is that, unlike Java, Kotlin has top-level declarations which can be grouped together using packages thus freeing you from the need to use special classes and reducing the boilerplate.

Companion objects

Similar to nested classes, nested objects can access private members of the enclosing the class given its instance. A useful implication of this is an ability to easily implement the Factory design pattern. There are cases when using the constructor directly is unwanted. You can't, for example, return null or instances of different types (conforming to the class type) depending on some pre-checks since a constructor call always returns an instance of its class or throws an exception. A possible solution is to mark a constructor as `private`, making it inaccessible outside the class, and define a nested object with a function which serves as a factory method and calls class constructor when necessary:

```kotlin
class Application private constructor(val name: String) {
    object Factory {
        fun create(args: Array<String>): Application? {
            val name = args.firstOrNull() ?: return null
            return Application(name)
        }
    }
}

fun main(args: Array<String>) {
    // Direct constructor call is not permitted
    // val app = Application(name)
    val app = Application.Factory.create(args) ?: return
```

```
    println("Application started: ${app.name}")
}
```

Note that in this case, we have to refer to the object name every time we call the factory method unless it's imported using the **import Application.Factory. create** directive. Kotlin allows you to solve this problem by turning the Factory object into the *companion*. A companion object is basically a nested object marked with a **companion** keyword. Such an object behaves just like any other nested object with one exception; you can refer to its members by the name of its enclosing class without mentioning the name of companion object itself. Using companions, we can make our previous example slightly more concise:

```
class Application private constructor(val name: String) {

    companion object Factory {

        fun create(args: Array<String>): Application? {

            val name = args.firstOrNull() ?: return null

            return Application(name)

        }

    }

}


fun main(args: Array<String>) {

    val app = Application.create(args) ?: return

    println("Application started: ${app.name}")

}
```

Although it's considered redundant, you can still refer to the companion object members using its name:

```
val app = Application.Factory.create(args) ?: return
```

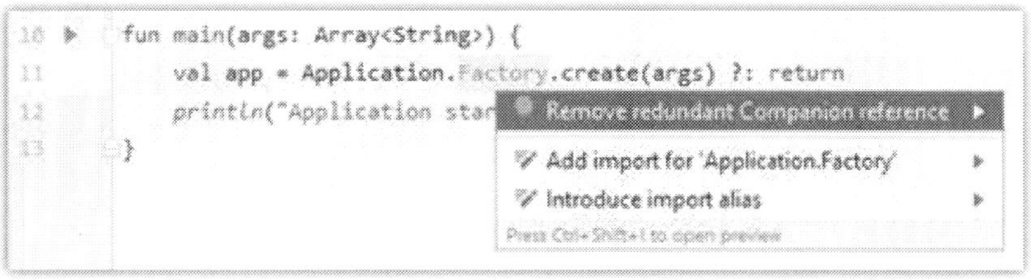

Figure 4.4: Redundant companion reference

IDE Tips: IntelliJ automatically warns you about unnecessary references to the companion and suggests removing them from the code (*Figure 4.4*):

For a companion object, you can also skip the name in the definition itself. This is the recommended approach:

```kotlin
class Application private constructor(val name: String) {

    companion object {

        fun create(args: Array<String>): Application? {

            val name = args.firstOrNull() ?: return null

            return Application(name)

        }

    }

}
```

When the companion name is omitted, the compiler assumes the default name `Companion`.

Note that the companion name *must* be mentioned explicitly when you import its members:

```kotlin
import Application.Companion.create // OK

import Application.create            // Error
```

A class may not have more than one companion:

```kotlin
class Application {

    companion object Factory

    companion object Utils   // Error: only one companion is allowed

}
```

It's also an error to use the **companion** modifier for a top-level object or an object nested into another object. In the former case, you lack a class definition to bind the companion to, while in the latter companion is basically redundant.

Java vs. Kotlin: Companion objects in Kotlin may be considered a counterpart of Java's static context. Like statics, companion members share the same global state and can access any member of an enclosing class regardless of its visibility. The crucial difference, however, is that their global state is an object instance. This gives much more flexibility than Java's statics as companion objects may have supertypes and passed around like any other object. In *Chapter 8, Understanding Class Hierarchies* and *Chapter 11, Domain-Specific Languages,* we'll see how companion objects can be combined with inheritance and language conventions to produce more expressive code.

Note also that the **init** blocks in companion objects can be used similar to Java static initializers.

Object expressions

Kotlin has a special kind of expression which creates a new object without an explicit declaration. This *object expression* is very similar to a Java anonymous class. Consider the following example:

```kotlin
fun main() {
    fun midPoint(xRange: IntRange, yRange: IntRange) = object {
        val x = (xRange.first + xRange.last)/2
        val y = (yRange.first + yRange.last)/2
    }


    val midPoint = midPoint(1..5, 2..6)
    println("${midPoint.x}, ${midPoint.y}") // (3, 4)
}
```

An object expression looks just like an object definition without a name and being an *expression* can be, for example, assigned to a variable like in the preceding example. Note that unlike classes and object expressions, named objects can't be declared inside functions:

```kotlin
fun printMiddle(xRange: IntRange, yRange: IntRange) {
    // Error
    object MidPoint {
        val x = (xRange.first + xRange.last)/2
        val y = (yRange.first + yRange.last)/2
    }
    println("${MidPoint.x}, ${MidPoint.y}")
}
```

The rationale behind this decision is that object definitions are supposed to represent singletons while local objects, if they were allowed, in general would have to be created anew upon every call of the enclosing function.

Since we've defined no explicit type for the object returned by the **midPoint()** function, you might be wondering what the return type is. The answer is a so called *anonymous object type* which represents a class with all the members defined in the object expression and a single instance. This type is not denotable in the language itself. It's just an internal representation of the object expression type used by the Kotlin compiler. We can still use expressions of anonymous type similar to any other class instances; for example, to access its members as evidenced by the **println()** call as mentioned earlier.

IDE Tips: If we try to look at the object expression type using the 'Show Expression Type' action (*Ctrl + Shift + P*/Cmd+Shift+P), IntelliJ will show us the "<anonymous object>" placeholder (*Figure 4.5*):

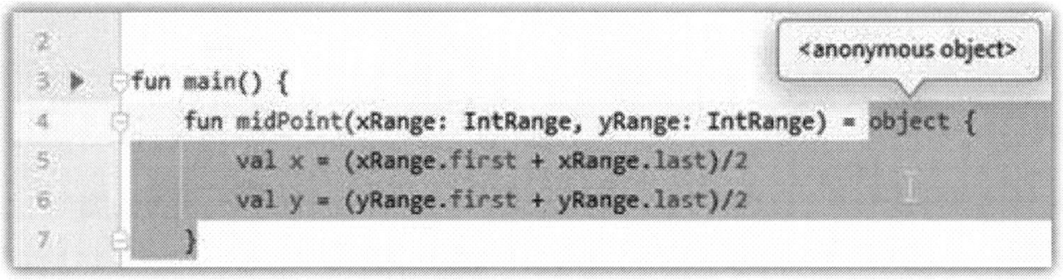

Figure 4.5: *Anonymous object type*

This example also demonstrates that a function with an object expression body has anonymous return type and the same is also true for local variables and properties:

```kotlin
fun main() {
    val o = object { // anonymous object type is inferred
        val x = readLine()!!.toInt()
        val y = readLine()!!.toInt()
    }
    println(o.x + o.y) // can access x and y here
}
```

Note, however, that anonymous types are only propagated to local or private declarations. If we, for example, were to declare the **midPoint()** function as a top-level one, we would get a compile-time error on attempt to access object members:

```kotlin
fun midPoint(xRange: IntRange, yRange: IntRange) = object {
    val x = (xRange.first + xRange.last)/2
    val y = (yRange.first + yRange.last)/2
}
```

```
fun main() {
    val midPoint = midPoint(1..5, 2..6)
    println("${midPoint.x}, ${midPoint.y}")
                                // Error: x and y are unresolved
}
```

Now the return type of the **midPoint()** function is not an anonymous type of our object expression, but rather it's a denotable supertype. Since our object has no explicit supertype, it's assumed to be Any. That's why **midPoint.x** reference becomes unresolved.

Similar to local functions and classes, object expressions can capture variables from the enclosing code. Mutable captured variables can be modified in the object's body. In this case, a compiler creates necessary wrappers to share the data similar to the local classes:

```
fun main() {
    var x = 1
    val o = object {
        fun change() {
            x = 2
        }
    }
    o.change()
    println(x) // 2
}
```

Note that unlike object declarations which are initialized lazily, object expressions are initialized immediately after their instance is created. For example, the following code will print **"x = 2"** since at the point, the **x** variable is read, the initialization code in the object expression has already been executed:

```
fun main() {
    var x = 1
    val o = object {
        val a = x++;
    }
    println("o.a = ${o.a}") // o.a = 1
    println("x = $x")       // x = 2
```

}

Just like Java's anonymous classes, object expressions are most useful when combined with class inheritance. They give you a concise way to describe a small modification based on the existing class without explicit subclass definition. We'll consider them in *Chapter 8, Understanding Class Hierarchies.*

Conclusion

In conclusion, let us summarize the things we've learned in this chapter. We now have a basic understanding of how to define and use custom types based on Kotlin classes, how to properly initialize class instances, and use singleton objects. We've learned to use different kinds of properties to program custom read/write behavior. Finally, we're now able to employ powerful type nullability mechanism for improving our program safety.

We'll revisit object-oriented aspects of Kotlin in the upcoming chapters. In particular, *Chapter 6, Using Special-Case Classes* will deal with special classes covering common programming patterns, while *Chapter 8, Understanding Class Hierarchies* will address the issue of inheritance and building class hierarchies.

In the next chapter, we'll switch to a different topic and get to know another major paradigm powering Kotlin development: the functional programming. We will introduce you to lambdas, discuss higher-order functions, and show how to use extension functions and properties for adding new features to existing types.

Points to remember

- Kotlin class definitions may contain constructors, member functions/properties as well as nested classes
- Unlike Java, Kotlin supports the simplified constructor syntax embedded in the class header.
- Properties combine simplicity of variable definitions with expressiveness of functions.
- The language allows the developer to explicitly distinguish between nullable and non-nullable types.
- Kotlin supports singletons in a form of object declarations.

Multiple choice questions

1. What is the default visibility level for Kotlin declarations placed at the top-

level or in a class body?

A. public

B. internal

C. protected

D. private

2. Choose all INCORRECT statements:

A. Secondary constructors always delegate to the primary one.

B. A class may have multiple secondary constructors.

C. A class is allowed to have no primary constructor.

D. A primary constructor is forbidden if a class has at least one secondary constructor.

3. Choose all correct statements regarding **lateinit** properties:

A. They might be nullable.

B. They may not be of primitive type.

C. They must be private.

D. They must be immutable.

4. What is a correct way to instantiate the Inner class in the following example?

```
class Outer(val n: Int = 0) {
    inner class Inner(val m: Int = 0)
}
```

A. **val** x = Outer.Inner(1)

B. **val** x = Outer(1).Inner(2)

C. val x = Outer().Inner

D. **val** x = Inner()

5. Which of the following denotes a valid Kotlin type that permits nullable values?

A. String?

B. Integer??

C. Array<Int>?

D. ByteArray

6. Choose all pieces of code which compile when placed instead of the following comment:

```
fun sum(a: Int?, b: Int?): Int? {
    // todo
}
```

A. **return** a+b

B. **return** if (a != **null** && b != **null**) a + b else **null**

C. **return** if (a != **null** || b != **null**) a + b else **null**

D. **return** (a ?: 0) + (b ?: 0)

7. What is a valid way to access foo property in the following code?

```
class MyClass {
    companion object MyComp {
        val foo = 123
    }
}
```

A. MyComp.foo

B. MyClass.foo

C. MyClass.MyComp.foo

D. MyClass.Companion.foo

Answers

1. A
2. A, D
3. B
4. B
5. A, C
6. B, D
7. B, C

Questions

1. Describe the basic class structure in Kotlin. How does it compare to Java classes?

2. What is a primary constructor?

3. What is a secondary constructor? How would you decide which constructor(s) a class should contain and whether secondary constructors are necessary?

4. What are the supported member visibilities in Kotlin? How do they differ

from the visibilities in Java?

5. What's difference between inner and non-inner nested classes in Kotlin? Compare them with Java's counterparts.

6. Can you define a class inside a function body? What are the limitations?

7. What's the gist of the late initialization mechanism? What's the advantage of using **lateinit** compared to a nullable property?

8. What are custom property accessors? Compare them with the conventional getter and setter methods in Java. Can you define an effectively read-only which behaves like a val for the class client? What about an effectively write-only property?

9. How can you achieve lazy computation with delegated properties? Compare lazy and **lateinit** properties.

10. What is object declaration? Compare Kotlin objects with common singleton implementation used in the Java development.

11. What are limitations of object declarations as compared to classes?

12. What's the difference between an ordinary object and a companion one?

13. Compare Kotlin companion objects with Java's statics. What is the Kotlin's counterpart of Java's anonymous classes? How do you use one?

Key terms

1. Primary constructor: A constructor defined in a class header.

2. Secondary constructor: A constructor defined in a class body together with other members of that class.

3. Nested class: A class defined in the body of another class.

4. Local class: A class defined in the body of a function or property accessor.

5. Nullable type: A type whose instances may hold the null value.

6. Not-null assertion operator (!!): A built-in Kotlin operator which smart-casts given a value to a non-nullable type throwing an exception if it happens to be null.

7. The Elvis operator (?:): A variety of branching expression which allows to substitute some replacement values if a given expression is null.

8. Property: A declaration which may be accessed using variable references syntax but allows a developer to customize read and write operations.

9. Property delegate: A special object which implements the property read/

write semantics.

10. Object declaration: A declaration which introduces both a class and its singleton value.

11. Companion object: A nested object declaration whose members may be accessed by a simplified syntax via its containing class name.

12. Object expression: An expression which introduces a class instance without explicit declaration.

CHAPTER 5

Leveraging Advanced Functions and Functional Programming

In this chapter, we'll address some advanced issues related to using functions and properties. The first section is devoted to the fundamentals of functional programming in Kotlin. We'll introduce you to a concept of a higher-order function, describe how to construct functional values using lambdas, anonymous functions and callable references, and show how inline functions can help you to use functional programming with almost zero runtime overheads. In the second section, we'll consider a matter of extension functions and properties which allow you to add new features to existing types without their modification.

Structure

In this chapter, we will cover the following topics:

- Functional programming in Kotlin
- Extensions

Objective

After reading this chapter, you will learn to make use of functional Kotlin features with higher-order functions, lambdas, and callable references as well as employ extension functions and properties for enriching existing types.

Functional programming in Kotlin

In this section, we will introduce you to the Kotlin features enabling the support of the functional paradigm. Functional programming is based around the idea of presenting the program code as a composition of functions manipulating immutable data. Functional languages allow treating functions like first-class values which means that they have the same basic capabilities as the value of any other type. In particular, they can be assigned to/read from variables as well as passed to/returned from functions. This enables definition of so called higher-order functions which manipulate other functional values like a data providing flexible mechanism for code abstraction and composition.

Higher-order functions

In the previous chapter, we saw some examples of using lambdas to perform computations. For example, the array constructor call takes a lambda which computes an array element given its index:

```kotlin
val squares = IntArray(5) { n -> n*n } // 0, 1, 4, 9, 16
```

In this section, we will take a more detailed look at lambdas and higher-order functions.

Suppose that we want to define a function which computes a sum of elements in an integer array:

```kotlin
fun sum(numbers: IntArray): Int {
    var result = numbers.firstOrNull()
        ?: throw IllegalArgumentException("Empty array")
    for (i in 1..numbers.lastIndex) result += numbers[i]
    return result
}


fun main() {
    println(sum(intArrayOf(1, 2, 3))) // 6
}
```

What if we want to generify this function to cover other kinds of aggregates like a product or min/max value? We can keep the basic iteration logic in the function itself and extract the computation of intermediate values into a functional parameter which can be supplied at the call site:

```kotlin
fun aggregate(numbers: IntArray, op: (Int, Int) -> Int): Int {
    var result = numbers.firstOrNull()
        ?: throw IllegalArgumentException("Empty array")
    for (i in 1..numbers.lastIndex) result = op(result, numbers[i])
    return result
}


fun sum(numbers: IntArray) =
    aggregate(numbers, { result, op -> result + op })


fun max(numbers: IntArray) =
    aggregate(numbers, { result, op -> if (op > result) op else result })


fun main() {
    println(sum(intArrayOf(1, 2, 3))) // 6
    println(sum(intArrayOf(1, 2, 3))) // 3
}
```

What distinguishes the **op** parameter is a **functional type (Int, Int) -> Int** describing values which can be called like functions. In our example, the op parameter can accept functional values which accept a pair of Int values and return some Int values as their result.

At the call site in the **sum()** and **max()** functions, we pass a lambda expression which denotes such a functional value. It's basically a definition of a local function without a name which uses a kind of simplified syntax. For example, in the following expression:

```kotlin
{ result, op -> result + op }
```

result and **op** play the role of function parameters while the expression after **->** computes the result. No explicit return statement is necessary in this case, and parameter types are inferred automatically from the context.

Let's now examine these features in more detail.

Functional types

The functional type describes values which can be used like functions. Syntactically, such a type is similar to a function signature and contains the following two components:

- A list of parentheses-enclosed argument types which determine which data can be passed to the functional value.

- A return type which determines the type of result returned by the value of functional type.

Note that the return type must be always specified explicitly even if it's the `Unit`.

For example, the type **(Int, Int) -> Boolean** represents a function which takes a pair of integers as its input and returns a **boolean** values as a result. Note that unlike the function definition, the return type and argument list in a function type notation are separated by the **->** character instead of a colon (**:**).

The value of the functional type can be invoked just like an ordinary function: **op(result, numbers[i])**. An alternative way is to use an **invoke()** method which takes the same arguments:

```
result = op.invoke(result, numbers[i])
```

Java vs. Kotlin: In Java 8+, any interface with a single abstract method (SAM) may be considered a functional type given appropriate context and instantiated with a lambda expression or method reference. In Kotlin, however, functional values always have a type of the form **(P1, …, Pn) -> R** and cannot be implicitly cast to an arbitrary SAM interface. So while the following code is valid in Java:

```java
import java.util.function.Consumer;


public class Main {
    public static void main(String[] args) {
        Consumer<String> consume = s -> System.out.println(s);
        consume.accept("Hello");
    }
}
```

The similar code in Kotlin will not compile:

```kotlin
import java.util.function.Consumer


fun main() {
    // Error: type mismatch
    val consume: Consumer<String> = { s -> println(s) }
```

```
    consume.accept("Hello")
}
```

Kotlin, however, **does** support simplified conversion between function types and SAM interfaces declared in Java for the sake of Kotlin/Java interoperability. We'll see examples of this conversion in *Chapter 12, Java Interoperability*.

Since version 1.4, Kotlin supports explicit conversion between Kotlin SAM interfaces and functional types. For this to work, you need to accompany interface declaration with the **fun** keyword:

```
fun interface IntOp {      // SAM interface
  fun op(value: Int): Int
}


interface NotQuiteIntOp { // Ordinary interface: no 'fun' keyword
  fun op(value: Int): Int
}


fun main() {
  val square: IntOp = IntOp { it*it }                    // Ok
  val cube: NotQuiteIntOp = NotQuiteIntOp { it*it*it } // Error
}
```

The parameter list may be empty if functions represented by a functional type do not take any parameters:

```
fun measureTime(action: () -> Unit): Long {
    val start = System.nanoTime()
    action()
    return System.nanoTime() - start
}
```

Note that parentheses around parameter types are mandatory even if the function type has a single parameter or none at all:

```
val inc: (Int) -> Int = { n -> n + 1 } // Ok
val dec: Int -> Int = { n -> n - 1 }   // Error
```

Values of functional types are not limited to function parameters. In fact, they may be used on equal terms with any other type. For example, you can store the functional value in a variable:

```kotlin
fun main() {
    val lessThan: (Int, Int) -> Boolean = { a, b -> a < b }
    println(lessThan(1, 2)) // true
}
```

Note that if you omit a variable type, the compiler won't have enough information to infer types of lambda parameters:

```kotlin
val lessThan = { a, b -> a < b } // Error
```

In such a case, you'll have to specify parameter types explicitly:

```kotlin
val lessThan = { a: Int, b: Int -> a < b } // Ok
```

Just like any other type, a functional type may be nullable. In this case, we enclose the original type in parentheses before adding a question mark:

```kotlin
fun measureTime(action: (() -> Unit)?): Long {
    val start = System.nanoTime()
    action?.invoke()
    return System.nanoTime() - start
}


fun main() {
    println(measureTime(null))
}
```

If we don't do that, the effect would be different: **() -> Unit?** will describe functions which return the value of **Unit?**.

Functional types may be nested in which case they represent higher-order functions themselves:

```kotlin
fun main() {
    val shifter: (Int) -> (Int) -> Int = { n -> { i -> i + n } }
    val inc = shifter(1)
    val dec = shifter(-1)
    println(inc(10)) // 11
```

```
    println(dec(10)) // 9
}
```

Note that -> is right-associative, so **(Int) -> (Int) -> Int** actually means **(Int) -> ((Int) -> Int)**, i.e., a function which takes an Int and returns another function which maps an **Int** to an **Int**. If we want it to mean the function which takes an **Int-to-Int** function and returns an **Int**, we have to use parentheses:

```
fun main() {
    val evalAtZero: ((Int) -> (Int)) -> Int = { f -> f(0) }
    println(evalAtZero { n -> n + 1 }) // 1
    println(evalAtZero { n -> n - 1 }) // -1
}
```

A functional type may include optional names for its parameters. They can be used for documentation purpose to clarify the meaning of a functional value represented by this type:

```
fun aggregate(
    numbers: IntArray,
    op: (resultSoFar: Int, nextValue: Int) -> Int
): Int {...}
```

IDE Tips: IntelliJ IDEA allows you to see these parameters' name using the "Parameter Info" feature which gives you hints about a function signature when you press *Ctrl + P* (Cmd+P) inside its call (*Figure 5.1*):

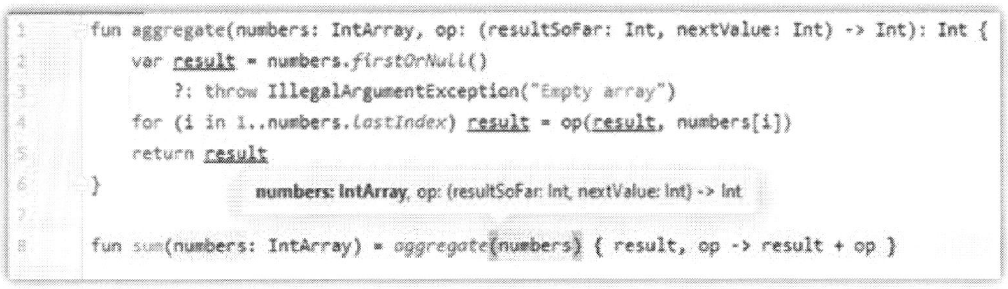

```
1    fun aggregate(numbers: IntArray, op: (resultSoFar: Int, nextValue: Int) -> Int): Int {
2        var result = numbers.firstOrNull()
3            ?: throw IllegalArgumentException("Empty array")
4        for (i in 1..numbers.lastIndex) result = op(result, numbers[i])
5        return result
6    }
7
8    fun sum(numbers: IntArray) = aggregate(numbers) { result, op -> result + op }
```

         numbers: IntArray, op: (resultSoFar: Int, nextValue: Int) -> Int

Figure 5.1: Viewing functional parameter names with "Parameter Info"

Lambdas and anonymous functions

How do we construct a particular value of a functional type? One way is to use a lambda expression which basically describes a function without giving it a name.

Let's, for example, define two more functions which compute the sum and maximum value using the **aggregate()** defined earlier:

```kotlin
fun sum(numbers: IntArray) =
    aggregate(numbers, { result, op -> result + op })


fun max(numbers: IntArray) =
    aggregate(numbers, { result, op -> if (op > result) op else result })


fun main() {
    println(sum(intArrayOf(1, 2, 3))) // 6
    println(sum(intArrayOf(1, 2, 3))) // 3
}
```

The expression

```kotlin
{ result, op -> result + op }
```

is called a *lambda expression*. Similarly to a function definition, it consists of

- Parameter list: **result, op**
- A list of expressions or statements which comprises the lambda body: **result + op**

Unlike the function definition, you can't specify a return type. It's inferred automatically from the lambda body. Also, the last expression in the body is treated as a lambda result, so you don't need to use an explicit return statement at the end.

Note that the lambda parameter list is not enclosed in parentheses. Parentheses around lambda parameters are reserved for the so called *destructuring declarations* which we'll cover in *Chapter 6, Using Special-Case Classes*.

When lambda is passed as the last argument, it can be placed outside parentheses. This is in fact the recommended code style we've already seen in the examples of array construction calls and lazy properties:

```kotlin
fun sum(numbers: IntArray) =
    aggregate(numbers) { result, op -> result + op }
fun max(numbers: IntArray) =
    aggregate(numbers) { result, op -> if (op > result) op else result }
```

IDE Tips: The IntelliJ plugin warns you about the cases when lambda can be passed outside an ordinary argument list and can automatically perform the necessary code changes.

When lambda has no arguments, an arrow symbol -> can be omitted:

```kotlin
fun measureTime(action: () -> Unit): Long {
    val start = System.nanoTime()
    action()
    return System.nanoTime() - start
}
val time = measureTime { 1 + 2 }
```

Kotlin also has a simplified syntax for lambdas with a single parameter. In such cases, we can omit both the parameter list and an arrow and refer to the parameter by the predefined name **it**:

```kotlin
fun check(s: String, condition: (Char) -> Boolean): Boolean {
    for (c in s) {
        if (!condition(c)) return false
    }
    return true
}


fun main() {
    println(check("Hello") { c -> c.isLetter() }) // true
    println(check("Hello") { it.isLowerCase() })  // false
}
```

IDE Tips: The IntelliJ plugin allows you to convert lambda with it into a lambda with an explicit parameter and vice versa. These actions are available via *Alt + Enter* menu when the caret is positioned on either the parameter reference, or parameter definition (*Figure 5.2*):

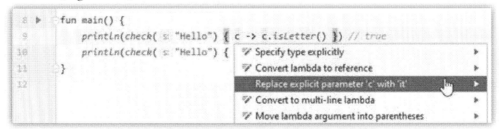

Figure 5.2: Converting explicit parameter to it

Since Kotlin 1.1, you can put underscore symbols (_) in place of unused lambda parameters:

```kotlin
fun check(s: String, condition: (Int, Char) -> Boolean): Boolean {
    for (i in s.indices) {
        if (!condition(i, s[i])) return false
    }
    return true
}


fun main() {
    println(check("Hello") { _, c -> c.isLetter() })            // true
    println(check("Hello") { i, c -> i == 0 || c.isLowerCase() }) // true
}
```

Another way to specify a functional value is to use an anonymous function:

```kotlin
fun sum(numbers: IntArray) =
    aggregate(numbers, fun(result, op) = result + op)
```

An anonymous function has almost the same syntax as an ordinary function definition, albeit with a few differences:

- An anonymous function doesn't have a name, so the fun keyword is immediately followed by a parameter list.

- Similar to lambdas, you can omit explicit specification of parameter types if they can be inferred from the context.

- Unlike a function definition, an anonymous function is an expression, so it can be, for example, passed to a function as an argument or assigned to a variable (this is the parallel similar difference between object definitions and anonymous object expressions).

Unlike lambdas, anonymous functions allow you specify the return type. In this regard, they follow the same rules as function definitions. The return type is optional (and can be inferred) if a function has an expression body, and must be explicit (unless it's the Unit) when using a block body:

```kotlin
fun sum(numbers: IntArray) =
    aggregate(numbers, fun(result, op): Int { return result + op })
```

Note that unlike lambdas, anonymous functions can't be passed outside the argument list.

IDE Tips: The IntelliJ plugin include actions for automatic conversion between lambdas and anonymous functions. To access it, you need to place an editor caret on lambda's opening brace or the **fun** keyword and press *Alt + Enter* (*Figure 5.3*):

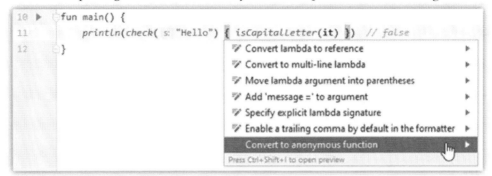

Figure 5.3: Converting a lambda expression to an anonymous function

Similar to local functions, lambdas and anonymous functions can access their *closure*, or variables defined in their containing declaration. In particular, they can change mutable variables from the outer scope:

```kotlin
fun forEach(a: IntArray, action: (Int) -> Unit) {
    for (n in a) {
        action(n)
    }
}


fun main() {
    var sum = 0
    forEach(intArrayOf(1, 2, 3, 4)) {
        sum += it
    }
    println(sum) // 10
}
```

Java vs. Kotlin: Java lambdas, on the contrary, may not modify any outer variables. This is similar to the case of modifying outer variables from local classes and anonymous objects we've discussed in *Chapter 4, Working with Classes and Objects*.

Callable references

In the previous section, we've seen how to construct a new functional value using lambdas and anonymous functions. But what if we already have a function definition and want to, for example, pass it as a functional value into some higher-order function? We can, of course, wrap it in a lambda expression like this:

```kotlin
fun check(s: String, condition: (Char) -> Boolean): Boolean {
    for (c in s) {
        if (!condition(c)) return false
    }
    return true
}


fun isCapitalLetter(c: Char) = c.isUpperCase() && c.isLetter()


fun main() {
    println(check("Hello") { c -> isCapitalLetter(c) }) // false
}
```

In Kotlin, however, there is a much more concise way to use an existing function definition as an expression of a functional type. This is achieved through the use of *callable references*:

```kotlin
fun main() {
    println(check("Hello", ::isCapitalLetter)) // false
}
```

The expression **::isCapitalLetter** denotes a function value which behaves exactly like the **isCapitalLetter()** function it refers.

IDE Tips: The IntelliJ plugin provides a pair of actions which can transform lambda expressions to callable references (if possible) and vice versa. These actions can be accessed via *Alt + Enter* menu (*Figure 5.4*):

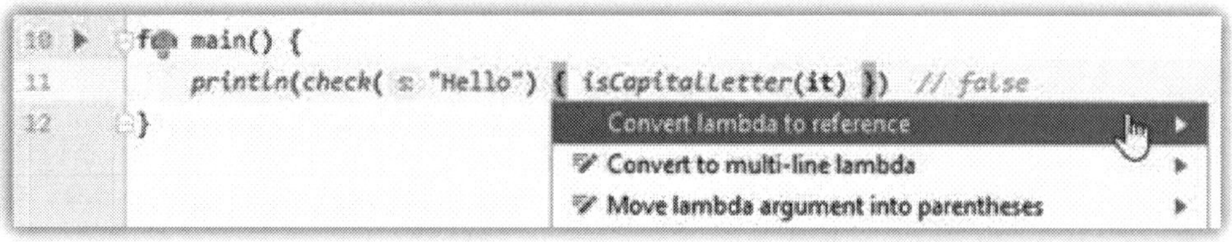

Figure 5.4: Converting lambda to a callable reference

The simplest kind of a callable reference is based on a top-level or local function. To compose such a reference, you just need to prefix function name with the :: operator:

```
fun evalAtZero(f: (Int) -> Int) = f(0)


fun inc(n: Int) = n + 1


fun main() {
    fun dec(n: Int) = n - 1

    println(evalAtZero(::inc)) // 1
    println(evalAtZero(::dec)) // -1
}
```

The callable reference may only mention a function by its simple name, so if a top-level function is located in another package, it must be imported first.

Applying the :: operator to a class name, you get a callable reference to its constructor:

```
class Person(val firstName: String, val familyName: String)


fun main() {
    val createPerson = ::Person
    createPerson("John", "Doe")
}
```

Another form of the :: operator introduced in Kotlin 1.1 is called a *bound callable reference*. You can use it to refer to a member function in a context of a given class instance:

```
class Person(val firstName: String, val familyName: String) {
    fun hasNameOf(name: String) = name.equals(firstName, ignoreCase
    = true)
}


fun main() {
```

```
val isJohn = Person("John", "Doe")::hasNameOf
println(isJohn("JOHN")) // true
println(isJohn("Jake")) // false
}
```

There is also a third form which allows you to refer to a member function without binding it to a particular instance. We'll discuss it in the section "Callable Reference with Receiver".

Note that callable references by themselves are not able to distinguish between overloaded functions. You have to provide an explicit type if the compiler is not able to choose a particular overload:

```
fun max(a: Int, b: Int) = if (a > b) a else b
fun max(a: Double, b: Double) = if (a > b) a else b


val f: (Int, Int) -> Int = ::max // Ok
val g = ::max                     // Error: ambiguous reference
```

The ability to specify a particular function signature in a callable reference may be added in a future version of Kotlin. For that reason, using parentheses after the callable reference is currently reserved to accommodate a possible refinement of syntax. If you want to use a callable reference in a call, you have to enclose it in parentheses:

```
fun max(a: Int, b: Int) = if (a > b) a else b


fun main() {
    println((::max)(1, 2)) // 2
    println(::max(1, 2))   // Error: this syntax is reserved for
                           // future use

}
```

The callable reference can also be constructed for Kotlin properties. Such references, however, are not functional values by themselves, but rather reflection objects containing the property information. Using the getter property, we can access the functional value corresponding to the getter function. For a **var** declaration, the setter property similarly allows you to refer to setter:

```kotlin
class Person(var firstName: String, var familyName: String)

fun main() {
    val person = Person("John", "Doe")
    val readName = person::firstName.getter    // bound reference to
                                               // getter
    val writeFamily = person::familyName.setter // bound reference
                                                // to setter
    println(readName())                         // John
    writeFamily("Smith")
    println(person.familyName)                  // Smith
}
```

Callable references to local variables are currently not supported, but may be added in a future version.

Java vs. Kotlin: Readers familiar with Java would probably recognize the similarity between Kotlin callable references and method references introduced in Java 8. Although their semantics is indeed very similar, there are some important differences. First, callable references are more varied due to the fact that Kotlin supports declarations which have no direct counterparts in Java such as top-level and local functions as well as properties. Second, while Kotlin callable references are first-class expressions, Java's method references only make sense in the context of some functional interface. They don't have a definite type of their own. On top of that, a callable reference is not just a functional value but also a reflection object which you can use to obtain the function or property attributes at runtime. In *Chapter 10, Annotations and Reflection*, we'll address the reflection API in more detail.

Inline functions and properties

Using higher-order functions and functional values is fraught with certain performance overheads, since each function is represented as an object. Moreover, when a lambda or an anonymous function in question uses variables from outer scope, it has to be created anew each time you pass it into a higher-order call to reflect a change of context. Invocations of functional values have to be dispatched through virtual calls which choose the function implementation at runtime as the compiler in general has no way to infer it statically.

Kotlin, however, provides a solution which can reduce runtime penalties of using functional values. The basic idea is to inline a higher-order function at its usage replacing a call with a copy of its body. To distinguish such a function, you need to mark with the **inline** modifier.

Suppose, for example, the function which searches a value in an integer array given a predicate, it must satisfy:

```
inline fun indexOf(numbers: IntArray, condition: (Int) -> Boolean): Int {
    for (i in numbers.indices) {
        if (condition(numbers[i])) return i
    }
    return -1
}


fun main() {
    println(indexOf(intArrayOf(4, 3, 2, 1)) { it < 3 }) // 2
}
```

Since the **indexOf()** function is inlined, the compiler will substitute its body instead of the function call. It means that the **main()** function will be basically equivalent to the code:

```
fun main() {
    val numbers = intArrayOf(4, 3, 2, 1)
    var index = -1
    for (i in numbers.indices) {
        if (numbers[i] < 3) {
            index = i
            break
        }
    }
    println(index)
}
```

Although inline functions can increase the size of the compiled code, when used reasonably they can boost performance especially when a function in question is relatively small. Many higher-order functions provided by the Kotlin standard library we'll see in *Chapter 7, Exploring Collections and I/O* are inline.

Note that unlike some programming languages supporting function inlining (such as C++), the **inline** modifier in Kotlin is not an optimization hint which may be ignored depending on the compiler decision. Kotlin functions marked with **inline** are *always* inlined when it's possible, and when inlining can't be performed, usage of the **inline** modifier is considered a compilation error.

The preceding example demonstrates that the **inline** modifier affects not just a function it's applied to, but also functional values which serve as its parameters. This in turn restricts what possible manipulations with such lambdas inside an inline function. Since inlined lambdas won't exist as a separate entity at runtime, they can't be, for example, stored in a variable or passed to a non-inline function. There are only two things we can do with an inlinable lambda; call it or pass as an inlinable argument into another inline function:

```
var lastAction: () -> Unit = {}
```

```
inline fun runAndMemorize(action: () -> Unit) {
    action()
    lastAction = action // Error
}
```

For the same reason, it's not allowed to inline values of a nullable functional type:

```
inline fun forEach(a: IntArray, action: ((Int) -> Unit)?) { // Error
    if (action == null) return
    for (n in a) action(n)
}
```

In such cases, we can forbid inlining of a particular lambda argument by marking it with the **noinlne** modifier:

```
inline fun forEach(a: IntArray, noinline action: ((Int) -> Unit)?) {
                                                            // Error
    if (action == null) return
    for (n in a) action(n)
}
```

Note that when a function has no inlinable parameters, it's usually not worth inlining at all since substituting its body at call site will unlikely make a significant difference at runtime. For that reason, the Kotlin compiler marks such functions with a warning.

What if we try to use private members in a public inline function? Since the body of the inline function is substituted instead of a call, it might allow some external code to break encapsulation. To avoid this, Kotlin forbids references to private members which may be leaked to the external code:

```kotlin
class Person(private val firstName: String, private val familyName: String) {

    inline fun sendMessage(message: () -> String) {

        println("$firstName $familyName: ${message()}") // Error

    }

}
```

Note that if we'd marked the **sendMessage()** function or its containing class with the private modifier, the code would've compiled since references to private members in the **sendMessage()** body wouldn't have leaked outside the **Person** class.

Starting from version 1.1, Kotlin supports inlining of property accessors. This may be useful for improving the performance of reading/writing a property by eliminating a function call:

```kotlin
class Person(var firstName: String, var familyName: String) {
    var fullName
        inline get() = "$firstName $familyName" // Inline getter
        set(value) { ... }                      // Non-inline setter
}
```

Apart from inlining individual accessors, you can also mark a property itself with the inline modifier. In this case, the compiler will inline both getter and setter (if the property is mutable):

```kotlin
class Person(var firstName: String, var familyName: String) {
    inline var fullName // Inline getter and setter
        get() = "$firstName $familyName"
        set(value) { ... }
}
```

Note that inlining is only supported for properties without the backing field. Also similar to functions, you may not refer to private declarations if your property is public:

```kotlin
class Person(private val firstName: String, private val familyName:
String) {
    inline var age = 0 // Error: property has a backing field
                       // Error: firstName and familyName are private
    inline val fullName get() = "$firstName $familyName"

}
```

Non-local control flow

Using higher-order functions raises some issues with instructions that break the normal control flow such as the **return** statement. Consider the following code:

```kotlin
fun forEach(a: IntArray, action: (Int) -> Unit) {
    for (n in a) action(n)
}


fun main() {
    forEach(intArrayOf(1, 2, 3, 4)) {
        if (it < 2 || it > 3) return
        println(it) // Error
    }
}
```

The intention was to return from lambda before printing a number if doesn't fit into a range. However, this code won't compile. This happens because a return statement by default is related to the nearest enclosing function defined with **fun**, **get** or **set** keywords. So in our example, we're trying to return from the main() function instead. Such a statement, also known as *non-local return*, is forbidden because on JVM, there is no efficient way that would allow a lambda to force the return of its enclosing function. One way to solve the problem is to use the anonymous function instead:

```kotlin
fun main() {
    forEach(intArrayOf(1, 2, 3, 4), fun(it: Int) {
        if (it < 2 || it > 3) return
        println(it)
    })
}
```

If we do want to return from a lambda *itself,* we need to qualify the return statement with a context name similar to the labelled **break** and **continue**. In general, the context name can be introduced by labeling a function literal expression:

```kotlin
val action: (Int) -> Unit = myFun@ {
    if (it < 2 || it > 3) return@myFun
    println(it)
}
```

When lambda is passed as an argument to a higher-order function, however, it's possible to use that function's name as a context without introducing an explicit label:

```kotlin
forEach(intArrayOf(1, 2, 3, 4)) {
    if (it < 2 || it > 3) return@forEach
    println(it)
}
```

Qualified returns are available in ordinary functions as well. You can use a function name as a context although usually such a qualification is redundant:

```kotlin
fun main(args: Array<String>) {
    if (args.isEmpty()) return@main
    println(args[0])
}
```

When lambda is inlined, we *can* use return statements to return from the enclosing function. This is possible because the lambda body is substituted into the call site together with a body of corresponding higher-order function, so the return statement would be treated as if it was placed directly in the body of **main()**:

```kotlin
inline fun forEach(a: IntArray, action: (Int) -> Unit) { ... }


fun main() {
    forEach(intArrayOf(1, 2, 3, 4)) {
        if (it < 2 || it > 3) return // Return from main
        println(it)
    }
}
```

There is a special case with calling inlinable lambda not directly in the body of a function it's passed to, but in a separate execution context like a local function or a method of local class. Even though such lambdas are inlined, they are not able to force the return of the caller function since even after inlining, they would occupy different frames of the execution stack. For reasons such usages of functional parameters are forbidden by default:

```
private inline fun forEach(a: IntArray, action: (Int) -> Unit) = object {
    fun run() {
        for (n in a) {
            action(n) // Error
        }
    }
}
```

To allow them, we need to mark a functional parameter with a **crossinline** modifier which leaves the functional value inlined but forbids using non-local returns inside a corresponding lambda:

```
private inline fun forEach(
    a: IntArray, crossinline action: (Int) -> Unit
) = object {
    fun run() {
        for (n in a) {
            action(n) // Ok
        }
    }
}

fun main() {
    forEach(intArrayOf(1, 2, 3, 4)){
        if (it < 2 || it > 3) return // Error
        println(it)
    }
}
```

Non-local control flow issues may also arise when using break and continue statements since they can target a loop enclosing the lambda. Currently, they are not supported even if the lambda in question is inlined, although such support may be added in a future language version:

```
while (true) {
    forEach(intArrayOf(1, 2, 3, 4)) {
        if (it < 2 || it > 3) break // Error
        println(it)
    }
}
```

Extensions

The need to extend an existing class is quite common in practice. As a program evolves, a developer may want to add new functions and properties to classes thus extending their API. But sometimes, simply adding new code to a class is not an option since a class in question may be a part of some library and its modification will require significant efforts if feasible at all. Putting all possible methods into a single class may also be impractical as not all of them are used together and therefore worth decoupling into several program units.

In Java, such extra methods are often packed into utility classes. A common example is **java.util.Arrays** and **java.util.Collections** classes which contain methods extending capabilities of Collection interfaces. The problem with such classes is that they often produce unnecessary boilerplate. For example, a typical usage of utility methods in Java may look like this:

```
int index = Collections.indexOfSubList(
    Arrays.asList("b", "c", "a"),
    Arrays.asList("a", "b")
)
```

Apart from clattering the source code, such calls do not allow you to make use of autocompletion available for class members in major IDEs such as IntelliJ and Eclipse.

That's the primary motivation behind Kotlin extensions which allow you to use functions and properties defined outside a class as if they were its members. Supporting the "open/closed" design principle, they allow you to extend existing classes without modifying them.

Extension functions

The Extension function is basically a function which can be called as if it were a member of some class. When you define such a function, you put a type of its receiver before its name separating them with a dot. Suppose we want to enrich the `String` type with a function which truncates the original string so that its length does not exceed the given threshold:

```
fun String.truncate(maxLength: Int): String {

    return if (length <= maxLength) this else substring(0, maxLength)

}
```

Once defined, this function can be used just like any member of the `String` class:

```
fun main() {
    println("Hello".truncate(10)) // Hello
    println("Hello".truncate(3))  // Hel
}
```

Note that inside the extension function body, the receiver value can be accessed via **this** expression similar to class members. Members and extensions of the receiver can also be accessed implicitly without this just like we've done with a **substring()** function call in the **truncate()** definition.

It's worth pointing out that extension functions by themselves are not able to break through the receiver type encapsulation. For example, since the extension function is defined outside the class, it can't access its private members:

```
class Person(val name: String, private val age: Int)


fun Person.showInfo() = println("$name, $age") // Error: can't access age
```

The extension function, however, may be declared inside a class body making it a member and extension at the same time. Such function is allowed to access private members just like any other function in the class body:

```
class Person(val name: String, private val age: Int) {
    fun Person.showInfo() = println("$name, $age")
                                        // Ok: age is accessible

}
```

We'll see how to use such functions later in this chapter.

IDE Tips: The IntelliJ plugin can convert a class member to an extension. This can be achieved with the "Convert member to extension" action available in Alt+Enter menu when the caret is positioned on the member name (*Figure 5.5*):

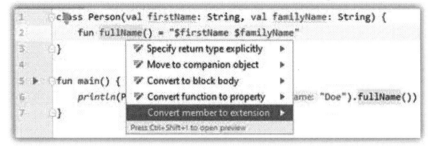

Figure 5.5: Converting member function to extension

Extension functions can be used in bound callable references similar to class members:

```kotlin
class Person(val name: String, val age: Int)


fun Person.hasName(name: String) = name.equals(this.name, ignoreCase
= true)


fun main() {
    val f = Person("John", 25)::hasName
    println(f("JOHN")) // true
    println(f("JAKE")) // false
}
```

What if you have the function with the same signature defined both as a class member and as an extension? Consider the following code:

```kotlin
class Person(val firstName: String, val familyName: String) {
    fun fullName() = "$firstName $familyName"
}


fun Person.fullName() = "$familyName $firstName"


fun main() {
    println(Person("John", "Doe").fullName()) // ???
}
```

In this example, we have two **fullName()** functions defined on the **Person** class which differ in whether they put **familyName** first or last. When faced with such ambiguity on the call site, the compiler always chooses the member function, so the preceding code will print "John Doe". It will also issue a warning telling you that the extension function **fullName()** is shadowed by a member of the Person class and thus can't be called. IDE provides an appropriate highlighting as well (*Figure 5.6*):

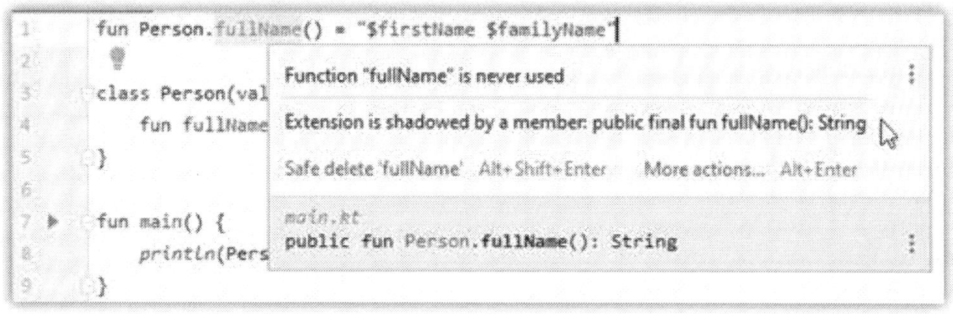

Figure 5.6: *"Shadowed extension" warning*

Favoring members over extensions prevents accidental modification of existing class behavior which otherwise could have led to hard-to-find errors. If it weren't the case we could have, for example, defined:

```
package bad
```

```
fun Person.fullName() = "$familyName $firstName"
```

Then, the meaning of **Person("John", "Doe").fullName()** call would depend on whether

```
import bad.fullName
```

is present in its containing file. This also protects members of built-in and JDK classes.

Note that the extension shadowing has a flipside. If you define an extension function first and *then* add the corresponding member to the class, the original call *will* change its meaning. This is, however, considered acceptable since class members comprising its primary API are supposed to change less frequently than its extension functions. This also simplifies interoperability with a Java code which doesn't have extensions at all.

Extension functions may be local. In particular, they may be nested into other extension functions. In such cases, this expression means the receiver of the innermost function. If you need to refer to the receiver of the outer function, instead you may use a qualified form of this which specifies the function name explicitly. This is also true for members of local classes or anonymous objects declared inside an extension function body:

```kotlin
private fun String.truncator(max: Int) = object {
    val truncated
        get() = if (length <= max) this@truncator else substring(0, max)

    val original
        get() = this@truncator
}

fun main() {
    val truncator = "Hello".truncator(3)
    println(truncator.original)   // Hello
    println(truncator.truncated)  // Hel
}
```

The syntax is basically the same as we've seen in the case of inner classes.

When the top-level extension function is defined in another package, it must always be imported before you can make a call. For example:

```kotlin
// util.kt
package util

fun String.truncate(maxLength: Int): String {
    return if (length <= maxLength) this else substring(0, maxLength)
}


// main.kt
package main

import util.truncate

fun main() {
    println("Hello".truncate(3))
}
```

The reason is that such a function can't be invoked by a qualified name since the qualifier position is taken by the receiver expression. The non-extension function, however:

```
fun truncate(s: String maxLength: Int): String {
    return if (s.length <= maxLength) s else s.substring(0, maxLength)
}
```

could've been called as **util.truncate("Hello", 3)** without an import directive.

Java vs. Kotlin: You might've been wondering how extension functions are represented on the JVM. The answer is actually quite simple: extension functions are compiled into methods with an additional parameter which represent the receiver expression. If we look at the bytecode generated for the **truncate()** function above, we'll see that it's basically equivalent to the following Java code:

```
public final class UtilKt {
    public static String truncate(String s, int maxLength) {
        return s.length() <= maxLength
                ? s
                : s.substring(0, maxLength)
    }
}
```

which corresponds to the non-extension Kotlin function:

```
fun truncate(s: String, maxLength: Int) =
    if (s.length <= maxLength) s else s.substring(0, maxLength)
```

In other words, extension functions are essentially a syntactic sugar over ordinary functions which allow you to call them like class members.

IDE Tips: The IntelliJ plugin includes an action which automatically converts an extension function to a non-extension one by changing its receiver to a parameter. To do it, you need to place a caret at the receiver type, choose "Convert receiver to parameter" from the *Alt + Enter* menu and enter a new parameter name (*Figure 5.7*). There is also an opposite action, "Convert parameter to receiver" which transforms an arbitrary function parameter to its receiver. The latter action is available via *Alt + Enter* when a caret is positioned on the parameter name.

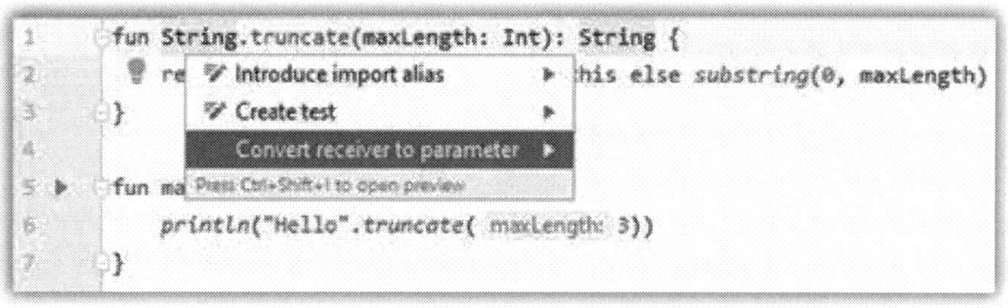

Figure 5.7: *"Convert receiver to parameter" action*

It's worth noting that an extension function, unlike member functions and properties, can be defined for a nullable receiver type. Since nullable types do not have their own members, this mechanism allows you to enrich them by introducing extension functions "from outside". Such extensions can then be invoked without the safe call operator:

```
// Nullable receiver
fun String?.truncate(maxLength: Int): String {
    if (this == null) return null
    return if (length <= maxLength) this else substring(0, maxLength)
}


fun main() {
    val s = readLine()     // nullable String
    println(s.truncate(3)) // ?. is not necessary here
}
```

Note that if the extension receiver has a nullable type, it's the responsibility of the extension function to handle a null value.

Extension properties

Similarly to functions, Kotlin allows you to define *extension properties* which can be accessed just like any member property. The syntax is also similar. To define an extension property, you prefix its name with a receiver type. Let's take a look at the following example:

```
val IntRange.leftHalf: IntRange
    get() = start..(start + endInclusive)/2
```

```kotlin
fun main() {
    println((1..3).leftHalf) // 1..2
    println((3..6).leftHalf) // 3..4
}
```

The preceding code defined an extension property **leftHalf** for the **IntRange** type. It computes the left half of the original range.

The crucial difference between the member and extension property is that the latter can't have a backing field since there is no reliable way to add some extra state to a class instance. It means that extension properties can neither have initializers, nor use the **field** keyword inside their accessors. They also can't be lateinit since such properties rely on backing fields. For the same reason, an extension property must always have an explicit getter and, if mutable, an explicit setter:

```kotlin
val IntArray.midIndex
    get() = lastIndex/2


var IntArray.midValue
    get() = this[midIndex]
    set(value) {
        this[midIndex] = value
    }


fun main() {
    val numbers = IntArray(6) { it*it } // 0, 1, 4, 9, 16, 25
    println(numbers.midValue)              // 4
    numbers.midValue *= 10
    println(numbers.midValue)              // 40
}
```

Extension properties, however, can use delegates. Bear in mind, though, that the delegate expression can't access the property receiver so in general, there is no point in declaring the lazy property as an extension since it would have the same value for each instance of the receiver type:

```kotlin
val String.message by lazy { "Hello" }
```

```kotlin
fun main() {
    println("Hello".message) // Hello
    println("Bye".message)   // Hello
}
```

Object definitions can be considered an exception since they have only one instance:

```kotlin
object Messages
```

```kotlin
val Messages.HELLO by lazy { "Hello" }
```

```kotlin
fun main() {
    println(Messages.HELLO)
}
```

In general, it's possible to create a delegate which is able to access the property receiver. We'll see how to do it in *Chapter 11, Domain-Specific Languages*.

Companion extensions

In *Chapter 4, Working with Classes and Objects*, we've introduced an idea of the companion object which is a special nested object whose members can be accessed by the name of its containing class. This useful feature covers extensions as well.

In the following example, we define an extension function for the companion object of the built-in **IntRange** class. The function can then be invoked via the class name:

```kotlin
fun IntRange.Companion.singletonRange(n: Int) = n..n
```

```kotlin
fun main() {
    println(IntRange.singletonRange(5))            // 5..5
    println(IntRange.Companion.singletonRange(3)) // 3..3
}
```

It's, of course, possible, to call such a function using the full companion name as well, like in **IntRange.Companion.singletonRange(3)**. The same idea also works for extension properties:

```kotlin
val String.Companion.HELLO
    get() = "Hello"
```

```kotlin
fun main() {
    println(String.HELLO)
    println(String.Companion.HELLO)
}
```

Note that the definition of extensions on the companion object is only possible if a class in question has explicit declaration of the companion even if it's empty:

```kotlin
class Person(val firstName: String, val familyName: String) {
    companion object
}
```

```kotlin
val Person.Companion.UNKNOWN by lazy { Person("John", "Doe") }
```

We can't, on the other side, define an extension for the companion object of **Any** since it doesn't exist:

```kotlin
// Error: Companion is undefined
fun Any.Companion.sayHello() = println("Hello")
```

Lambdas and functional types with the receiver

Similar to functions and properties, Kotlin allows you to utilize extension receivers for lambdas and anonymous functions. Such functional values are described by a special variety of functional types with the receiver. Let's rewrite our **aggregate()** example to use a functional value with the receiver instead of a two-argument function:

```kotlin
fun aggregate(numbers: IntArray, op: Int.(Int) -> Int): Int {
    var result = numbers.firstOrNull()
        ?: throw IllegalArgumentException("Empty array")
    for (i in 1..numbers.lastIndex) result = result.op(numbers[i])
    return result
}
```

```kotlin
fun sum(numbers: IntArray) = aggregate(numbers) { op -> this + op }
```

The receiver type is specified before the parameter type list and is separated with a dot:

```kotlin
Int.(Int) -> Int
```

In this case, any lambda passed as an argument gets an implicit receiver which we can access using **this** expression:

```
{ op -> this + op }
```

Similarly, we can use an extension syntax for anonymous functions. The receiver type is specified just before function's parameter list:

```
fun sum(numbers: IntArray) = aggregate(numbers, fun Int.(op: Int) =
this + op)
```

Unlike extension function definitions, a functional value with the receiver can be called as a non-extension function with the receiver placed before all succeeding arguments. We could've written, for example:

```
fun aggregate(numbers: IntArray, op: Int.(Int) -> Int): Int {
    var result = numbers.firstOrNull()
        ?: throw IllegalArgumentException("Empty array")
    for (i in 1..numbers.lastIndex) {
        result = op(result, numbers[i]) // Non-extension call
    }
    return result
}
```

Basically, non-literal values of a functional type with the receiver are freely interchangeable with values of the corresponding type where the receiver is used as the first parameter as if they have the same type. This is possible because such values have essentially the same runtime representation:

```
val min1: Int.(Int) -> Int = { if (this < it) this else it }
val min2: (Int, Int) -> Int = min1
val min3: Int.(Int) -> Int = min2
```

Note, however, that while it's possible to invoke a functional value with the receiver as either an extension or non-extension (with the receiver placed as the first argument), functional values without receivers can be invoked using a non-extension syntax only:

```
fun main() {
    val min1: Int.(Int) -> Int = { if (this < it) this else it }
    val min2: (Int, Int) -> Int = min1
    println(3.min1(2))  // Ok: calling min1 as extension
```

```
    println(min1(1, 2)) // Ok: calling min1 as non-extension
    println(3.min2(2))  // Error: Can't call min2 as extension
    println(min2(1, 2)) // Ok: Calling min2 as non-extension
}
```

Lambdas with the receiver give you a powerful tool which can be used for building DSL-like API. We'll address this issue in *Chapter 11, Domain-Specific Languages*.

Callable references with receiver

In Kotlin, you can also use callable references which define functional values with receivers. Such references may be based on either the class member, or extension declarations. Syntactically, they are similar to bound callable references, but qualified by a receiver **type** instead of an expression:

```
fun aggregate(numbers: IntArray, op: Int.(Int) -> Int): Int {
    var result = numbers.firstOrNull()
        ?: throw IllegalArgumentException("Empty array")
    for (i in 1..numbers.lastIndex) result = result.op(numbers[i])
    return result
}


fun Int.max(other: Int) = if (this > other) this else other


fun main() {
    val numbers = intArrayOf(1, 2, 3, 4)
    println(aggregate(numbers, Int::plus)) // 10
    println(aggregate(numbers, Int::max))  // 4
}
```

In the preceding code, **Int::plus** refers to the member function **plus()** (which does exactly the same as **+** operator) of the built-in class Int, while **Int::max** refers to the extension function defined in the containing file. The syntax is the same in both cases.

Thanks to implicit casting between extension and non-extension functional types we've mentioned in the previous section, it's also possible to use non-receiver callable references in the context where the functional type with the receiver is expected. For example, we could've passed a two-argument callable reference **::max** for a parameter of type **Int.(Int) -> Int**:

```
fun aggregate(numbers: IntArray, op: Int.(Int) -> Int): Int {
    var result = numbers.firstOrNull()
        ?: throw IllegalArgumentException("Empty array")
    for (i in 1..numbers.lastIndex) result = result.op(numbers[i])
    return result
}

fun max(a: Int, b: Int) = if (a > b) a else b

fun main() {
    println(aggregate(intArrayOf(1, 2, 3, 4), ::max))
}
```

The converse is true as well. Callable references with the receiver can be used when the expected functional type is a non-receiver one. In a slightly modified example, callable references to member and extension functions are used as values of a two-argument functional type **(Int, Int) -> Int**:

```
fun aggregate(numbers: IntArray, op: (Int, Int) -> Int): Int {
    var result = numbers.firstOrNull()
        ?: throw IllegalArgumentException("Empty array")
    for (i in 1..numbers.lastIndex) result = op(result, numbers[i])
    return result
}

fun Int.max(other: Int) = if (this > other) this else other

fun main() {
    println(aggregate(intArrayOf(1, 2, 3, 4), Int::plus)) // 10
    println(aggregate(intArrayOf(1, 2, 3, 4), Int::max))  // 4
}
```

Note that callable references are not supported for extensions functions declared as class members as currently there is no way to specify multiple receiver types for a :: expression.

Scope functions

The Kotlin standard library includes a set of functions which allow you to introduce a temporary scope where you can refer to the value of given *context expression*. Sometimes, this can be helpful to avoid an explicit introduction of local variables in containing the scope to hold an expression value and simplify the code. These functions are usually called *scope functions.*

The basic effect is a simple execution of a lambda you will provide as an argument. The difference comes from the combination of the following aspects:

- Whether the context expression is passed as a receiver or an ordinary argument.
- Whether the lambda is an extension or not.
- Whether the function returns the value of lambda or the value of the context expression.

Overall there are five standard scope functions: **run**, **let**, **with**, **apply**, **also**. In this section, we'll discuss how to use them to simplify your code. All scope functions are inline and thus do not entail any performance overhead.

Note that scope functions should be used with care as abusing them can make your code less readable and more prone to errors. In general, it's worth avoiding the nested scope functions as you might get easily confused about the meaning of **this** or **it**.

run / with

The **run()** function is an extension which accepts an extension lambda and returns its result. The basic use pattern is a configuration of an object state followed by a computation of a result value:

```
class Address {
    var zipCode: Int = 0
    var city: String = ""
    var street: String = ""
    var house: String = ""

    fun post(message: String): Boolean {
        "Message for ${zipCode, $city, $street, $house}: $message"
        return readLine() == "OK"
```

```
        }
    }


fun main() {
    val isReceived = Address().run {
        // Address instance is available as this
        zipCode = 123456
        city = "London"
        street = "Baker Street"
        house = "221b"
        post("Hello!") // return value
    }
    if (!isReceived) {
        println("Message is not delivered")
    }
}
```

Without a run, we'd have to introduce a variable for the `Address` instance thus making it available for the rest of the function body which may be undesirable if we need that instance for a single **post()** action. Using functions like **run()** gives you more fine-grained control over visibility of local declarations.

Note that the result may also be of the type **Unit**:

```
fun Address.showCityAddress() = println("$street, $house")


fun main() {
    Address().run {
        zipCode = 123456
        city = "London"
        street = "Baker Street"
        house = "221b"
        showCityAddress()
    }
}
```

The **with()** function is very similar to **run():** the only difference is that **with()** is not an extension, so the context expression is passed as an ordinary argument rather than the receiver. The common use of this function is a grouping of calls to member functions and properties of the context expression under the same scope:

```kotlin
fun main() {

    val message = with (Address("London", "Baker Street", "221b")) {

        "Address: $city, $street, $house"

    }

    println(message)

}
```

In the preceding example, we're making use of the fact that the members of **this** instance can be accessed without the qualifier. Without the scope function, we'd have to write the following:

```kotlin
fun main() {
    val addr = Address("London", "Baker Street", "221b")
    val message = "Address: ${addr.city}, ${addr.street}, ${addr.house}"
    println(message)
}
```

Thus, introducing an additional variable and explicitly qualifying all members of **Address** with a particular instance **addr**.

run without context

The Kotlin standard library also provides an overloaded version of **run()** which doesn't have a context expression and just returns the value of lambda. The lambda itself has neither the receiver, nor parameters.

The primary use case for this function is using a block in some context which requires an expression. Consider, for example, the following code:

```kotlin
class Address(val city: String, val street: String, val house: String) {
    fun asText() = "$city, $street, $house"
}


fun main() {
```

```
    val address = Address("London", "Baker Street", "221b")
    println(address.asText())
}
```

What if we want to read address components from the standard input? We could've introduced a separate variable for each of them:

```
fun main() {
    val city = readLine() ?: return
    val street = readLine() ?: return
    val house = readLine() ?: return
    val address = Address(city, street, house)
    println(address.asText())
}
```

But that would place them in the same scope as any other local variable of **main()** while variables like **city** only make sense in the context of creating a particular **Address** instance. Inlining all the variables and getting something like:

```
fun main() {
    val address = Address(readLine() ?: return,
                          readLine() ?: return,
                          readLine() ?: return)
    println(address.asText())
}
```

is rather a bad choice since we are looking at such code we can immediately tell what each **readLine()** is supposed to mean. The idiomatic solution is given by **run()**:

```
fun main() {
    val address = run {
        val city = readLine() ?: return
        val street = readLine() ?: return
        val house = readLine() ?: return
        Address(city, street, house)
    }
    println(address.asText())
}
```

Since run is an inline function, we can use return statements inside its lambda to exit the outer function as if it's some built-in control structure.

Note that using a block statement by itself doesn't work since such a block is treated as lambda. That's the reason the **run()** function is added to the standard library:

```
fun main() {
    val address = {
        val city = readLine() ?: return
                                // Error: return is not allowed
        val street = readLine() ?: return
                                // Error: return is not allowed
        val house = readLine() ?: return
                                // Error: return is not allowed
        Address(city, street, house)
    }
    println(address.asText()) // Error: no asText() method
}
```

let

The **let** function is similar to **run** but accepts a single-argument lambda instead of an extension one. The value of context expression is thus represented by the lambda argument. The return value of let is the same as that of its lambda. This function is often used to avoid introduction of a new variable in the outer scope:

```
class Address(val city: String, val street: String, val house: String) {
    fun post(message: String) {}
}


fun main() {
    Address("London", "Baker Street", "221b").let {
        // Address instance is accessible via it parameter
        println("To city: ${it.city}")
        it.post("Hello")
    }
}
```

Similar to other lambdas, you can introduce a custom parameter name for the purpose of readability or disambiguation:

```kotlin
fun main() {
    Address("London", "Baker Street", "221b").let { addr ->
        // Address instance is accessible via addr parameter
        println("To city: ${addr.city}")
        addr.post("Hello")
    }
}
```

A common use case of let is a concise way to pass a nullable value to a non-nullable function with a safety check. In the previous chapter, we've learned about a safe call operator that allows you to invoke a function with a nullable receiver. But what if the value in question must be passed as an ordinary parameter. Consider the following example:

```kotlin
fun readInt() = try {
    readLine()?.toInt()
} catch (e: NumberFormatException) {
    null
}


fun main(args: Array<String>) {
    val index = readInt()
    val arg = if (index != null) args.getOrNull(index) else null
    if (arg != null) {
        println(arg)
    }
}
```

The **getOrNull()** function returns an array item if the given index is valid and null otherwise. Since its parameter is non-nullable, we can't pass a result of **readInt()** function to **getOrNull():** hence the if check which enables smart cast to a non-nullable type. We can, however, simplify the code by using let:

```kotlin
val arg = index?.let { args.getOrNull(it) }
```

The let call is only executed when the index is not null, so the compiler knows that its parameter is non-nullable inside lambda.

apply / also

The **apply()** function is an extension which takes an extension lambda and return the value of its receiver. A common use of this function is a configuration of object state which, as opposed to **run()**, is not followed by immediate computation of some result value:

```
class Address {
    var city: String = ""
    var street: String = ""
    var house: String = ""


    fun post(message: String) { }
}


fun main() {
    val message = readLine() ?: return
    Address().apply {
        city = "London"
        street = "Baker Street"
        house = "221b"
    }.post(message)
}
```

There is also a similar function **also()** which takes a single-argument lambda instead:

```
fun main() {
    val message = readLine() ?: return
    Address().also {
        it.city = "London"
        it.street = "Baker Street"
        it.house = "221b"
    }.post(message)
}
```

Extensions as class members

In a previous section, we've discussed a possibility of declaring an extension function as a class member. Let's now take a closer look at such extensions.

When you define an extension function or property inside a class, such a definition automatically gets *two* receivers as opposed to a single one for ordinary members and top-level extensions. The instance of the receiver type mentioned in the extension definition is called an *extension receiver*, while the instance of the class containing the extension is called the *dispatch receiver*. Both receivers can be denoted by **this** expression qualified with either the containing class name (for dispatch receiver), or the name of the extension (for the extension receiver). Unqualified **this** expression, as usually, refer to the receiver of the nearest enclosing declaration, so usually it's the same as the extension receiver unless you use it inside some local declaration such as class, nested extension function or a lambda with the receiver.

Let's consider an example which illustrates both kinds of receivers:

```kotlin
class Address(val city: String, val street: String, val house: String)


class Person(val firstName: String, val familyName: String) {
    fun Address.post(message: String) {
                    // implicit this: extension receiver (Address)
        val city = city
                    // unqualified this: extension receiver (Address)
        val street = this.city
                    // qualified this: extension receiver (Address)
        val house = this@post.house
                        // implicit this: dispatch receiver (Person)
        val firstName = firstName
                        // qualified this: dispatch receiver (Person)
        val familyName = this@Person.familyName
        println("From $firstName, $familyName at $city, $street, $house:")
        println(message)
    }

    fun test(address: Address) {
```

```
        // Dispatch receiver: implicit
        // Extension receiver: explicit
        address.post("Hello")
    }
}
```

When we invoke the **post()** function inside **test()**, the dispatch receiver is supplied automatically since **test()** is a member of the **Person** class. The extension receiver, on the other hand, is passed explicitly as the **address** expression.

Similarly, we can call the **post()** function when the current instance of the **Person** class is supplied in a different way: for example, as an extension receiver or an instance of the outer class:

```
class Address(val city: String, val street: String, val house: String)


class Person(val firstName: String, val familyName: String) {
    fun Address.post(message: String) { }


    inner class Mailbox {
        fun Person.testExt(address: Address) {
            address.post("Hello")
        }
    }
}


fun Person.testExt(address: Address) {
    address.post("Hello")
}
```

What if we have a receiver of the **Address** type instead? Suppose we want to call the **post()** inside the **Address** class body:

```
class Address(val city: String, val street: String, val house: String) {
    fun test(person: Person) {
        person.post("Hello") // Error: method post() is not defined
    }
}
```

```kotlin
class Person(val firstName: String, val familyName: String) {
    fun Address.post(message: String) { }
}
```

This doesn't work because the dispatch receiver of the type **Person** must be already in scope. The problem can be solved by using one of the scope functions which can wrap the **post()** call inside an extension lambda with a **Person** receiver:

```kotlin
class Address(val city: String, val street: String, val house: String) {
    fun test(person: Person) {
        with(person) {
            // Implicit dispatch and extension receivers
            post()
        }
    }
}


class Person(val firstName: String, val familyName: String) {
    fun Address.post(message: String) { }
}
```

This trick can also be used to call **post()** outside the **Address** or **Person** class as well their extensions:

```kotlin
class Address(val city: String, val street: String, val house: String)

class Person(val firstName: String, val familyName: String) {
    fun Address.post(message: String) { }
}


fun main() {
    with(Person("John", "Watson")) {
        Address("London", "Baker Street", "221b").post("Hello")
    }
}
```

These examples demonstrate that rules regarding functions and properties with double receivers can become quite confusing. For that reason, it's generally recommended to restrict their scope to the containing declaration:

```kotlin
class Address(val city: String, val street: String, val house: String)


class Person(val firstName: String, val familyName: String) {
    // Can't be used outside Person class
    private fun Address.post(message: String) { }


    fun test(address: Address) = address.post("Hello")
}
```

One particularly confusing and error-prone case that's worth avoiding is when both dispatch and extension receivers have the same type:

```kotlin
class Address(val city: String, val street: String, val house: String) {
    fun Address.post(message: String) { }
}
```

An interesting example of the double-receiver member is an extension declared inside an object (in particular, a companion object). Such extensions may be imported and used similarly to top-level ones:

```kotlin
import Person.Companion.parsePerson


class Person(val firstName: String, val familyName: String) {
    companion object {
        fun String.parsePerson(): Person? {
            val names = split(" ")
          return if (names.size == 2) Person(names[0], names[1]) else null
        }
    }
}


fun main() {
    // instance of Person.Companion is supplied implicitly
    println("John Doe".parsePerson()?.firstName) // John
}
```

In most cases, though, using top-level extensions is more preferable since it leads to a more simple and readable code.

Conclusion

Let's sum up the basic things we have picked in this chapter. We've learned to use functional types and higher-order functions to abstract and compose pieces of code in the form of functions. We've also seen various forms of constructing a functional value and discussed the capabilities of function inlining. Finally, we have gone through the major uses cases of extension functions and properties which allow you to add new features to existing types.

In the next chapter, we're going to revisit the object-oriented programming and discuss special varieties of classes aimed at simplifying common programming patterns like enumerations and data classes.

Points to remember

- Kotlin supports first-class values of functional types which can be stored in variables as well as passed into and returned from another functions.
- Functional values can be constructed in two ways: by defining new function via the lambda/anonymous function syntax or by using an existing function/class method in the form of a callable reference.
- Kotlin functions and properties can be inlined meaning that their body gets substituted in place of their calls.
- Existing types can be enhanced by adding extension functions and properties.
- The standard library includes a set of functions which allow you to introduce a new scope where given context expression can be used as either parameter, or receiver.

Questions

1. What's a higher-order function?
2. Describe the syntax of lambda expression. How do they compare with lambdas in Java?
3. What is a functional type? What's the difference between functional types in Kotlin and functional interfaces in Java?
4. Compare functional types with the receiver and the ones without.

5. What are the differences between lambdas and anonymous functions? When would you prefer an anonymous function over lambda?

6. Describe the pros and cons of inline functions. What are the limitations?

7. What is a callable reference? Describe callable reference forms. How do they compare with method references in Java?

8. Describe the behavior of return statements inside lambdas and anonymous functions. What is a qualified return statement?

9. Compare inlining modes of functional parameters: default, **noinline**, **crossinline**.

10. How to define an extension function? Do extensions modify the classes they apply to?

11. How would you use a companion object extension?

12. What are limitations of extension properties?

13. Describe the forms of **this** expression. What are the uses of qualified **this**?

14. What are the specifics of declaring extension functions inside classes?

15. What are the scope functions? How would you decide which scope function better fits for the particular task at hand?

Key terms

- Functional value: An object which can be invoked like a function (via its `invoke()` method).

- Lambda: A functional value expression in the form of a code block with optional arguments and return type.

- Callable reference: An expression which wraps the existing function or method into a functional value which can be stored and passed around like any other object.

- Inline function: A function whose body is substituted in a place of a call instead of performing a call itself

- Non-local return: A **return** statement which can terminate enclosing function from inside a lambda that is passed as its argument.

- Extension function/property: A function/property which is defined with an explicit receiver of some type and can be invoked as if it were a member of that type.

CHAPTER 6

Using Special-Case Classes

In this chapter, we will discuss special kinds of classes designed to simplify the implementation of some common programming patterns. Namely, we'll address the usage of enums to describe types with a restricted set of instances, the concise representation of data with data classes, and experimental lightweight wrappers with almost zero runtime overhead.

Structure

- Enum classes
- Data classes
- Inline classes

Objective

After reading this chapter, you will learn to use special varieties of classes such as enums and data classes to solve common programming tasks. Get a basic understanding of inline classes and their usage on the example of unsigned integer types.

Enum classes

An **enum** (short of "enumeration") class is a special variety of class which can represent a limited set of predefined constants. The simplest form is just a list of constant names enclosed inside the **enum class** body:

```
enum class WeekDay {
    MONDAY, TUESDAY, WEDNESDAY, THURSDAY, FRIDAY, SATURDAY, SUNDAY
}


fun WeekDay.isWorkDay() =
    !(this == WeekDay.SATURDAY || this == WeekDay.SUNDAY)


fun main() {
    println(WeekDay.MONDAY.isWorkDay())   // true
    println(WeekDay.SATURDAY.isWorkDay()) // false
}
```

Enums allow more type-safe representations of limited value sets as compared to, say, integers or strings since you don't have to check whether a value in the question is out of possible range. The compiler ensures that any variable of a particular enum type can take only one of the values specified in its body.

Java vs. Kotlin: Kotlin enums are defined with a pair of keyword **enum class** as opposed to just **enum** in Java. The **enum** keyword itself is soft and can be used as an identifier in any other context.

Note that compile-time constants enum values are usually written in upper case.

Enums are somewhat similar to object declarations in a sense that they define a set of global constants representing instances of a particular type. Similarly to objects, they are not permitted in contexts where there is no guarantee that such a definition can be available as a global constant. You can't, for example, put an enum definition into an inner class or function body:

```
fun main() {
    enum class Direction { NORTH, SOUTH, WEST, EAST } // Error
}
```

Exhaustive when expressions

Just like values of any other type, enum variables may be compared against particular values using a **when** expression. There is, however, an additional benefit when using enums; you can omit an **else** branch if the when expression is *exhaustive*, i.e., it contains branches for all possible values of an enum type:

```
enum class Direction {
    NORTH, SOUTH, WEST, EAST
}
```

```
fun rotateClockWise(direction: Direction) = when (direction) {
    Direction.NORTH -> Direction.EAST
    Direction.EAST -> Direction.SOUTH
    Direction.SOUTH -> Direction.WEST
    Direction.WEST -> Direction.NORTH
}
```

The exhaustive form of the **when** expression decreases the chance of writing a code which may break on a context change like adding a new enum value. Suppose that we've added an **else** branch instead:

```
fun rotateClockWise(direction: Direction) = when (direction) {
    Direction.NORTH -> Direction.EAST
    Direction.EAST -> Direction.SOUTH
    Direction.SOUTH -> Direction.WEST
    Direction.WEST -> Direction.NORTH
    else -> throw IllegalArgumentException("Invalid direction:
    $direction")
}
```

This code works fine until we add new values for the **Direction** enum:

```
enum class Direction {
    NORTH, SOUTH, WEST, EAST,
    NORTH_EAST, NORTH_WEST, SOUTH_EAST, SOUTH_WEST
}
```

Now, a call like `rotateClockWise(Direction.NORTH_EAST)` will throw an exception. If we, however, use an **else** free form, an error can be captured at compile-time as the compiler can complain about the non-exhaustive **when** expression in the `rotateClockWise()` body.

Java vs. Kotlin: Note that unlike Java's **switch** statement which requires you to use *unqualified* names of enum values in **case** clauses, Kotlin enum constants used in a **when** expression must be qualified with the name of the enum class unless imported. Compare the preceding `rotateClockWise()` function with a similar Java method:

```
public Direction rotateClockWise(Direction d) {
    switch (d) {
        case NORTH: return Direction.EAST;
        case EAST: return Direction.SOUTH;
        case SOUTH: return Direction.WEST;
        case WEST: return Direction.NORTH;
    }
    throw new IllegalArgumentException("Unknown value: " + d);
}
```

We can void explicit qualification of cnum constants by importing them at the beginning of the containing file:

```
import Direction.*

enum class Direction {
    NORTH, SOUTH, WEST, EAST
}

fun rotateClockWise(direction: Direction) = when (direction) {
    NORTH -> EAST
    EAST -> SOUTH
    SOUTH -> WEST
    WEST -> NORTH
}
```

Internally exhaustive **when** expressions include an implicit **else** branch which throws a special exception of the **NoWhenBranchMatchedException** class when no branch matches a subject expression.

IDE Tips: The IntelliJ plugin can detect unnecessary **else** branches and suggest you to drop them if the **when** expression is exhaustive as shown in *Figure 6.1* (as shown on the Error: Reference source not found):

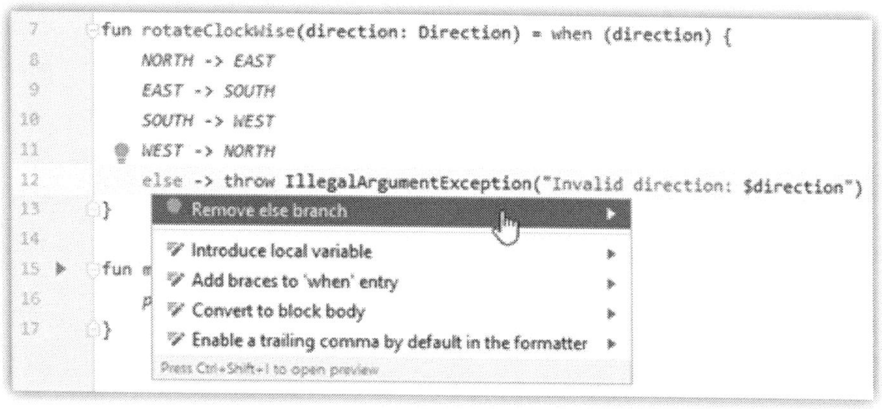

Figure 6.1: Redundant else *branch in an exhaustive* when *expression*

Declaring enums with custom members

Similarly to other classes, enums may have their own members. Besides that, you can define your own extension functions and properties as evidenced by the preceding example.

The enum class may include any definitions permitted for an ordinary class, including functions, properties, primary and secondary constructors, initialization blocks, inner/non-inner nested classes, and objects (whether companion or not). Any such declarations in an enum class body must be placed *after* the enum constant list. The constant list itself in this case must be terminated by a semicolon (it's one of those rare cases when a semicolon in Kotlin can't be omitted). The members declared in an enum class body are available for all its constants:

```kotlin
enum class WeekDay {
    MONDAY, TUESDAY, WEDNESDAY, THURSDAY, FRIDAY, SATURDAY, SUNDAY;

    val lowerCaseName get() = name.toLowerCase()
    fun isWorkDay() = !(this == SATURDAY || this == SUNDAY)
}


fun main() {
    println(WeekDay.MONDAY.isWorkDay())        // true
```

```
    println(WeekDay.WEDNESDAY.lowerCaseName) // wednesday
}
```

When an enum class has a constructor, you need to place an appropriate call in the definition of each enum constant:

```
enum class RainbowColor(val isCold: Boolean) {
    RED(false), ORANGE(false), YELLOW(false),
    GREEN(true), BLUE(true), INDIGO(true), VIOLET(true);


    val isWarm get() = !isCold
}


fun main() {
    println(RainbowColor.BLUE.isCold) // true
    println(RainbowColor.RED.isWarm)  // true
}
```

The enum constants may also have a body with their own definitions. Note, however, that an anonymous type introduced by such constants (we've already mentioned them in *Chapter 4, Working with Classes and Objects*) are not exposed to the outside code which means that you can't access members introduced in the enum constant body outside the body itself:

```
enum class WeekDay {
    MONDAY { fun startWork() = println("Work week started") },
    TUESDAY, WEDNESDAY, THURSDAY, FRIDAY, SATURDAY, SUNDAY
}
```

```
fun main() = WeekDay.MONDAY.startWork() // Error
```

Such members are generally helpful when they are used to provide the implementation of virtual methods in the enum class itself or some supertype. We'll defer such examples till *Chapter 8, Understanding Class Hierarchies*.

Note that currently all nested classes defined in an enum constant body must be inner.

Using common members of enum classes

All enum classes in Kotlin are implicit subtypes of the `kotlin.Enum` class which contains a set of common functions and properties available for any enum value. Besides a few API differences, this class is quite similar to its Java counterpart, `java.lang.Enum`. On the JVM, it's indeed represented by the Java's `Enum`.

Any enum value has a pair of properties, `ordinal` and `name` which contain the zero-based index of its definition in the enum class body and value name, respectively:

```
enum class Direction {
    NORTH, SOUTH, WEST, EAST;
}


fun main() {
    println(Direction.WEST.name)    // WEST
    println(Direction.WEST.ordinal) // 2
}
```

Values of a particular enum class are comparable with each other according to the order of their definition in the enum body. Similarly to Java, the enum equality is based on their identity:

```
fun main() {
    println(Direction.WEST == Direction.NORTH)    // false
    println(Direction.WEST != Direction.EAST)     // true
    println(Direction.EAST < Direction.NORTH)     // false
    println(Direction.SOUTH >= Direction.NORTH)   // true
}
```

The comparison operations on enum values basically work on their indices as given by the **ordinal** property.

Java vs. Kotlin: Even though both Java and Kotlin enums implicitly implement the **Comparable** interface, you can't apply the operator such as < or > to enum values in Java.

Each enum class also has a set of implicit methods which can be invoked on a class name similarly to members of a companion object. The **valueOf()** method returns a enum value given its name or throws an exception if a name is not valid:

```kotlin
fun main() {
    println(Direction.valueOf("NORTH"))        // NORTH
    println(Direction.valueOf("NORTH_EAST")) // Exception: Invalid name
}
```

The **values()** method gives you an array of all enum values in the order of their definition. Note that the array is created anew on each call so changes to one of them do not affect others:

```kotlin
enum class WeekDay {
    MONDAY, TUESDAY, WEDNESDAY, THURSDAY, FRIDAY, SATURDAY, SUNDAY
}
```

private val weekDays = WeekDay.values()**val** WeekDay.nextDay **get()** = weekDays[(ordinal + 1) % weekDays.size]Since Kotlin 1.1 you can use generic top-level functions **enumValues()** and **enumValueOf()** instead of **values()** and **valueOf()** methods respectively:

```kotlin
fun main() {
    val weekDays = enumValues<WeekDay>()
    println(weekDays[2])                         // WEDNESDAY
    println(enumValueOf<WeekDay>("THURSDAY")) // THURSDAY
}
```

Data classes

Kotlin provides a useful feature to declare classes with a primary goal of storing some data. This feature, called *data classes,* allows you to automatically use generated implementations of some basic operations like equality or conversion to `String`. With data classes, you can also take advantage of destructuring declarations which give you an option to extract class properties putting them into separate local variables with a single and concise language construct. In this section, we'll consider the possibilities of data classes.

Data classes and their operations

Consider, for example, the following class:

```kotlin
class Person(val firstName: String, val familyName: String, val age: Int)
```

What if we want to compare its instances by equality? Similarly to Java, the value of referential types is by default considered equal if they have the same identity, i.e., refer to the same object. The values of instance fields are not taken into account:

```kotlin
fun main() {
    val person1 = Person("John", "Doe", 25)
    val person2 = Person("John", "Doe", 25)
    val person3 = person1
    println(person1 == person2) // false, different identities
    println(person1 == person3) // true, the same identity
}
```

If we need a custom equality for the out class, we usually implement it with the **equals()** method (more on this in *Chapter 7, Exploring Collections and I/O* and *Chapter 8, Understanding Class Hierarchies*) accompanied with the corresponding **hashCode()** method which allows you to use class instances as keys in collections like HashMap. For a certain variety of classes, called *data classes*, Kotlin can generate these methods automatically based on a list of class properties. Let's modify our example slightly:

```kotlin
data class Person(
    val firstName: String,
    val familyName: String,
    val age: Int
)

fun main() {
    val person1 = Person("John", "Doe", 25)
    val person2 = Person("John", "Doe", 25)
    val person3 = person1
    println(person1 == person2) // true
    println(person1 == person3) // true
}
```

Now, both comparisons yield **true** since the compiler automatically provides implementation of the equality operation which compares values of the properties declared in the primary constructor. This also applies to the hash code which depends on the same set of properties.

Note that comparisons of property values are based on their **equals()** method too, so how deep the equality goes depends on the type of the properties involved. Consider the following example:

```
data class Person(
    val firstName: String,
    val familyName: String,
    val age: Int
)
data class Mailbox(val address: String, val person: Person)


fun main() {
    val box1 = Mailbox("Unknown", Person("John", "Doe", 25))
    val box2 = Mailbox("Unknown", Person("John", "Doe", 25))
    println(box1 == box2) // true
}
```

Since **String, Person,** and **MailBox** implement content-based equality, the comparison of **MailBox** instances depend on its own address property as well as the properties of the corresponding Person instance. If we, however, drop the **data** modifier before the **Person** class, the result will change since the **person** properties will be compared by their identity:

```
class Person(
    val firstName: String,
    val familyName: String,
    val age: Int
)
data class Mailbox(val address: String, val person: Person)


fun main() {
    val box1 = Mailbox("Unknown", Person("John", "Doe", 25))
    val box2 = Mailbox("Unknown", Person("John", "Doe", 25))
    println(box1 == box2) // false: Person instances have different
                                                          identities
}
```

The **hashCode()** method similarly returns an object hash code which depends on hash codes of all properties declared in the primary constructor.

Aside of the **equals()/hashCode()** generation data classes provide an implementation of the **toString()** method which converts a class instance to string:

```
fun main() {
    val person = Person("John", "Doe", 25)
    println(person) // Person(firstName=John, familyName=Doe, age=25)
}
```

Note that only properties declared as parameters of the primary constructor are used in the equality/hash code/string conversion. Any other properties do not affect the result:

```
data class Person(val firstName: String, val familyName: String) {
    var age = 0
}
```

```
fun main() {
    val person1 = Person("John", "Doe").apply { age = 25 }
    val person2 = Person("John", "Doe").apply { age = 26 }
    println(person1 == person2) // true
}
```

Any data class implicitly provides the **copy()** function which allows you to create a copy of the current instance with a possible change of some properties. It has the same signature as the data class primary constructor, but accompanies each parameter with a default equal to the current value of the corresponding property. The **copy()** function is usually invoked with a named argument syntax for better code readability:

```
fun Person.show() = println("$firstName $familyName: $age")
fun main() {
    val person = Person("John", "Doe", 25)
    person.show()                                   // John Doe: 25
    person.copy().show()                            // John Doe: 25
    person.copy(familyName = "Smith").show()        // John Smith: 25
    person.copy(age = 30, firstName = "Jane").show() // Jane Doe: 30
}
```

The ability to easily copy an instance encourages the usage of immutable data classes. Although the **var** properties are allowed, it's often reasonable to design data classes as immutable. Using immutable data simplifies reasoning about your code and makes it less error-prone, especially in multi-threaded projects. Immutability is a prerequisite for a proper usage of object as a map key; violating immutability in such cases may lead to quite unexpected behavior as we'll see in *Chapter 7, Exploring Collections and I/O.*

The Kotlin standard library includes two general-purpose data classes which can be used to hold a pair or a triplet of values:

```kotlin
fun main() {
    val pair = Pair(1, "two")
    println(pair.first + 1)     // 2
    println("${pair.second}!") // two!

    val triple = Triple("one", 2, false)

    println("${triple.first}!") // one!
    println(triple.second - 1)  // 1
    println(!triple.third)       // true
}
```

Pairs can also be constructed using the infix operation to:

```kotlin
val pair = 1 to "two"
println(pair.first + 1)     // 2
println("${pair.second}!") // two!
```

Note that in most cases, using custom data classes is more reasonable since they allow you to choose meaningful names for both a class and its properties, thus improving the code readability.

Java vs. Kotlin: Kotlin data classes are very similar to the concept of *record classes* which had been introduced in Java 14 for the same purpose of reducing boilerplate when writing simple data holder classes. Starting from Kotlin 1.5 both kinds of classes can easily interoperate in the JVM-targeted codebases (see *Chapter 12, Java Interoperability* for details).

Apart from the autogenerated functions we've seen earlier, data classes give you a useful ability to extract their constituent properties into separate variables within a single definition. In the following section, we'll consider how to do it using *destructuring declarations*.

Destructuring declarations

Consider the following example:

```kotlin
import kotlin.random.Random
data class Person(
    val firstName: String,
    val familyName: String,
    val age: Int
)
fun newPerson() = Person(
    readLine()!!,
    readLine()!!,
    Random.nextInt(100)
)
fun main() {
    val person = newPerson()
    val firstName = person.firstName
    val familyName = person.familyName
    val age = person.age
    if (age < 18) {
        println("$firstName $familyName is under-age")
    }
}
```

We will extract values of the Person properties and use them in a subsequent computation. But since Person is a data class, we will use a much more concise syntax to define the corresponding local variables:

```kotlin
val (firstName, familyName, age) = person
```

This is a *destructuring declaration* which generalizes a local variable syntax by allowing you to use a parentheses-enclosed list of identifiers instead of a single variable name. Each name corresponds to a separate variable definition which is initialized by a corresponding property from a data class instance written after the = sign.

Note that properties are mapped to the variables according to their position in the data class constructor rather than their name. So while the code:

```
val (firstName, familyName, age) = Person("John", "Doe", 25)

println("$firstName $familyName: $age")
```

produces the expected result **"John Doe: 25"**, the following lines:

```
val (familyName, firstName, age) = Person("John", "Doe", 25)

    println("$firstName $familyName: $age")
```

will give you **"Doe John: 25"**.

IDE Tips: For this specific case, when variable names in the destructuring declaration match the data class properties but are written in a wrong order, the IntelliJ plugin reports a warning which may help to locate a source of a possible bug. It's recommended that you either rename a variable so that it does match the property, or change its position in the destructuring declaration (see an example on the Error: Reference source not found) as shown in *Figure 6.2*:

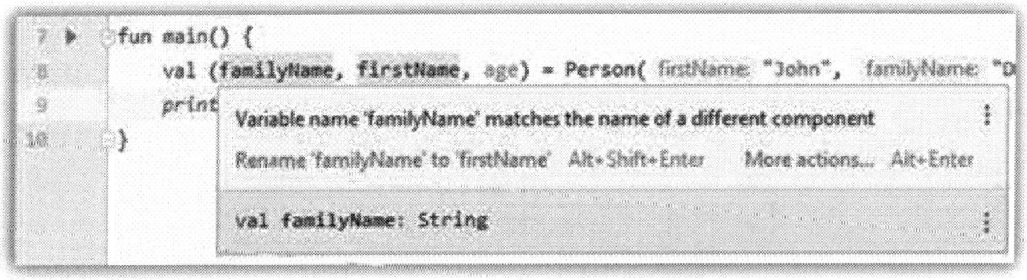

Figure 6.2: Wrong ordering of variables in destructuring declaration

A destructuring declaration as a whole may not have a type. It's possible, however, to specify explicit types for a component variable whenever it's necessary:

```
val (firstName, familyName: String, age) = Person("John", "Doe", 25)
```

A destructuring declaration may include fewer components than there are properties in a data class. In this case, missing properties at the end of the constructor are not extracted:

```
val (firstName, familyName) = Person("John", "Doe", 25)
println("$firstName $familyName") // John Doe
val (name) = Person("John", "Doe", 25)
println(name)                         // John
```

What if you need to skip some properties that come at the beginning or in the middle? Since Kotlin 1.1, you can replace unused components with the _ symbol similar to unused parameters of a lambda expression:

```kotlin
val (_, familyName) = Person("John", "Doe", 25)

println(familyName) // Doe
```

Replacing **val** with **var** you get a set of mutable variables:

```kotlin
var (firstName, familyName) = Person("John", "Doe", 25)
firstName = firstName.toLowerCase()
familyName = familyName.toLowerCase()
println("$firstName $familyName") // john doe
```

Note that the **val/var** modifier applies to all components of destructuring declarations, so you may either declare all variables mutable, or declare them all immutable without intermediate options.

Destructuring can also be used in the **for** loops:

```kotlin
val pairs = arrayOf(1 to "one", 2 to "two", 3 to "three")
for ((number, name) in pairs) {
    println("$number: $name")
}
```

Since Kotlin 1.1, it's possible to destructure a lambda parameter:

```kotlin
fun combine(person1: Person,
            person2: Person,
            folder: ((String, Person) -> String)): String {
    return folder(folder("", person1), person2)
}


fun main() {
    val p1 = Person("John", "Doe", 25)
    val p2 = Person("Jane", "Doe", 26)
    // Without destructuring:
    println(combine(p1, p2) { text, person -> "$text ${person.age}" })
    // With destructuring:
    println(combine(p1, p2) { text, (firstName) -> "$text $firstName" })
```

```
println(combine(p1, p2) { text, (_, familyName) -> "$text $familyName"
})
}
```

Note that unlike the ordinary lambda parameter list, destructured parameters are enclosed in parentheses.

Since destructuring declarations are currently only supported for local variables, they can't be declared in a class body or at the top level in a file:

```
data class Person(
  val firstName: String,
  val familyName: String,
  val age: Int
)
val (firstName, familyName) = Person("John", "Doe", 25) // Error
```

Note that as of now, destructuring declarations can't be nested:

```
data class Person(
  val firstName: String,
  val familyName: String,
  val age: Int
)
data class Mailbox(val address: String, val person: Person)

fun main() {
    val (address, (firstName, familyName, age)) =
        Mailbox("Unknown", Person("John", "Doe", 25)) // Error
}
```

While data classes provide destructuring support out of the box, in general it may be implemented for any Kotlin type. In *Chapter 11, Domain-Specific Languages*, we'll discuss how to do it using the operator overloading conventions.

Inline classes

Creating wrapper classes is quite common in programming practice; after all, this is a gist of the well-known Adapter design pattern. Suppose, for example, we want our program to have a concept of currency. Although money quantity is essentially a number, we'd prefer not to mix it with other numbers which may have a very different meaning. So we will introduce some wrapper classes and utility functions:

```kotlin
class Dollar(val amount: Int) // amount in cents
class Euro(val amount: Int)   // amount in cents
```

```kotlin
fun Dollar.toEuro() = …
fun Euro.toDollar() = …
```

The problem with such an approach is a runtime overhead which comes from the necessity to create an extra object whenever we're introducing a new monetary amount. The problem becomes even more significant when the wrapped value is a primitive as we have in the case of our currency classes since direct manipulation of numeric values doesn't require any object allocation at all. Using wrapper classes instead of primitives prevent many optimizations and take a toll on the program performance.

To solve such issues, Kotlin 1.3 has introduced a new variety of classes which is called an *inline class*.

Defining an inline class

To define an inline class, you need to add the inline keyword before its name:

```kotlin
inline class Dollar(val amount: Int) // amount in cents
inline class Euro(val amount: Int)   // amount in cents
```

Such a class must have a single immutable property declared in the primary constructor. At runtime, a class instance will be represented as a value of this property without creating any wrapper objects. That's the origin of the term "inline class"; similarly, inline functions whose bodies are substituted instead of their calls, the data contained in an inline class is substituted instead of its usages.

Inline classes may have their own properties and functions:

```kotlin
inline class Dollar(val amount: Int) {
    fun add(d: Dollar) = Dollar(amount + d.amount)

    val isDebt get() = amount < 0
}
```

```kotlin
fun main() {
    println(Dollar(15).add(Dollar(20)).amount) // 35
    println(Dollar(-100).isDebt)               // true
}
```

Inline class properties, however, may not have any state. The reason is that such a state would have to be inlined together with a property in the primary constructor, and currently, the Kotin compiler supports only single-property inlining. This means that no backing fields, no lateinit, or delegated (including lazy) properties are possible. Inline class properties may have only explicit accessors like the **isDebt** in our example.

It's possible to define the **var** properties in the inline class body, although it usually makes a little sense because the inline class may not have a mutable state.

Another restriction is an inability to use initialization blocks. This is explained by the fact that the inline class constructor may not execute any custom code since at runtime, the constructor call to Dollar(15) must behave just like a simple mention of number 15.

In *Chapter 2, Language Fundamentals*, we've mentioned that primitive values may be implicitly boxed if the program tries to use them in some context which requires a reference to a real object such as assigning them to a variable of the nullable type. The same also applies to inline classes; for the sake of the optimization compiler, we will prefer using unwrapped values whenever possible. When it's not an option, however, the compiler will fall back to using your class as if it wasn't an inline one. For a good approximation of the compiler behavior, you may use the following rule of thumb: an inline class instance can be inlined whenever it's used as exactly the value of the corresponding type without casting to something else. Consider the following example:

```kotlin
fun safeAmount(dollar: Dollar?) = dollar?.amount ?: 0
```

```kotlin
fun main() {
    println(Dollar(15).amount)        // inlined
    println(Dollar(15))               // not inlined: used as Any?
    println(safeAmount(Dollar(15)))   // not inlines: used as Dollar?
}
```

One more point worth noting is an experimental status of inline classes. At the moment, the design of this language feature is not finalized and may change in a future version. For this reason, any definition of inline classes in Kotlin 1.3 is by default accompanied with a compiler warning. This warning may be suppressed by passing a special command-line argument **XXLanguage:+InlineClasses** to the Kotlin compiler.

IDE Tips: When using IntelliJ, you can automatically enable or disable inline classes (or any other experimental language features such as unsigned integers) in your project by choosing an appropriate action from the Alt+Enter menu on the highlighted element as shown in *Figure 6.3* (as shown on the Error: Reference source not found):

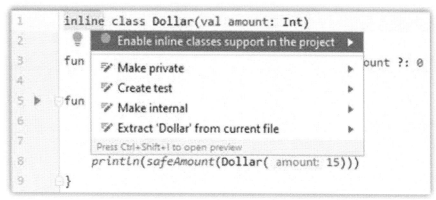

Figure 6.3: Enabling inline classes in IntelliJ project

Unsigned integers

Since version 1.3, the Kotlin standard library includes a set of unsigned integer types implemented on top of the built-in signed types using inline classes. Just like inline classes in general, these types comprise an experimental feature, so currently their usages produce a warning unless you explicitly permit them in your project as shown in *Figure 6.4* (see the Error: Reference source not found):

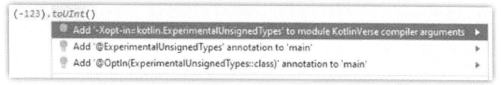

Figure 6.4: Enabling unsigned types support in the IntelliJ Project

The name of each unsigned type is similar to the name of each signed counterpart with an extra U letter (*Table 6.1*):

Type	Size (in bytes)	Range
UByte	1	0 .. 255
UShort	2	0 .. 65535
UInt	4	$0 .. 2^{32} - 1$
ULong	8	$0 .. 2^{64} - 1$

Table 6.1: Unsigned Integer types

To denote an unsigned value, you can add u or U suffix to an integer literal. The type of the literal is determined by its expected type such as the type of variable initialized by this value. If no expected type is specified, the literal type is supposed to be either UInt, or ULong depending on its size:

```
val uByte: UByte = 1u      // explicit UByte
val uShort: UShort = 100u // explicit UShort
val uInt = 1000u           // UInt inferred automatically
val uLong: ULong = 1000u  // explicit ULong
val uLong2 = 1000uL        // explicit ULong due to L suffix
```

Signed and unsigned types are compatible with each other, though, so you can't, for example, assign an unsigned value to a variable of a signed type and vice versa:

```
val long: Long = 1000uL  // Error
```

Unsigned and signed types can be converted into another using one of the **toXXX()** methods:

```
println(1.toUByte())        // 1,     Int -> UByte
println((-100).toUShort()) // 65436, Int -> UShort
println(200u.toByte())      // -56,   UInt -> Byte
println(1000uL.toInt())     // 1000,  ULong -> Int
```

Unsigned type API is quite similar to that of signed integer types. In particular, any pair of unsigned values can be combined by arithmetic operators **+, -, *, /, %**:

```
println(1u + 2u) // 3
println(1u - 2u) // 4294967295
println(3u * 2u) // 6
println(5u / 2u) // 2
println(7u % 3u) // 1
```

You can't, however, combine signed values with unsigned ones:

```
println(1u + 2) // Error
println(1 + 2u) // Error
```

Also, unlike signed types, unsigned integers do not support the unary minus operation. This makes sense since they can't denote negative values:

```
println(-1u) // Error
```

Unsigned values can be used in increment/decrement expressions and augmented assignments:

```
var uInt: UInt = 1u
++uInt
uInt -= 3u
```

And support basic bitwise operations such as inversion, AND, OR and XOR:

```
val ua: UByte = 67u  // 01000011
val ub: UByte = 139u // 10001011
println(ua.inv())    // 10111100: 188
println(ua or ub)    // 11001011: 203
println(ua xor ub)   // 11001000: 200
println(ua and ub)   // 00000011: 3
```

`UInt` and `ULong` also supports left and right bitwise shifts:

```
val ua = 67u      // 0..0001000011
println(ua shr 2) // 0..0000010000: 16
println(ua shl 2) // 0..0100001100: 268
```

Note that the bit count is specified as a value of the ordinary **Int** rather than **UInt**. Also, there is no separate **ushr** operation for unsigned right shifts because for unsigned integers, it behaves exactly like **shr**.

Similar to ordinary integers, unsigned values can be compared using the `<, >, <=, >=, ==` and `!=` operations:

```
println(1u < 2u)             // true
println(2u >= 3u)            // false
println(2u + 2u == 1u + 3u) // true
```

The Kotlin standard library also includes a set of auxiliary types which represent arrays of unsigned integers: **UByteArray**, **UShortArray**, **UIntArray**, **ULongArray**.

These are also inline classes backed by the corresponding array classes like **IntArray**. Unsigned array types can be constructed in a similar way to arrays we've faced so far:

```
val uBytes = ubyteArrayOf(1u, 2u, 3u)
val squares = UIntArray(10) { it*it }
```

There are also unsigned counterparts for range and progression types which can be constructed using the **..** operator as well as operations like **until** or **downTo**:

```
1u .. 10u              // 1, 2, 3, 4, 5, 6, 7, 8, 9, 10
1u .. 10u step 2       // 1, 3, 5, 7, 9
1u until 10u           // 1, 2, 3, 4, 5, 6, 7, 8, 9
10u downTo 1u          // 10, 9, 8, 7, 6, 5, 4, 3, 2, 1
10u downTo 1u step 3 // 10, 7, 4, 1
```

Conclusion

This chapter has introduced us to some special varieties of classes aimed at solving particular programming problems. We learned to use enums to describe limited sets of objects with common functions and properties and seen how to employ data classes to concisely define simple holders of data as well as use destructuring for extraction of data classes properties. Finally, we took a look at possibilities of experimental inline classes introduced in Kotlin 1.3 for the purpose of creating lightweight wrappers and examined unsigned integer types based on the Kotlin inline classes.

In the next chapter, we will focus on the Kotlin standard library. In particular, we will cover basic collection types, give more extensive treatments to arrays and strings, and consider I/O and networking capabilities as well as some useful utility functions.

Points to remember

- The enum class is a built-in way to restrict class instances to a fixed set of constants.
- Data classes provide a concise syntax to define a simple data holder.
- Destructuring declarations allow extraction of multiple values from a given object within a single variable definition.
- Inline classes allow you to define zero-overhead wrappers. The Standard library, in particular, uses them to implement unsigned integers.

Questions

1. What is an enum class? What built-in operations are available for enums?

2. What's the specifics of using **when** expressions with enum classes?

3. How can you define an enum class with custom functions or properties?

4. What is a data class? Which operations are generated automatically for any data class? How to copy a data class instance?

5. What is a destructuring declaration? Where can you use one?

6. What's the purpose of inline classes? What requirements a class must satisfy in order to be inline?

7. Describe Kotlin unsigned types and their built-in operations. What are their specifics as compared to signed integers?

Key terms

*   Enum class: A special class representing some limited set of constants with their own methods and properties.

*   Data class: A class providing automatic implementation of common methods for data holder objects such as equality, hash code, copying, and destructuring.

*   Destructuring declaration: A multi-variable definition that is initialized by a value supporting destructuring methods such as `component1()`, `component2()`, etc.

*   Inline class: A wrapper class whose values at runtime are represented by values of a wrapped type.

CHAPTER 7
Exploring Collections and I/O

In this chapter, we'll take a look at two major components of the Kotlin standard library. The first part will be devoted to the collections API. Then, we'll discuss common collection types together with their basic operations and give a comprehensive treatment of various manipulations with collections and their data such as element access utilities, testing collection predicates, filtering and extracting collection parts, aggregation, transformation, and ordering. In the second part, we'll focus on I/O API and talk about utilities which simplify both creation of I/O streams and access to their data as well some common file system operations.

Structure

- Collections
- Files and I/O streams

Objective

Get an understanding of Kotlin collection types and learn to use its standard library for concise and idiomatic manipulations with collection data as well as use I/O stream API extensions.

Collections

A **collection** is an object designed to store a group of elements. In *Chapter 2*, we discussed one example of such objects, namely, *arrays* which allow you to keep a fixed number of elements belonging to some common type. The Kotlin standard library, though, provides far richer collection capabilities, including both various classes based on different data structures (such as arrays, linked lists, hash tables, and so on) as well comprehensive API for manipulating collections and their data: filtering, aggregation, transformation, ordering, etc. In this section, we'll give a detailed account of what a collection library can offer to Kotlin developers.

It's worth noting that almost all collection-manipulating operations are inline functions so the ease of their use doesn't involve any performance penalties related to function calls and lambdas.

Collection types

Collection types in Kotlin can be divided into four basic categories: arrays, iterables, sequences, and maps. Since arrays have already been a major topic in Chapter 2, In this section, we'll focus on the remaining three categories.

Similar to arrays, collection types are generic. When specifying a type of particular collection, you also need to specify a type of its elements; for example, **List<String>** means a list of strings, while **Set<Int>** means a set of Int values.

The outline of basic collection types can be represented by the following diagram (*Figure 7.1*):

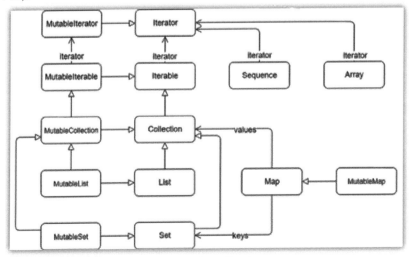

Figure 7.1: Kotlin collection types

Iterables

An iterable, represented by the **Iterable\<T>** type, represents a collection which is generally both eager and stateful. The statefulness means that such collection stores contain elements in its instance rather than keeping some generator function which can retrieve them lazily. Eagerness, on the other hand, means that collection elements are initialized at the moment of its creation instead of being computed lazily at some later point.

The **Iterable** type itself is rather similar to its Java counterpart. It provides a single **iterator()** method which returns an object capable of traversing its elements. This allows you to use Kotlin's **for** loop with any iterable:

```
val list = listOf("red", "green", "blue") // Create new List
for (item in list) {
    print(item + " ")
} // Prints red green blue
```

Java vs Kotlin: The Kotlin's Iterator type is basically the same as Java's. It contains two methods: **hasNext()** which checks whether the iterator has reached the end of collection, and **next()** which returns the next collection element. The only difference is the absence of the **remove()** method which is moved to **MutableIterator** instead.

A major feature of Kotlin iterables, as compared to Java, is a distinction between mutable and immutable collections. The content of immutable collections can't change after they are created, while mutable collections can generally be updated at any time by adding or removing elements. Note that collection mutability has nothing to do with mutability of a variable keeping a reference to collection instance. It means the ability to change the data this reference points to. You can, for example, keep a mutable collection in an immutable variable; in this case, you can't change the variable making it refer to some other collection, but *can*, for example, add or remove collection elements:

```
val list = ArrayList<String>()
list.add("abc")              // Ok: changing collection data
list = ArrayList<String>() // Error: can't reassign immutable variable
```

The basic type of mutable iterable is represented by the MutableIterable interface which can create a **MutableIterator**.

A useful feature of immutable collection types is their *covariance*. It means that if **T** is a subtype of **U**, then **Iterable\<T>** is a subtype of **Iterable\<U>**. This is also true for other collection-related types like **Iterator**, **Collection**, **List**, **Set,** and **Map**. This, in particular, allows you write the following code:

```
fun processCollection(c: Iterable<Any>) {…}
```

```
fun main() {
    val list = listOf("a", "b", "c") // List<String>
    processCollection(list)      // Ok: passing List<String> as List<Any>
}
```

This, however, does not work for a mutable collection. Otherwise, we could have written the code which, for example, adds an integer to a list of string.

```
fun processCollection(c: MutableCollection<Any>) { c.add(123) }
```

```
fun main() {
    val list = arrayListOf("a", "b", "c") // ArrayList<String>
    processCollection(list)                // !!!
}
```

In *Chapter 9, Generics*, we'll address the issue of covariance in more detail.

Collections, lists, and sets

An important subcategory of iterables is represented by the **Collection** interface and its mutable subtype, **MutableCollection**. This is a basic class for many standard implementations of iterables. **Collection** inheritors, in turn, typically belong to one of the following kinds:

- A list (represented by interfaces **List** and **MutableList**) is an ordered collection of elements with index-based element access. Common implementations of lists are **ArrayList** with fast random access by index and **LinkedList** which can quickly add or remove elements but requires the linear time to find the existing element by its index.

- A set is a collection of unique elements. Element ordering varies depending on the implementation:

  - **HashSet** is based on the hash table implementation and orders elements according to their hash codes. In general, such ordering depends on particular implementations of the **hashCode()** method so can be considered unpredictable.

  - **LinkedHashSet** is also based on the hash table but retains the insertion order. In other words, elements are iterated in the same order as they've been inserted into the set.

- **TreeSet** is an implementation based on binary search trees which maintain stable element ordering according to some comparison rule which may be implemented by elements themselves (if they implement the **Comparable** interface), or provided in the form of separate **Comparator** object.

On the JVM platform, concrete classes implementing these interfaces are represented by corresponding JDK collections. Well-known Java classes like **HashMap** or **ArrayList** are seamlessly integrated into the Kotlin library.

Java vs Kotlin: In the Kotlin code, there is usually no need to use classes from the **java.util** package. Most standard collections like ArrayList can be referred via aliases in the **kotlin.collections** package which is automatically imported to all Kotlin files.

Sequences

Similar to iterables, **sequences** provide the **iterator()** method which can be used to traverse their content. The intent behind them, however, is different since a sequence is supposed to be lazy. Most of sequence implementations do not initialize their elements at the moment of instantiation and compute them only on demand. Many sequence implementations are also stateless which means that they keep only a constant amount of data required to lazily generated collection elements. Iterables, on the other hand, usually spend an amount of memory proportional to the number of elements.

Unlike iterables, most of the sequence implementations are internal and are not intended to be used directly. Instead, new sequences are created by special functions which we'll discuss in the upcoming sections.

Java vs Kotlin: Readers familiar with Java might recognize the similarity between sequences and streams introduced in Java 8. Since the Kotlin 1.2 standard library provides **asSequence()** extension function which can be used to wrap Java stream into a Kotlin sequence.

Maps

A **map** is a set of key-value pairs where keys are unique. Although the map is not a subtype of Collection by itself, its content may be presented as such. You can, in particular, get a set of all keys, a collection of all values, and a set of key-value pairs represented by **Map.Entry,** and **MutableMap.MutableEntry** interfaces.

Since maps contain two different kinds of elements (keys and values), their types have two parameters; for example, **Map<Int, String>** is a map with associate **Int** keys with **String** values.

Standard implementations of maps include **HashMap**, **LinkedHashMap,** and **TreeMap** which have properties similar to that of corresponding implementations of **Set**.

AbstractMap and **AbstractMutableMap** classes can be used as placeholders for implementing your own maps.

Comparables and comparators

Similarly to Java, Kotlin supports the **Comparable** and **Comparator** types which can be used in some collection operations. Comparable instances possess a natural ordering. Each of them has the **compareTo()** function which can be used to compare it with other instances of the same type. So by making your type of an inheritor of **Comparable**, you can automatically allow operations like **<** and **>** and, on top of it, you can apply ordering operations for a collection with the corresponding element type. Suppose we want our Person class to have the natural order based on the full name. The implementation would look like this:

```
class Person(
    val firstName: String,
    val familyName: String,
    val age: Int
) : Comparable<Person> {
    val fullName get() = "$firstName $familyName"

    override fun compareTo(other: Person) = fullName.compareTo(other.
    fullName)
}
```

The convention about the **compareTo()** function is the same as in Java. It returns a positive number when the current instance is greater than **other**, a negative number when it's smaller, and zero when both instances are equal. An implementation of **compareTo()** is supposed to be compatible with the **equals()** function.

In many cases, a given class can be compared in multiple ways. For example, we can order a collection of Person instances by their first or family names only, by age, or by various combinations of these properties. For this reason, the Kotlin library provides a concept of comparator. Similarly to Java, an instance of the **Comparator<T>** class provides the **compare()** function which takes two instances of a type T and returns the comparison result following the same convention as **compareTo()**. In Kotlin, comparators can be concisely constructed based on a comparison lambda:

```
val AGE_COMPARATOR = Comparator<Person> { p1, p2 ->
    p1.age.compareTo(p2.age)
}
```

Alternatively, you can use the **compareBy()** or **compareByDescending()** function to provide a comparable value to be used instead of the original object:

```
val AGE_COMPARATOR = compareBy<Person> { it.age }
val REVERSE_AGE_COMPARATOR = compareByDescending<Person> { it.age }
```

The comparator instance can then be passed into some ordering-aware function like **sorted()** or **maxOrNull()**. You can find examples in the upcoming sections on aggregating functions and collection ordering.

Creating a collection

In *Chapter 2, Language Fundamentals,* we saw how to create array instances using either constructors or standard functions like **arrayOf()**. Many standard collection classes may be constructed in a similar way. For example, such classes **ArrayList** or **LinkedHashSet** can be created by an ordinary constructor call just like in Java:

```
val list = ArrayList<String>()
list.add("red")
list.add("green")
println(list) // [red, green]

val set = HashSet<Int>()
set.add(12)
set.add(21)
set.add(12)
println(set)  // [12, 21]

val map = TreeMap<Int, String>()
map[20] = "Twenty"
```

```
map[10] = "Ten"
println(map)  // {10=Ten, 20=Twenty}
```

We also have functions similar to **arrayOf()** which take a variable argument list and produce an instance of some standard collection class:

- **emptyList()/emptySet():** This is an instance of the immutable empty list/set (similar to the **emptyXXX()** methods of the JDK **Collections** class).
- **listOf()/setOf():** This creates a new immutable list/set backed by the argument array (for lists, it's basically the same as Java's **Arrays.asList()**).
- **listOfNotNull():** This creates a new immutable list with nulls filtered out.
- **mutableListOf()/mutableSetOf():** This creates a default implementation of the mutable list/set (internally, it's **ArrayList** and **LinkedHashSet**, respectively).
- **arrayListOf():** This creates a new **ArrayList**.
- **hashSetOf()/linkedSetOf()/sortedSetOf():** This creates a new instance of **HashSet/LinkedHashSet/TreeSet,** respectively.

Let's consider some examples:

```
val emptyList = emptyList<String>()
println(emptyList)   // []
emptyList.add("abc") // Error: add is unresolved


val singletonSet = setOf("abc")
println(singletonSet)      // [abc]
singletonSet.remove("abc") // Error: remove is unresolved


val mutableList = mutableListOf("abc")
println(mutableList) // [abc]
mutableList.add("def")
mutableList[0] = "xyz"
println(mutableList) // [xyz, def]


val sortedSet = sortedSetOf(8, 5, 7, 1, 4)
println(sortedSet) // [1, 4, 5, 7, 8]
sortedSet.add(2)
```

```
println(sortedSet) // [1, 2, 4, 5, 7, 8]
```

Similar functions are also provided for constructing maps:

- **emptyMap():** This is an instance of the immutable empty map.
- **mapOf():** This creates a new immutable map (internally, it's a LinkedHashMap).
- **mutableMapOf():** This creates a default implementation of the mutable map (internally, it's **LinkedHashMap**).
- **hashMapOf()/linkedMapOf()/sortedMapOf():** This creates a new instance **HashMap/LinkedHashMap/TreeMap**.

Note that the preceding map functions take a variable argument list of the **Pair** objects which can be concisely constructed by the **to** infix operation:

```
val emptyMap = emptyMap<Int, String>()
println(emptyMap)      // {}
emptyMap[10] = "Ten" // Error: set is unresolved


val singletonMap = mapOf(10 to "Ten")
println(singletonMap)      // {10=Ten}
singletonMap.remove("abc") // Error: remove is unresolved


val mutableMap = mutableMapOf(10 to "Ten")
println(mutableMap) // {10=Ten}
mutableMap[20] = "Twenty"
mutableMap[100] = "Hundred"
mutableMap.remove(10)
println(mutableMap) // {20=Twenty, 100=Hundred}


val sortedMap = sortedMapOf(3 to "three", 1 to "one", 2 to "two")
println(sortedMap) // {1=one, 2=two, 3=three}
sortedMap[0] = "zero"
println(sortedMap) // {0=zero, 1=one, 2=two, 3=three}
```

Alternatively, you can create a mutable map and fill it using the **set()** method or indexing operator to avoid the creation of excessive **Pair** instances.

Lists can also be constructed that are similar to arrays by specifying their size and a function which maps the index to the element value:

```
println(List(5) { it*it }) // [0, 1, 4, 9, 16]
```

```
val numbers = MutableList(5) { it*2 }
println(numbers) // [0, 2, 4, 6, 8]
numbers.add(100)
println(numbers) // [0, 2, 4, 6, 8, 100]
```

The simplest way to create a sequence of known elements is to use a **sequenceOf()** function which takes a **vararg**. Alternatively, you can convert an existing collection such as an array, iterable, or a map into the sequence by calling the **asSequence()** function:

```
println(sequenceOf(1, 2, 3).iterator().next())            // 1
println(listOf(10, 20, 30).asSequence().iterator().next()) // 10
println(
    mapOf(1 to "One", 2 to "Two").asSequence().iterator().next()
)                                                          // 1=One
```

Note that calling **asSequence()** on map gives you a sequence of map entries.

Another option is to create a sequence based on some generator function. This case is implemented by a pair of **generateSequence()** functions. The first one takes a parameterless function which computes the next sequence element. Sequence generation proceeds until this function returns null. For example, the following code creates a sequence which reads the program input until it encounters a non-number or the input is exhausted:

```
val numbers = generateSequence { readLine()?.toIntOrNull() }
```

The second **generateSequence()** function takes an initial value and single-parameter function which generates a new sequence element based on the previous one. Just like in the first case, the generation stops when this function returns null:

```
// Infinite sequence (with overflow): 1, 2, 4, 8,...
val powers = generateSequence(1) { it*2 }
// Finite sequence: 10, 8, 6, 4, 2, 0
val evens = generateSequence(10) { if (it >= 2) it - 2 else null }
```

Since Kotlin 1.3, one more way to construct a sequence is to use a special builder which allows you to provide sequence elements in parts. The builder is implemented by the **sequence()** function which accepts an extension lambda with the **SequenceScope** receiver type. This type introduces a set of functions which can be used to append elements to a new sequence:

- **yield()**: This adds a single element.

- **yieldAll()**: This adds all elements of the specified iterator, iterable, or sequence.

Note that elements are added lazily. The **yield()/yieldAll()** calls are executed only when the corresponding chunk of sequence is requested. Consider the following example:

```
val numbers = sequence {
    yield(0)
    yieldAll(listOf(1, 2, 3))
    yieldAll(intArrayOf(4, 5, 6).iterator())
    yieldAll(generateSequence(10) { if (it < 50) it*3 else null })
}
println(numbers.toList()) // [0, 1, 2, 3, 4, 5, 6, 10, 30, 90]
```

The sequence builder implemented by the **sequence()/yield()/yieldAll()** functions is in fact an example of suspendable computations, a powerful Kotlin feature which gets especially useful in multi-threaded applications. We'll defer its detailed treatment till *Chapter 13, Concurrency*.

The final group of functions we'd like to mention in this section deals with collection conversion; for example, they allow you to create a list based on the content of array or turn a sequence into a set:

```
println(
    listOf(1, 2, 3, 2, 3).toSet()
) // [1, 2, 3]
println(
    arrayOf("red", "green", "blue").toSortedSet()
) // [blue, green, red]
println(
    mapOf(1 to "one", 2 to "two", 3 to "three").toList()
```

```
) // [(1, one), (2, two), (3, three)]
println(
    sequenceOf(1 to "one", 2 to "two", 3 to "three").toMap()
) // {1=one, 2=two, 3=three}
```

You can find a complete list of the conversion functions in the standard library reference at kotlinlang.org/api/latest/jvm/stdlib. Conversion functions follow certain conventions, namely, functions whose name starts with "to" (such as **toList()** or **toMap()**) create a separate copy of the original collection, while those which start with "as" (such as **asList()**) create a view which reflects any changes in the original collection.

IDE Tips: Do not hesitate using the IDE completion (available by *Ctrl* + Space / Cmd + Space) to help you with choosing the conversion function or any other method (see example in *Figure 7.2*):

Figure 7.2: *Using completion to choose conversion function*

New collections may also be created on the basis of existing ones through operations like filtering, transforming, or sorting. We'll cover such cases in the upcoming sections.

Basic operations

In this section, we'll take a look at basic operations available for Kotlin collection types.

One common operation supported by all collections is iteration. Arrays, iterables, sequences, and maps support the **iterator()** function. Although, the instance of the Iterator object returned by this function can definitely be used to traverse collection elements, this is rarely needed in practice since Kotlin provides more concise ways to do the same job.

In particular, the presence of the **iterator()** function allows us to use the for loop with any collection as we've already seen in the "Iterables" section. One thing worth pointing out is that for maps, the iterator returns instances of **Map.Entry**. In Kotlin, map entries support destructuring which allows writing map iteration as follows:

```
val map = mapOf(1 to "one", 2 to "two", 3 to "three")
for ((key, value) in map) {
    println("$key -> $value")
}
```

The preceding code would print the following:

```
1 -> one
2 -> two
3 -> three
```

This also goes for lambdas which accept a map entry as their parameter.

An alternative is to use the **forEach()** extension function which executes a supplied lambda for each collection element:

```
intArrayOf(1, 2, 3).forEach { println(it*it) }
listOf("a", "b", "c").forEach { println("'$it'") }
sequenceOf("a", "b", "c").forEach { println("'$it'") }
mapOf(1 to "one", 2 to "two", 3 to "three").forEach { (key, value) ->
    println("$key -> $value")
}
```

If you want to additionally take element indices into account, there is a more general **forEachIndexed()** function:

```
listOf(10, 20, 30).forEachIndexed { i, n -> println("$i: ${n*n}") }
```

Basic features of the collection type include:

- **The size** property which gives you a number of elements.
- **The isEmpty()** function which returns true if the collection has no elements.
- **The contains()/containsAll()** functions which check whether the collection contains a specific element or all elements of another collection.

A call to the **contains()** function may be replaced by the **in** operator:

```
val list = listOf(1, 2, 3)
println(list.isEmpty())                 // false
```

```
println(list.size)                      // 3
println(list.contains(4))               // false
println(2 in list)                      // true
println(list.containsAll(listOf(1, 2))) // true
```

Note that the behavior of **contains()/containsAll()** depends on the proper implementation of the **equals()** method. If you use instances of your own classes as collection elements, make sure to implement content-based equality when necessary.

The **MutableCollection** introduces methods for adding and removing elements. Consider the following example:

```
val list = arrayListOf(1, 2, 3)
list.add(4)                        // Add single:      [1, 2, 3, 4]
list.remove(3)                     // Remove single: [1, 2, 4]
list.addAll(setOf(5, 6))           // Union:          [1, 2, 4, 5, 6]
list.removeAll(listOf(1, 2))       // Difference:     [4, 5, 6]
list.retainAll(listOf(5, 6, 7))    // Intersection:   [5, 6]
list.clear()                       // Remove all:     []
```

You can also use **+=** and **-=** operators instead of **add()/remove()/addAll()/removeAll()** calls:

```
list += 4
list -= 3
list += setOf(5, 6)
list -= listOf(1, 2)
```

Both mutable and immutable collections support the **+** and **–** operators which produce a new collection leaving the original untouched:

```
println(listOf(1, 2, 3) + 4)           // [1, 2, 3, 4]

println(listOf(1, 2, 3) - setOf(2, 5)) // [1, 3]
```

You can also use **+=** and **-=** with the immutable collection but with a very different semantics. For the immutable collection, they act as abbreviations for assignments and thus can be applied only to mutable variables:

```
val readOnly = listOf(1, 2, 3)
readOnly += 4 // Error: can't assign to val
var mutable = listOf(1, 2, 3)
```

```
mutable += 4  // Correct
```

Such code, however, should be avoided in general since it implicitly creates a new collection object on each assignment which may affect a program performance.

IDE Tips: The IntelliJ plugin warns you about such assignments suggesting you to use mutable collection instead of immutable one (see *Figure 7.3*):

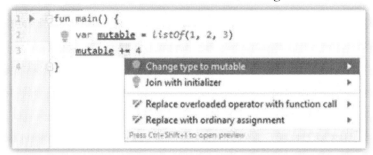

Figure 7.3: *Replacing immutable collection with mutable*

The list introduces some methods to access its elements by an index similar to arrays:

```
val list = listOf(1, 4, 6, 2, 4, 1, 7)
println(list.get(3))         // 2
println(list[2])             // 6
println(list[10])            // Exception
println(list.indexOf(4))     // 1
println(list.lastIndexOf(4)) // 4
println(list.indexOf(8))     // -1
```

Note that the indexing notation is generally more preferable than a call to the **get()** method. When the list is mutable, its elements may also be changed by an index:

```
val list = arrayListOf(1, 4, 6, 2, 4, 1, 7)
list.set(3, 0)   // [1, 4, 6, 0, 4, 1, 7]
list[2] = 1      // [1, 4, 1, 0, 4, 1, 7]
list.removeAt(5) // [1, 4, 1, 0, 4, 7]
list.add(3, 8)   // [1, 4, 1, 8, 0, 4, 7]
```

The **subList()** function creates a wrapper over a particular segment of the list specified by start (inclusive) and end (exclusive) indices. The view shares data with the original collection and in the case of the mutable list reflects changes in its data:

```
val list = arrayListOf(1, 4, 6, 2, 4, 1, 7)
```

```
val segment = list.subList(2, 5) // [6, 2, 4, 1]
list[3] = 0
println(segment[1]) // 0
segment[1] = 8
println(list[3])    // 8
```

Sets do not introduce any additional operations by themselves. Their implementation of common **Collection** methods, however, ensures that no duplicates are added to a set.

The methods of Map allow you to retrieve a value by a key as well as provide access to the full key set and value collection. Let's consider an example:

```
val map = mapOf(1 to "I", 5 to "V", 10 to "X", 50 to "L")
println(map.isEmpty())              // false
println(map.size)                   // 4
println(map.get(5))                 // V
println(map[10])                    // X
println(map[100])                   // null
println(map.getOrDefault(100, "?")) // ?
println(map.getOrElse(100) { "?" }) // ?
println(map.containsKey(10))        // true
println(map.containsValue("C"))     // false
println(map.keys)                   // [1, 5, 10, 50]
println(map.values)                 // [I, V, X, L]
println(map.entries)                // [1=I, 5=V, 10=X, 50=L]
```

MutableMap introduces basic modification methods as well support of + and – operators:

```
val map = sortedMapOf(1 to "I", 5 to "V")
map.put(100, "C")             // {1=I, 5=V, 100=C}
map[500] = "D"                // {1=I, 5=V, 100=C, 500=D}
map.remove(1)                 // {5=V, 100=C, 500=D}
map.putAll(mapOf(10 to "X")) // {5=V, 10=X, 100=C, 500=D}
map += 50 to "L"              // {5=V, 10=X, 50=L, 100=C, 500=D}
map += mapOf(2 to "II",
```

```
          3 to "III")       // {2=II, 3=III, 5=V, 10=X, 50=L, 100=C,
                               500=D}
map -= 100                   // {2=II, 3=III, 5=V, 10=X, 50=L, 500=D}
map -= listOf(2, 3)          // {5=V, 10=X, 50=L, 500=D}
```

The comment about **+=** and **-=** operators with respect to mutable and immutable collection is also valid for maps. Note also that while **+** operators take key-value pairs, – operators take keys.

Accessing collection elements

Apart from basic collection operations, the Kotlin standard library contains a set of extension functions that simplify access to individual collection elements which we'll discuss in this section.

The **first()/last()** functions return, respectively the first and the last element of a given collection throwing a **NoSuchElementException** if the collection is empty. There are also "safe" versions called **firstOrNull()/lastOrNull()** which return null when no elements are found:

```
println(listOf(1, 2, 3).first())         // 1
println(listOf(1, 2, 3).last())          // 3
println(emptyArray<String>().first())       // Exception
println(emptyArray<String>().firstOrNull()) // null
val seq = generateSequence(1) { if (it > 50) null else it * 3 }
println(seq.first())                     // 1
println(seq.last())                      // 81
```

These functions may also be passed a predicate in which case they will look for the first or the last element matching the corresponding condition:

```
println(listOf(1, 2, 3).first { it > 2 })      // 3
println(listOf(1, 2, 3).lastOrNull { it < 0 })  // null
println(intArrayOf(1, 2, 3).first { it > 3 })   // Exception
```

The **single()** function returns the element of a singleton collection. If the collection is empty or contains more than one element, **single()** throws an exception. Its safe counterpart, **singleOrNull()**, returns null in both cases:

```
println(listOf(1).single())                 // 1
println(emptyArray<String>().singleOrNull())  // null
println(setOf(1, 2, 3).singleOrNull())       // null
```

```
println(sequenceOf(1, 2, 3).single())          // Exception
```

The **elementAt()** function allows you to retrieve the collection element by its index. It generalizes the **get()** function of lists and can be applied to any array, iterable, or sequence. Bear in mind, though, that applying this function to a non-random access list will in general take time proportional to the value of the index.

In the case of an invalid index, **elementAt()** throws an exception. There are also variants which provide a safer behavior when the index violates collection bounds: **elementAtOrNull()** which simply returns null and **elementAtOrElse()** which returns the value of the supplied lambda:

```
println(listOf(1, 2, 3).elementAt(2))                          // 3
println(sortedSetOf(1, 2, 3).elementAtOrNull(-1))            // null
println(arrayOf("a", "b", "c").elementAtOrElse(1) { "???" }) // b
val seq = generateSequence(1) { if (it > 50) null else it * 3 }
println(seq.elementAtOrNull(2))                                // 9
println(seq.elementAtOrElse(100) { Int.MAX_VALUE })          // 81
println(seq.elementAt(10))                              // Exception
```

One more thing to mention here is the support of destructuring of arrays and lists which allows you to extract up to first 5 elements. Note, however, that destructuring will throw an exception if you try to extract more elements than there is in a collection:

```
val list = listOf(1, 2, 3)
val (x, y) = list        // 1, 2
val (a, b, c, d) = list // Exception
```

Collective conditions

Checking whether some collection satisfies certain conditions is a quite common task. For this reason, the Kotlin library includes a set of functions implementing basic checks such as testing given the predicate against collection elements.

The **all()** function returns true if *all* collection elements satisfy a given predicate. This function can be applied to any collection object, including arrays, iterables, sequences, and maps. In the case of maps, the predicate parameter is a map entry:

```
println(listOf(1, 2, 3, 4).all { it < 10 })      // true
println(listOf(1, 2, 3, 4).all { it % 2 == 0 }) // false
println(
    mapOf(1 to "I", 5 to "V", 10 to "X")
```

```
        .all { it.key == 1 || it.key % 5 == 0 }
)                                              // true
// 1, 3, 9, 27, 81
val seq = generateSequence(1) { if (it < 50) it*3 else null }
println(seq.all { it % 3 == 0 })               // false
println(seq.all { it == 1 || it % 3 == 0 })    // true
```

The **none()** function tests the opposite condition. It returns true when there is *no* collection element satisfying a predicate:

```
println(listOf(1, 2, 3, 4).none { it > 5 }) // true
println(
    mapOf(1 to "I", 5 to "V", 10 to "X").none { it.key % 2 == 0 }
)                                              // false
// 1, 3, 9, 27, 81
val seq = generateSequence(1) { if (it < 50) it*3 else null }
println(seq.none { it >= 100 })                // true
```

One more function of this kind is **any()** which returns true when a predicate is satisfied by at least one collection element:

```
println(listOf(1, 2, 3, 4).any { it < 0 })     // false
println(listOf(1, 2, 3, 4).any { it % 2 == 0 }) // true
println(
    mapOf(1 to "I", 5 to "V", 10 to "X").any { it.key == 1 }
)                                              // true
// 1, 3, 9, 27, 81
val seq = generateSequence(1) { if (it < 50) it*3 else null }
println(seq.any { it % 3 == 0 })               // true
println(seq.any { it > 100 })                  // false
```

For an empty collection, the **all()** and **none()** functions return true while any() returns false. All the three functions can be expressed in terms of one another using the relationships reminiscent of the De Morgan's law:

```
c.all { p(it) } == c.none { !p(it) }

c.none { p(it) } == !c.any { p(it) }
```

Keep in mind that **all()**, **none()**, and **any()** may run forever when applied to an infinite sequence. For example, the following code will never terminate:

```
// 0, 1, 2, 3, 4, 0, 1, 2, 3, 4, 0,...
val seq = generateSequence(0) { (it + 1) % 5 }
println(seq.all { it < 5 })
```

The **any()** and **none()** functions also have overloads which do not take any parameters and simply check whether the collection in question is empty:

```
println(emptyList<String>().any())  // false

println(emptyList<String>().none()) // true

println(listOf(1, 2, 3).any())       // true

println(listOf(1, 2, 3).none())      // false
```

These overloads generalize the **isNotEmpty()/isEmpty()** functions which are available for arrays, instances of Collection and Map types, but not for arbitrary iterables or sequences.

Aggregation

Aggregation is a computation of a single value based on the collection content such as summing up collection elements or finding a maximum value. The Kotlin library provides a set of functions which can be used for this purpose. In the previous section, we covered a group of functions which test some collective conditions such as **any()** or **all()**. They can be considered a special kind of aggregates computing a Boolean value.

Aggregate functions in general shouldn't be applied to infinite sequences as they (with an exception of **count()** below) will never return in such a case.

The aggregation functions can be divided into three basic groups. The first one includes functions which computes commonly used aggregates such as sum, min, or max. Let's take a closer look at what they can do.

The **count()** function gives you the number of elements in a collection. It can be applied to any collection object, including arrays, iterables, sequences, and maps and thus generalizes the size property available for arrays, maps, and Collection instances.

Note that **count()** throws an exception if the number of elements exceeds **Int. MAX_VALUE**. This, in particular, happens when **count()** is invoked on an infinite sequence:

```
// 0, 1, 2, 3, 4, 0, 1, 2, 3, 4, 0,...
val seq = generateSequence(0) { (it + 1) % 5 }

// Throws an exception after iterating through Int.MAX_VALUE elements

println(seq.count())
```

The **count()** function has an overload which takes a predicate applied to collection elements. In this case, it returns the number of collection elements satisfying a given condition:

```
println(listOf(1, 2, 3, 4).count { it < 0 })        // 0
println(listOf(1, 2, 3, 4).count { it % 2 == 0 }) // 2
println(
    mapOf(1 to "I", 5 to "V", 10 to "X").count { it.key == 1 }
)                                                   // 1
// 1, 3, 9, 27, 81
val seq = generateSequence(1) { if (it < 50) it*3 else null }
println(seq.count { it % 3 == 0 })                  // 4
println(seq.count { it > 100 })                     // 0
```

The **sum()** function computes an arithmetic sum for a numeric array, iterable, or sequence:

```
println(listOf(1, 2, 3, 4).sum())                             // 10
println(doubleArrayOf(1.2, 2.3, 3.4).sum())                  // 6.9
// Summing 1, 3, 9, 27, 81
println(generateSequence(1) { if (it < 50) it*3 else null }.sum())
// 121
```

The type of return value depends on the element type of the original collection similar to an ordinary **+** operation; for example, summing up the collection of bytes will get you an **Int**, while applying **sum()** to, say, a **LongArray** will result in a value of **Long**.

Summation can also be applied to a collection of arbitrary element type provided it can be converted to a number. This can be achieved with **sumBy()** and **sumByDouble()** which takes a conversion function as a parameter. The difference is that **sumBy()** converts the collection elements to **Int** values (or **UInt** when applied to a collection of unsigned integers), while **sumByDouble()** converts them to **Double**:

```
println(listOf(1, 2, 3, 4).sumByDouble { it/4.0 })    // 2.5
```

```
println(arrayOf("1", "2", "3").sumBy { it.toInt() }) // 6
// X, XX, XXX, XXXX, XXXXX
val seq = generateSequence("X") { if (it.length >= 5) null else it + "X" }
println(seq.sumBy { it.length })                        // 15
```

The **average()** function similarly computes an arithmetic average of a numeric array, iterable, or sequence. The result is always a value of Double:

```
println(listOf(1, 2, 3, 4).average())          // 2.5
println(doubleArrayOf(1.2, 2.3, 3.4).average()) // 2.3000000000000003
// Averaging 1, 3, 9, 27, 81
val seq = generateSequence(1) { if (it < 50) it*3 else null }
println(.average())                             // 24.2
```

When the collection is empty, the **average()** always returns **Double.NaN**. For a non-empty collection, **c.average()** is essentially the same as **c.sum().toDouble()/c.count()**. Similarly to the **count()** function, the **average()** will throw an exception if the collection contains more than **Int.MAX_VALUE** elements.

The **minOrNull()** and **maxOrNull()** functions compute, respectively the smallest and the largest value for an array/iterable/sequence of a comparable values:

```
println(intArrayOf(5, 8, 1, 4, 2).minOrNull())             // 1
println(intArrayOf(5, 8, 1, 4, 2).maxOrNull())             // 8
println(listOf("abc", "w", "xyz", "def", "hij").minOrNull()) // abc
println(listOf("abc", "w", "xyz", "def", "hij").maxOrNull()) // xyz
// 1, -3, 9, -27, 81
val seq = generateSequence(1) { if (it < 50) -it * 3 else null }
println(seq.minOrNull())                                    // -27
println(seq.maxOrNull())                                    // 81
```

Similarly to summation, min/max can be computed for collections of non-comparable elements by providing a function which converts them to comparables. This behavior is implemented in the **minByOrNull()** and **maxByOrNull()** functions:

```
class Person(val firstName: String, val familyName: String, val age:
Int) {
    override fun toString() = "$firstName $familyName: $age"
}
```

```
fun main() {
    val persons = sequenceOf(
        Person("Brook", "Watts", 25),
        Person("Silver", "Hudson", 30),
        Person("Dane", "Ortiz", 19),
        Person("Val", "Hall", 28)
    )
    println(persons.minByOrNull { it.firstName })  // Brook Watts: 25
    println(persons.maxByOrNull { it.firstName })  // Val Hall: 28
    println(persons.minByOrNull { it.familyName }) // Val Hall: 25
    println(persons.maxByOrNull { it.familyName }) // Brook Watts: 28
    println(persons.minByOrNull { it.age })          // Dane Ortiz: 19
    println(persons.maxByOrNull { it.age})           // Silver Hudson: 30
}
```

Alternatively, you can use **minWith()/maxWith()** which accepts a comparator instance instead of a conversion function. In the following example, we will use different comparators to impose ordering by the full name with the first name coming either first, or last:

```
class Person(val firstName: String, val familyName: String, val age: Int) {
    override fun toString() = "$firstName $familyName: $age"
}


val Person.fullName get() = "$firstName $familyName"
val Person.reverseFullName get() = "$familyName $firstName"


val FULL_NAME_COMPARATOR = Comparator<Person> { p1, p2 ->
    p1.fullName.compareTo(p2.fullName)
}


val REV_FULL_NAME_COMPARATOR = Comparator<Person> { p1, p2 ->
    p1.reverseFullName.compareTo(p2.reverseFullName)
}
```

```kotlin
fun main() {
    val seq = sequenceOf(
        Person("Brook", "Hudson", 25),
        Person("Silver", "Watts", 30),
        Person("Dane", "Hall", 19),
        Person("Val", "Ortiz", 28)
    )
    println(seq.minWithOrNull(FULL_NAME_COMPARATOR))
                                             // Brook Hudson: 25
    println(seq.maxWithOrNull(FULL_NAME_COMPARATOR))
                                             // Val Ortiz: 28
    println(seq.minWithOrNull(REV_FULL_NAME_COMPARATOR))
                                             // Dane Hall: 19
    println(seq.maxWithOrNull(REV_FULL_NAME_COMPARATOR))
                                             // Silver Watts: 30
}
```

All variants of min/max aggregates return **null** when applied to an empty collection.

The min/max functions we mentioned earlier were in fact introduced in Kotlin 1.4 as a replacement for older ones: **min()/max(), minBy()/maxBy()**, and **minWith()/maxWith()**. The reason for the change was a somewhat inconsistent naming of original functions since they return **null** on the empty collection and nullable collection function in the Kotlin standard library tend to have the **OrNull** suffix in their name. The older variants like **min()** and **max()** can still be used in Kotlin 1.4 but the compiler will now issue a warning as they are considered deprecated.

The second group of aggregate functions deals with combining collection elements into strings. The basic function is **joinToString()** which in its simplest form doesn't take any parameters:

```kotlin
println(listOf(1, 2, 3).joinToString()) // 1, 2, 3
```

By default, the elements are converted to String using their **toString()** method and concatenated together with space-commas which serve as separators. In many cases, though, you'd need a custom conversion which can be supplied by a lambda parameter. Suppose we want to present our values in the binary numeral system:

```kotlin
println(listOf(1, 2, 3).joinToString { it.toString(2) }) // 1, 10, 11
```

Apart from that it's possible to specify the following optional parameters:

- **separator**: A string inserted between elements (", " by default).
- **prefix** and **postfix**: A string inserted at the beginning and at the end of the resulting string, respectively (both empty by default).
- **limit**: A maximum number of elements to show (-1 by default which means the number is not limited).
- **truncated**: When **limit** is non-negative, it specifies a string which is added instead of skipped elements ("..." by default).

The **joinToString()** is available for any array, iterable, and sequence. Here is an example illustrating different options:

```
val list = listOf(1, 2, 3)
println(list.joinToString(prefix = "[", postfix = "]")) // [1, 2, 3]
println(list.joinToString(separator = "|"))             // 1|2|3
println(list.joinToString(limit = 2))                   // 1, 2, ...
println(list.joinToString(
    limit = 1,
    separator = " ",
    truncated = "???"
))                                                      // 1 ???
```

The Kotlin library also includes a more general function **joinTo()** which appends characters to an arbitrary **Appendable** instance such as **StringBuilder** instead of producing a new string:

```
import java.lang.StringBuilder

fun main() {
    val builder = StringBuilder("joinTo: ")
    val list = listOf(1, 2, 3)
    println(list.joinTo(builder, separator = "|")) // joinTo: 1|2|3
}
```

The third group we will cover in this section allows you to implement your own custom aggregates based on functions which combine a pair of values. This group is represented by the **fold()/reduce()** functions and their varieties.

The **reduce()** function takes a two-parameter function where the first parameter contains an accumulated value and the second one contains the current collection element. The aggregation proceeds as follows:

1. Initialize an accumulator to the value of the first element.

2. For each successive element, combine the current value of the accumulator with an element and assign the result back to the accumulator.

3. Return the value of the accumulator.

If the collection is empty, the **reduce()** throws an exception since the accumulator can't be initialized.

Let's consider an example. In the following code, we will use **reduce()** to compute a product of numbers and concatenation of strings:

```
println(intArrayOf(1, 2, 3, 4, 5).reduce { acc, n -> acc * n })  // 120

println(listOf("a", "b", "c", "d").reduce { acc, s -> acc + s }) // abcd
```

If the aggregation rule depends on the element indices, you may use a **reduceIndexed()** function which passes the current index as the first parameter of the aggregator operation. Suppose we want to modify the preceding example to sum only elements on odd positions:

```
println(intArrayOf(1, 2, 3, 4, 5)
    .reduceIndexed { i, acc, n -> if (i % 2 == 1) acc * n else acc })
                                                                    // 8
println(listOf("a", "b", "c", "d")
    .reduceIndexed { i, acc, s -> if (i % 2 == 1) acc + s else acc })
                                                                  // abd
```

Note that the first element is processed regardless of our constraint. If you want to choose the initial value by yourself, you can use the **fold()/foldIndexed()** functions instead of **reduce()/reduceIndexed()**. On top of it, they allow you to use the accumulator of a type which differs from that of collection elements:

```
println(
    intArrayOf(1, 2, 3, 4).fold("") { acc, n -> acc + ('a' + n - 1) }
) // abcd
println(
    listOf(1, 2, 3, 4).foldIndexed("") { i, acc, n ->
        if (i % 2 == 1) acc + ('a' + n - 1) else acc
    }
```

```
) // bd
```

Unlike **reduce()**, **fold()** doesn't fail on an empty collection since the initial value is supplied by the programmer.

The **reduce()/reduceIndexed()** and **fold()/foldIndexed()** are available for any array, iterable, or sequence. Each of these functions has a counterpart which processes elements in a reverse order starting from the last one. Such functions have a "Right" word in their name and are available only for arrays and lists since these objects provide an easy way to traverse them backward:

```
println(
    arrayOf("a", "b", "c", "d").reduceRight { s, acc -> acc + s }
) // dcba
println(
    listOf("a", "b", "c", "d").reduceRightIndexed { i, s, acc ->
        if (i % 2 == 0) acc + s else acc
    }
) // dca
println(
    intArrayOf(1, 2, 3, 4).foldRight("") { n, acc -> acc + ('a' + n - 1) }
) // dcba
println(
    listOf(1, 2, 3, 4).foldRightIndexed("") { i, n, acc ->
        if (i % 2 == 0) acc + ('a' + n - 1) else acc
    }
) // ca
```

Keep the difference in the parameter order for lambdas passed to the "left" and "right" varieties of fold/reduce. In the "left" version, the accumulator comes before the current element, while in the "right" version, the order is reversed.

Filtering

The Kotlin standard library provides a bunch of extension functions that can be used to filter collections leaving out elements which do not satisfy given conditions. A filtering operation does not modify an original collection. It either produces an entirely new one or puts all accepted elements into some existing mutable collection distinct from the original one.

The most basic filtering operation is given by the **filter()** function. Its predicate takes the current element as its single parameter and returns **true** if that element is accepted and **false** otherwise. The function is applicable to arrays, iterables, maps, and sequences with the return type determined as follows:

- filtering **Array<T>** or **Iterable<T>** gives you a **List<T>**
- filtering a **Map<K, V>** gives you a **Map<K, V>**
- filtering a **Sequence<T>** gives you a **Sequence<T>**

This function is also applicable to primitive array types such as **IntArray** with the result being a **List** with a corresponding boxed element type such as **List<Int>**. Keep this in mind as applying **filter()** to such arrays will force boxing of filtered elements.

Let's consider an example of applying **filter()** to various collection objects:

```
// List: [green, blue, green]
println(listOf("red", "green", "blue", "green").filter { it.length > 3 })
// List: [green, blue]
println(setOf("red", "green", "blue", "green").filter { it.length > 3 })
// List: [green, blue, green]
println(arrayOf("red", "green", "blue", "green").filter { it.length > 3 })
// List: [2, 4]
println(byteArrayOf(1, 2, 3, 4, 5).filter { it % 2 == 0 })
// Map: {X=10, L=50}
println(
    mapOf("I" to 1, "V" to 5, "X" to 10, "L" to 50).filter { it.value > 5 }
)
// Sequence
val seq = generateSequence(100) {
    if (it != 0) it/3 else null
}.filter { it > 10 }
// Converted to list: [100, 33, 11]
println(seq.toList())
```

Note that in the case of a map, the predicate parameter takes a value of the corresponding map entry. If you want to filter only by the key or value, you may use either the **filterKeys()** or **filterValues()** function:

```
val map = mapOf("I" to 1, "V" to 5, "X" to 10, "L" to 50)

println(map.filterKeys { it != "L" })   // {X=10, V=5, X=10}

println(map.filterValues { it >= 10 }) // {X=10, L=50}
```

The **filterNot()** function allows you to filter by the negative condition; in other words, a collection element is accepted when the corresponding predicate returns **false**:

```
// [red]
println(listOf("red", "green", "blue").filterNot { it.length > 3 })
// {I=1, V=5}
println(
    mapOf("I" to 1, "V" to 5, "X" to 10, "L" to 50).filterNot {
it.value > 5 }
)
```

Note that **filterKeys()** and **filterValues()** do not have a negative version like **filterNot()**.

If your filtering condition depends on the element index as well as its value, you can use a **filterIndexed()** function whose lambda takes an additional index parameter. This function is available for arrays, iterables, and sequences, but not for maps:

```
val list = listOf("red", "green", "blue", "orange")
// [green, blue]
println(list.filterIndexed { i, v -> v.length > 3 && i < list.lastIndex })


val seq = generateSequence(100) { if (it != 0) it/3 else null }
// [33, 11, 3, 1]
println(seq.filterIndexed { i, v -> v > 0 && i > 0 }.toList())
```

The standard library also includes filtering functions based on some common conditions which often arise in practice. One of them is **filterNotNull()** which filters out null values. It always produces a collection with the non-nullable element type:

```
val list = listOf("red", null, "green", null, "blue")
// Error: it is nullable here
list.forEach { println(it.length) }
// Ok: it is non-nullable
```

```
list.filterNotNull().forEach { println(it.length) }
```

IDE Tips: IntelliJ includes an out-of-the-box inspection which warns you about redundant **filterNotNull()** calls when the collection is question already has a non-nullable element type. You can easily drop the extra filter through Alt+Enter menu (as shown in *Figure 7.4*):

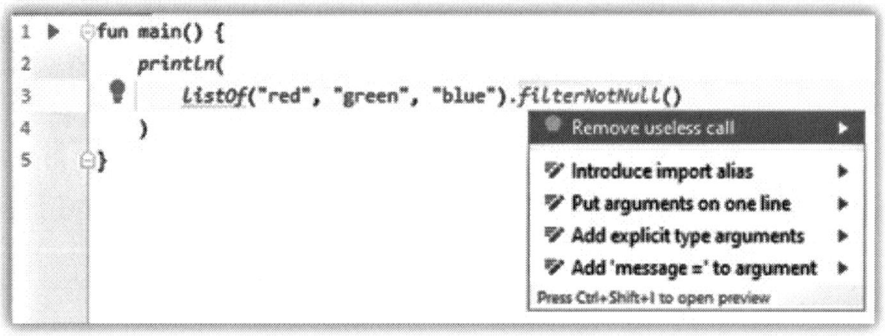

Figure 7.4: *Removing useless filter*

Another common case is covered by the **filterIsInstance()** function which leaves only elements conforming to the specific type. The collection returned by this function has the same element type you specify in its call:

```
val hotchpotch = listOf(1, "two", 3, "four", 5, "six")
val numbers = hotchpotch.filterIsInstance<Int>()
val strings = hotchpotch.filterIsInstance<String>()
println(numbers.filter { it > 2 })        // [3, 5]
println(strings.filter { it != "two" }) // [four, six]
```

The filtering functions we've seen so far produce new immutable collections on each call. What if we need to put the filtering results into some existing mutable collection? In this case, we can use special versions of filter functions which take additional parameters for the target collection where they put accepted values. The names of these functions have "To" added to them:

```
val allStrings = ArrayList<String>()
// Added: green, blue
listOf("red", "green", "blue").filterTo(allStrings) { it.length > 3 }
// Added: one, two, three
arrayOf("one", null, "two", null, "three").filterNotNullTo(allStrings)
// abcde, bcde, cde, de, e,
val seq = generateSequence("abcde") {
```

```
        if (it.isNotEmpty()) it.substring(1) else null
}
// Added: abcde, bcde, cde
seq.filterNotTo(allStrings) { it.length < 3 }
// [green, blue, one, two, three, abcde, bcde, cde]
println(allStrings)
```

"To" versions are available for **filter()**, **filterNot()**, **filterIndexed()**, **filterIsInstance()**, and **filterNotNull()** functions. Note that an attempt to use the original collection as a target would in general lead to Concurrent ModificationException due to adding elements during the collection traversal:

```
val list = arrayListOf("red", "green", "blue")
list.filterTo(list) { it.length > 3 } // Exception
```

Apart from various kinds of filtering, the Kotlin standard library includes the **partition()** function which splits the original collection into a pair where the first collection gets elements satisfying a given predicate, while the second gets those which do not. Consider the following example:

```
val (evens, odds) = listOf(1, 2, 3, 4, 5).partition { it % 2 == 0 }
println(evens) // [2, 4]
println(odds)  // [1, 3, 5]
```

Unlike **filter()** and its varieties, **partition()** always returns a pair of lists even when applied to a sequence:

```
val seq = generateSequence(100) { if (it == 0) null else it/3 }
val (evens, odds) = seq.partition { it % 2 == 0 }
println(evens) // [100, 0]
println(odds)  // [33, 11, 3, 1]
```

Note that **partition()** is not supported for maps.

Transformation

Various transformation functions included in the Kotlin standard library give you the ability to produce a new collection by changing each element of the existing one according to a given rule and then combining the results in some way. These functions can be divided into three basic categories: mapping, flattening, and associating.

Mapping transformation applies a given function to each element of the original collection. The results then become elements of the new collection. The basic function of this kind is **map()** which can be applied to any collection object, including arrays, iterables, sequences, and maps. The result is a sequence when applied to a sequence and a list otherwise:

```
println(setOf("red", "green", "blue").map { it.length }) // [3, 5, 4]
println(listOf(1, 2, 3, 4).map { it*it })                // [1, 4, 9, 16]
println(byteArrayOf(10, 20, 30).map { it.toString(16) }) // [a, 14, 1e]
// 50, 16, 5, 1, 0
val seq = generateSequence(50) { if (it == 0) null else it / 3 }
println(seq.map { it*3 }.toList()) // [150, 48, 15, 3, 0]
```

You can also use the **mapIndexed()** function if your transformation needs to take element indices into account:

```
// [(0, 0), (1, 1), (2, 4), (3, 9), (4, 16), (5, 25)]
println(List(6) { it*it }.mapIndexed { i, n -> i to n })
```

The **map()** and **mapIndexed()** functions also have variants which automatically filter out null values in the resulting collection. Semantically, they are similar to calling **filterNotNull()** after **map()** or **mapIndexed()**:

```
println(
   arrayOf("1", "red", "2", "green", "3").mapNotNull { it.toIntOrNull()
}
) // [1, 2, 3]
println(
    listOf("1", "red", "2", "green", "3").mapIndexedNotNull { i, s ->
        s.toIntOrNull()?.let { i to it }
    }
) // [(0, 1), (2, 2), (4, 3)]
```

IDE Tips: IntelliJ can detect and simplify redundant usages of **mapNotNull()/ mapIndexedNotNull()** suggesting to replace them by **map()/mapIndexed()** calls (see *Figure 7.5* for example). It also warns you about the explicit combination of **map()** and **filterNotNull()** calls which can be simplified to **mapNotNull()**. You can see an example in *Figure 7.6*:

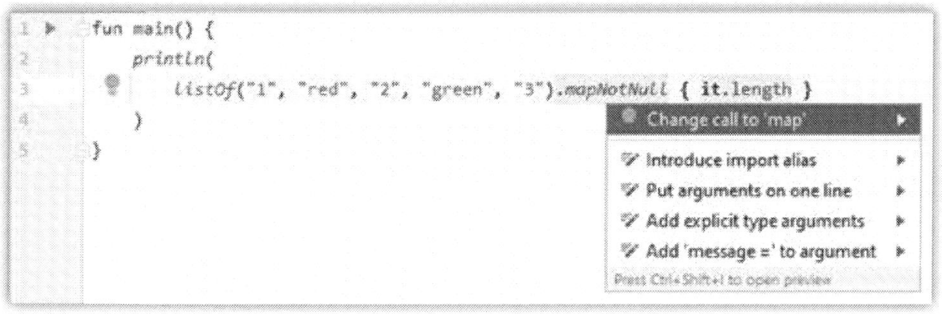

Figure 7.5: *Simplifying redundant call to mapNotNull()*

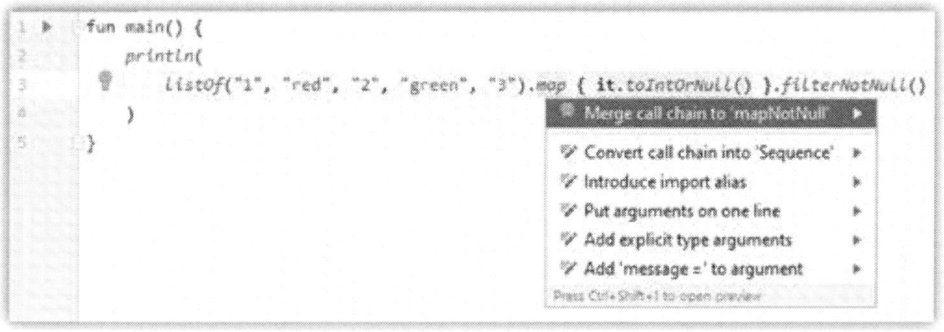

Figure 7.6: *Merging* **map-filterNotNull** *chained call*

The **map()** function can be applied to maps in which case the transformation takes map entries as its input and produces a list. Additionally, you can use **mapKeys()**/ **mapValues()** functions which transform only the keys or values, respectively and return a new *map*:

```
val map = mapOf("I" to 1, "V" to 5, "X" to 10, "L" to 50)
println(map.map { "${it.key} ${it.value}" })   //[I 1, V 5, X 10, L 50]
println(map.mapKeys { it.key.toLowerCase() })   //{i=1, v=5, x=10, l=50}
println(map.mapValues { it.value.toString(16) }) //{I=1, V=5, X=a, L=32}
```

Each of the **mapXXX()** functions also comes with a version which puts the resulting element into some existing mutable collection rather than creating a new one. Similarly to filters, these functions contain "To" in their names:

```
val result = ArrayList<String>()
listOf(1, 2, 3).mapTo(result) { it.toString() }
arrayOf("one", "two", "three").mapIndexedTo(result) { i, s -> "${i
+ 1}: s" }
sequenceOf("100", "?", "101", "?", "110").mapNotNullTo(result) {
    it.toIntOrNull(2)?.toString()
```

```
}
println(result) // [1, 2, 3, 1: s, 2: s, 3: s, 4, 5, 6]
```

The flattening operations transform each element of the original collection into a new collection and then glue the resulting collection together. This kind of transformation is implemented by the **flatMap()** function which produces a sequence when applied to a sequence and a list when applied to any other collection:

```
// [a, b, c, d, e, f, g, h, i]
println(setOf("abc", "def", "ghi").flatMap { it.asIterable() })
// [1, 2, 3, 4]
println(listOf(1, 2, 3, 4).flatMap { listOf(it) })
// [1, 1, 2, 1, 2, 3]
Array(3) { it + 1 }.flatMap { 1..it }
```

The **flatten()** function can be applied to any collection whose elements are collection themselves to glue them into a single collection. It can be considered a simplified version of **flatMap()** with trivial transformation:

```
println(
    listOf(listOf(1, 2), setOf(3, 4), listOf(5)).flatten()
)                                                    // [1, 2, 3, 4, 5]
println(Array(3) { arrayOf("a", "b") }.flatten()) // [a, b, a, b, a, b]
println(
    sequence {
        yield(sequenceOf(1, 2))
        yield(sequenceOf(3, 4))
    }.flatten().toList()
)                                                    // [1, 2, 3, 4]
```

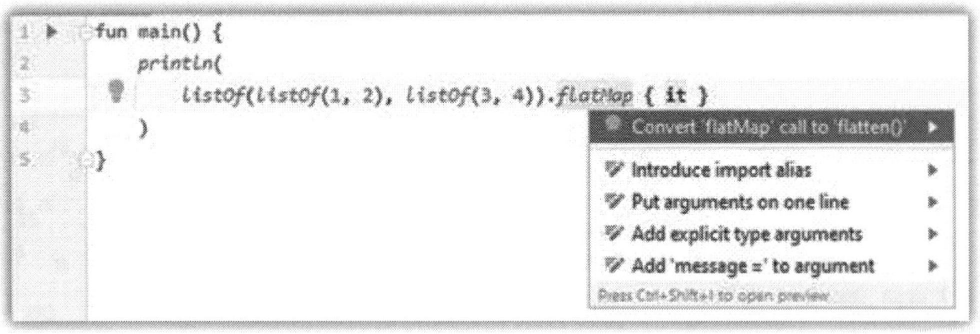

Figure 7.7: Replacing trivial **flatMap()** *call with* **flatten()**

IDE Tips: The IntelliJ plugin can detect trivial calls to flatMap suggesting to replace them with flatten (see *Figure 7.7*).

Similarly to map(), the **flatMap()** has a version which appends resulting elements to an existing collection:

```
val result = ArrayList<String>()
listOf(listOf("abc", "def"), setOf("ghi"))
    .flatMapTo(result) { it }
sequenceOf(sequenceOf(1, 2), sequenceOf(3, 4))
    .flatMapTo(result) { it.map { "$it" } }
println(result) // [abc, def, ghi, 1, 2, 3, 4]
```

One more transformation kind we'd like to cover in this section is an association which allows you to build maps based on a given transformation function and using the original collection elements as either map keys, or map values. The first case is implemented by the **associateWith()** function which generates map values using the original collection as a source of keys:

```
println(
    listOf("red", "green", "blue").associateWith { it.length }
) // {red=3, green=5, blue=4}
println(
    generateSequence(1) { if (it > 50) null else it*3 }
        .associateWith { it.toString(3) }
) // {1=1, 3=10, 9=100, 27=1000, 81=10000}
```

Note that **associateWith()** function is not applicable to arrays.

The **associateBy()** function similarly treats collection elements as values and uses the supplied transformation function to produce map keys. Not that if there are multiple values corresponding to a single key, only one is retained in the resulting map:

```
// {3=red, 5=green, 4=blue}
println(listOf("red", "green", "blue").associateBy { it.length })
// {1=15, 2=25, 3=35}
println(intArrayOf(10, 15, 20, 25, 30, 35).associateBy { it/10 })
// {1=1, 10=3, 100=9, 1000=27, 10000=81}
println(
```

```
    generateSequence(1) { if (it > 50) null else it*3 }
        .associateBy { it.toString(3) }
)
```

Finally, the **associate()** function transforms the collection element to produce both a key and value:

```
println(
    listOf("red", "green", "blue")
        .associate { it.toUpperCase() to it.length }
) // {RED=3, GREEN=5, BLUE=4}
println(
    intArrayOf(10, 15, 20, 25, 30, 35).associate { it to it/10 }
) // {10=1, 15=1, 20=2, 25=2, 30=3, 35=3}
println(
    generateSequence(1) { if (it > 50) null else it*3 }
        .associate {
            val s = it.toString(3)
            "3^${s.length - 1}" to s
        }
) // {3^0=1, 3^1=10, 3^2=100, 3^3=1000, 3^4=10000}
```

A similar effect can also be achieved by **associateBy()** overloads which take a separate transformation function for keys and values:

```
println(
    listOf("red", "green", "blue").associateBy(
        keySelector = { it.toUpperCase() },
        valueTransform = { it.length }
    )
) // {RED=3, GREEN=5, BLUE=4}
```

Association functions also have "To" variants (such as **associateByTo()**) which put produced entries into an existing mutable map.

Extracting subcollections

In the filtering section, we discussed a set of functions which allow you to extract a part of the original collection retaining only elements satisfying a certain condition.

In this section, we'll consider functions which serve a similar purpose but extract collection parts based on other criteria.

In the *Basic operations* section, we mentioned the `subList()` function which gives you a view of a list segment. The **slice()** function performs a similar task but uses the integer range instead of a pair of integers to represent segment bounds. The **slice()** can be applied to arrays as well as lists:

```
// 0, 1, 4, 9, 16, 25
println(List(6) { it*it }.slice(2..4)) // [4, 9, 16]
```

```
// 0, 1, 8, 27, 64, 125
println(Array(6) { it*it*it }.slice(2..4)) // [8, 27, 64]
```

In the case of list, it works similar to the **subList()** method producing a wrapper of the original collection which reflects a given segment. In the case of an array, the result is a new list containing array elements with specified indices.

If you want to extract an array segment as another array, you can use **sliceArray()** instead:

```
val slice = Array(6) { it*it*it }.sliceArray(2..4).contentToString()
```

There is also a more general version of **slice()/sliceArray()** which takes an iterable of integers and uses them as indices. In other words, it allows you to extract an arbitrary subsequence of the original list or array:

```
println(List(6) { it*it }.slice(listOf(1, 2, 3))) // [1, 4, 9]
println(Array(6) { it*it*it }.slice(setOf(1, 2, 3))) // [1, 8, 27]
println(
    Array(6) { it*it*it }.sliceArray(listOf(1, 2, 3)).contentToString()
) // [1, 8, 27]
```

The **take()/takeLast()** functions are used to extract a given number of iterable or array elements starting from the first or the last one, respectively:

```
println(List(6) { it*it }.take(2))         // [0, 1]
println(List(6) { it*it }.takeLast(2))     // [16, 25]
println(Array(6) { it*it*it }.take(3))     // [0, 1, 8]
println(Array(6) { it*it*it }.takeLast(3)) // [27, 64, 125]
```

The **take()** function can also be applied to a sequence in which case it returns a new sequence containing the first element of the original one:

```kotlin
val seq = generateSequence(1) { if (it > 100) null else it*3 }

println(seq.take(3).toList()) // [1, 3, 9]
```

The **drop()/dropLast()** functions can be considered a complement to **take()/takeLast()**. They return the remaining elements when a given number of the first/last ones is removed:

```kotlin
println(List(6) { it*it }.drop(2))          // [4, 9, 16, 25]
println(List(6) { it*it }.dropLast(2))      // [0, 1, 4, 9]


println(Array(6) { it*it*it }.drop(3))      // [27, 64, 125]
println(Array(6) { it*it*it }.dropLast(3))  // [0, 1, 8]


val seq = generateSequence(1) { if (it > 100) null else it*3 }
println(seq.drop(3).toList())               // [27, 81, 243]
```

The take/drop operations also come in versions which take a predicate on collection elements rather than a number. These versions take/drop elements only up to the first one violating a given condition:

```kotlin
val list = List(6) { it * it }
println(list.takeWhile { it < 10 })          // [0, 1, 4, 9]
println(list.takeLastWhile { it > 10 })      // [16, 25]
println(list.dropWhile { it < 10 })          // [16, 25]
println(list.dropLastWhile { it > 10 })      // [0, 1, 4, 9]


val seq = generateSequence(1) { if (it > 100) null else it*3 }
println(seq.takeWhile { it < 10 }.toList()) // [1, 3, 9]
println(seq.dropWhile { it < 10 }.toList()) // [27, 81, 243]
```

The **chunked()** functions introduced in Kotlin 1.2 allow you to split an iterable or sequence into lists (called chunks) whose size does not exceed a given threshold. The simplest form of **chunked()** takes just a maximum chunk size:

```kotlin
// 0, 1, 4, 9, 16, 25, 36, 49, 64, 81
val list = List(10) { it*it }
println(list.chunked(3)) // [[0, 1, 4], [9, 16, 25], [36, 49, 64], [81]]
```

```
// 1, 3, 9, 27, 81, 243, 729
val seq = generateSequence(1) { if (it > 300) null else it*3 }
println(seq.chunked(3).toList()) // [[1, 3, 9], [27, 81, 243], [729]]
```

Note that **chunked()** returns a list of chunks when applied to an iterable, and a sequence of chunks when applied to a sequence.

The more general version allows you to specify a function which transforms each chunk into an arbitrary value. The result is a list or sequence composed of transformation results. The following code replaces each chunk from the preceding example by the sum of its elements:

```
// 0, 1, 4, 9, 16, 25, 36, 49, 64, 81
val list = List(10) { it*it }
println(list.chunked(3) { it.sum() })          // [5, 50, 149, 81]


// 1, 3, 9, 27, 81, 243, 729
val seq = generateSequence(1) { if (it > 300) null else it*3 }
println(seq.chunked(3) { it.sum() }.toList()) // [13, 351, 729]
```

The **windowed()** function also introduced in Kotlin 1.2 allows you to extract all segments of a given slide visible through a kind of "sliding window". Like **chunked()**, it produces a list of lists when applied to an iterable and a sequence of lists when applied to a sequence:

```
// 0, 1, 4, 9, 16, 25
val list = List(6) { it*it }
// [[0, 1, 4], [1, 4, 9], [4, 9, 16], [9, 16, 25]]
println(list.windowed(3))


// 1, 3, 9, 27, 81, 243
val seq = generateSequence(1) { if (it > 100) null else it*3 }
// [[1, 3, 9], [3, 9, 27], [9, 27, 81], [27, 81, 243]]
println(seq.windowed(3).toList())
```

Similarly to **chunked()**, you can supply a transformation function which aggregates elements of each window:

```
// 0, 1, 4, 9, 16, 25
val list = List(6) { it*it }
```

```
println(list.windowed(3) { it.sum() })              // [5, 14, 29, 50]
```

```
// 1, 3, 9, 27, 81, 243
val seq = generateSequence(1) { if (it > 100) null else it*3 }
println(seq.windowed(3) { it.sum() }.toList()) // [13, 39, 117, 351]
```

Additionally, you can specify optional parameters which affect the sliding window behaviour:

- **step**: The distance between indices of the first element in a pair of adjacent windows (1 by default).
- **partialWindows**: This includes windows of smaller size at the end of the collection (false by default).

Let's see an example using these options:

```
// 0, 1, 4, 9, 16, 25
val list = List(6) { it*it }
// Only elements with even indices (0 and 2) produce windows:
// [[0, 1, 4], [4, 9, 16]]
println(list.windowed(3, step = 2))
// Added two partial windows at the end:
// [[0, 1, 4], [1, 4, 9], [4, 9, 16], [9, 16, 25], [16, 25], [25]]
println(list.windowed(3, partialWindows = true))
```

There is also a separate function for building two-element windows: **zipWithNext()**. Unlike **windowed()**, it produces lists and sequences of pairs rather than lists:

```
// 0, 1, 4, 9, 16, 25
val list = List(6) { it*it }
// [(0, 1), (1, 4), (4, 9), (9, 16), (16, 25)]
println(list.zipWithNext())
```

```
// 1, 3, 9, 27, 81, 243
val seq = generateSequence(1) { if (it > 100) null else it*3 }
// [(1, 3), (3, 9), (9, 27), (27, 81), (81, 243)]
println(seq.zipWithNext().toList())
```

Accordingly, its aggregation version uses a function which takes a pair of collection elements instead of a list:

```
// [0, 4, 36, 144, 400]
println(List(6) { it*it }.zipWithNext { a, b -> a * b })
```

Ordering

The standard library includes functions which sort collection elements according to a given ordering. The simplest of them is the **sorted()** function which can be applied to any array/iterable/sequence of comparable values to sort them based on their natural ordering. The **sortDescending()** function is similar but sorts elements in reverse:

```
println(intArrayOf(5, 8, 1, 4, 2).sorted()) // [1, 2, 4, 5, 8]
println(
    intArrayOf(5, 8, 1, 4, 2).sortedDescending()
)                                               // [8, 5, 4, 2, 1]
println(
    listOf("abc", "w", "xyz", "def", "hij").sorted()
)                                               // [abc, def, hij, w, xyz]
println(
    listOf("abc", "w", "xyz", "def", "hij").sortedDescending()
)                                               // [xyz, w, hij, def, abc]
// 1, -3, 9, -27, 81
val seq = generateSequence(1) { if (it < 50) -it * 3 else null }
println(seq.sorted().toList())                  // [-27, -3, 1, 9, 81]
println(seq.sortedDescending().toList())    // [81, 9, 1, -3, -27]
```

These functions return **Sequence** when applied to a sequence. Note, though, that the sequence returned is stateful and sorts the entire collection at the first attempt to access its elements.

When applied to an array or iterable, the result is always a **List**. For arrays, you can use a similar pair of **sortedArray()/sortedArrayDescending()** functions which return an array instead of the list.

If collection elements are not comparable, you can still sort them by using one of **sorted()** alternatives which allows you to specify a custom ordering: **sortedBy()**/ **sortedWith()**. The convention is similar to the one we've seen for the **minOrNull()**/

maxOrNull() aggregation functions. **sortedBy()** takes a function which converts collection elements to comparables, while **sortedWith()** takes a comparator. There is also a reversed version of **sortedBy()** which is called **sortedByDescending()**:

```kotlin
class Person(val firstName: String, val familyName: String, val age:
Int) {
    override fun toString() = "$firstName $familyName: $age"
}


val Person.fullName get() = "$firstName $familyName"
val Person.reverseFullName get() = "$familyName $firstName"


val FULL_NAME_COMPARATOR = Comparator<Person> { p1, p2 ->
    p1.fullName.compareTo(p2.fullName)
}


val REVERSE_FULL_NAME_COMPARATOR = Comparator<Person> { p1, p2 ->
    p1.reverseFullName.compareTo(p2.reverseFullName)
}


fun main() {
    val persons = listOf(
        Person("Brook", "Hudson", 25),
        Person("Silver", "Watts", 30),
        Person("Dane", "Hall", 19),
        Person("Val", "Ortiz", 28)
    )
    println(persons.sortedWith(FULL_NAME_COMPARATOR))
    println(persons.sortedWith(FULL_NAME_COMPARATOR))
    println(persons.sortedWith(REVERSE_FULL_NAME_COMPARATOR))
    println(persons.sortedWith(REVERSE_FULL_NAME_COMPARATOR))
    println(persons.sortedBy { it.age })
    println(persons.sortedByDescending { it.age })
}
```

All sorting functions we've seen so far put sorted elements into a new collection leaving the original one untouched. In the case of arrays and mutable lists, though, we can modify the original collection instead and sort its elements in place. This is implemented by the **sort()** and **sortDescending()** functions:

```
val array = intArrayOf(4, 0, 8, 9, 2).apply { sort() }
println(array.contentToString()) // [0, 2, 4, 8, 9]
val list = arrayListOf("red", "blue", "green").apply { sort() }
println(list)                    // [blue, green, red]
```

A separate group of functions can be used to reverse elements in iterables and arrays. The basic case is handled by the **reversed()** function which returns a new list with the original elements reversed:

```
println(intArrayOf(1, 2, 3, 4, 5).reversed())       // [5, 4, 3, 2, 1]

println(listOf("red", "green", "blue").reversed()) // [blue, green, red]
```

For arrays, you can also use the **reversedArray()** function which produces a new array instead of a list.

The **reverse()** function can be used to reverse elements of a mutable list or array without creating a new collection (note the similarity with **sort()** vs **sorted()**/ **sortedArray()**):

```
val array = intArrayOf(1, 2, 3, 4, 5).apply { reverse() }.contentToString()
println(array) // [5, 4, 3, 2, 1]
val list = arrayListOf("red", "green", "blue").apply { reverse() }
println(list) // [blue, green, red]
```

The **asReversed()** function is similar to **reversed()** in the sense that it returns a new list. The list produced is, however, just a wrapper over the original. Both lists share the same data which makes **asReversed()** more efficient in terms of memory usage. When applied to a mutable list, it returns a mutable wrapper. Changes in either list are automatically reflected in the other (unlike the collection produced by the **reversed()** function):

```
val list = arrayListOf("red", "green", "blue")
val reversedCopy = list.reversed()
val reversedMirror = list.asReversed()
list[0] = "violet"
println(list)             // [violet, green, blue]
```

```
println(reversedCopy)    // [blue, green, red]
println(reversedMirror) // [blue, green, violet]
```

Note that **asReversed()** is available only for lists.

One more function we'd like to mention in this section is **shuffled()**. When applied to an iterable, it produces a new list with original elements rearranged in a random order:

```
println(listOf(1, 2, 3, 4, 5).shuffled())
```

Mutable lists can be similarly modified in place using **shuffle()**:

```
arrayListOf(1, 2, 3, 4, 5).shuffle()
```

Note that sequences and arrays do not support either of these functions.

Files and I/O streams

In this section, we'll address the part of the Kotlin standard library which deals with input/output operations. The features we will cover are based around the existing Java API for files, I/O streams, and URLs. In this regard, the Kotlin standard library provides a set of useful extension functions and properties which simplify a usage of I/O-related classes already present in the JDK.

Stream utilities

The Kotlin standard library includes a bunch of helper extensions for Java I/O streams. These functions simplify access to the stream content and implement some more complex patterns such as copying and automatic stream finalization. In this section, we'll take a closer look at these features.

The following functions allow you to retrieve the entire stream content:

```
fun InputStream.readBytes(): ByteArray

fun Reader.readText(): String

fun Reader.readLines(): Line<String>
```

Keep in mind the difference between the latter two functions and the **readLine()** method of the **BufferedReader**. While **readLine()** retrieves a *single line* from the stream, **readText()/readLines()** read the stream till the end and returns its entire content as either a single string, or a list of individual lines. Consider the following example:

```kotlin
import java.io.*

fun main() {
    FileWriter("data.txt").use { it.write("One\nTwo\nThree") }
    // One
    FileReader("data.txt").buffered().use { println(it.readLine()) }
    // One Two Three
    FileReader("data.txt").use { println(it.readText().replace('\n',
' ')) }
    // [One, Two, Three]
    println(FileReader("data.txt").readLines())
}
```

Note that unlike **readText()**, the **readLines()** function automatically closes its stream on completion.

Kotlin allows direct iteration over buffered streams, although the API is a bit different for binary and text data. In the case of **BufferedOutputStream**, we have the **iterator()** function which, in particular, allows us to use such streams in the **for** loop to iterate over individual bytes:

```kotlin
FileInputStream("data.bin").buffered().use {
    var sum = 0
    for (byte in it) sum += byte
}
```

BufferedReader, on the other hand, provides the **lineSequence()** function which gives you a sequence over its lines:

```kotlin
FileReader("data.bin").buffered().use {
    for (line in it.lineSequence()) println(line)
}
```

Similar capabilities, albeit in a more indirect form, are available for an arbitrary **Reader** instance. The **forEachLine()** and **useLines()** functions allow you to iterate over individual lines. When using them you don't have to worry about closing the stream since they perform it automatically:

```kotlin
import java.io.*

fun main() {
    FileWriter("data.txt").use { it.write("One\nTwo\nThree") }
    // One, Two, Three
    FileReader("data.txt").useLines { println(it.joinToString()) }
    // One/Two/Three
    FileReader("data.txt").forEachLine { print("$it/") }
}
```

The difference is that the lambda of **forEachLine()** accepts the current line and is invoked upon each iteration, while the lambda of **useLines()** takes a sequence over all lines.

It's also possible to transfer data between streams using the **copyTo()** function which has two overloaded versions for binary and text streams:

```kotlin
fun InputStream.copyTo(
    out: OutputStream,
    bufferSize: Int = DEFAULT_BUFFER_SIZE
): Long
fun Reader.copyTo(out: Writer, bufferSize: Int = DEFAULT_BUFFER_
SIZE): Long
```

The return value gives you an actual number of bytes or characters copied. The following sample demonstrates the usage of **copyTo()**:

```kotlin
import java.io.*

fun main() {
    FileWriter("data.txt").use { it.write("Hello") }

    val writer = StringWriter()
    FileReader("data.txt").use { it.copyTo(writer) }
    println(writer.buffer)          // Hello

    val output = ByteArrayOutputStream()
```

```
FileInputStream("data.txt").use { it.copyTo(output) }
println(output.toString("UTF-8")) // Hello
}
```

One more function that we will consider in this section provides a safe way to work with streams and other resources which need explicit finalization. The **use()** function can be invoked on any instance of **java.io.Closeable** type (and **java.lang.AutoCloseable** since Kotlin 1.2). It then executes a supplied lambda, properly finalizes the resource (whether an exception is thrown or not), and then returns the result of the lambda:

```
val lines = FileReader("data.bin").use { it.readLines() }
```

Java vs Kotlin: This function serves the same purpose as try-with-resources statement introduced in Java 7.

The preceding code is roughly equivalent to the explicit **try** block:

```
val reader = FileReader("data.bin")
val lines = try {
    reader.readLines()
} finally {
    reader.close()
}
```

IDE Tips: IntelliJ can automatically detect such **try** blocks and suggest converting them into the **use()** function calls via the Alt+Enter menu on the **try** keyword (as shown in *Figure 7.8*):

Creating streams

The standard library includes a set of functions that simplify the creation of Java I/O streams. In this section, we'll take a look at the basic cases.

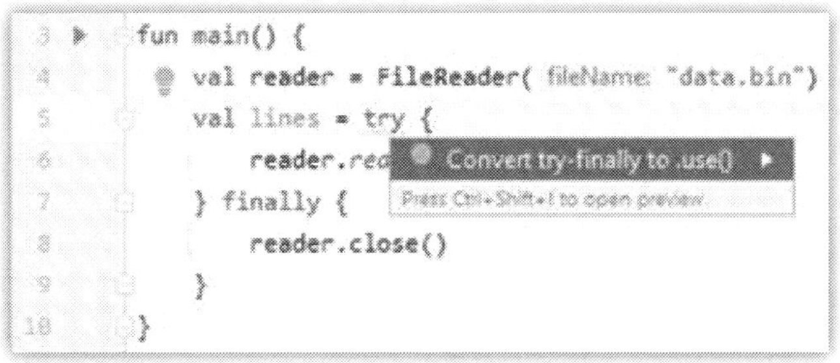

Figure 7.8: Converting explicit try block into use() call

Using **bufferedReaders()/bufferedWriter()** extensions, you can create a **BufferedReader/BufferedWriter** instance for a particular File object:

```kotlin
import java.io.File


fun main() {
    val file = File("data.txt")
    file.bufferedWriter().use { it.write("Hello!") }
    file.bufferedReader().use { println(it.readLine()) } // Hello!
}
file.writer(charset = Charsets.US_ASCII).use { it.write("Hello!") }
```

There is also a similar pair of **reader()/writer()** extension functions which create a **FileReader/FileWriter** object without bufferization.

The **printWriter()** function creates a **PrintWriter** instance suitable for formatted output.

The reader/writer-related functions allow you to optionally specify encoding charset (defaulting to UTF-8), and the buffered versions have an extra optional parameter for the buffer size. The default buffer size is given by **DEFAULT_BUFFER_SIZE** constant which currently corresponds to 8 kilobytes:

```kotlin
file.bufferedReader(
    charset = Charsets.US_ASCII,
    bufferSize = 100
).use { println(it.readLine()) }
```

The Charsets object contains a set of constants for some standard charsets such as US-ASCII or different UTF variants.

If you want to work with a binary file, you can similarly use **inputStream()/ outputStream()** functions to create an appropriate stream instance:

```kotlin
import java.io.File


fun main() {
    val file = File("data.bin")
    file.outputStream().use { it.write("Hello!".toByteArray()) }
    file.inputStream().use { println(String(it.readAllBytes())) } // Hello!
}
```

Several functions give you the ability to create I/O streams based on the content of a **String** or **ByteArray**. The **byteInputStream** creates an **ByteArrayInputStream** with a string as its source:

```
println("Hello".byteInputStream().read().toChar())                    // H

println("Hello".byteInputStream(Charsets.US_ASCII).read().toChar()) // H
```

The **reader()** function similarly creates a **StringReader** instance:

```
println("One\nTwo".reader().readLines()) // [One, Two]
```

The **inputStream()** function constructs a **ByteArrayInputStream** using a ByteArray as its source:

```
println(byteArrayOf(10, 20, 30).inputStream().read())
```

It's also possible to use a portion of the byte array using the overloaded version of **inputStream()** which takes an offset and a portion size:

```
val bytes = byteArrayOf(10, 20, 30, 40, 50)

println(bytes.inputStream(2, 2).readBytes().contentToString())

                                                      // [30, 40]
```

The standard library also includes some extensions simplifying stream piping. The following set of functions can be used to construct a **Reader**, a **BufferedReader,** or a **BufferedInputStream** based on the general instance of the **InputStream** class:

```
fun InputStream.reader(charset: Charset = Charsets.UTF_8):
InputStreamReader


fun InputStream.bufferedReader(
    charset: Charset = Charsets.UTF_8
): BufferedReader


fun InputStream.buffered(
    bufferSize: Int = DEFAULT_BUFFER_SIZE
): BufferedInputStream
```

Similar functions (named **writer()**, **bufferedWriter(),** and **buffered()**) are also available for **OutputStream** piping it to a **Writer**, a **BufferedWriter**, or a **BufferedOutputStream**. The following example gives you a taste of them:

```kotlin
import java.io.FileInputStream
import java.io.FileOutputStream

fun main() {
    val name = "data.txt"
    FileOutputStream(name).bufferedWriter().use  {   it.write("One\
nTwo") }
    val line = FileInputStream(name).bufferedReader().use {
    it.readLine() }
    println(line) // One
}
```

The **buffered()** function is also defined for Reader and Writer:

```kotlin
fun Reader.buffered(bufferSize: Int = DEFAULT_BUFFER_SIZE):
BufferedReader
```

```kotlin
fun Writer.buffered(bufferSize: Int = DEFAULT_BUFFER_SIZE):
BufferedWriter
```

URL utilities

The Kotlin library provides a couple of helper functions for retrieving data over network connections associated with URL objects:

```kotlin
fun URL.readText(charset: Charset = Charsets.UTF_8): String
```

```kotlin
fun URL.readBytes(): ByteArray
```

The **readText()** function reads the entire content of an input stream corresponding to the URL instance using the specified charset. The **readBytes()** function similarly retrieves the content of a binary stream as an array of bytes.

Since both functions load the entire stream content blocking the calling thread till completion, they shouldn't be used to download large files.

Accessing file content

The Kotlin standard library allows you to access file content using special functions without explicitly mentioning I/O streams. These functions are helpful in such cases as reading/writing an entire file, appending data to existing file, or processing file line-by-line.

The following functions allow you to manipulate the text content:

- **readText()**: This reads the entire content of a file as a single string.
- **readLines()**: This reads the entire content of a file splitting it by line separators and returning a list of strings.
- **writeText()**: This sets the file content to a given String rewriting it if necessary.
- **appendText()**: This adds a specified string to the content of a given file.

The usage of these functions is demonstrated by the following example:

```kotlin
import java.io.File


fun main() {
    val file = File("data.txt")
    file.writeText("One")
    println(file.readText())  // One
    file.appendText("\nTwo")
    println(file.readLines()) // [One, Two]
    file.writeText("Three")
    println(file.readLines()) // [Three]
}
```

Each of the text-related functions may accept an optional parameter of the **Charset** type specifying text encoding.

For the binary files, you can use similar functions which work with byte arrays instead of strings:

```kotlin
import java.io.File


fun main() {
    val file = File("data.bin")
    file.writeBytes(byteArrayOf(1, 2, 3))
    println(file.readBytes().contentToString()) // [1, 2, 3]
    file.appendBytes(byteArrayOf(4, 5))
    println(file.readBytes().contentToString()) // [1, 2, 3, 4, 5]
    file.writeBytes(byteArrayOf(6, 7))
```

```
    println(file.readBytes().contentToString()) // [6, 7]
}
```

Another group of functions allows you to process file content in blocks without reading it entirely. This is helpful for handling large files which can't be efficiently put in memory as a whole.

The **forEachLine()** function allows you to process text content line-by-line without reading an entire file:

```
import java.io.File


fun main() {
    val file = File("data.txt")
    file.writeText("One\nTwo\nThree")
    file.forEachLine { print("/$it") } // /One/Two/Three
}
```

The **useLines()** function passes a line sequence to the given lambda which can compute some result which is then returned by the **useLines()**:

```
import java.io.File


fun main() {
    val file = File("data.txt")
    file.writeText("One\nTwo\nThree")
    println(file.useLines { lines -> lines.count { it.length > 3 } }) // 1
}
```

Similar to other text-related file functions, you can pass the optional Charset parameter to **forEachLine()** and **useLines()**.

To process a binary file, you can use the **forEachBlock()** function. Its lambda accepts a **ByteArray** buffer and an integer which tells how many bytes were read on the current iteration. The following code, for example, outputs the sum of all bytes in the **data.bin** file:

```
import java.io.File


fun main() {
    val file = File("data.bin")
```

```
    var sum = 0
    file.forEachBlock { buffer, bytesRead ->
        (0 until bytesRead).forEach { sum += buffer[it] }
    }
    println(sum)
}
```

By default, the buffer size is implementation-dependent, but you can specify it as an optional **blockSize** parameter. Note that the buffer size can't be smaller than some implementation-specific threshold. In Kotlin 1.3, the default and minimum buffer sizes are 4096 and 512 bytes, respectively.

File system utilities

In this section, we'll discuss the standard library functions which simplify file system operations such as copying and removing files as well as traversing the directory structure.

The **deleteRecursively()** function allows you to delete a given file together with all its children, including nested directories. The result is true if the deletion completes successfully and false otherwise. In the latter case, the deletion may be partial; for example, if some nested directories can't be deleted. This function serves as a counterpart for the **mkdirs()** method present in the Java API:

```
import java.io.File

fun main() {
    File("my/nested/dir").mkdirs()
    val root = File("my")
    println("Dir exists: ${root.exists()}")                     // true
    println("Simple delete: ${root.delete()}")                  // false
    println("Dir exists: ${root.exists()}")                     // true
    println("Recursive delete: ${root.deleteRecursively()}")    // true
    println("Dir exists: ${root.exists()}")                     // false
}
```

The **copyTo()** function copies its receiver to another file and returns the copy:

```kotlin
import java.io.File

fun main() {
    val source = File("data.txt")
    source.writeText("Hello")
    val target = source.copyTo(File("dataNew.txt"))
    println(target.readText()) // Hello
}
```

By default, the target file is not overwritten, so if it already exists the **copyTo()** function throws **FileAlreadyExistsException**. You can, however, specify the optional overwrite parameter to enforce the copying:

```kotlin
import java.io.File

fun main() {
    val source = File("data.txt").also { it.writeText("One") }
    val target = File("dataNew.txt").also { it.writeText("Two") }
    source.copyTo(target, overwrite = true)
    println(target.readText()) // One
}
```

The **copyTo()** function can be applied to directories as well, but it doesn't copy its files and subdirectories and simply creates an empty directory corresponding to the target path. If you want to copy the directory together with its content, there is a separate **copyRecursively()** function:

```kotlin
import java.io.File

fun main() {
    File("old/dir").mkdirs()
    File("old/dir/data1.txt").also { it.writeText("One") }
    File("old/dir/data2.txt").also { it.writeText("Two") }
    File("old").copyRecursively(File("new"))
    println(File("new/dir/data1.txt").readText()) // One
    println(File("new/dir/data2.txt").readText()) // Two
}
```

Similar to **copyTo(),** this function allows you to specify the overwriting policy using the overwrite parameter (false by default). Additionally, you can set an action which is invoked on **IOException** when copying a particular file. This can be done using the optional onError parameter which accepts a lambda of the type **(File, IOException) -> OnErrorAction**. The result value determines how the **copyRecursively()** function would deal with a problematic file:

- **SKIP:** This skips the file and continues the copying.
- **TERMINATE:** This stops the copying.

Being the last parameter, the **onError** lambda can be passed outside parentheses:

```
File("old").copyRecursively(File("new")) { file, ex -> OnErrorAction.
SKIP }
```

The default action is to rethrow an **IOException** back to the caller.

The **walk()** function implements traversal of the directory structure according to the depth-first search algorithm. The optional parameter specifies the traversal direction:

- **TOP_DOWN:** This visits parent before children (default value).
- **BOTTOM_UP:** This visits children before parent.

The return value is a sequence of File instances. The following example demonstrates the usage of different traversal modes:

```
import java.io.File
import kotlin.io.FileWalkDirection.*


fun main() {
    File("my/dir").mkdirs()
    File("my/dir/data1.txt").also { it.writeText("One") }
    File("my/dir/data2.txt").also { it.writeText("Two") }
    println(File("my").walk().map { it.name }.toList())
    println(File("my").walk(TOP_DOWN).map { it.name }.toList())
    println(File("my").walk(BOTTOM_UP).map { it.name }.toList())
}
```

You can also use the **walkTopDown()** and **walkBottomUp()** functions instead of **walk(TOP_DOWN)** and **walk(BOTTOM_UP)** calls, respectively.

The sequence returned by the **walk()** function belongs to the special **FileTreeWalk** class. Apart from the common sequence functionality, this class allows you to specify additional traversal options. The **maxDepth()** function sets a maximum depth of the traversed subtree:

```
println(File("my").walk().maxDepth(1).map { it.name }.toList()) // [my, dir]
```

The **onEnter()** and **onLeave()** functions set up actions performed when the traversal enters and leaves a directory. The onEnter() accepts a **(File) -> Boolean** lambda whose return value determines whether a directory (and its children) should be visited at all. The **onLeave()** accepts **(File) -> Unit** lambda. The **onFail()** function allows you to specify an action which is called on **IOException** when trying to access the directory's children. The action takes the form of **(File, IOException) -> Unit** lambda which accepts the problematic directory and a corresponding exception.

Since all four functions return the current instance of **FileTreeWalk**, they can be chained as shown in the following example:

```
println(
        File("my")
             .walk()
             .onEnter { it.name != "dir" }
             .onLeave { println("Processed: ${it.name}") }
             .map { it.name }
             .toList()
```

The preceding code would print:

Processed: my

[my]

The **dir** directory would be filtered out by the **onEnter()** action.

The default actions are as follows: always return true for **onEnter()**, do nothing for **onLeave()**, and throw an exception for **onFail()**. The maximum tree depth is **Int.MAX_VALUE** by default making it effectively unconstrained.

The **createTempFile()/createTempDir()** functions can be used to create a temporary file or directory, respectively:

```
val tmpDir = createTempDir(prefix = "data")

val tmpFile = createTempFile(directory = tmpDir)
```

Both functions have the same set of parameters:

```
fun createTempDir(
    prefix: String = "tmp",
    suffix: String? = null,
    directory: File? = null
): File
```

The **createTempFile()** is essentially the same as the JDK method **File.createTempFile()**.

Conclusion

In this chapter, we learned that a major part of the Kotlin standard library is aimed at manipulation of collections. We learned different collection types such as arrays, iterables, sequences, and maps, discussed their basic API and operations covering various collection use cases such as accessing elements and subcollections, filtering, aggregation, transformations, and sorting. In the second part of this chapter, we took a look at I/O utilities aimed at simplifying creation of streams, access to their data and common file system operation such as deleting and copying.

In the next chapter, we will revisit the subject of object-oriented programming and discuss how the concepts of class inheritance and delegation can be used in Kotlin applications.

Points to remember

- Kotlin distinguishes between mutable and immutable collection types.
- Apart from stored collections, Kotlin supports sequences which are generated and consumed on-demand.
- The standard library contains a multitude of top-level and extension functions implementing major operations on collection data, including but not limited to filtering, aggregation, grouping, transformation, and ordering.

Multiple choice questions

1. Which of the following types exist in both mutable and immutable versions?

    A. Set

    B. Map

    C. Sequence

    D. Iterable

2. What's the result of the += operator in the following example?

```kotlin
var list = ArrayList<String>()
list += "test"
```

    A. `list.add("test")`

    B. `list = list + "test"`

    C. compilation error

    D. runtime exception

3. What's the result of the -= operator in the following example?

```kotlin
val list = ArrayList<String>()
list -= "test"
```

    A. `list.remove("test")`

    B. `list = list - "test"`

    C. compilation error

    D. runtime exception

4. Which of the following functions can be used to check whether a sequence is empty?

    A. `isEmpty()`

    B. `size()`

    C. `any()`

    D. `all()`

5. Which of the following sorting functions accepts a comparator?

    A. `sorted()`

    B. `sortedWith()`

    C. `sortedBy()`

    D. `sort()`

6. What is the result of the following expression?

```kotlin
intArrayOf(1, 2, 3, 4, 5)
  .map { it*it }
  .filter { it < 10 }
  .reduce { acc, n -> 2*acc - n }
```

    A. -12

    B. 13

C. 14

D. -13

7. What is the result of the following expression?

```
intArrayOf(1, 2, 3, 4, 5).joinToString(
    prefix = "{",
    separator = "1",
    postfix = "}"
) { "${it - 1}" }
```

A. {10111213141}

B. {112131415}

C. {011121314}

D. {11121314151}

8. Which of the following functions returns the content of the text file as a single string?

A. `read()`

B. `readLines()`

C. `readBytes()`

D. `readText()`

Answers

1. A, B, D
2. C
3. A
4. C
5. C
6. D
7. C
8. D

Questions

1. Give an outline of collection types in Kotlin. What are the key differences from the Java collections library?

2. Which basic operations are provided by collection types?

3. Describe various ways to iterate over collection elements.

4. What common functions can be used to access collection elements?

5. What common aggregates are available in the Kotlin library?

6. Describe the fold/reduce operations.

7. What is the purpose of `all()`/`any()`/`none()` functions?

8. Describe collection filtering functions.

9. How one can extract a subcollection?

10. What standard transformations can be applied to collections? Describe features of mapping, flattening, and association.

11. Describe collection ordering utilities provided by the Kotlin standard library.

12. Describe stream creation and conversion utilities.

13. What functions can be used to access content of the File or I/O stream?

14. Describe file system utility function.

CHAPTER 8
Understanding Class Hierarchies

This chapter continues with the discussion of object-oriented aspects of Kotlin introduced in *Chapter 4, Working with Classes and Objects* and *Chapter 6, Using Special-Case Classes*. We'll introduce the concept of class inheritance and explain how to define subclasses. We'll also consider designing complex class hierarchies using abstract classes, interfaces, and class delegation. The features of interest also include sealed classes which implement the concept of algebraic data types suited for the definition of restricted class type hierarchies and type checking enabling powerful Kotlin smart casts.

Structure

In this chapter, we will cover the following topics:

- Inheritance
- Abstract classes and interfaces

Objective

We will get an understanding of how inheritance and overriding works in Kotlin and learn to use Kotlin object-oriented capabilities to build class hierarchies.

Inheritance

In order to represent "is-a" relationship between domain concepts, most object-oriented languages use a concept of inheritance. When class A (a subclass or a derived class) inherits class B (a superclass or a base class) all instances of A are automatically considered instances of B. As a consequence class A gets all members and extensions defined for B. This relation is transitive. If class B, in turn, inherits some class C, A is also considered a subclass (albeit indirect) of C.

In Kotlin, similar to Java, classes support only single inheritance which means that any class may not have more than one superclass. If you don't specify a superclass explicitly, the compiler automatically assumes that your class inherits from built-in class Any. Thus, all classes in a given program form a well-defined inheritance tree which is usually called a *class hierarchy*.

In the upcoming sections, we'll discuss the basics of class inheritance in Kotlin, how to define a subclass, how superclass members are inherited and overridden, and which common methods are available for any object via the Any class.

Declaring a subclass

To inherit from a given class, you need to add its name preceded by the : symbol after the primary constructor in your class definition:

```kotlin
open class Vehicle {
    var currentSpeed = 0

    fun start() {
        println("I'm moving")
    }

    fun stop() {
        println("Stopped")
    }
}


open class FlyingVehicle : Vehicle() {
    fun takeOff() {
```

```
        println("Taking off")
    }


    fun land() {
        println("Landed")
    }
}
```

```
class Aircraft(val seats: Int) : FlyingVehicle()
```

Java vs. Kotlin: In Kotlin there are now special keywords like **extends** and **implements** in Java. Instead inheritance is always denoted by colon symbol (:).

Note the parentheses are added after **Vehicle** and **FlyingVehicle** in the definitions of their subclasses. This is in fact a call to the superclass constructor where you put necessary arguments to the super class initialization code.

You've probably noticed the **open** keyword near the **Vehicle** and **FlyingVehicle** definitions. This modifier marks the corresponding classes as *open for inheritance* thus allowing them to serve as superclasses. The **Aircraft**, on the other hand, has no such modifier and by default is considered *final*. If you attempt to inherit from a final class, the compiler will report an error:

```
class Airbus(seats: Int) : Aircraft(seats) // Error: Aircraft is final
```

Java vs Kotlin: Mind the difference between the default class behavior in Java and Kotlin. In Java, any class is open by default and must be explicitly marked as final if you want to forbid inheriting from it. In Kotlin, however, the default is final. If you want some class to be inheritable, you must declare it as open.

As evidenced in practice, classes which are not specifically designed with inheritance in mind may suffer from the so called "fragile base class" problem when changes in a base class lead to an incorrect behavior in subclasses because the superclass no longer satisfies their assumptions. For that reason, it's highly recommended to carefully design and document inheritable classes making such assumptions explicit.

Instances of subclasses are also instances of their superclasses and also inherit super class members:

```
val aircraft = Aircraft(100)
val vehicle: Vehicle = aircraft // implicit cast to supertype
vehicle.start()                 // calling Vehicle method
```

```
vehicle.stop()              // calling Vehicle method
aircraft.start()            // calling Vehicle method
aircraft.takeOff()          // calling FlyingVehicle method
aircraft.land()             // calling FlyingVehicle method
aircraft.stop()             // calling Vehicle method
println(aircraft.seats)     // accessing Aircraft own property
```

Some classes do not support inheritance to the full extent. In particular, data classes are always final and can't be declared as open:

open data class Person(**val** name: String, **val age**: Int) *// Error*

Initially, it was also forbidden to inherit the data class from another class, but this limitation was removed in Kotlin 1.1.

Inline classes, on the other hand, currently can neither extend other classes nor serve as superclasses themselves:

```
class MyBase
open inline class MyString(val value: String)                // Error
inline class MyStringInherited(val value: String): MyBase() // Error
```

Objects (including companions) can be freely inherited from open classes:

```
open class Person(val name: String, val age: Int) {
    companion object : Person("Unknown", 0)
}
object JohnDoe : Person("John Doe", 30)
```

You can't, however, inherit from an object or declare it open since each object is supposed to have only one instance.

A powerful feature of inheritance is a so called ad-hoc polymorphism which allows you to provide different implementations of a superclass member for particular subclasses and choose them depending on the actual instance class at runtime. In Kotlin, this can be achieved by *overriding* a member of the superclass. Consider the following classes:

```
open class Vehicle {
    open fun start() {
        println("I'm moving")
    }
}
```

```kotlin
    fun stop() {
        println("Stopped")
    }
}


class Car : Vehicle() {
    override fun start() {
        println("I'm riding")
    }
}


class Boat : Vehicle() {
    override fun start() {
        println("I'm sailing")
    }
}
```

The **Vehicle** class provides common implementation of the **start()** method which is then overridden by its inheritors, **Car** and **Boat**. Note that the **start()** method in the **Vehicle** class is marked as open which makes it overridable in subclasses, while its implementations in **Car** and **Boat** are marked with the **override** keyword. Now, calls on values of the type **Vehicle** are dispatched depending on their runtime class. If you run the following code:

```kotlin
fun startAndStop(vehicle: Vehicle) {
    vehicle.start()
    vehicle.stop()
}


fun main() {
    startAndStop(Car())
    startAndStop(Boat())
}
```

You'll get:

```
I'm riding
```

Stopped

I'm sailing

Stopped

The **stop()** method, on the other hand, is final since it's not explicitly marked as open. It can't be overridden and is simply inherited by subclasses.

Java vs Kotlin: It's worth pointing out two major differences between overriding in Kotlin and Java. First, similarly to classes, Kotlin functions and properties are final by default and must be explicitly marked with the **open** keyword to permit overriding in subclasses, while in Java, methods are implicitly open so if you want to forbid their overriding you have to do it with the explicit **final** modifier. Second, overridden members in Kotlin *must* be always accompanied by the **override** keyword; failing to do so produces a compilation error. In Java, on the other hand, explicit marking of overriding methods is optional, although it's considered a good practice to use the **@Override** annotation. Enforcing explicit marking of overridden members in Kotlin helps to prevent the "accidental override" problem where you can add a member which just happens to match some super class and overrides its implementation leading to unexpected program behavior and hard-to-fine bugs.

It's worth pointing out an important difference between members and extensions. While class members can be overridden (provided they are not final) and thus chosen based on the runtime class of a particular instance, extensions are always resolved *statically*. In other words, when calling an extension compiler always chooses it on the base of a statically known receiver type. Consider the following example:

```kotlin
open class Vehicle {
    open fun start() {
        println("I'm moving")
    }
}


fun Vehicle.stop() {
    println("Stopped moving")
}


class Car : Vehicle() {
    override fun start() {
        println("I'm riding")
```

```
    }
}


fun Car.stop() {
    println("Stopped riding")
}


fun main() {
    val vehicle: Vehicle = Car()
    vehicle.start() // I'm riding
    vehicle.stop()  // Stopped moving
}
```

It's clear that a program calls **start()** defined in the **Car** class because it's resolved dynamically depending on the runtime type of the **vehicle** variable (which is **Car**). The **stop()**, however, is chosen depending on the static type of **vehicle** (which is **Vehicle**), so the function called is **Vehicle.stop()**.

Note that the signature of an overridden member must match with that of its superclass version:

```
open class Vehicle {
    open fun start(speed: Int) {
        println("I'm moving at $speed")
    }
}


class Car : Vehicle() {
    override fun start() { // Error: wrong signature
        println("I'm riding")
    }
}
```

You can, however, replace the return type with its supertype:

```
open class Vehicle {
    open fun start(): String? = null
}
```

```kotlin
open class Car : Vehicle() {
    final override fun start() = "I'm riding a car"
}
```

If you declare the overridden member final, it won't be overridden further in subclasses:

```kotlin
open class Vehicle {
    open fun start() {
        println("I'm moving")
    }
}


open class Car : Vehicle() {
    final override fun start() {
        println("I'm riding a car")
    }
}


class Bus : Car() {
    override fun start() { // Error: start() is final in Car
        println("I'm riding a bus")
    }
}
```

Properties can be overridden too. Apart from placing their implementations in the subclass body, you also have an option to override them as primary constructor parameters:

```kotlin
open class Entity {
    open val name: String get() = ""
}


class Person(override val name: String) : Entity()
```
Immutable properties can be overridden by mutable ones:
```kotlin
open class Entity {
```

```kotlin
    open val name: String get() = ""
}


class Person() : Entity() {
    override var name: String = ""
}
```

Similar to Java, Kotlin has a special access modifier which restricts the member scope to its inheritors. Such members are marked with the **protected** keyword:

```kotlin
open class Vehicle {
    protected open fun onStart() { }

    fun start() {
        println("Starting up...")
        onStart()
    }
}


class Car : Vehicle() {
    override fun onStart() {
        println("It's a car")
    }
}


fun main() {
    val car = Car()
    car.start()   // Ok
    car.onStart() // Error: onStart is not available here
}
```

Java vs Kotlin: Mind the difference between the **protected** modifier in Kotlin and Java. While both languages permit to access protected members from inheritor classes, Java also allows you to use them from *any code located in the same package*. In Kotlin, that's forbidden. Currently, it doesn't have an access modifier which restricts the declaration scope to a containing package.

Sometimes, an overridden version of a function or property needs to access its original version to reuse its code. In this case, you can prefix your member reference with the **super** keyword (the syntax is similar to **this**, but you can access an inherited member instead of the current one):

```kotlin
open class Vehicle {
    open fun start(): String? = "I'm moving"
}


open class Car : Vehicle() {
    override fun start() = super.start() + " in a car"
}


fun main() {
    println(Car().start()) // I'm moving in a car
}
```

IDE Tips: The IntelliJ plugin includes a special action which can help you to generate stubs for overriding members. To access it, you can use the *Ctrl + O/Cmd + O* shortcut inside a class body. The IDE then displays a dialog box where you can choose superclass members to override (as shown in *Figure 8.1*):

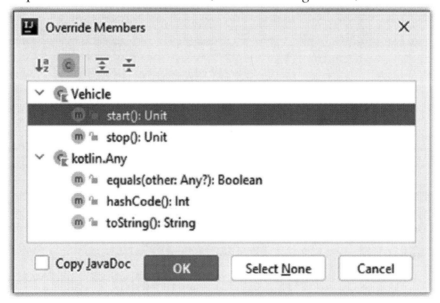

Figure 8.1: "Override Members" dialog

Subclass initialization

In *Chapter 4, Working with Classes and Objects*, we discussed how constructors are used to initialize an instance state of a particular class. When creating an instance of the subclass, your program also needs to call the initialization code defined in its superclasses. The superclass initialization must come first since it may create an environment used by a subclass code. In Kotlin, this order is enforced automatically. When your program attempts to create an instance of some class **A**, it gets a chain of its superclasses and then calls their constructors starting from the hierarchy root (that is, the **Any** class) and finishing with a constructor of **A**. Let's take a look at an example demonstrating the order of initialization:

```kotlin
open class Vehicle {
    init {
        println("Initializing Vehicle")
    }
}

open class Car : Vehicle() {
    init {
        println("Initializing Car")
    }
}

class Truck : Car() {
    init {
        println("Initializing Truck")
    }
}

fun main() {
    Truck()
}
```

When this is run, this program will print the following:

```
Initializing Vehicle

Initializing Car

Initializing Truck
```

Confirming the preceding idea that initialization proceeds from the superclass to the subclass.

We've already mentioned that parentheses that come after the superclass name in the subclass definition in fact constitute a call to its constructor. So far, we didn't have to pass some arguments there since super classes in our examples have been using default constructors. What if we need to provide them with some data too? The simplest case is when a superclass has exactly one constructor:

```kotlin
open class Person(val name: String, val age: Int)


class Student(name: String, age: Int, val university: String) :
    Person(name, age)


fun main() {
    Student("Euan Reynolds", 25, "MIT")
}
```

In the preceding example, the primary constructor of the Student class passes three of its parameters to the constructor of the Person superclass using a so called *delegating call*: **Person(firstName, familyName, age)**.

Similar to ordinary constructor calls, delegating calls are equally applicable to both primary and secondary constructors:

```kotlin
open class Person {
    val name: String
    val age: Int

    constructor(name: String, age: Int) {
        this.name = name
        this.age = age
    }
}
```

```kotlin
class Student(name: String, age: Int, val university: String) :
    Person(name, age)
```

What if we want to use a secondary constructor in the **Student** class? In this case, delegating a call is specified after the constructor signature:

```kotlin
open class Person(val name: String, val age: Int)


class Student : Person {
    val university: String


    constructor(name: String, age: Int, university: String) :
            super(name, age) {
        this.university = university

    }
}
```

The **super** keyword tells the compiler that our secondary constructor delegates to the corresponding constructor of the superclass. This syntax resembles a delegation to another constructor of the same class which is denoted by **this** keyword instead (see *Chapter 4, Working with Classes and Objects*). Another difference as compared to the call in the primary constructor is the absence of parentheses after the superclass name: **Person** instead of **Person()**; the reason is that our class does not have a primary constructor and delegating is put into a secondary one instead.

Java vs Kotlin: Unlike Java, calls between constructors – whether they belong to the same class, or class and its superclass – are never put into the constructor body. In Kotlin, you use a delegating call syntax for that.

Note that if a class **do** has a primary constructor, its secondary constructor may not delegate to the superclass:

```kotlin
open class Person(val name: String, val age: Int)


class Student() : Person { // Error: call to Person constructor is expected
    val university: String


    constructor(name: String, age: Int, university: String) :
            super(name, age) {
                // Error: can't invoke Person constructor here
```

```
        this.university = university
    }
}
```

A more interesting case is when a superclass has different constructors and we want its subclass to support more than one of them. In this case, the use of secondary constructors becomes the only option:

```
open class Person {
    val name: String
    val age: Int

    constructor(name: String, age: Int) {
        this.name = name
        this.age = age
    }

    constructor(firstName: String, familyName: String, age: Int) :
            this("$firstName $familyName", age)
}

class Student : Person {
    val university: String

    constructor(name: String, age: Int, university: String) :
            super(name, age) {
        this.university = university
    }

    constructor(
        firstName: String,
        familyName: String,
        age: Int,
        university: String
```

```
    ) :
            super(firstName, familyName, age) {
        this.university = university
    }
}


fun main() {
    Student("Euan", "Reynolds", 25, "MIT")
    Student("Val Watts", 22, "ETHZ")
}
```

In fact, the preceding use case was one of the primary reasons to add a secondary constructor to the language. This becomes especially important if you take into account the interoperability with Java code which doesn't distinguish between primary and secondary constructors.

One more issue we'd like to point out in this section is a so called "leaking this" problem. Consider the following code:

```
open class Person(val name: String, val age: Int) {
    open fun showInfo() {
        println("$name, $age")
    }

    init {
        showInfo()
    }
}


class Student(
    name: String,
    age: Int,
    val university: String
) : Person(name, age) {
    override fun showInfo() {
```

```
        println("$name, $age (student at $university)")
    }
}


fun main() {
    Student("Euan", "Reynolds", 25, "MIT")
}
```

If you run this program, the output will look like this:

```
Euan Reynolds, 25 (student at null)
```

Why does the university variable happen to be null? The reason is that the method **showInfo()** is invoked in the superclass initializer. It's a virtual function, so the program will call its overriding version in the Student class, but since Person initializer runs before that of Student, the university variable is not yet initialized at the moment of the **showInfo()** call. The reason this situation is called "leaking this" is because the super class "leaks" the current instance to code which in general may depend on the uninitialized part of the instance state. A more explicit example would look like this:

```
open class Person(val name: String, val age: Int) {
    override fun toString() = "$name, $age"


    init {
        println(this) // potentially dangerous
    }
}


class Student(
    name: String,
    age: Int,
    val university: String
) : Person(name, age) {
    override fun toString() = super.toString() + "(student at $university)"
}
```

```kotlin
fun main() {
    Student("Euan Reynolds", 25, "MIT")
                                // Euan Reynolds, 25 (student at null)
}
```

The issue of "Leaking this" poses a rare case when a variable of a non-nullable type in Kotlin may in fact turn out null.

IDE Tips: The IntelliJ plugin includes an inspection which flags such calls and **this** usages as potentially unsafe displaying an appropriate warning (as shown in *Figure 8.2*):

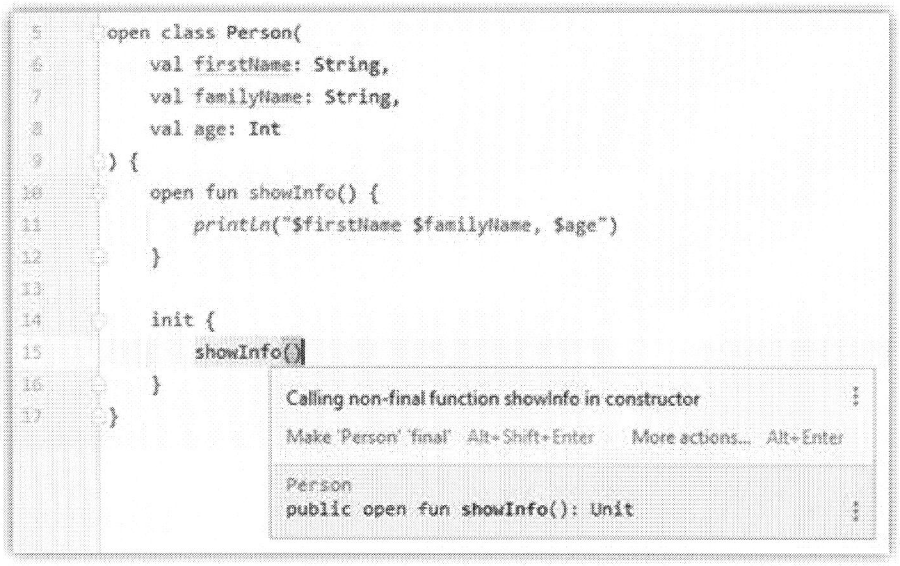

Figure 8.2: Warning on non-final function call inside constructor

Type Checking and Casts

Since a variable of some class may refer to any instance of its subtypes at runtime, it's useful to have a means to check whether a particular instance corresponds to a more specific type and cast it to that type when necessary. Consider, for example, the following code:

```kotlin
val objects = arrayOf("1", 2, "3", 4)
```

From the compiler's point of view, objects is an array of Any since Any is a minimal common supertype which covers all its elements. But what if we want to use some String- or Int-specific operations? Applying them to array elements directly won't work since they have `Any` type and thus do not support more specific functions or properties:

```
for (obj in objects) {
    println(obj*2) // Error: * is not supported for Any
}
```

Kotlin provides a solution in the form of type checking and casting operators. The **is** operator returns true if its left operand has a given type. Let's change our example slightly:

```
for (obj in objects) {
    println(obj is Int)
}
```

When we run the program, it prints the following:

```
false
```

```
true
```

```
false
```

```
true
```

The null value as expected is considered an instance of any nullable type, but doesn't belong to non-nullable ones:

```
println(null is Int)     // false
println(null is String?) // true
```

Kotlin also supports inverted operation which is expressed by **!is** operator:

```
val o: Any = ""
println(o !is Int)    // true
println(o !is String) // false
```

Note that **is/!is** operators are only applicable when the static type of their left operand is a supertype of the type at the right. The following check produced a compilation error since it's meaningless to test an Int value against String when the compiler knows statically that String is not an Int subtype:

```
println(12 is String) // Error
```

Both **is** and **!is** operators have the same precedence as **in** and **!in**.

Java vs Kotlin: The **is** operator is very similar to Java's **instanceof**. Bear in mind, however, that they diverge in their treatment of null. While **instanceof** always returns false when applied to null. The result of the **is** operator depends on whether its right-hand type is nullable or not.

In *Chapter 4, Working with Classes and Objects*, we introduced a concept of smart casts which allowed us to automatically refine a variable's type from a nullable to non-nullable one after comparing it with null. This useful feature is supported for is/!is checks as well. For example:

```kotlin
val objects = arrayOf("1", 2, "3", 4)

var sum = 0

for (obj in objects) {

    if (obj is Int) {

        sum += obj // type of obj is refined to Int here

    }

}

println(sum) // 6
```

The **is/!is** checks and smart casts are also supported in the **when** expressions where you can use them as a special kind of condition similar to **in/!in**:

```kotlin
val objects = arrayOf("1", 2, "3", 4)

var sum = 0

for (obj in objects) {

    when (obj) {

        is Int -> sum += obj            // obj has Int type here

        is String -> sum += obj.toInt() // obj has String type here

    }

}

println(sum) // 10
```

Java vs Kotlin: Starting from the JDK 14, Java supports its own smart casts in the form of an experimental pattern matching feature. Currently, it supports **instanceof** matching which can be compared to **is/!is** checks in Kotlin. It's worth noting, however, that while Kotlin smart casts refine the type information of an *existing* variable, Java pattern matching require a programmer to declare a separate variable to hold the cast result. Compare, for example, the following statement in Kotlin:

```
if (obj is String) {
    println(obj.length) // obj has 'String' type here
}
```

With a similar Java code:

```
if (obj instanceof String s) {        // obj type is unchanged
    System.out.println(s.length()); // s has 'String' type
}
```

Earlier, we've already mentioned that a compiler permits a smart cast only when it can ensure that the variable type does not change before its check and the usage. Now, we can express the smart cast rules more precisely.

First, smart casts are not allowed for properties and variables with custom accessors since a compiler can't guarantee that its return value won't change after the check. This also includes properties and local variables which use delegates:

```
class Holder {
    val o: Any get() = ""
}


fun main() {
    val o: Any by lazy { 123 }
    if (o is Int) {
        println(o*2)                // Error: smart cast is not possible
    }
    val holder = Holder()
    if (holder.o is String) {
        println(holder.o.length) // Error: smart cast is not possible
    }
}
```

Open member properties also fall into this category since they can be overridden in subtypes and given a custom accessor:

```
open class Holder {
    open val o: Any = ""
}
```

```
fun main() {
    val holder = Holder()
    if (holder.o is String) {
        println(holder.o.length) // Error: smart cast is not possible
    }
}
```

Mutable local variables can't be smart cast when their value is explicitly changed between the check and the read, or if they are modified in some lambda (the latter means that their value may change when lambda is invoked which in general is unpredictable):

```
fun main() {
    var o: Any = 123
    if (o is Int) {
        println(o + 1)     // Ok: smart cast to Int
        o = ""
        println(o.length) // Ok: smart cast to String
    }
    if (o is String) {
        val f = { o = 123 }
        println(o.length) // Error: smart cast is not possible
    }
}
```

Mutable properties, on the other hand, can't use smart casts since their value can be changed at any time by some other code.

It's worth noting that immutable local variables without delegates always support smart casts which is one more argument for preferring them over mutable ones.

When smart casts are not available, though, we can use explicit operators to coerce a given value to some type. Kotlin supports two operators of this kind: **as** and its safe version **as?**. The difference lies in their treatment of values which do not conform to the target type: while as throws an exception, **as?** simply returns null:

```
val o: Any = 123
println((o as Int) + 1)                 // 124
```

```
println((o as? Int)!! + 1)              // 124
println((o as? String ?: "").length)    // 0
println((o as String).length)           // Exception
```

Check the difference between expressions like **o as String?** and **o as? String.** They have the same value when **o** is a value of **String?** (including null), but behave differently when it's not:

```
val o: Any = 123
println(o as? String) // null
println(o as String?) // Exception
```

Also, note that attempt to cast null to non-nullable type produces an exception at runtime:

```
println(null as String) // Exception
```

Java vs Kotlin: The **as** operator is similar to the Java cast expression except the null treatment. In Java, casting always leave null unchanged, while in Kotlin, the result depends on the nullability of the target type.

Common methods

The **kotlin.Any** class is a root of the Kotlin class hierarchy. Every other class is its direct or indirect inheritor. When you don't specify an explicit superclass in your class definition, the compiler automatically assumes that it's **Any**. The members of this class are therefore available for all values. Let's take a look at how it's defined:

```
open class Any {
    public open operator fun equals(other: Any?): Boolean
    public open fun hashCode(): Int
    public open fun toString(): String
}
```

The operator keyword here means that the **equals()** method can be invoked in an operator form (via == or !=). We'll discuss the operator syntax later in *Chapter 11, Domain-Specific Languages.*.

These methods define basic operations which can be performed on any non-nullable value:

- structural equality (== and !=)
- computation of hash code which is used by some collection types like **HashSet** or **HashMap**

- default conversion to **String**

Java vs Kotlin: Readers familiar with Java will surely recognize Any definition as a somewhat minimalistic version of **java.lang.Object**. In fact, on the JVM runtime values of Any are represented as Object instances.

In *Chapter 6, Using Special-Case Classes*, we've already discussed an example of using referential equality in which the compiler automatically provides for any data class. Now, we'll see how to implement the custom equality operation for an arbitrary Kotlin class. Consider the following code:

```kotlin
class Address(
    val city: String,
    val street: String,
    val house: String
)


open class Entity(
    val name: String,
    val address: Address
)


class Person(
    name: String,
    address: Address,
    val age: Int
): Entity(name, address)


class Organization(
    name: String,
    address: Address,
    val manager: Person
) : Entity(name, address)
```

By default, these classes implement only referential equality inherited from the **Any** class. So if we try, for example, to use them as collection elements, we may face a problem since two instances with equal properties are not considered equal themselves:

```kotlin
fun main() {
    val addresses = arrayOf(
        Address("London", "Ivy Lane", "8A"),
        Address("New York", "Kingsway West", "11/B"),
        Address("Sydney", "North Road", "129")
    )
    println(addresses.indexOf(Address("Sydney", "North Road", "129")))
                                                                    // -1
}
```

The problem can be fixed by overriding the **equals()** method and implementing content-based equality. A simple implementation would look like this:

```kotlin
override fun equals(other: Any?): Boolean {
    if (other !is Address) return true
    return city == other.city &&
            street == other.street &&
            house == other.house
}
```

Now, the **index()** call from the preceding example finds our **Address** object and returns 2.

Note that the **equals()** method is commonly used in its operator form **==** or **!=**. These operators may also be applied to nullable values. When the left operand is null, they simply compare the right one with null referentially. The original referential equality is implemented by **===** and **!==** operators; their behavior, unlike that of **==** and **!=**, can't be overridden in the user code:

```kotlin
val addr1 = Address("London", "Ivy Lane", "8A")
val addr2 = addr1                              // the same instance
val addr3 = Address("London", "Ivy Lane", "8A") // different, but equal
println(addr1 === addr2) // true
println(addr1 == addr2)  // true
println(addr1 === addr3) // false
println(addr1 == addr2)  // true
```

Java vs Kotlin: In Java, on the opposite, == and != operators implement referential equality, while content-based is expressed by an explicit call to **equals()**. The latter must also be guarded against a possible null value of its receiver object to avoid NPE.

Just like in Java, a custom implementation of the **equals()** method must be accompanied by a corresponding **hashCode()**. Both implementations must be related so that any pair of equal objects (from the **equals()** point of view) always have the same hash code. This is because some collections (such as **HashSet**) use **hashCode()** to find a value in the hash table first and then use the **equals()** method to filter through all candidates with the same hash code. If equal objects have different hash codes, such collections will filter them out even before calling **equals()**. A possible **hashCode()** implementation which is compatible with the preceding **equals()** method can look like this:

```
override fun hashCode(): Int {
    var result = city.hashCode()
    result = 31 * result + street.hashCode()
    result = 31 * result + house.hashCode()
    return result
}
```

IDE Tips: The IntelliJ plugin warns you about classes which provide implementation of **equals()**, but not **hashCode()**, or vice versa. It also allows you to add the missing method by automatically generating some reasonable implementation (see *Figure 8.3*):

The general requirements for **equals()** implementations are basically the same as in Java:

- No non-null object must be equal to null
- Each object must be equal to itself
- Equality must be symmetric: **a == b** must entail **b == a**
- Equality must be transitive: **a == b** and **b == c** must entail **a == c**

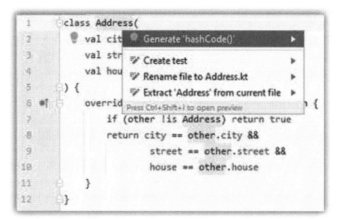

Figure 8.3: *Using IDE inspection to generate missing hashCode() method*

IDE Tips: The IntelliJ plugin can automatically generate implementations of the **equals()** and **hashCode()** methods based on the class properties. These methods are quite similar to the ones provided for data classes and would give reasonable equality behavior in most situations. In the remaining cases, you may use them as a good starting point for writing your own implementations.

To generate methods, choose "**equals()** and **hashCode()**" in the "Generate" menu which is displayed by the *Alt + Insert* shortcut inside a class definition (see *Figure 8.4*):

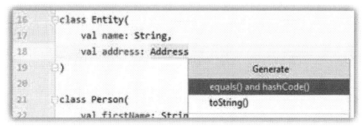

Figure 8.4: *"Generate" menu*

When a class in question is an open one, the IDE will suggest you to generate methods which also support instances of its subclasses. If you agree, then instances of different subclasses may happen to be equal which is not always desirable. In our example, we won't use this option since we want instances of **Person** and **Organization** to be distinct from each other.

You can then proceed with choosing properties which should be used in generated methods (as shown in *Figure 8.5*). Note that only properties chosen for **equals()** can be used in **hashCode()**. This ensures that both methods are compatible in a sense that equal objects always have the same hash code:

Figure 8.5: Choosing properties for `equals()` *method implementation*

Applying this action to the **Entity** class will produce the following code:

```
open class Entity(
    val name: String,
    val address: Address
) {
    override fun equals(other: Any?): Boolean {
        if (this === other) return true
        if (javaClass != other?.javaClass) return false

        other as Entity

        if (name != other.name) return false
        if (address != other.address) return false

        return true
    }

    override fun hashCode(): Int {
        var result = name.hashCode()
        result = 31 * result + address.hashCode()
        return result
    }
}
```

Properties are compared by delegating to their own implementation of **equals()** and **hashCode()**. Array types comprise an exception. Since they do not have their own content-based equality implementation, the generated code will use **contentEquals()** and **contentHashCode()** (or **contentDeepEquals()**/**contentDeepHashCode()** when applied to properties of multidimensional array types).

If the superclass has its own non-trivial implementation of **equals()/hashCode()**, the corresponding implementation in the superclass will automatically include a call to its super counterpart. For example, applying "Generate **equals()/hashCode()**" to the **Person** class, we get the following code:

```kotlin
class Person(
    name: String,
    address: Address,
    val age: Int
): Entity(name, address) {
    override fun equals(other: Any?): Boolean {
        if (this === other) return true
        if (javaClass != other?.javaClass) return false
        if (!super.equals(other)) return false

        other as Person

        if (age != other.age) return false

        return true
    }

    override fun hashCode(): Int {
        var result = super.hashCode()
        result = 31 * result + age
        return result
    }
}
```

Similar to Java, all Kotlin classes have a **toString()** method which provides the default **String** representation of a given instance. By default, such a representation is composed of a class name and an object's hash code, so in most cases it's worth overriding to get more readable information:

```kotlin
class Address(
    val city: String,
    val street: String,
    val house: String
) {
    override fun toString() = "$city, $street, $house"
}


open class Entity(
    val name: String,
    val address: Address
)


class Person(
    name: String,
    address: Address,
    val age: Int
): Entity(name, address) {
    override fun toString() = "$name, $age at $address"
}


class Organization(
    name: String,
    address: Address,
    val manager: Person?
) : Entity(name, address) {
    override fun toString() = "$name at $address"
}
```

```kotlin
fun main() {
    // Euan Reynolds, 25 at London, Ivy Lane, 8A
    println(Person("Euan  Reynolds",  Address("London",  "Ivy  Lane",
    "8A"), 25))
    // Thriftocracy, Inc. at Perth, North Road, 129
    println(
        Organization(
            "Thriftocracy, Inc.",
            Address("Perth", "North Road", "129"),
            null
        )
    )
}
```

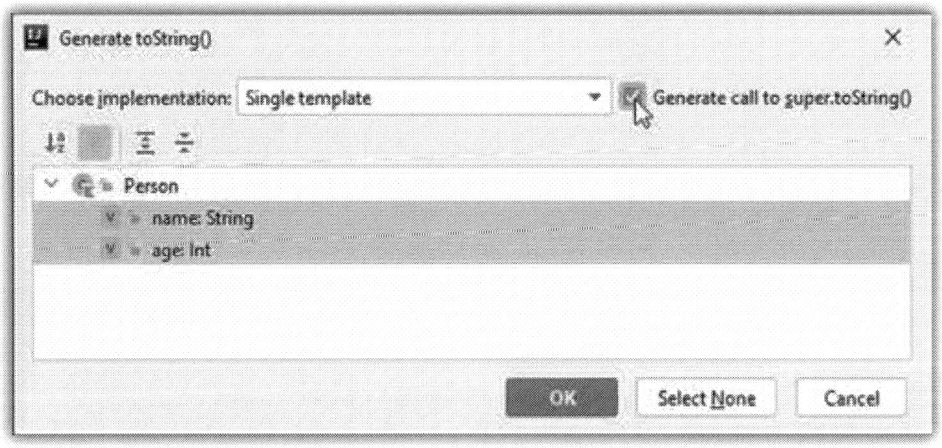

Figure 8.6: Choosing properties to use in toString()

IDE Tips: IntelliJ also allows you to generate a simple **toString()** implementation similar to the **equals()/hashCode()** methods. To do it, you just need to select the **"toString()"** option in the "Generate" menu (see *Figure 8.6*) and then choose properties you want to use in **toString()**. You may choose to generate the resulting string as either a single string template, or concatenation expression. If the superclass already has some nontrivial **toString()** implementation, you may additionally choose whether to add a **super.toString()** call. The example of this dialog is shown in *Figure 8.6*:

Here is the result of applying the "Generate **toString()**" action to our **Person** class:

```kotlin
class Person(
    val name: String,
    val age: Int,
    address: Address
): Entity(address) {
    override fun toString(): String {
        return "Person(name='$name', age=$age) ${super.toString()}"
    }
}
```

The Kotlin standard library also includes the **toString()** extension which is defined for **Any?** type. This function simply delegates to the receiver's **toString()** member when it's not null and returns "null" string otherwise. This allows you to use **toString()** on both nullable and non-nullable values.

Abstract classes and interfaces

So far all superclasses we've seen can have their own instances. Sometimes, however, this is undesirable because classes may also represent abstract concepts which do not have instances by themselves and are only instantiated through more specific cases. For example, our earlier example involved the **Entity** class subclassed by **Person** and **Organization**. While it makes sense to have objects representing particular persons and organizations, an entity by itself is an abstract notion, so it's basically meaningless to create an instance of "just" **Entity** rather than one of its specific subclasses. In the upcoming sections, we'll deal with Kotlin aspects which allow us to define and use such abstract types.

Abstract classes and members

Similar to Java, Kotlin supports *abstract classes* which can't be instantiated directly but instead serve only as super types for other classes. In order to mark the class as abstract, you use a corresponding modifier keyword:

```kotlin
abstract class Entity(val name: String)

// Ok: delegation call in subclass
class Person(name: String, val age: Int) : Entity(name)
```

```kotlin
val entity = Entity("Unknown") // Error: Entity can't be instantiated
```

Abstract classes, as you can see in the preceding example, may have their own constructors. The difference from non-abstract classes is that the abstract class constructor may only be invoked as a part of delegation call in the subclass definition. In the following code, the secondary constructor delegates to the constructor of the abstract class:

```kotlin
abstract class Entity(val name: String)

class Person : Entity {
    constructor(name: String) : super(name)
    constructor(
        firstName: String,
        familyName: String
    ) : super("$firstName $familyName")
}
```

Another feature of abstract classes allows you to declare *abstract* members. An abstract member defines a basic shape of a function or property such as its name, parameters and return type, but omits any implementation details. When a non-abstract class inherits such members from its abstract parent, they *must* be overridden and given an implementation:

```kotlin
import kotlin.math.PI

abstract class Shape {
    abstract val width: Double
    abstract val height: Double

    abstract fun area(): Double
}

class Circle(val radius: Double) : Shape() {
    val diameter get() = 2*radius
    override val width get() = diameter
    override val height get() = diameter
```

```kotlin
    override fun area() = PI*radius*radius
}


class Rectangle(
    override val width: Double,
    override val height: Double
) : Shape() {
    override fun area() = width*height
}


fun Shape.print() {
    println("Bounds: $width*$height, area: ${area()}")
}


fun main() {
    // Bounds: 20.0*20.0, area: 314.1592653589793
    Circle(10.0).print()
    // Bounds: 3.0*5.0, area: 15.0
    Rectangle(3.0, 5.0).print()
}
```

Since abstract members are not supposed to have an implementation by themselves, their definitions are subject to some limitations. In particular:

- Abstract properties may not have initializers, explicit accessors, or **by** clauses.
- Abstract functions may not have a body.
- Both abstract properties and functions must explicitly specify their return type since it can't be inferred automatically.

Note that abstract members are implicitly **open**, so you don't need to explicitly mark them as such.

IDE Tips: On top of the "Override Members" action we've seen in the "Overriding Class Members" section, IntelliJ has a similar action which is called "Implement Members". The action is available by either the *Ctrl + I* shortcut and produces a dialog similar to that of "Override Members", but lists only those members that are *yet to be implemented* (see the example for the **Circle** class in *Figure 8.7*):

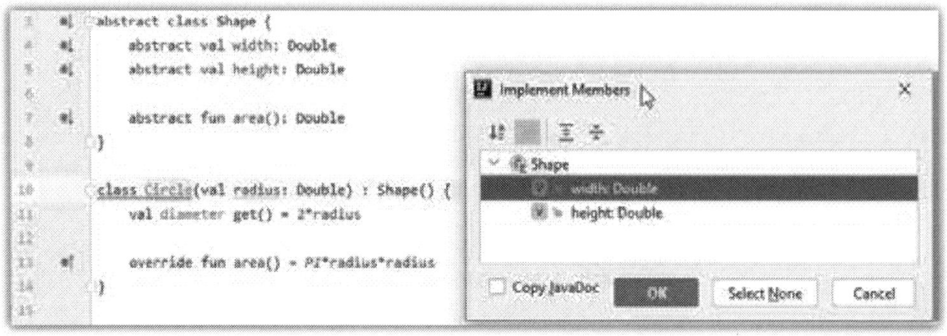

Figure 8.7: "Implement Members" dialog

An alternative option is to use one of the quick fixes available from the *Alt + Enter* menu invoked on the class name or keyword (note red highlighting in *Figure 8.7*). These quick fixes allow you, among other things, to implement abstract properties as constructor parameters (see the **Rectangle** class for an example), or simply mark the current class as **abstract**.

Interfaces

Kotlin interfaces are conceptually pretty much similar to their Java counterparts, especially after the introduction of default methods in Java 8. So basically an interface is a type which can contain methods and properties (both abstract and non-abstract), but can't define neither instance state nor constructors.

Unlike classes, an interface definition is introduced by the **interface** keyword:

```kotlin
interface Vehicle {
    val currentSpeed: Int

    fun move()
    fun stop()
}
```

Interface members are abstract by default, so if you don't provide an implementation (like in the preceding code), the abstract modifier is automatically assumed. You can, of course, write it explicitly, but that is considered redundant.

Interfaces can be supertypes for both classes and other interfaces. When a non-abstract class inherits an interface, it must provide implementations for all abstract members (and may optionally override non-abstract ones). Similar to class-to-class inheritance, implementations of interface members *must* be marked with the **override** keyword:

```kotlin
interface FlyingVehicle : Vehicle {
    val currentHeight: Int

    fun takeOff()
    fun land()
}


class Car : Vehicle {
    override var currentSpeed = 0
        private set

    override fun move() {
        println("Riding...")
        currentSpeed = 50
    }

    override fun stop() {
        println("Stopped")
        currentSpeed = 0
    }
}


class Aircraft : FlyingVehicle {
    override var currentSpeed = 0
        private set
    override var currentHeight = 0
        private set

    override fun move() {
        println("Taxiing...")
        currentSpeed = 50
    }
```

```kotlin
    override fun stop() {
        println("Stopped")
        currentSpeed = 0
    }

    override fun takeOff() {
        println("Taking off...")
        currentSpeed = 500
        currentHeight = 5000
    }

    override fun land() {
        println("Landed")
        currentSpeed = 50
        currentHeight = 0
    }
}
```

Note an absence of **()** after the supertype name in the definitions of all three types. This is explained by the fact that, unlike classes, interfaces have no constructors and thus no code to call upon the subclass initialization.

Java vs Kotlin: Note that in Kotlin, all possible cases of inheritance (class from class, interface from interface, and class from interface) are denoted by the same symbol (:) as opposed to Java which requires you to use the **implements** keyword when the class inherits from an interface and **extends** in all other cases.

Similarly to Java, Kotlin interfaces are not allowed to inherit from classes. The Any class can be considered an exception of sort since it's implicitly inherited by each Kotlin class and interface.

Interface functions and properties may also have implementations:

```kotlin
interface Vehicle {
    val currentSpeed: Int
    val isMoving get() = currentSpeed != 0
```

```kotlin
    fun move()

    fun stop()


    fun report() {
        println(if (isMoving) "Moving at $currentSpeed" else "Still")
    }
}
```

These implementations are considered implicitly **open** and thus can be overridden by inheritors. Marking interface member as **final** is a compilation error:

```kotlin
interface Vehicle {
    final fun move() {} // Error
}
```

You may, however, use extension functions and properties as an alternative to final members:

```kotlin
fun Vehicle.relativeSpeed(vehicle: Vehicle) =
    currentSpeed - vehicle.currentSpeed
```

Similarly to classes, interface methods can be overridden by inheriting interfaces:

```kotlin
interface Vehicle {
    fun move() {
        println("I'm moving")
    }
}


interface Car : Vehicle {
    override fun move() {
        println("I'm riding")
    }
}
```

IDE Tips: The "Override Members" and "Implement Members" actions we discussed in the previous sections are also available inside interface bodies.

Since interfaces are not allowed to define the state, they can't contain properties with backing fields. In particular, properties with initializers and delegates are forbidden:

```kotlin
interface Vehicle {
    val currentSpeed = 0        // Error
    val maxSpeed by lazy { 100 } // Error
}
```

The interface itself is also implicitly abstract. Unlike abstract classes, however, interfaces are forbidden to define any constructors:

```kotlin
interface Person(val name: String) // Error


interface Vehicle {
    constructor(name: String)      // Error
}
```

Just like in Java, Kotlin interfaces support multiple inheritances. Let's consider an example:

```kotlin
interface Car {
    fun ride()
}


interface Aircraft {
    fun fly()
}


interface Ship {
    fun sail()
}


interface FlyingCar : Car, Aircraft


class Transformer : FlyingCar, Ship {
    override fun ride() {
        println("I'm riding")
    }
}
```

```
    override fun fly() {
        println("I'm flying")
    }

    override fun sail() {
        println("I'm sailing")
    }
}
```

Both the **FlyingCar** interface and **Transformer** class inherit from more than one interface at once, thus getting all their members. In the case of the non-abstract **Transformer** class, we also have to implement all inherited members.

An interesting issue arises when a single type inherits from more than one different interface which has members with the same signatures. In this case, they are effectively merged into a single member which is then inherited by a subtype. Suppose that our **Car** and **Ship** interfaces do not have a common supertype other than Any:

```
interface Car {
    fun move()
}

interface Ship {
    fun move()
}

class Amphibia : Car, Ship {
    override fun move() {
        println("I'm moving")
    }
}
```

In the preceding code, both variants of the **move()** method are abstract, so we have to implement it in the non-abstract **Amphibia** class. However, even if some of them do have implementations, the compiler will still force us to provide an explicit implementation to resolve a possible ambiguity:

```kotlin
interface Car {
    fun move() {
        println("I'm riding")
    }
}


interface Ship {
    fun move()
}


class Amphibia : Car, Ship {
    override fun move() {
        super.move() // Calling inherited implementation from Car
    }
}


fun main() {
    Amphibia().move() // I'm riding
}
```

When more than one supertype provides an implementation of such a "merged" member, the super-call itself becomes ambiguous. In this case, you may have an extended form of super qualified with a supertype name:

```kotlin
interface Car {
    fun move() {
        println("I'm riding")
    }
}


interface Ship {
    fun move() {
        println("I'm sailing")
    }
}
```

```
}

class Amphibia : Car, Ship {
    override fun move() {
        super<Car>.move()
                // Call inherited implementation in Car interface
        super<Ship>.move()
                // Call inherited implementation in Ship interface
    }
}

fun main() {
    /*
       I'm riding
       I'm sailing
    */
    Amphibia().move()
}
```

Java vs Kotlin: Java 8 uses the qualified form of **super** for the same purpose: **Ship. super.move()**.

Since version 1.1, the Kotlin compiler can generate non-abstract interface members in the form of Java 8 default methods. In *Chapter 12, Java Interoperability*, we'll discuss such interoperability issues in more detail.

The limitations concerning the use of state and constructors in interfaces are in fact explained by their support of multiple inheritances. The primary goal was to avoid the infamous "diamond inheritance problem". Consider the following classes:

```
interface Vehicle {
    val currentSpeed: Int
}

interface Car : Vehicle

interface Ship : Vehicle
```

```kotlin
class Amphibia : Car, Ship {
    override var currentSpeed = 0
        private set
}
```

If an instance state was allowed, the **Vehicle** interface may define **currentSpeed** as a state variable. As a result, the **Amphibia** class would inherit *two* copies of **currentSpeed**: one from the **Car** and another from Ship (both of which would inherit it from **Vehicle**). The Kotlin design prevents the problem at the expense of disallowing state in interfaces. A restriction on the constructor definition is related to the importance of having a predictable initialization order of program state. Allowing them for interfaces would require you to extend initialization order rules (see the "Subclass Initialization" section) to cover multiple inheritance which can become quite cumbersome to follow, especially if some interfaces occur more than once in the supertype graph (like **Vehicle** in the preceding example).

Sealed classes

Sometimes, the concepts we want to represent in a program may come in a fixed set of variants. In *Chapter 6, Using Special-Case Classes,* we introduced an idea of the **enum** class which allows you to represent a predetermined set of constants with the same common type. For example, we can use it to represent a result of some computation as being either success or error:

```kotlin
enum class Result {
    SUCCESS, ERROR
}


fun runComputation(): Result {
    try {
        val a = readLine()?.toInt() ?: return Result.ERROR
        val b = readLine()?.toInt() ?: return Result.ERROR
        println("Sum: ${a + b}")
        return Result.SUCCESS
    } catch (e: NumberFormatException) {
        return Result.ERROR
```

```
        }
}


fun main() {
    val message = when (runComputation()) {
        Result.SUCCESS -> "Completed successfully"
        Result.ERROR -> "Error!"
    }
    println(message)
}
```

In some cases, however, different variants may have their own attributes. For example, a state of successful completion may be accompanied by a produced result, while a state of error may carry some information about its cause. Similar to examples we've already discussed in this chapter such concepts can be modeled with a class hierarchy where the root abstract class expresses the concept in general and its subclasses serve as representations of particular variants. Let's refine our example and add some members to Success and Error cases:

```
abstract class Result {
    class Success(val value: Any) : Result() {
        fun showResult() {
            println(value)
        }
    }


    class Error(val message: String) : Result() {
        fun throwException() {
            throw Exception(message)
        }
    }
}


fun runComputation(): Result {
    try {
```

```
        val a = readLine()?.toInt()
            ?: return Result.Error("Missing first argument")
        val b = readLine()?.toInt()
            ?: return Result.Error("Missing second argument")
        return Result.Success(a + b)
    } catch (e: NumberFormatException) {
        return Result.Error(e.message ?: "Invalid input")
    }
}


fun main() {
    val message = when (val result = runComputation()) {
        is Result.Success -> "Completed successfully: ${result.value}"
        is Result.Error -> "Error: ${result.message}"
        else -> return
    }
    println(message)
}
```

But this implementation is not flawless. It doesn't allow you to express the fact that the set of **Result** variants is restricted to **Success** and **Error**. In particular, nothing prevents some client code from adding a new subclass, say:

```
class MyStatus: Result()
```

It's also the reason why we have to add the **else** clause to the **when** expression. The compiler can't ensure that the result variable will always hold an instance of either Success, or **Error** and forces us to deal with remaining cases as well.

In Kotlin, this problem can be overcome courtesy of sealed classes. Let's change our class definition by adding the **sealed** modifier:

```
sealed class Result {
    class Success(val value: Any) : Result() {...}

    class Error(val message: String) : Result() {...}
}
```

When the class is marked as sealed, its inheritors may be declared in either its body as nested classes and objects, or as top-level classes in the same file (the latter option was introduced in Kotlin 1.1). Outside these scopes, the sealed class is effectively final and can't be inherited from.

The latter rule will be partially relaxed in Kotlin 1.5 where sealed class inheritors may be put into different files provided they all share the same package as shown in *Figure 8.8*:

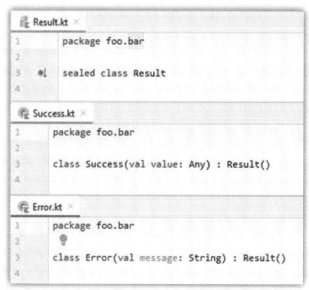

Figure 8.8: *Placing sealed class hierarchy in multiple files (Kotlin 1.5 only)*

Note that the sealed class is also abstract, so you can't create its instance directly. The idea is that any instance of a sealed class must be created through one of its subclasses:

```
val result = Result() // Error: can't instantiate an abstract class
```

In fact, sealed class constructors are **private** by default, and declaring them with some other visibility modifier is considered a compile-time error

Similar to enums, sealed classes support the exhaustive form of the **when** expression that allows us to avoid redundant **else** branches:

```
val message = when (val result = runComputation()) {
    is Result.Success -> "Completed successfully: ${result.value}"
    is Result.Error -> "Error: ${result.message}"
}
```

Note that inheritance restriction only covers direct subclasses of a sealed class. The subclasses itself may have their own inheritors provided they are not final:

```
// Result.kt
sealed class Result {
    class Success(val value: Any) : Result()


    open class Error(val message: String) : Result()
}
```

```
// util.kt
class FatalError(message: String): Result.Error(message)
```

Since Kotlin 1.1, sealed classes may extend other classes as well. This, in particular, allows them classes to have subclasses which are also sealed:

```
sealed class Result


class Success(val value: Any) : Result()


sealed class Error : Result() {
    abstract val message: String
}


class ErrorWithException(val exception: Exception): Error() {
    override val message: String get() = exception.message ?: ""
}


class ErrorWithMessage(override val message: String): Error()
```

Thanks to the data class inheritance also introduced in 1.1, it's possible to use data classes as parts of sealed class hierarchy. This allows us to combine advantages given by both data and sealed classes. Consider, for example, classes which represent the syntactic tree of simple arithmetic expressions:

```
sealed class Expr


data class Const(val num: Int): Expr()
```

```kotlin
data class Neg(val operand: Expr): Expr()
data class Plus(val op1: Expr, val op2: Expr): Expr()
data class Mul(val op1: Expr, val op2: Expr): Expr()

fun Expr.eval(): Int = when (this) {
    is Const -> num
    is Neg -> -operand.eval()
    is Plus -> op1.eval() + op2.eval()
    is Mul -> op1.eval() * op2.eval()
}

fun main() {
    // (1 + 2) * 3
    val expr = Mul(Plus(Const(1), Const(2)), Const(3))
        //   Mul(op1=Plus(op1=Const(num=1),   op2=Const(num=2)),
op2=Const(num=3))
    println(expr)
    println(expr.eval()) // 9
    // 2 * 3
    val expr2 = expr.copy(op1 = Const(2))
    // Mul(op1=Const(num=2), op2=Const(num=3))
    println(expr2)
    println(expr2.eval()) // 6
}
```

Note that the **sealed** modifier can't be applied to interfaces in Kotlin 1.4 and prior versions. As a result, subclasses comprising a sealed hierarchy can't inherit from some other class since multiple class inheritance is forbidden in Kotlin.

The situation is going to change after the release of Kotlin 1.5 which, among other things, adds support of sealed interfaces. From the developer's point of view, sealed interfaces work similar to their class counterparts and effectively give you the ability to apply sealed hierarchies in those cases when using classes that are not appropriate; for example, if multiple inheritance is needed.

To demonstrate this improvement, let's rewrite our expression types with the interface as a root type:

```
sealed interface Expr
```

```
data class Const(val num: Int): Expr
data class Neg(val operand: Expr): Expr
data class Plus(val op1: Expr, val op2: Expr): Expr
data class Mul(val op1: Expr, val op2: Expr): Expr
```

Just like with sealed classes such a hierarchy supports exhaustiveness checks in **when** expressions.

Java vs Kotlin: Java 15 has introduced an experimental feature of sealed classes/ interfaces which is expected to reach a stable state in the upcoming Java 16 release. The key difference from a similar Kotlin concept is that sealed classes/interfaces in Java must explicitly list the allowed direct inheritors in the hierarchy root declarations (unless those inheritors are defined in the same compilation unit) as well as a requirement to explicitly mark direct inheritors as either final, sealed, or non-sealed.

Note that exhaustiveness checks similar to the ones supported by Kotlin **when** expressions is not implemented yet and is planned for a later version of JDK.

A **sealed** class implementation may also be an object. Suppose we want to refine our Result example to distinguish successful state without the produced value:

```
sealed class Result {
    object Completed : Result()
    class ValueProduced(val value: Any) : Result()
    class Error(val message: String) : Result()
}
```

When all direct inheritors are objects, a sealed class effectively behaves like an **enum**.

IDE Tips: If you want to refactor an **enum** class into a sealed one, the IntelliJ plugin can give a good starting point thanks to the corresponding intention action available via *Alt + Enter* menu (see *Figure 8.9*). As a result **enum** constants are converted into singletons implementing an abstract sealed class.

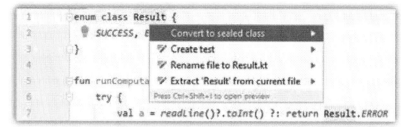

Figure 8.9: *Converting enum class to sealed class hierarchy*

On top of it, IntelliJ supports a reverse transformation. If all direct inheritors of a sealed class are represented by object declarations, you can turn it into a sealed class replacing its implementations by **enum** constants (as shown in *Figure 8.10*):

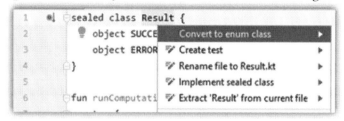

Figure 8.10: *Converting sealed class to enum*

Delegation

In the preceding section, we saw that Kotlin classes are final by default. The goal is to encourage the though-out design of inheritable classes and prevent accidental inheritance from classes which are not supposed to have subclasses. This helps to mitigate the "fragile base class" problem we discussed earlier.

What if still need to extend or change behavior of some existing class but can't inherit from it? In this case, we can use the well-known delegation pattern which allows us to reuse the existing classes. If we want to create an implementation of some interface, we can take an instance of the existing implementation, wrap it inside an instance of our class, and delegate our methods to it when necessary.

Let's consider an example. Suppose we have the following types:

```
interface PersonData {
    val name: String
    val age: Int
}
```

```kotlin
open class Person(
    override val name: String,
    override val age: Int
): PersonData


data class Book(val title: String, val author: PersonData) {
    override fun toString() = "'$title' by ${author.name}"
}


fun main() {
    val valWatts = Person("Val Watts", 30)
    val introKotlin = Book("Introduction to Kotlin", valWatts)
    println(introKotlin) // 'Introduction to Kotlin' by Val Watts
}
```

Suppose that we want writers to have pen names allowing them to pose as another person.

```kotlin
class Alias(
    private val realIdentity: PersonData,
    private val newIdentity: PersonData
) : PersonData {
    override val name: String
        get() = newIdentity.name
    override val age: Int
        get() = newIdentity.age
}
```

We now can use this class to create person aliases:

```kotlin
fun main() {
    val valWatts = Person("Val Watts", 30)
    val johnDoe = Alias(valWatts, Person("John Doe", 25))
    val introJava = Book("Introduction to Java", johnDoe)
    println(introJava) // 'Introduction to Java' by John Doe
}
```

The problem of such an approach is the amount of boilerplate code you have to generate to delegate all necessary methods and properties to another object. Luckily for us Kotlin has a built-in support for delegates. All you have to do is specify a delegate instance after the by keyword following a superinterface name:

```kotlin
class Alias(
    private val realIdentity: PersonData,
    private val newIdentity: PersonData
) : PersonData by newIdentity
```

Now, all members the Alias inherits from the **PersonData** interface are implemented by delegating to corresponding calls on the **newIdentity** instance. We may also override some of them to change the implementation behavior:

```kotlin
class Alias(
    private val realIdentity: PersonData,
    private val newIdentity: PersonData
) : PersonData by newIdentity {
    override val age: Int get() = realIdentity.age
}


fun main() {
    val valWatts = Person("Val Watts", 30)
    val johnDoe = Alias(valWatts, Person("John Doe", 25))
    println(johnDoe.age) // 30
}
```

In general, the delegate expression can be anything you can use in the class initialization. When necessary, the compiler automatically creates a field to store the delegate value. So we can, for example, drop **val** on **newIdentity** making it a simple parameter:

```kotlin
class Alias(
    private val realIdentity: PersonData,
    newIdentity: PersonData
) : PersonData by newIdentity
```

But we can't delegate it to a property defined in the class body:

```kotlin
class Alias(

    private val realIdentity: PersonData

): PersonData by newIdentity { // Error: newIdentity is not available here

    val newIdentity = Person("John Doe", 30)

}
```

Combining the delegation with object expressions can be useful to create an implementation with slightly different behavior than the original object:

```kotlin
fun PersonData.aliased(newIdentity: PersonData) =
    object : PersonData by newIdentity {
        override val age: Int get() = this@aliased.age
    }
```

```kotlin
fun main() {
    val valWatts = Person("Val Watts", 30)
    val johnDoe = valWatts.aliased(Person("John Doe", 25))
    println("${johnDoe.name}, ${johnDoe.age}") // John Doe, 30
}
```

Note that a class may only delegate an implementation of *interface* members. The following code, for example, produces an error since Person is a *class*:

```kotlin
class Alias(
    private val realIdentity: PersonData,
    private val newIdentity: PersonData
) : Person by newIdentity // Error: only interfaces can be delegated to
```

The bottom line is as follows: class delegation allows you to combine advantages of composition and inheritance with minimal boilerplate, thus encouraging you to follow the well-known "composition over inheritance" principle.

Conclusion

In this chapter, we got an insight into the powerful inheritance mechanism of the Kotlin type system. We discussed how to define subclasses, how class initialization fits into the picture of class hierarchy, and learned how to use member overriding for changing the base class behavior in subclasses. We also learned to employ tools aimed at representation of abstract concepts such as abstract classes and interfaces. Finally, we explored features implementing two useful inheritance-related patterns, namely, sealed classes and delegation.

In the next chapter, we'll focus on the topic of generics, a special feature of the Kotlin type system giving you the ability to parameterize your declarations with unknown types which are provided later at the use site.

Points to remember

1. Kotlin classes and class members are final by default. In order to make them open/overridable, you need to explicitly declare them as such.

2. Checking the variable type with the **is** operation automatically refines its compile-time type in the respective scope, thus avoiding the need of manual type casting.

3. Explicit type casting has a safe form (**as?**) which returns **null** when cast fails rather than throwing an exception.

4. Sealed classes have predetermined set of direct inheritors.

5. Delegation allows you to implement some interface by automatically redirecting its member calls to a given object.

Multiple choice questions

1. Choose all valid statements regarding interfaces.

   A. They may inherit multiple interfaces.

   B. They may inherit multiple classes.

   C. They are not allowed to have constructors except the primary one.

   D. They are allowed to contain non-abstract members.

2. Choose all valid statements regarding abstract classes.

   A. They can be implemented using **by**-delegation.

   B. They may inherit multiple interfaces.

   C. They are final by default.

   D. They may inherit multiple classes.

3. Choose valid places where direct inheritors of a sealed class can be declared as of Kotlin 1.5.

   A. Inside a sealed class body

   B. In the same file as the sealed class

C. In the same package as the sealed class

D. Anywhere

4. What method is responsible for structural equality (==/!=)?

A. `isEqual()`

B. `equals()`

C. `==()`

D. `eq()`

5. Given that the following class definition is valid what statements are guaranteed to be true about `Super`?

```
class MyClass : Super {
    constructor(): super(123)
}
```

A. `Super` is an interface

B. `Super` has a non-default constructor

C. `Super` is abstract

D. `Super` is not final

Answers

1. A, D
2. B, D
3. A, B, C
4. B
5. B, D

Questions

1. How to define a subclass in Kotlin? What conditions must a class satisfy in order to be inheritable?

2. Point out the major differences between class inheritance in Java and Kotlin.

3. How the class instance is initialized when its class is an inheritor? How the superclass initialization is enforced in Java? Compare both approaches.

4. Describe the purpose of `is`/`as`/`as?` operators. How can they be compared to Java type checks and casts?

5. Name the common methods defined in the Any class. Describe basic guidelines for their implementations.

6. What is an abstract class and an abstract class member? What rules govern abstract class/member implementations?

7. What are the differences between abstract classes and interfaces? Compare interfaces in Kotlin and Java.

8. What are the specifics of interface inheritance? Describe differences between member overriding for classes and interfaces.

9. What is a sealed class hierarchy? How would you implement such hierarchy in Java?

10. Describe how class delegation works in Kotlin.

CHAPTER 9
Generics

In this chapter, we will discuss generics, a powerful feature of the Kotlin type system that allows you to write a code which manipulates data of some unknown types. We'll see how to define and use generics declarations, address issues of type erasure and reification concerned with generics representation at runtime, and focus on an important concept of variance which can help you with improving flexibility of generics by means of extending a subtyping relation to different substitutions of the same generic type. We will also highlight a related topic, that is, a concept of type alias which will allow you to introduce alternative names for existing types.

Structure

- Type parameters
- Variance
- Type aliases

Objective

After reading this chapter, you will learn the basics of generic declarations in Kotlin and their difference from Java as well as get an understanding of how to use reified type parameters and variance to design more flexible generic APIs.

Type parameters

In the preceding chapters, we've already seen quite a few examples of using generic types such as arrays and various collection classes as well as generic functions and properties like **map()**, **filter()**, **sorted()**, and so on. In this section, we will discuss how you can generify your own code to improve its flexibility and make use of more advanced features of the Kotlin type system.

Generic declarations

In order to make a declaration generic, we need to add one or more *type parameters* to it. Such parameters can then be used inside the declaration in place of ordinary types. When declaration is used; for example, when we construct an instance of a class or call a function, we need to supply actual types instead of type parameters:

```
val map = HashMap<Int, String>()
val list = arrayListOf<String>()
```

Sometimes, these *type arguments* can be omitted since the compiler can infer them from context:

```
// use explicit type to infer type arguments of HashMap class
val map: Map<Int, String> = HashMap()
// use argument types of arrayListOf() call to infer its type arguments
val list = arrayListOf("abc", "def")
```

Java vs. Kotlin: Mind the difference between passing type arguments to generic functions in Kotlin vs generic methods in Java. While Java requires angle brackets to be put right after the dot, like in **Collections.<String>emptyList()**, in Kotlin such arguments are passed after the function name **emptyList<String>**. When calling a class constructor, though, the syntax is similar; **new ArrayList<String>()** in Java vs **ArrayList<String>()** in Kotlin.

Also note that Java supports automatic inference of type arguments when calling a class constructor, but unlike Kotlin uses a so-called *diamond operator*:

```
Map<Int, String> map = new HashMap<>() // not new HashMap() !!!
```

The reason is a necessity to maintain a backward compatibility with the older code written before generics were added in Java 5.

Let's see how to create generic declarations of our own. Suppose we want to define a class representing a tree which can store values of a given type:

```kotlin
class TreeNode<T>(val data: T) {
    private val _children = arrayListOf<TreeNode<T>>()

    var parent: TreeNode<T>? = null
        private set

    val children: List<TreeNode<T>> get() = _children

    fun addChild(data: T) = TreeNode(data).also {
        _children += it
        it.parent = this
    }

    override fun toString() =
        _children.joinToString(prefix = "$data {", postfix = "}")
}

fun main() {
    val root = TreeNode("Hello").apply {
        addChild("World")
        addChild("!!!")
    }
    println(root) // Hello {World {}, !!! {}}
}
```

Type parameters of a class are written inside angle brackets which are put right after the class name. Type parameters may have arbitrary names, but the conventional code style is to use capital letters like **T, U, V,** and so on. Inside a class type, parameters can be used to define types of variables, properties, or functions or as argument types for other generic declarations.

Java vs Kotlin: When a generic class or an interface is used to specify a data type, it must be accompanied by corresponding type arguments. Unlike Java, you can't have a variable of type TreeNode. You need to specify a type argument for **T**, like **TreeNode<String>** or **TreeNode<U>** where **U** is some other type parameter.

When you call a generic class constructor, explicit type arguments are often unnecessary since in many cases, the compiler can infer them from the context. That's why we do not need to specify **<String>** in **TreeNode("Hello")** call above. An important exception is the delegation call to the super class constructor. Let's change our example a bit:

```
open class DataHolder<T>(val data: T)
                     // Passing actual type as supertype argument
class StringDataHolder(data: String) : DataHolder<String>(data)
                     // Passing type parameter as supertype argument
class TreeNode<T>(data: T) : DataHolder<T>(data) { ... }
```

Unlike the ordinary constructor call, a compiler does not infer type arguments in delegation calls, so you always have to provide them explicitly. Compare the two cases:

```
// Error: need to explicitly specify DataHolder<String>
class StringDataHolder(data: String) : DataHolder(data)
// Ok: DataHolder<String> is inferred automatically
fun stringDataHolder(data: String) = DataHolder(data)
```

Note that type parameters are not inherited. You pass them to supertype similarly to constructor parameters, so **T** in **TreeNode** and **T** in **DataHolder** are separate declarations. In fact, we could've used different names for them:

```
class TreeNode<U>(data: U) : DataHolder<U>(data) { ... }
```

Functions and properties defined in generic classes may access their type parameters as demonstrated by the preceding **addChild()** and **children** definitions. Additionally, you can make a property or a function generic by adding type parameters of its own:

```
fun <T> TreeNode<T>.addChildren(vararg data: T) {
    data.forEach { addChild(it) }
}


fun <T> TreeNode<T>.walkDepthFirst(action: (T) -> Unit) {
    children.forEach { it.walkDepthFirst(action) }
    action(data)
}
```

```kotlin
val <T> TreeNode<T>.depth: Int
    get() = (children.asSequence().map { it.depth }.maxOrNull() ?: 0) + 1


fun main() {
    val root = TreeNode("Hello").apply {
        addChildren("World", "!!!")
    }
    println(root.depth) // 2

}
```

Note that the type parameter list is placed after the **fun** keyword rather than the declaration name as opposed to a generic class. Similar to generic class constructors, you may omit the explicit type argument in generic function calls when they can be inferred from the context. IntelliJ IDEA provides a quickfix action to drop redundant type parameters as shown on Figure 9.1:

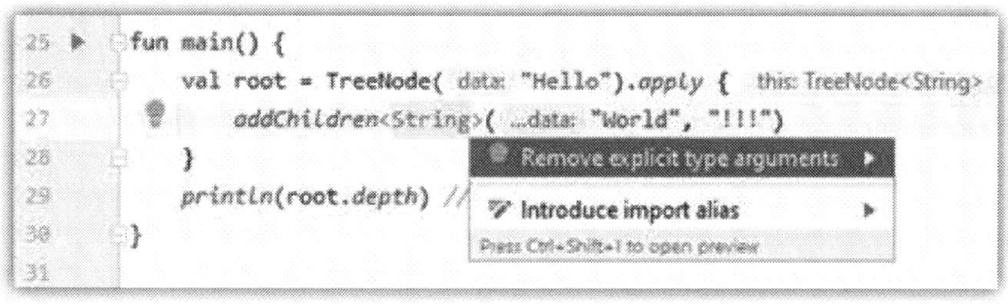

Figure 9.1: Redundant type arguments

Only extension properties may have their own type parameters. The reason is that the non-extension property effectively represents a single value. Therefore, it can't be used to read/write values of different types depending on supplied type arguments:

```kotlin
var <T> root: TreeNode<T>? = null // Error: T must be used in receiver type
```

For the same reason, it's not forbidden to add type parameters to object declarations:

```kotlin
object EmptyTree<T> // Error: type parameters are not allowed for objects
```

Property references do not support type arguments so for generic properties they are always inferred using the receiver type. For that reason, declaring the generic property with type parameters which are not actually used in its receiver is a compile-time error:

```kotlin
// Error: explicit type arguments are forbidden here
val minDepth = TreeNode("").depth<String>
```

```
// Error: T is not used in receiver type
val <T> TreeNode<String>.upperCaseData get() = data.toUpperCase()
```

Bounds and constraints

By default, type parameters do not impose any restrictions on their values and behave as if they are synonymous to **Any?** type. Sometimes, though, implementation of the generic class, function, or property requires some additional information about the data they manipulate. Expanding our **TreeNode** example; suppose that we want to define a function which computes an average value among all tree nodes. Such an operation is applicable to numeric trees so we want the type element to be a subtype of **Number**. In order to do this, we declare a type parameter with **Number** as *upper bound*:

```
fun <T : Number> TreeNode<T>.average(): Double {
    var count = 0
    var sum = 0.0
    walkDepthFirst {
        count++
        sum += it.toDouble()
    }
    return sum/count
}
```

When the type parameter has an upper bound, the compiler will check whether corresponding type arguments are subtypes of that bound. By default, the upper bound is assumed to be **Any?** so if you don't specify it explicitly, a type parameter may accept any Kotlin type. The following calls are valid since Int and Double are subtypes of **Number**:

```
val intTree = TreeNode(1).apply {
    addChild(2).addChild(3)
    addChild(4).addChild(5)
}
println(intTree.average()) // 3.0

val doubleTree = TreeNode(1.0).apply {
    addChild(2.0)
```

```
    addChild(3.0)
}
println(doubleTree.average()) // 2.0
```

Calling **average()** on tree of strings, however, produces a compilation error:

```
val stringTree = TreeNode("Hello").apply {
    addChildren("World", "!!!")
}
println(stringTree.average()) // Error: String is not subtype of Number
```

Note that using the final class as an upper bound is meaningless since there are no other types which can be substituted for such type parameter. In this case, the compiler reports a warning:

```
// Can be replaced by a non-generic function
// fun TreeNode<Int>.sum(): Int {...}
fun <T : Int> TreeNode<T>.sum(): Int { // Warning
    var sum = 0
    walkDepthFirst { sum += it }
    return sum
}
```

A type parameter bound may refer the type parameter itself in which case it's called recursive. For example, if our tree contains instances of a comparable interface, we may find a node with the maximum value:

```
fun <T : Comparable<T>> TreeNode<T>.maxNode(): TreeNode<T> {
    val maxChild = children.maxByOrNull { it.data } ?: return this
    return if (data >= maxChild.data) this else maxChild
}


fun main() {
    // Double is subtype of Comparable<Double>
    val doubleTree = TreeNode(1.0).apply {
        addChild(2.0)
        addChild(3.0)
    }
```

```
println(doubleTree.maxNode().data) // 3.0


// String is subtype of Comparable<String>
val stringTree = TreeNode("abc").apply {
    addChildren("xyz", "def")
}
println(stringTree.maxNode().data) // xyz
```
}

Bounds can also refer to preceding type parameters. We can make use of that fact to write a function which appends tree elements to a mutable list:

```
fun <T, U : T> TreeNode<U>.toList(list: MutableList<T>) {
    walkDepthFirst { list += it }
}
```

Since **U** is a subtype of **T,** the preceding function may accept lists of more general elements. For example, we can append trees of **Int** and **Double** to a list of **Number** (which is their common supertype):

```
fun main() {
    val list = ArrayList<Number>()
    TreeNode(1).apply {
        addChild(2)
        addChild(3)
    }.toList(list)
    TreeNode(1.0).apply {
        addChild(2.0)
        addChild(3.0)
    }.toList(list)
}
```

Java vs Kotlin: The upper bounds of Kotlin type parameters are quite similar to their Java counterparts; the major difference being the syntax: T extends Number in Java vs. **T** : **Number** in Kotlin.

A particularly common case is constraining the type parameter to be not null. To do this, we need to use the non-nullable type as its upper bound:

```
fun <T: Any> notNullTreeOf(data: T) = TreeNode(data)
```

The type parameter syntax allows you to specify only one upper bound. In some cases, though, we may need to impose multiple restrictions on a single type parameter. This can be achieved by using a slightly more elaborate syntax of *type constraint*. Suppose that we have a pair of interfaces:

```
interface Named {
    val name: String
}


interface Identified {
    val id: Int
}
```

And we want to define a registry of objects which have both a name and an identifier:

```
class Registry<T> where T : Named, T : Identified {
    val items = ArrayList<T>()
}
```

The **where** clause is added before the declaration body and lists type parameters with their bounds.

Now that we've got a taste of the generics syntax, we can move to the next topic which deals with generics representation at runtime.

Type erasure and reification

In the preceding examples, we've seen that type parameters can be used to specify types of variables, properties, and functions inside generic declarations. There are cases, however, when type parameters can't replace actual types. Consider, for example, the following code:

```
fun <T> TreeNode<Any>.isInstanceOf(): Boolean =
    data is T && children.all { it.isInstanceOf<T>() } // Error
```

The intention is to write a function which checks whether the given tree node and all its children conform to the specific type **T**. The compiler, however, reports an error on data **is** **T** expression, and the reason is so-called *type erasure*.

The readers familiar with Java will probably recognize similar limitation of Java generics. It comes from the fact that generics only appeared in Java 5, so newer versions of the compiler and virtual machine had to maintain the existing representation of types for the purpose of backward compatibility with the older code. As a result, the JVM information about type arguments is effectively erased from code (thus the *type erasure* term), and types like **List<String>** or **List<Number>** merge into the same type **List**.

In Kotlin, generics are available from the version 1.0 but due to JVM being its major platform, it suffers from the same type erasure problem. At runtime, the generic code can't distinguish between different versions of its parameter types, so checks like **data is T** above basically makes no sense: The **isInstance()** function just has no way to know what **T** means when it's called. For the same reason, it's meaningless to use the is operator for the generic type with arguments; although in this case, the compiler will report either an error, or a warning depending on whether type arguments correspond to type parameters:

```
val list = listOf(1, 2, 3) // List<Int>

list is List<Number> // Warning: List<Int> is a subtype of List<Number>

list is List<String> // Error: List<Int> is not a subtype of List<String>
```

What if we need to just check that our value is a list without clarifying its element type? We can't just write list is **List** because generic types in Kotlin must always be accompanied by type arguments. A correct check looks like this:

```
list is List<*>

map is Map<*, *>
```

where ***** basically means some unknown type and replaces a single type argument. This syntax is in fact a special case of so-called *projections* which we'll discuss a bit later.

In some cases, though, the compiler has enough information to ensure that type check is valid and doesn't report warnings/errors. In following example, the check basically is concerned about the relationship between **List** and **Collection** interfaces rather than their particular types such as **List<Int>** and **Collection<Int>**:

```
val collection: Collection<Int> = setOf(1, 2, 3)

if (collection is List<Int>) {

    println("list")

}
```

Note that casts to generic types with non-* arguments are permitted but always produce a warning since their behavior involves a certain risk. While they allow you to work around limitations of generics, they also may defer the actual type error till runtime. For example, both the following expressions are compiled with warning, but the first completes normally, while the second one throws an exception:

```
val n = (listOf(1, 2, 3) as List<Number>)[0] // OK

val s = (listOf(1, 2, 3) as List<String>)[0] // Exception
```

The exception in the latter case happens only when the value of a list element (which has type Int) is assigned to the variable of (statically known) type String.

In Java, you mostly have to rely on casts or use reflection to work around type erasure. Both approaches have their drawbacks since casts may mask a problem and leaf to error afterwards, while using the reflection API may impact performance. Kotlin, however, offers you a third option which doesn't suffer from neither of these weaknesses.

Reification means that the type parameter information is retained at runtime. How a compiler does circumvent type erasure? The answer is that reified type parameters are only available for inline functions. Since the function body is inlined at the call site where type arguments are provided, the compiler always knows which actual type corresponds to type parameters in a particular inlined call.

To make the parameter reified, we need to mark it with a corresponding keyword. Let's use this feature to fix our **isInstanceOf()** function. Since inline functions can't be recursive, we'll have to rewrite its implementation to some extent:

```
fun <T> TreeNode<T>.cancellableWalkDepthFirst(
    onEach: (T) -> Boolean
): Boolean {
    val nodes = Stack<TreeNode<T>>()
    nodes.push(this)
    while (nodes.isNotEmpty()) {
        val node = nodes.pop()
        if (!onEach(node.data)) return false
        node.children.forEach { nodes.push(it) }
    }
    return true
}


inline fun <reified T> TreeNode<*>.isInstanceOf() =
    cancellableWalkDepthFirst { it is T }
```

In the preceding code, we've extracted the actual tree traversal logic into a separate non-inline function **cancellableWalkDepthFirst()** to prevent inlining of the loop itself. Now, when we call this function, say, in the following way:

```
fun main() {
    val tree = TreeNode<Any>("abc").addChild("def").addChild(123)
    println(tree.isInstanceOf<String>())
}
```

The compiler will inline **isInstanceOf()** substituting the actual type **String** instead of **T**, and the code that gets executed will look like this:

```
fun main() {
    val tree = TreeNode<Any>("abc").addChild("def").addChild(123)
    println(tree.cancellableWalkDepthFirst { it is String })
}
```

As opposed to approaches used in Java, reified type parameters give you both safe (no unchecked casts) and fast (thanks to inlining) solution. Note, however, that using the inline function tends to increase the size of the compiled code, but this issue can be mitigated by extracting heavy portions of code into separate non-inline functions (like we did with **cancellableWalkDepthFirst()**). Also since reified type parameters are only supported for inline functions, you can't use them with classes or properties.

Reified type parameters still have their own limitations which distinguish them from full-fledged types. In particular, it's currently not possible to call the constructor or access companion members via reified type parameters:

```
inline fun <reified T> factory() = T() // Error
```

Also, you can't substitute the non-reified type parameter instead of a reified one:

```
fun <T, U> TreeNode<*>.isInstanceOfBoth() =
    isInstanceOf<T>() && isInstanceOf<U>()
```

The reason is type erasure again. Since we can't know actual types substituted for **T** and **U** in **isInstanceOfBoth()**, we have to make way to safely inline either of **isInstanceOf()** calls.

This concludes our basic discussion of Kotlin generics. Now, we'll move to a more advanced topic of variance which allows you to improve flexibility of generics by controlling the producer/consumer aspects of type behavior.

Variance

Variance is an aspect of the generic type which describes how its particular substitutions are related to each other in terms of subtyping. In the previous chapters, we've already seen examples of generic types with different variance. Arrays and mutable collections, for example, do not preserve subtyping of their arguments. Even though, **String** is a subtype of **Any, Array<String>** is not considered a subtype of **Array<Any>** (neither **Array<Any>** is considered a subtype of **Array<String>**). Immutable collections, like **List** or **Set**, on the other hand, do preserve subtyping, so **List<String>** is a subtype of **List<Any>**:

```
val objects: List<Any> = listOf("a", "b", "c") // Correct
```

Reasonable use of variance may improve flexibility of your API without having to trade off its type safety. In the following sections, we'll discuss the meaning of variance and how it's used with Kotlin generics.

Variance: Distinguishing producers and consumers

Generics classes and interfaces can give rise to an unlimited set of types produced by substituting different type arguments instead of their type parameters. By default, all substitutions of a particular type are not considered subtypes of each other regardless of relationships between their arguments. In this case, we say that the generic type is *invariant* (relative to some of its type parameters). For example, the built-in **Array** class, mutable collection classes as well as our **TreeNode** class are all invariant. The following example shows that **TreeNode<String>** is not considered a subtype of **TreeNode<Any>**:

```
val node: TreeNode<Any> = TreeNode<String>("Hello") // Error
```

Some types, like immutable collections, on the other hand preserve subtyping of their arguments. In the following section, we'll discuss language features which allow you to control how subtyping affects your own generic classes, but first we need to understand why some generic classes can preserve inheritance while others cannot.

The distinction is based on the way a type handles the values of its type parameter (say, T). All generic types may be divided into three categories:

1. *Producers* which have only operations which return values of T but never take them as input.

2. *Consumers* whose operations only take values of T as input but never return them.

3. All remaining types which do not fall into either of the groups above.

It turns out that in general, types from the last group (ones that are neither producers, nor consumers) can't preserve subtyping without breaking type safety. To understand why it happens, let's consider an example with our **TreeNode** class. Suppose for a moment that subtyping is permitted and we can assign **TreeNode<String>** to **TreeNode<Any>**. Consider the following code:

```
val stringNode = TreeNode<String>("Hello")

val anyNode: TreeNode<Any> = stringNode

anyNode.addChild(123)

val s = stringNode.children.first() // ???
```

Now, the problem is clear. Since you can add a child of any type to **TreeNode<Any>**, assigning **stringNode** to **anyNode** makes it possible to add the Int child to an original tree of **String**! If such an assignment is allowed, the program would fail with the exception when trying to cast **stringNode.children.first()** to **String**. In other words, we'd have violated the contract of **TreeNode<String>** by putting the integer value into one of its children nodes.

Java vs Kotlin: Readers familiar with Java would recognize a similarity with infamous **ArrayStoreException** which may happen due to array assignments. That's in fact the reason why in Kotlin, as opposed to Java, array types do *not* preserve subtyping.

When we consider type A subtype of type **B,** we assume that values of **A** can be used in any context which requires a value of **B**. This is clearly not the case here. The type **TreeNode<Any>** has an ability to add child nodes of any type, while **TreeNode<String>** don't; it only can add children of type **String**. That's the reason why **TreeNode<String>** can't be a subtype of **TreeNode<Any>**.

Why immutable collections like **List<T>** are different? The reason is that they do not have operations like **addChild():** their members only produce values of **T** but never consume them. So the basic contract of **List<Any>** is its ability to retrieve values of **Any**. Similarly, the contract of **List<String>** is its ability to retrieve values of **String**. But since **String** is a subtype of **Any**, that automatically makes **List<String>** capable to retrieve values of **Any** as well. In other words, subtyping of **List<String>** and **List<Any>** does not endanger type safety, and the compiler permits us to make use of this property. We can say that such types are *covariant* with respect to their type argument. All producer-like types can be made covariant in Kotlin.

Many built-in immutable types like **Pair, Triple, Iterable, Iterator,** and so on are covariant. On top of that, functional types are covariant with respect to their return types:

```
val stringProducer: () -> String = { "Hello" }
val anyProducer: () -> Any = stringProducer
println(anyProducer()) // Hello
```

Note that covariance is not the same as immutability. Covariance (with respect to **T**) just forbids taking values of **T** as input, so it's possible to have a mutable type which still can be made covariant. Consider, for example, a putative list which can only delete its elements by index but can't add new ones:

```
interface NonGrowingList<T> {
    val size: Int
    fun get(index: Int): Int
    fun remove(index: Int)
}
```

It's clearly mutable but behaves covariantly: for example, **NonGrowingList<String>** is capable of everything the **NonGrowingList<Any>** can.

The reverse is also true. Types representing immutable objects may behave non-covariantly. For example:

```
interface Set<T> {
    fun contains(element: T): Boolean
}
```

The preceding type might be immutable, but it's not a producer and thus can't preserve subtyping. While **Set<Any>** can take any value as its input, **Set<String>** can take only strings.

What about consumer-like types? They obviously can't preserve subtyping in keeping with the preceding arguments. It turns out, though, that they preserve subtyping in the *opposite direction*. To understand what it means, let's consider two substitutions of the **Set<T>** type such as **Set<Int>** and **Set<Number>**. The contract of **Set<T>** can be reduced to the ability to handle elements of **T** by the **contains()** function. So **Set<Number>** can handle any **Number** and **Set<Int>** can handle any **Int**. But **Int** is a subtype of **Number**, so **Set<Number>** can handle any Int as well. In other words, **Set<Number>** behaves like a subtype of **Set<Int>**. In Kotlin, you can, in fact, enable this subtyping by declaring **T** *contravariant*.

Function types, for example, are contravariant with respect to their argument types:

```
val anyConsumer: (Any) -> Unit = { println(it) }
val stringConsumer: (String) -> Unit = anyConsumer
stringConsumer("Hello") // Hello
```

So for a given generic type **X<T,...>**, we have the following options in terms of variance with respect to **T**:

- **X** behaves like a producer; in this case, we can declare **T** covariant so that **X<A>** will be a subtype of **X<B>** whenever **A** is a subtype of **B**.

- **X** behaves like a consumer; we then can me **T** contravariant: **X<A>** will be a subtype of **X<B>** whenever **B** is a subtype of **A**.

- In all remaining cases, **T** has to remain invariant.

In the following section, we'll see how variance is expressed in Kotlin.

Variance at the declaration site

In Kotlin, variance of a type parameter can be specified in two ways: either in declaration itself, or on its usage site when substituting particular type arguments. In this section, we'll focus on the first approach which is called *declaration-site variance*.

By default, type parameters are considered invariant which means that their generic types do not preserve subtyping of corresponding type arguments (as well its reversed version). Consider, for example, the simplified version of List type with array-based immutable implementation:

```
interface List<T> {
    val size: Int
    fun get(index: Int): T
}


class ListByArray<T>(private vararg val items: T) : List<T> {
    override val size: Int get() = items.size

    override fun get(index: Int) = items[index]
}
```

Suppose we define a function which takes a pair of lists and returns their concatenation delegating to either of the original **List** instances:

```
fun <T> concat(list1: List<T>, list2: List<T>) = object : List<T> {
    override val size: Int
        get() = list1.size + list2.size

    override fun get(index: Int): T {
        return if (index < list1.size) {
            list1.get(index)
        } else {
            list2.get(index - list1.size)
        }
    }
}
```

Now, everything goes smoothly until we try to use this function to combine lists of related types, say, **List<Number>** and **List<T>**:

```
val numbers = ListByArray<Number>(1, 2.5, 3f)
val integers = ListByArray(10, 30, 30)
val result = concat(numbers, integers) // Error
```

The reason is an invariance of parameter **T:** due to that **List<Int>** is not considered a subtype of **List<Int>** (and vice versa), so we can't pass a **List<Int>** variable into a function which expects **List<Number>**.

This is, however, too restrictive. A quick glance at the **List** interface reveals that it actually behaves like a producer type. Its operations only return values of **T** but never take them as input. In other words, this type can be safely made covariant. To do this, we mark parameter **T** with the **out** keyword:

```
interface List<out T> {
    val size: Int
    fun get(index: Int): T
}
```

Now, the **concat()** call works as expected because the compiler understands that **List<Int>** is a subtype of **List<Number>**.

The producer part is crucial here because the compiler wouldn't let us define the parameter as covariant otherwise. Let's consider a mutable version of **List**:

```
interface MutableList<T> : List<T> {
```

```
    fun set(index: Int, value: T)
}
```

Trying to make **T** in **MutableList** covariant will lead to a compilation error:

```
interface MutableList<out T> : List<T> {
    fun set(index: Int, value: T) // Error: T occurs in 'in' position
}
```

It happens because of the **set** function which takes an input value of **T,** thus acting as its consumer. The basic rule is as follows: a type parameter may only be declared covariant if all its occurrences happen to be in 'out' positions where the 'out' position basically mean usages where its values is produced rather than consumed such as the return type of a property or function, or covariant type argument of generic type. For example, the following type is valid since all usages of parameter **T** are in 'out' positions:

```
interface LazyList<out T> {
    // usage as return type
    fun get(index: Int): T

    // usage as out type argument in return type
    fun subList(range: IntRange): LazyList<T>

    // return part of functional type is 'out' position as well
    fun getUpTo(index: Int): () -> List<T>
}
```

The 'in' positions similarly cover the usages where values are consumed like arguments of function calls and contravariant type arguments.

Note that constructor parameters are exempted from these checks because a constructor is called before an instance of generic type exists (it's called to create it in the first place). For this reason, we can make the **ListByArray** implementation covariant as well:

```
class ListByArray<out T>(private vararg val items: T) : List<T> { ... }
```

Similarly, we can use the in keyword to declare the type parameter contravariant. This is possible when its generic type acts as a consumer, that is, the type parameter itself has no usages in 'in' positions. For example:

```kotlin
class Writer<in T> {

    // usages as function argument
    fun write(value: T) {
        println(value)
    }


    // combining out List argument with in position as function argument
    // gives in position again
    fun writeList(values: Iterable<T>) {
        values.forEach { println(it) }
    }
}


fun main() {
    val numberWriter = Writer<Number>()
    // Correct: Writer<Number> can also handle integers
    val integerWriter: Writer<Int> = numberWriter
    integerWriter.write(100)
}
```

The **TreeNode** class from our earlier example can't be made neither covariant, nor contravariant since its type parameter has usages in both 'in' (for example, the **addChild()** function) and 'out' positions (like **data** or **children** properties). We have no other options apart from leaving it as invariant as it was originally. Suppose if we want to make a copy of a tree with all its children? Then, our **TreeNode** instance acts solely as a producer since the only members we need for that task are **data** and **children** properties. Can we somehow convince the Kotlin compiler that **TreeNode** is used covariantly in such case? In fact, the answer is yes, and the language tool we need for that is a use-site variance also called a projection.

Use-site variance with projections

Another way to specify a variance is to place the out/in keyword before a type argument in a particular usage of generic type. This construct, also called a *projection* is useful for types which are invariant in general, but can be used as either producers, or consumers depending on the context.

Suppose if we want to implement a function which adds a copy of existing tree to another tree as a child. Let's start with invariant definition:

```kotlin
fun <T> TreeNode<T>.addSubtree(node: TreeNode<T>): TreeNode<T> {
    val newNode = addChild(node.data)
    node.children.forEach { newNode.addSubtree (it) }
    return newNode
}
```

This function works well when both trees have the same type:

```kotlin
fun main() {
    val root = TreeNode("abc")
    val subRoot = TreeNode("def")
    root.addSubtree(subRoot)
    println(root) // abc {def {}}
}
```

But what if we want to, say, add a tree of **Int** to a tree of **Number**? This operation is actually well-defined since **Int** is a subtype of **Number** and adding Int-based nodes to a Number tree does not violate any assumptions about its type. But since **TreeNode<T>** is invariant and we've specified that both trees have the same element type **T**, the compiler won't let us do it:

```kotlin
val root = TreeNode<Number>(123)
val subRoot = TreeNode(456.7) // Error
```

The **TreeNode<T>** type has to remain invariant since it contains both members which can return values of **T** (like **data** property) and those which take **T** values as their input (like **addChild()** function), so we can't use declaration-site variance here. However, in the context of the **addSubtree()** function, a tree we pass as an argument is used exclusively as a producer. This allows us to achieve our goal by marking the necessary type argument as **out**:

```kotlin
fun <T> TreeNode<T>.addSubtree(node: TreeNode<out T>): TreeNode<T> {
    val newNode = addChild(node.data)
    node.children.forEach { newNode.addSubtree(it) }
    return newNode
}
```

```
fun main() {
    val root = TreeNode<Number>(123)
    val subRoot = TreeNode(456.7)
    root.addSubtree(subRoot)
    println(root) // 123 {456.7 {}}
}
```

Alternatively, we could've introduced the additional type parameter bounded by the first one to represent elements of the added tree:

```
fun <T, U : T> TreeNode<T>.addSubtree(node: TreeNode<U>): TreeNode<T> {
    val newNode = addChild(node.data)
    node.children.forEach { newNode.addSubtree(it) }
    return newNode
}
```

Using out-projection, we can avoid extra type parameters and solve our problem in a more concise way.

The **TreeNode<out T>** is called a projected type. The projection **out T** means that we do not know the actual type argument of **TreeNode:** only that it must be a subtype of **T**. You can think of **TreeNode<out T>** as a version of **TreeNode<T>** which only exposes operations that act as producers with respect to **T**. For example, we can use properties such **data**, **children**, **depth**, or functions like **walkDepthFirst()** since they do not take values of **T** as their input. Consumer operations like **addChild()** member or **addChildren()** extension are available but not actually usable as any attempt to call them on out-projected type produces a compilation error:

```
fun processOut(node: TreeNode<out Any>) {
    node.addChild("xyz") // Error: addChild() is projected out
}
```

The in-projections can be used similarly to enforce the usage of the type as a consumer. For example, we could've written our tree-adding function in the following form:

```
fun <T> TreeNode<T>.addTo(parent: TreeNode<in T>) {
    val newNode = parent.addChild(data)
    children.forEach { it.addTo(newNode) }
}
```

Now, the receiver is a tree being added while a parameter represents its new parent. Thanks to in-projection such a function can add **TreeNode<T>** to a tree containing elements of any supertype of **T**:

```kotlin
fun main() {
    val root = TreeNode<Number>(123)
    val subRoot = TreeNode(456.7)
    subRoot.addTo(root)
    println(root) // 123 {456.7 {}}
}
```

Java vs Kotlin: Kotlin projections play essentially the same role as Java **extends**/**super** wildcards. For example, **TreeNode<out Number>** and **TreeNode<in Number>** are equivalent to Java's **TreeNode<? extends Number>** and **TreeNode<? super Number>,** respectively.

Note that using projections when the corresponding type argument has declaration-site variance is basically meaningless. When the projection matches the parameter variance, the compiler reports a warning since using the projection in such case in redundant. On the other hand, when projections do not match, the compiler considers this a compilation error. For example:

```kotlin
interface Producer<out T> {
    fun produce(): T
}


interface Consumer<in T> {
    fun consume(value: T)
}


fun main() {
    val inProducer: Producer<in String>
                                    // Error: conflicting projection
    val outProducer: Producer<out String> // out is redundant
    val inConsumer: Consumer<in String>    // in is redundant
    val outConsumer: Consumer<out String>
                                    // Error: conflicting projection
}
```

Similarly to Java wildcards, projections give you a possibility to use invariant types in a more flexible way by representing types constrained by either a producer, or consumer role. On top of it, Kotlin has a special way to denote a generic whose argument can be replaced by any possible type: a *star projection*.

Star projections

Star projections denoted by ***** are used to indicate that the argument type can be anything within its bounds. Since Kotlin only supports upper bounds for type parameters, this amounts to saying that the type argument can be any subtype of the corresponding bounding type. Let's consider an example:

```
// Can be any list since its element type is only bounded by Any?
val anyList: List<*> = listOf(1, 2, 3)
// Can be any object comparable with itself (due to T : Comparable<T>
bound)
val anyComparable: Comparable<*> = "abcde"
```

In other words, a star projection effectively behaves like an out projection applied to a type parameter bound.

Java vs Kotlin: Star projection can be considered a Kotlin counterpart of Java's ? wildcard, so **TreeNode<*>** in Kotlin has basically the same meaning as **TreeNode<?>** in Java.

In the section on type erasure and refinement, we've seen that star-projected types can be used in type-checking operations:

```
val any: Any = ""
any is TreeNode<*>
```

Since the type parameter of **TreeNode** is bounded by **Any?,** we can also write this using an explicit out projection:

```
any is TreeNode<out Any?> // Ok
```

If we, however, try to replace **Any?** with some other type, the compiler will report an error since such a check is impossible due to type erasure:

```
any is TreeNode<out Number> // Error
```

It's important to keep in mind the difference between ***** and using the type parameter bound as a non-projection argument, like in **TreeNode<*>** vs. **TreeNode<Any?>**. While **TreeNode<Any?>** is a tree which can contain the value of any type, **TreeNode<*>** represents the tree whose nodes are characterized by the same common type **T,** but that **T** is unknown to us. For this reason, we can't use **TreeNode** operations which behave like consumers of **T** values. Since we don't know the actual type, we also don't know what values are acceptable for them. That's exactly the meaning of the out projection we've discussed in the previous section.

To put it short, star projections allow you to concisely represent the generic type when particular arguments are not relevant or simply not known.

Note that when the type parameter has more than one bound, * can't be replaced with an explicit out projection because the type intersection is not denotable in the Kotlin source code:

```kotlin
interface Named {
    val name: String
}


interface Identified {
    val id: Int
}


class Registry<T> where T : Named, T : Identified


// the bound is intersection of Named and Identified
var registry: Registry<*>? = null
```

Another difference between * and explicit out is that * are allowed for type parameters with the declaration-site variance. In this case, the compiler doesn't report warnings/errors:

```kotlin
interface Consumer<in T> {
    fun consume(value: T)
}


interface Producer<out T> {
    fun produce(): T
}


fun main() {
    val starProducer: Producer<*> // the same as Producer<Any?>
```

```
    val starConsumer: Consumer<*> // the same as Consumer<Nothing>
}
```

When applied to a type argument in the contravariant position (like in **Consumer<*>**), star projection in fact produces a type argument of **Nothing**. Thus, we can't pass anything to the **consume()** function because **Nothing** has no values.

Type aliases

In conclusion, we will discuss a language feature which is not directly related to generics but comes very handy when you have to deal with complex generic types: the type aliases.

The idea of type aliases added in Kotlin 1.1 is allowing you to introduce alternative names for existing types. The primary goal of such a construct is to provide short names for otherwise long types such as generic or functional ones. Type alias definition is introduced with the typealias keyword which is followed by an alias name and its definition separated by the = symbol:

```
typealias IntPredicate = (Int) -> Boolean

typealias IntMap = HashMap<Int, Int>
```

Now, we can use the preceding names instead of the right-hand sides of their definitions:

```
fun readFirst(filter: IntPredicate) =
    generateSequence { readLine()?.toIntOrNull() }.firstOrNull(filter)


fun main() {
    val map = IntMap().also {
        it[1] = 2
        it[2] = 3
    }
}
```

One more useful case is providing short names for nested classes:

```
sealed class Status {
    object Success : Status()
    class Error(val message: String) : Status()
}
```

```
typealias StSuccess = Status.Success

typealias StError = Status.Error
```

Similar to classes, type aliases may have type parameters which allow us to introduce aliases for generic types:

```
typealias ThisPredicate<T> = T.() -> Boolean

typealias MultiMap<K, V> = Map<K, Collection<V>>
```

You may also restrict their scope by using visibility modifiers:

```
private typealias MyMap = Map<String, String>

                                        // visible in current file only
```

As of now (Kotlin 1.3) type aliases may only be introduced at top-level. For example, it's not possible to declare them inside functions or as class members:

```
fun main() {
    typealias A = Int // Error
}
```

Another restriction is that you can't declare bounds or constraints for type parameters of generic type alias:

```
typealias ComparableMap<K : Comparable<K>, V> = Map<K, V> // Error
```

The important thing to note is that type aliases never introduce new types, just give an additional way to refer to existing ones. This, in particular, means that type aliases are completely interchangeable with their original types:

```
typealias A = Int


fun main() {
    val n = 1
    val a: A = n
    val b: Int = a
}
```

As you already know, type aliases are not the only way to introduce new names for existing types, so it's useful to understand major differences between language features which can be used for similar purposes.

Import aliases, for example, give you an ability to introduce alternative names as a part of import directives. Unlike type aliases, they also support functions and properties, but do not allow you to introduce generic aliases. Besides, their scope is always limited to the containing file, while public type aliases have more wider scope.

It's also possible to introduce a new type name by inheriting from, say, a generic or functional type. This option allows you to define generic types as well as control the new name visibility. The major difference with type aliases is that such definitions create a *new type*, namely, a subtype of the original one, so their compatibility is one-way:

```kotlin
class MyMap<T> : HashMap<T, T>()


fun main() {
    val map: Map<String, String> = MyMap()
                                        // Ok, MyMap is subtype of Map
    val myMap: MyMap<String> = map           // Error
}
```

While you can't inherit from a final class, you can introduce an alias for it.

Inline classes are also similar to type aliases in a sense that may have the same runtime representation as their original type. The crucial difference, however, is that inline classes introduce new types which are not compatible with their originals. For example, a value of **UInt** can't be assigned to variable of **Int** (and vice versa) without an explicit conversion.

Conclusion

This chapter has brought us to the concept of generics which give you an additional tool for designing abstractions in the Kotlin code. Now, you should be able to design your own generic APIs as well use more advanced concepts like reified type parameters and variance for writing more concise, efficient, and type-safe code. Among other things, we've introduced a useful feature of type aliasing that allows you to introduce alternative type names and simplify handling of complicated generic and functional types.

In the next chapter, we will take a closer look at two interrelated topics. The first one would be annotations which allow you specify various metadata for your program elements. In Kotlin, annotations, among others, are used for fine-tuning of interoperability with code which we'll also cover in *Chapter 12, Java Interoperability*. The second major topic of *Chapter 10, Annotations and Reflection*, would be a reflection which gives you an API to introspect a program structure and dynamically invoke your code.

Points to remember

1. Kotlin classes, functions and properties may have type parameters which allow them to be applicable to data of multiple different types. Such declarations are called generic. When used generic declarations are supplied with specific types in place of corresponding type parameters

2. Type parameters may have bounds which restrict their possible types to subtypes of some given base type.

3. The variance determines whether two particular instantiations of a generic type are related to each other via subtyping. The major use case for variance is distinguishing producer and consumer types at the type system level.

4. In Kotlin variance may be specified both in the declaration of generic class/interface/alias (declaration-site variance) as well as at its particular usage (use-site variance)

5. Type aliases allow the user to introduce alternative names for existing types. They might be generic similar to classes and interfaces.

Questions

1. How can you define a generic class, function, or property in Kotlin?

2. Describe how to specify constraints for type parameters. How are they compared to Java's?

3. What is type erasure? Describe limitations of type parameters vs. ordinary types.

4. How can you circumvent type erasure using reified type parameters? What are their limitations?

5. What is a variance? Why variance is important for a generic code?

6. Describe how declaration-site variance is used in Kotlin.

7. Compare use-site variance in Kotlin with Java wildcards.

8. Describe the purpose of star projections.

9. Describe type alias syntax. How can they be compared with related languages features such as import aliases and inheritance?

CHAPTER 10

Annotations and Reflection

In this chapter, we will cover two major topics. The first part will be devoted to annotations which allow you to bind metadata to Kotlin declarations and later access them at runtime. We'll explain how to define and apply your own annotations and look at some built-in annotations which affect the compilation of the Kotlin source code.

The second will introduce us to the Reflection API which defines a set of types comprising runtime representation of Kotlin declarations. We'll discuss how to obtain reflection objects, access their attributes, and use callables to dynamically invoke functions and properties.

Structure

In this chapter, we will cover the following topics:

- Annotations
- Reflection

Objectives

After reading this chapter, you will learn to apply annotations in the Kotlin source code as well as declare your own annotation classes. You will get an understanding of how to use the Kotlin Reflection API to obtain runtime information about Kotlin declarations and dynamically invoke functions and properties.

Annotations

Annotation is a special kind of Kotlin class which allows you to define custom metadata and bind them to elements of your source code: declarations, expressions, or whole files. Similar to their Java counterparts, Kotlin annotations can be accessed at runtime. This ability is used extensively by various frameworks and processing tools which rely on annotations for configuration and code instrumentation purposes.

Defining and using annotation classes

The syntax of annotation usage is rather similar to that of Java. The most basic case is annotating a declaration when you put a @-prefixed annotation name into its modifier list. For example, when using a test framework such as Junit, you can mark test methods using the annotation **@Test**:

```
class MyTestCase {
    @Test
    fun testOnePlusOne() {
        assert(1 + 1 == 2)
    }
}
```

Java vs Kotlin: Unlike Java, some Kotlin annotations may also be applied to expressions. For example, the built-in **@Suppress** annotation can be used to suppress compiler warnings for a particular expression in the source file:

```
val s = @Suppress("UNCHECKED_CAST") objects as List<String>
```

If you have multiple annotations for the same source file element, you may group them inside square brackets:

```
@[Synchronized Strictfp] // the same as @Synchronized @Strictfp
fun main() { }
```

If you want to apply an annotation to a primary constructor, you need to use an explicit **constructor** keyword:

```
class A @MyAnnotation constructor ()
```

In *Chapter 4, Working with Classes and Objects*, we already used a similar syntax to make a primary constructor private.

To define an annotation, you need to declare a class marked with a special **annotation** modifier:

```
annotation class MyAnnotation

@MyAnnotation fun annotatedFun() { }
```

Java vs Kotlin: Keep in mind the difference between the annotation definition in Kotlin and Java. While Java annotations have a syntactic form of an *interface*, Kotlin annotations comprise a special kind of *classes*.

Unlike ordinary classes, annotation classes may not have members, secondary constructors, or initializers:

```
annotation class MyAnnotation {
    val text = "???" // Error
}
```

Since Kotlin 1.3 you can, however, add nested classes, interfaces, and objects (including companions) to the annotation body:

```
annotation class MyAnnotation {
    companion object {
        val text = "???"
    }
}
```

If you want to add custom attributes to your annotation, you may do so via constructor parameters. When such an annotation is used, you need to provide actual values for parameters similar to a class constructor call:

```
annotation class MyAnnotation(val text: String)


@MyAnnotation("Some useful info") fun annotatedFun() { }
```

Note that annotation parameters must always be marked as **val**.

Java vs Kotlin: Java annotation attributes are specified in the form of parameterless methods. In Kotlin, however, you need to use constructor parameters which also play the role of properties.

Similar to ordinary constructors, you may use default values and varargs:

```kotlin
annotation class Dependency(vararg val componentNames: String)
annotation class Component(val name: String = "Core")


@Component("I/O")
class IO


@Component("Log")
@Dependency("I/O")
class Logger


@Component
@Dependency("I/O", "Log")
class Main
```

Even though every Kotlin annotation is a kind of class, you can't instantiate them the way you do it with ordinary classes:

```kotlin
annotation class Component(val name: String = "Core")

val ioComponent = Component("IO") // Error
```

Annotations can only be constructed using the preceding **@** syntax. To retrieve an actual annotation instance (if it's preserved at runtime), you may use the Reflection API which we'll discuss in the upcoming sections.

Annotation classes can't have explicit supertypes and can't be inherited. They automatically inherit from the **Any** class and empty the **Annotation** interface which serves as a common supertype for all annotation classes.

Since annotations arguments are evaluated at compilation time, you may not place arbitrary computations there. Furthermore, a compiler limits the range of possible types you may use for annotation parameters:

- primitive types such as Int, Boolean, or Double
- String
- enums
- other annotations
- class literals
- arrays of the types above

Note also that such parameters may not be nullable because JVM does not allow you to store nulls in annotation attributes.

When you use another annotation as an argument, you don't need to put the **@** prefix before its name. Instead, you need to write an annotation like an ordinary constructor call. Let's rework our previous example a bit:

```
annotation class Dependency(vararg val componentNames: String)
annotation class Component(
    val name: String = "Core",
    val dependency: Dependency = Dependency()
)


@Component("I/O")
class IO


@Component("Log", Dependency("I/O"))
class Logger


@Component(dependency = Dependency("I/O", "Log"))
class Main
```

Annotation parameters may have an explicit array type, without using a vararg. When using such an annotation, you may construct an array using the standard **arrayOf()** function:

```
annotation class Dependency(val componentNames: Array<String>)


@Component(dependency = Dependency(arrayOf("I/O", "Log")))
class Main
```

Since Kotlin 1.2, you may also use a more concise syntax by enclosing array elements inside square brackets:

```
annotation class Dependency(val componentNames: Array<String>)


@Component(dependency = Dependency(["I/O", "Log"]))
class Main
```

Such *array literals* are currently only supported inside annotations.

The class literal gives you a representation of a class as a reflection object of type **KClass**. This type serves as a Kotlin counterpart of the **Class** type used in the Java language. The class literal consists of a class name followed by :**:class**. Let's modify our component/dependency example to use class literals instead of names:

```
import kotlin.reflect.KClass


annotation class Dependency(vararg val componentClasses: KClass<*>)
annotation class Component(
    val name: String = "Core",
    val dependency: Dependency = Dependency()
)


@Component("I/O")
class IO


@Component("Log", Dependency(IO::class))
class Logger


@Component(dependency = Dependency(IO::class, Logger::class))
class Main
```

Java vs Kotlin: Note that instances of **java.lang.Class** may not be used in Kotlin annotations. During the JVM-targeted compilation, however, Kotlin class literals are automatically converted into Java's.

There are cases when a single declaration in a Kotlin source file corresponds to multiple language elements which may have annotations. For example, if we have the following class:

```
class Person(val name: String)
```

Then, **val name: String** serves as a shorthand declaration for a constructor parameter, a class property with getter, and a backing field which is used to store a property value. Since each of those elements may have their own annotations, Kotlin allows you to specify a particular annotation target at its use site.

The use-site target is represented by a special keyword which is placed before the annotation name and is separated by: character. For example, if we want to place some annotation on a property getter, we use the **get** keyword:

```
class Person(@get:A val name: String)
```

Most of the use-site targets are related to various components of a property. Such targets can be applied to any top-level or class property as well as the **val/var** parameter of a primary constructor:

- **property**: This represents a property itself.
- **field**: This represents the backing field (applicable only to properties which do have a backing field).
- **get**: This represents the property getter.
- **set**: This represents the property setter (applicable only to mutable properties).
- **param**: This represents the constructor parameter (applicable only to **val**/**var** parameters).
- **setparam**: This represents the parameter of a property setter (applicable only to mutable properties).
- **delegate**: This represents the field which stores the delegate object (applicable only to a delegated property, see *Chapter 11*, *Domain-Specific Languages*, for details).

The **get/set** targets allow you to annotate property accessors even when they are not explicitly present in your code (like the **val** parameter in the preceding example). The same goes for the **setparam** target which has the same effect as the annotation setter parameter directly.

Annotations with the use-site target can be also be grouped using the **[]** syntax. In this case, the target is applied to all of them. So the definition:

```
class Person(@get:[A B] val name: String)
```

Is basically equivalent to:

```
class Person(@get:A @get:B val name: String)
```

The **receiver** target applies the annotation to a receiver parameter of the extension function or property:

```
class Person(val firstName: String, val familyName: String)


fun @receiver:A Person.fullName() = "$firstName $familyName"
```

Finally, the **file** target means that the annotation is applied to the entire file. Such annotations must be placed at the beginning of the Kotlin file, before import and package directives:

```
@file:JvmName("MyClass")

fun main() {
    println("main() in MyClass")
}
```

At runtime file, annotations are kept in the file facade class which contains top-level functions and properties. In *Chapter 12, Java Interoperability*, we'll discuss a group of file-level annotations (like the @JvmName) which affect how such facade classes are visible from the Java code.

Now, we'll look at some built-in annotations which have a special meaning in the context of the Kotlin code.

Built-in annotations

Kotlin includes several built-in annotations which have special meaning in the context of a compiler. Some of them can be applied to annotation classes themselves and allow you to specify options which affect the usage of target annotations. Most of them serve as counterparts for similar meta-annotations available in Java language.

The **@Retention** controls how annotation is stored. Similar to Java's **@ Retention** interface, you can choose among the three options represented by the **AnnotationRetention** enum:

- **SOURCE:** The annotation exists at compile-time only and is not stored in the compiler's binary output.
- **BINARY:** The annotation is stored in the compiler's output, but remains invisible for the Reflection API.
- **RUNTIME:** The annotation is stored in the compiler's binary output and can be accessed via reflection.

By default, Kotlin annotations have the RUNTIME retention, so you don't have to worry about their availability via the Reflection API. Note that expression annotations currently can't be preserved at runtime, so both the BINARY and RUNTIME retentions are forbidden for them:

```
@Target(AnnotationTarget.EXPRESSION)
annotation class NeedToRefactor // Error: must have SOURCE retention
```

In such a case, you have to specify the SOURCE retention explicitly:

```
@Target(AnnotationTarget.EXPRESSION)
```

```
@Retention(AnnotationRetention.SOURCE)
annotation class NeedToRefactor // Ok
```

Java vs Kotlin: Keep in mind the difference between the default retention policies in Java and Kotlin. In case of Java, it's **RetentionPolicy.CLASS** (an equivalent of Kotlin's **AnnotationRetention.BINARY**) which means that Java annotations are not available via reflection unless you explicitly change their retention to RUNTIME.

The **@Repeatable** specifies that the annotation can be applied to the same element more than once:

```
@Repeatable
@Retention(AnnotationRetention.SOURCE)
annotation class Author(val name: String)
```

```
@Author("John")
@Author("Harry")
class Services
```

By default, annotations are not repeatable, and if you try to apply a non-repeatable annotation multiple times, the compiler will report an error:

```
@Deprecated("Deprecated")
@Deprecated("Even    more    deprecated")  //  Error:  non-repeatable
annotation
class OldClass
```

Note also that currently repeatable annotations can't be kept at runtime and so must have the explicit SOURCE retention.

The **@MustBeDocumented** specifies that the annotation must be included in the documentation since it's considered part of the public API. This annotation plays the same role as Java's @Documented and is supported by Dokka, the standard Kotlin documentation engine (similar to how @Documented is supported by the Javadoc tool).

The **@Target** indicates which kinds of language elements are supported by the annotation. Possible kinds are specified as a vararg of constants from the **AnnotationTarget** enum:

- **CLASS:** Any class, interface, or object, including annotation classes themselves
- **ANNOTATION_CLASS:** Any annotation class; this effectively allows you to define your own meta-annotations.

- **TYPEALIAS:** Any type alias definition
- **PROPERTY:** Any property, including val/var parameters of a primary constructors (but not local variables)
- **FIELD:** Backing field of a property

LOCAL_VARIABLE: Local variables only (excluding parameters)

VALUE_PARAMETER: Parameters of constructors, functions, and property setters

CONSTRUCTOR: Primary and secondary constructors only

FUNCTION: Functions, including lambdas and anonymous functions (but not constructors or property accessors)

PROPERTY_GETTER/PROPERTY_SETTER: Property getters/setters only

FILE: The annotation can be applied to an entire file.

TYPE: Any type specification like the type of a variable, parameter, or the return value of a function

EXPRESSION: Any expression

The **TYPE_PARAMETER** constant is reserved for a future use but currently is not supported. As a consequence, you yet can't apply annotations to type parameters of generic declarations.

When **@Target** is not specified, the annotation can be applied to any language element except type alias, type parameter, type specification, expression, and file. So if you want your annotation to be applicable to, say, file, you have to specify it explicitly.

Java vs Kotlin: The **AnnotationTarget** class is quite similar to the **ElementType** enum found in the JDK. Keep in mind the difference, though between their **TYPE** constants. In Kotlin, **AnnotationType.TYPE** refers to type *specification* (which corresponds to **ElementType.TYPE_USAGE** in Java), while **ElementType.TYPE** means actual declaration of a class or interface (similar to **AnnotationTarget. CLASS**).

Note also that, unlike Java, Kotlin doesn't support package-level annotations (thus no counterpart for **ElementType.PACKAGE**). You can, however, define annotation at the level of a source file. In *Chapter 12, Java Interoperability*, we'll see how file annotations can be used to tune Java-Kotlin interoperability.

The following annotations are equivalent to the corresponding Java modifiers:

- **@Strictfp:** This restricts the precision of floating-point operations for better portability between different platforms.

- **@Synchronized:** This forces the annotated function or property accessor to acquire/release the monitor before/after executing the body.
- **@Volatile:** This makes updates of the annotated backing field immediately visible to other threads.
- **@Transient:** This indicates that the annotated field is ignored by the default serialization mechanism.

Since **@Synchronized** and **@Volatile** are related to concurrency support, we'll defer their detailed treatment till *Chapter 13, Concurrency.*

The **@Suppress** annotation allows you to suppress some compiler warnings specified by their internal names. This annotation may be applied to any target, including expressions and files. For example, you can use them to disable spurious warnings related to casts when you're certain that your code is valid:

```kotlin
val strings = listOf<Any>("1", "2", "3")

val numbers = listOf<Any>(1, 2, 3)   // No warning:

val s = @Suppress("UNCHECKED_CAST") (strings as List<String>)[0]

                                     // Unchecked cast warning:

val n = (numbers as List<Number>)[1]
```

The annotation affects all code inside the element it's applied to. You can, for example, suppress all warnings inside a particular function:

```kotlin
@Suppress("UNCHECKED_CAST")

fun main() {
    val strings = listOf<Any>("1", "2", "3")

    val numbers = listOf<Any>(1, 2, 3)

    val s = (strings as List<String>)[0] // No warning

    val n = (numbers as List<Number>)[1] // No warning

    println(s + n) // 12
}
```

Or inside the entire file if you use **@Suppress** with **file** use-site target:

```kotlin
@file:Suppress("UNCHECKED_CAST")


val strings = listOf<Any>("1", "2", "3")

val numbers = listOf<Any>(1, 2, 3)
```

```kotlin
fun takeString() = (strings as List<String>)[0] // No warning
fun takeNumber() = (numbers as List<Number>)[1] // No warning


@Suppress("UNCHECKED_CAST")
fun main() {
    println(takeString() + takeNumber()) // 12
}`
```

IDE Tips: There is no need to look up warnings names or memorize them as IntelliJ can insert @Suppress annotations automatically. To do that, press *Alt + Enter* while your caret is placed within the warning region (see *Figure 10.1*) and choose one of "Suppress..." actions from the "Annotator" submenu. These actions are applicable to warnings reported by IDE inspections as well.

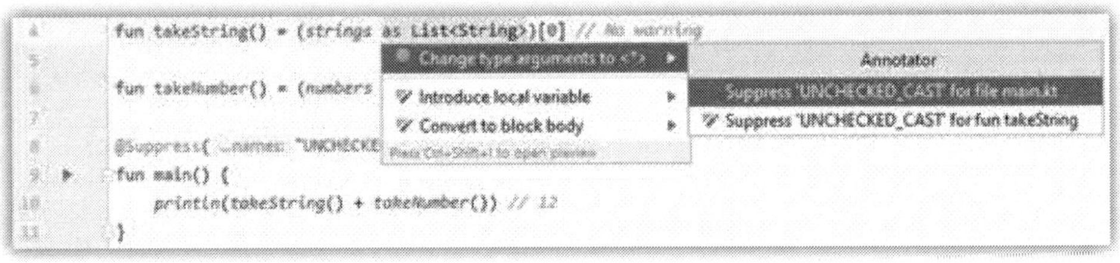

Figure 10.1: Suppressing compiler warning

Another useful annotation, **@Deprecated**, is pretty much similar to its Java counterpart. When you mark some declaration as deprecated, the client code is discouraged from using it. In IDE, usages of deprecated declarations are displayed in strike-through font (as shown in *Figure 10.2*). When using @Deprecated, you need to specify a message which usually clarifies why this declaration is deprecated and/or what user should use instead:

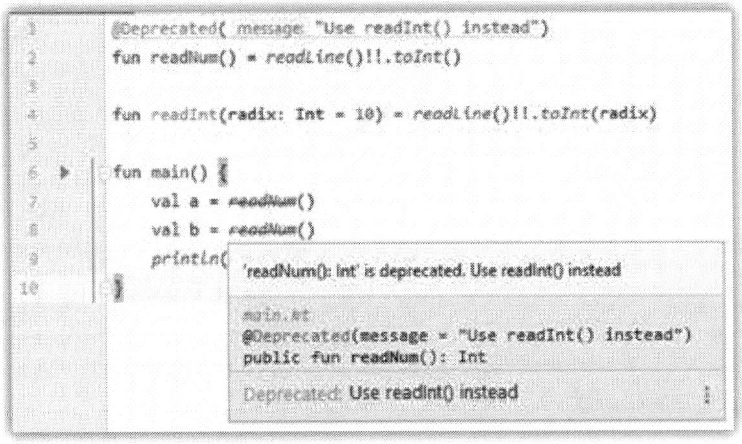

Figure 10.2: Deprecated declaration

Unlike Java, **@Deprecated** in Kotlin provides additional features. First, you can specify a string with a replacement expression. In this case, deprecated usage can automatically be changed into the desired form by using the corresponding quick-fix from the *Alt + Enter* menu (a shown in *Figure 10.3*). Suppose that we want to replace **readNum()** with **readInt()** above. Then, we can write:

```
@Deprecated(
    "Use readInt() instead", // Message
    ReplaceWith("readInt()") // Replacement expression
)
fun readNum() = readLine()!!.toInt()
```

Figure 10.3: Using quick-fix to replace a deprecated usage

Note that **ReplaceWith** is an annotation too. That's why you can place it inside the **@Deprecated** usage. **@ReplaceWith**, however, can't be used by itself. If you look at its definition:

```
@Target()
@Retention(BINARY)
@MustBeDocumented
public annotation class ReplaceWith(
    val expression: String,
    vararg val imports: String
)
```

You see that it has no supported targets. It can only be constructed as a part of another annotation like **@Deprecated**.

The additional vararg parameter of **ReplaceWith** allows you to specify a list of necessary imports to add on the replacement. This is useful if the replacement code refers to declarations from the non-default/non-current package.

Another feature is an ability to choose the severity of deprecation which is represented by the **DeprecationLevel** enum:

- **WARNING:** Usages of deprecated declarations are reported as warnings; this is the default behavior.

- **ERROR:** Usages of deprecated declarations are reported as compilation errors.

- **HIDDEN:** Deprecated declaration can't be accessed at all.

Using deprecation levels allows you to implement the smooth deprecation policy which is especially relevant for team development. First, you deprecate the declaration with the default level, so that its existing usages are reported as warnings. This gives developers time to replace them without breaking the compilation of the code. Then, you raise the deprecation error to ERROR, thus prohibiting newly introduced usages of the deprecated code. When you ensure that no one' going to use this code again, you may safely drop it from your code base.

Figure 10.4 shows an example of using **ERROR** level to forbid using the **readNum()** function:

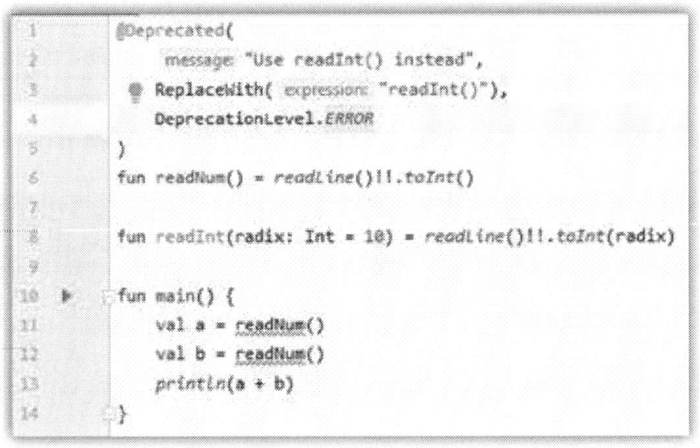

```
@Deprecated(
    message: "Use readInt() instead",
  ReplaceWith( expression: "readInt()"),
    DeprecationLevel.ERROR
)
fun readNum() = readLine()!!.toInt()

fun readInt(radix: Int = 10) = readLine()!!.toInt(radix)

fun main() {
    val a = readNum()
    val b = readNum()
    println(a + b)
}
```

Figure 10.4: *Deprecating declaration with ERROR level*

Some built-in annotations like **@Throws, @JvmName,** or **@NotNull** are used for tuning Java/Kotlin interoperability. We'll cover them in *Chapter 12, Java Interoperability.*

Reflection

The Reflection API is a set of types, functions, and properties which gives you an access to runtime representations of classes, functions, and properties. This is especially useful when your code has to work with classes which are not available at compile time but still conform to some common contract. For example, you may load classes dynamically as plugins and call their members knowing their signature.

In the following section, we'll discuss what elements comprise the Kotlin Reflection API and give examples of their use.

Java vs Kotlin: Note that Kotlin Reflection is not self-sufficient. In some cases like class search and loading, we have to rely on the facilities provided by the Java Reflection API. When it comes to manipulating Kotlin-specific aspects of your code (like properties or objects), using the Kotlin API gives you a more concise and idiomatic way to access them at runtime.

Reflection API overview

The Reflection classes reside in the **kotlin.reflect** package and can be loosely divided into two basic groups: *callables* which deal with the representation of properties and functions (including constructors) and *classifiers* which provide a runtime representation of classes and type parameters. *Figure 10.5* gives an overview of basic reflection types:

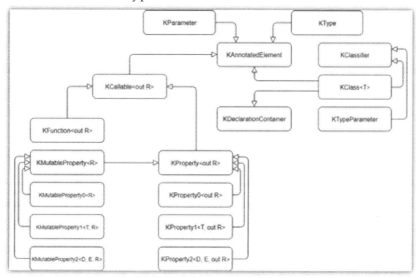

Figure 10.5: *Basic Reflection types*

All reflection types are descendants of **KAnnotatedElement** which allows you to access annotations defined for a particular language element such as a function, property, or class. **KAnnotatedElement** has a single property which returns a list of annotation instances:

```
public val annotations: List<Annotation>
```

Let's revisit our earlier example with **@Componet/@Dependency** annotations:

```
import kotlin.reflect.KClass

annotation class Dependency(vararg val componentClasses: KClass<*>)
annotation class Component(
```

```kotlin
    val name: String = "Core",
    val dependency: Dependency = Dependency()
)


@Component("I/O")
class IO


@Component("Log", Dependency(IO::class))
class Logger


@Component(dependency = Dependency(IO::class, Logger::class))
class Main
```

Suppose that we want to retrieve annotations associated with the **Main** class. We can do so by using the **annotations** property on its class literal:

```kotlin
fun main() {
    val component = Main::class.annotations
        .filterIsInstance<Component>()
        .firstOrNull() ?: return
    println("Component name: ${component.name}")
    val depText = component.dependency.componentClasses
            .joinToString { it.simpleName ?: "" }
    println("Dependencies: $depText")
}
```

If you run the preceding code, you will get:

```
Component name: Core
Dependencies: IO, Logger
```

In the following sections, we'll consider the API of more specific types related to classifiers and callables.

Classifiers and types

In terms of Kotlin Reflection, a *classifier* is a declaration which defines a type. Such declarations are represented by the **KClassifier** interface which currently has two more specific varieties:

- **KClass<T>** which represents a declaration of some class, interface, or object with the compile-time type **T**.

- **KTypeParameter** which represents a type parameter of some generic declaration.

Note that type aliases currently have no representation in the Reflection API. This, in particular, means that even though you may apply annotations to type aliases, such an annotation can't be retrieved at runtime. Type alias support is expected to be added in future releases of Kotlin.

Since **KClassifier** doesn't define members of its own, let's go straight to the specifics of classes and type parameters.

There are two basic ways to obtain an instance of **KClass**. The first it to use a class literal syntax we've already seen in the sections about annotations:

```
println(String::class.isFinal) // true
```

Apart from classes, this syntax is also supported for reified type parameters. In *Chapter 9, Generics*, we mentioned that type parameters of generic inline functions may be reified which means that the compiler substitutes actual types instead of them when the inlining function body at its call site. Let's define the following **cast()** function:

```
inline fun <reified T> Any.cast() = this as? T
```

Now, when we call this function, for example:

```
val obj: Any = "Hello"
println(obj.cast<String>())
```

The compiler will actually generate a code:

```
val obj: Any = "Hello"

println(obj as? String)
```

You may also use the **::class** syntax for an arbitrary expression to obtain a runtime class of its resulting value:

```
println((1 + 2)::class) // class kotlin.Int

println("abc"::class)    // class kotlin.String
```

Another way to get a **KClass** is to use the **kotlin** extension property to convert an instance of the **java.lang.Class**. This is especially useful to find a class dynamically by its qualified name. Since Kotlin Reflection doesn't have its own class search API yet, it has to rely on a platform-specific one:

```kotlin
val stringClass = Class.forName("java.lang.String").kotlin
```

```kotlin
println(stringClass.isInstance("Hello")) // true
```

The opposite conversion is given by the java extension property:

```kotlin
println(String::class.java) // class java.lang.String
```

Let's now look at the **KClass** API. The first group of the **KClass** members allows you to determine if a class of interest has a particular modifier:

```kotlin
val isAbstract: Boolean
```

```kotlin
val isCompanion: Boolean
```

```kotlin
val isData: Boolean
```

```kotlin
val isFinal: Boolean
```

```kotlin
val isInner: Boolean
```

```kotlin
val isOpen: Boolean
```

```kotlin
val isSealed: Boolean
```

Another property from the same group, **visibility**, gives you a visibility level of a class declaration as an instance of the **KVisibility** enum:

```kotlin
enum class Kvisibility {
    PUBLIC,
    PROTECTED,
    INTERNAL,
    PRIVATE
}
```

Note that visibility may be null if it can't be denoted in the Kotlin source code. For example, when **KClass** represents a local class.

The next group of properties allows you to retrieve a class name:

```kotlin
val simpleName: String?
```

```kotlin
val qualifiedName: String?
```

The **simpleName** property returns a simple name which was used in its source code. When the class has no name (for example, a class representing an object expression), the result is null.

The **qualifiedName** property similarly gives you a qualified name of a class which includes a full name of the containing package. When the class is local or nested into the local, the result is null since such classes can't be used from the top level and thus have no qualified name. The same goes for classes which have no name in the source code.

You can also use the **jvmName** extension property which gives you a qualified name of a class from the Java's point of view. This name may differ from the one given by **qualifiedName**. Some built-in Kotlin types do not have their own JVM representation and rely on existing Java classes instead. The **Any** class, for example, does not exist as a separate Java class; for Java code, it's basically the same as **java.lang.Object**:

```
println(Any::class.qualifiedName) // kotlin.Any
```

```
println(Any::class.jvmName)       // java.lang.Object
```

The **isInstance()** function allows you to check whether a given object is an instance of a class represented by its receiver. This function works similarly to the is operator when applied to a non-nullable type:

```
println(String::class.isInstance("")) // true
```

```
println(String::class.isInstance(12)) // false
```

```
println(String::class.isInstance(null)) // false
```

The next group of the **KClass** properties provides access to its member declarations:

- **constructors:** This is a collection of both primary and secondary constructors as instances of the **KFunction** type.
- **members:** This is a collection of member functions and properties represented by the **KCallable** instances, including all members inherited from supertypes.
- **nestedClasses:** This is a collection of nested classes and objects, including companions.
- **typeParameters:** This is a list of type parameters represented by the **KTypeParameter** type (when the class in question is not generic, the list is empty).

For example, in the following code, we use reflection to dynamically create an instance of the **Person** class and then call its **fullName()** function:

```
class Person(val firstName: String, val familyName: String) {
    fun fullName(familyFirst: Boolean): String = if (familyFirst) {
        "$familyName $firstName"
    } else {
```

```
            "$firstName $familyName"
    }
}


fun main() {
    val personClass = Class.forName("Person").kotlin
    val person = personClass.constructors.first().call("John", "Doe")
    val fullNameFun = personClass.members.first { it.name == "fullName" }
    println(fullNameFun.call(person, false)) // John Doe
}
```

When **KClass** represents object declarations, the constructors property always returns you an empty collection. To obtain an actual instance, you may use the **objectInstance** property:

```
object O {
    val text = "Singleton"
}


fun main() {
    println(O::class.objectInstance!!.text) // Singleton
}
```

When **KClass** does not represent an object, **objectInstance** is null.

Finally, for a sealed class (**isSealed == true**), you can also get a list of all direct inheritors via the **sealedSubclasses** property.

One more piece of information you can get from a **KClass** is supertype information provided by the **supertypes** property which returns a list of the **KType** instances. We'll get to the **KType** API a bit later, but for now let's consider a simple example:

```
open class GrandParent


open class Parent : GrandParent()


interface IParent
```

```kotlin
class Child : Parent(), IParent
```

```kotlin
fun main() {
    println(Child::class.supertypes) // [Parent, IParent]
}
```

Note that the **supertypes** property returns only *immediate* supertypes (thus **GrandParent** is absent in the preceding output), so if you want to access indirect ones, you'll have to perform an inheritance graph traversal.

Another classifier variety is represented by the **KTypeParameter** interface. Compared to **KClass,** it's rather simple and provides only four properties:

```kotlin
val isReified: Boolean
```

```kotlin
val name: String
```

```kotlin
val upperBounds: List<KType>
```

```kotlin
val variance: KVariance
```

The **upperBounds** give you a list of upper bound types similar to the **supertypes** property of **KClass**. The list is never empty as every type parameter has a bound (which is **Any?** by default). There may also be more than one bound if the type parameter is used in the type constraint. For example:

```kotlin
interface MyMap<K : Any, out V>
```

```kotlin
fun main() {
    val typeParameters = MyMap::class.typeParameters
    // K : [kotlin.Any], V : [kotlin.Any?]
    println(typeParameters.joinToString { "${it.name} : ${it.upperBounds}" })
}
```

The variance property returns a constant of the **KVariance** enum which represents **declaration-site variance of a type parameter:**

```kotlin
enum class KVariance { INVARIANT, IN, OUT }
```

Now, let's look at how types are represented in Kotlin Reflection through the **KType** interface. A Kotlin type is characterized by the following aspects:

- Nullability given by the **isMarkedNullable** property which distinguishes, say, **List<String>** and **List<String>?**.

- Classifier (given by the samename property) which refers to the class, interface, or object declaration defining the type; for example, the **List** part of **List<String>**.

- List of type arguments given by the arguments property: **<String>** for **List<String>**, **<Int, Boolean>** for **Map<Int, Boolean>** and so on.

The type argument is represented by the **KTypeProjection** interface which contains information about the type itself as well its use-site variance:

```
val type: kotlin.reflect.KType?
```

```
val variance: kotlin.reflect.KVariance?
```

Both properties return null for the star projection *.

This wraps up our overview of classifier types. In the following section, we'll focus on the callable part of the Reflection API.

Callables

The notion of a *callable* unites properties and functions which you can *call* to obtain some result. In the Reflection API, they are represented by a generic interface **KCallable<out R>** where R denotes either the return type of a function or a type of a property.

One way to get an instance of **KCallable** is to use callable references we've discussed in *Chapter 5, Leveraging Advanced Functions and Functional Programming*:

```
fun combine(n: Int, s: String) = "$s$n"


fun main() {
    println(::combine.returnType) // kotlin.String
}
```

You can also access member functions and properties via the corresponding **KClass** instance. Note, however, that the Reflection API currently doesn't allow you to obtain top-level callables this way.

Let's now take a look at common members defined in **KCallable** itself. Similar to **KClass,** we have a group of properties which allow you to check the presence of certain modifiers:

```
val isAbstract: Boolean
```

```
val isFinal: Boolean
```

```kotlin
val isOpen: Boolean
val isSuspend: Boolean
```

```kotlin
val visibility: KVisibility?
```

We haven't yet come across the **suspend** modifier corresponding to the **isSuspend** property. This modifier is used to define callables which support suspendable computations. In *Chapter 13, Concurrency*, we'll discuss this issue in more detail.

The next group of properties represents a signature of a property or a function:

```kotlin
val name: String
val typeParameters: List<KTypeParameter>
val parameters: List<KParameter>
val returnType: KType
```

Note that for members and extensions, the first parameter is reserved for a receiver. When callable is a member and extension at the same time, the second parameter is reserved as well. For example:

```kotlin
import kotlin.reflect.KCallable


val simpleVal = 1


val Int.extVal get() = this


class A {
    val Int.memberExtVal get() = this
}


fun main() {
    fun printParams(callable: KCallable<*>) {
        println(
            callable.parameters.joinToString(prefix = "[", postfix =
"]") {
                it.type.toString()
            }
```

```
        )
    }


    // []
    printParams(::simpleVal)
    // [kotlin.Int]
    printParams(Int::extVal)
    // [A, kotlin.Int]
    printParams(A::class.members.first { it.name == "memberExtVal" })
}
```

The **KParameter** interface contains information about the function/constructor parameter or receiver(s) of a member/extension declaration:

```
val index: Int
val isOptional: Boolean
val isVararg: Boolean
val name: String?
val type: KType
```

The **isOptional** property returns true when the parameter has a default value; the value itself is currently not available via reflection. Note also that the parameter name may be null if its name is not available or simply wasn't present in the source code. The latter goes for parameters representing receiver values.

The kind property indicates whether **KParameter** corresponds to the ordinary value, or dispatch/extension receiver. It can return one of the constants defined in the **KParameter.Kind** enum:

- **INSTANCE:** This is the dispatch receiver of the member declaration.
- **EXTENSION_RECEIVER:** This is the extension receiver of the extension declaration.
- **VALUE:** This is an ordinary parameter.

KCallable also defines the **call()** member which allows you to dynamically invoke the backing callable:

```
fun call(vararg args: Any?): R
```

In the case of a function-based callable, the **call()** invokes the function itself; if the callable corresponds to a property, the getter is used instead. We've already seen an example of using **call()** to invoke the constructor and member function. Let's take a look at the property example as applied to the same **Person** class:

```
fun main() {
    val person = Person("John", "Doe")
    val personClass = person::class
    val firstName = personClass.members.first { it.name == "firstName" }
    println(firstName.call(person)) // John
}
```

An alternative **callBy()** function allows you to pass arguments in the form of a map:

```
fun callBy(args: Map<KParameter, Any?>): R
```

Let's now move to more specialized callable kinds. The KProperty interface adds checks for property-specific modifiers:

```
val isConst: Boolean
```

```
val isLateinit: Boolean
```

You may also access the property getter as an instance of the **KFunction** type:

```
val myValue = 1
```

```
fun main() {
    println(::myValue.getter()) // 1
}
```

The **KMutableProperty** extends **KProperty** by adding a setter:

```
var myValue = 1
```

```
fun main() {
    ::myValue.setter(2)
    println(myValue) // 2
}
```

The **KProperty** also has subtypes **KProperty0**, **KProperty1,** and **KProperty2** representing properties without the receiver, with a single receiver (either dispatch, or extension) and with a pair of receivers (member extension), respectively. These subtypes refine types of getters by making them implement the corresponding functional type. That feature allowed us to use `::myValue.getter` as a function in the preceding example. Similar subtypes with refined setters are defined for `KMutableProperty` as well.

The final reflection type we will consider is the **KFunction** which quite expectedly represents functions and constructors. The only members added to this interface are related to function-specific modifiers checks:

`val` isInfix: Boolean

`val` isInline: Boolean

`val` isOperator: Boolean

`val` isSuspend: Boolean

The **isInfix** and **isOperator** checks are related to operator functions which we'll cover in *Chapter 11, Domain-Specific Languages*.

Note that **KFunction** by itself doesn't implement any functional type since it can represent functions with different arity. Specific implementations of **KFunction**, however, may also implement some functional type. We've already seen that using the example of accessors defined in **KProperty0/KProperty1/KProperty2**. Another important case is callable references which always conform to the proper functional type. For example:

```kotlin
import kotlin.reflect.KFunction2


fun combine(n: Int, s: String) = "$s$n"


fun main() {
    val f: KFunction2<Int, String, String> = ::combine
    println(f(1, "2")) // 12
}
```

You can see that the callable reference in this example has a **KFunction2<Int, String, String>** type which is a subtype of **(Int, String) -> String**. Note, however, that unlike **KProperty0** and similar types, **KFunction0/KFunction1/…** only exists during compilation. At runtime they're represented by synthetic classes similar to the one created for lambdas.

One more thing worth noting is the ability to access callables with restricted visibility. In some cases, you may need to, say, reflectively call a private function. In Java, an attempt to do this may produce an exception, so in general you have to make the reflection object "accessible" by calling **setAccessible(true)** beforehand. In Kotlin, you can use the **isAccessible** property for the same purpose:

```kotlin
import kotlin.reflect.KProperty1

import kotlin.reflect.jvm.isAccessible


class SecretHolder(private val secret: String)


fun main() {
    val secretHolder = SecretHolder("Secret")
    val secretProperty = secretHolder::class.members
        .first { it.name == "secret" } as KProperty1<SecretHolder, String>
    secretProperty.isAccessible = true
    println(secretProperty.get(secretHolder))
}
```

Conclusion

This chapter has brought us to the topic of annotations and reflection. We discussed how to annotate pieces of the Kotlin code and obtain associated metadata at runtime, explored major built-in annotations, and explained how to define your own annotation classes. We also introduced you to the Kotlin Reflection API. Now, you're familiar with how to access attributes of both classifiers and callables and use them in a dynamic fashion.

In the next chapter, we will address the subject of designing your own APIs in a way that resembles domain-specific languages bringing an air of declarative programming into your codebase.

Questions

1. How to define a new annotation? Compare the Kotlin annotation syntax with that of Java.

2. How annotations are used in Kotlin code?

3. Which built-in annotations are available in Kotlin?

4. What is an annotation use-site target? How is it related to targets specified by @Target meta-annotation?

5. What are the basic types comprising the Kotlin Reflection API?

6. Describe the class literal and callable reference syntax.

7. Describe the KClass API. How to convert between KClass and Java's class instances?

8. Describe the KCallable API.

Chapter 11
Domain-Specific Languages

Domain-specific language (DSL) is a language tailored at a specific function or domain. Such languages are heavily used in software development to deal with various tasks such as describing software configurations, test specification, workflow rules, UI design, data manipulation, and so on. The main advantage of DSLs is their simplicity. Instead of relying on low-level constructs of general-purpose languages such as Java, you can use domain-specific primitive thus dealing with a task in its own terms. The approach, however, has some drawbacks as it can be difficult to embed the DSL code into a general-purpose program because they are written in different languages. As a result DSL programs are usually stored outside their host code or simply embedded into string literals which complicate compile-time validation and code assistance in IDE.

Kotlin, however, can offer you a solution. In this chapter, we'll address a set of features which allow you to design DSLs that can be seamlessly combined with a rest of the Kotlin code. The basic idea is to design a special API which can be used in way resembling domain-specific language. So while your code may look like it's written in some different language, it still remains a valid Kotlin code. In other words, you get both advantages of the domain-specific approach and the power of compiled languages, including strong type-safety guarantees.

Structure

In this chapter, we will cover the following topics:

- Operator overloading
- Delegated properties
- Higher-order functions and DSLs

Objective

After reading this chapter, you will learn advanced features of Kotlin which help the developer to design API in the form of domain-specific languages.

Operator overloading

Operator overloading is a languages feature which allows you to assign custom meaning to built-in Kotlin operators like **+**, **-**, *****, **/**, and so on. In the previous chapters, we saw how + semantics vary depending on the type of values it applies to: arithmetic sum for numbers, concatenation for strings, appending an element for collection, and so on. This is possible because + is *overloaded*, i.e., has many different implementations.

In Kotlin, operators are in general just a syntactic sugar over calls to functions with a specific signature. In order to implement an operator, you just need to define an extension or member function following a certain convention and mark it with the **operator** keyword. For example, by defining the following:

```kotlin
operator fun String.times(n: Int) = repeat(n)
```

We extend the ***** operator (corresponding to the **times()** function) to the **String/Int** pairs which in turn allows us to write:

```kotlin
println("abc" * 3) // abcabcabc
```

Since operators are backed by some functions, we can always replace them by ordinary calls. For example, the preceding code has the same meaning as:

```kotlin
println("abc".times(3))
```

Even the built-in operations like addition can be written in this form, although in case of primitive types operations like addition or subtraction are optimized by compiler to avoid actual function calls for the sake of performance:

```kotlin
val x = 1.plus(2) // the same as 1 + 2
```

IDE Tips: The IntelliJ plugin can convert the explicit call of operator function into the corresponding unary/binary expression. To do that, you just need to press *Alt + Enter* on the operator token or function name and choose an appropriate conversion action. *Figure 11.1* shows an example of such a conversion which replaces the `times()` call with binary *.

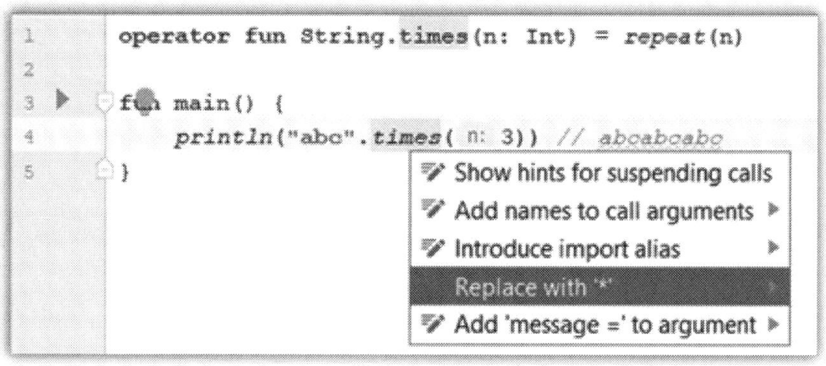

```
1    operator fun String.times(n: Int) = repeat(n)
2
3  ▶  ⬭ fun main() {
4        println("abc".times( n: 3)) // abcabcabc
5    ⬭ }
```

⬚ Show hints for suspending calls	
⬚ Add names to call arguments	▶
⬚ Introduce import alias	▶
Replace with '*'	▶
⬚ Add 'message =' to argument	▶

Figure 11.1: *Converting explicit call to operator form*

In the following section, we'll talk about conventions related to various Kotlin operators and consider some examples of their implementation.

Unary operations

Overloadable unary operators include prefix +, - and !. When you use such operators, the compiler automatically unfolds them into a call of an appropriate function (*Table 11.1*):

Expression	Meaning
+e	e.unaryPlus()
-e	e.unaryMinus()
!e	e.not()

Table 11.1: *Unary operator conventions*

The functions may be either members or extensions defined for the type of the argument expression. They may not have any parameters and their result type becomes the type of the whole unary expression.

Consider, for example, an enum class which represents basic RGB colors as well as their combinations:

```
enum class Color {
```

```
    BLACK, RED, GREEN, BLUE, YELLOW, CYAN, MAGENTA, WHITE
}
```

Using the **not()** convention, we can introduce the ! operator as a shorthand for complementary colors:

```
enum class Color {
    BLACK, RED, GREEN, BLUE, YELLOW, CYAN, MAGENTA, WHITE;

    operator fun not() = when (this) {
        BLACK -> WHITE
        RED -> CYAN
        GREEN -> MAGENTA
        BLUE -> YELLOW
        YELLOW -> BLUE
        CYAN -> RED
        MAGENTA -> GREEN
        WHITE -> BLACK
    }
}


fun main() {
    println(!Color.RED)  // CYAN
    println(!Color.CYAN) // RED
}
```

By defining operator functions as extensions, you can support respective operations for expressions of arbitrary types. For example:

```
operator fun <T> ((T) -> Boolean).not(): (T) -> Boolean = { !this(it) }
```

Using the preceding function, we can now apply the ! operator to any single-parameter predicate:

```
fun isShort(s: String) = s.length <= 4
fun String.isUpperCase() = all { it.isUpperCase() }


fun main() {
```

```
    val data = listOf("abc", "abcde", "ABCDE", "aBcD", "ab")
    println(data.count(::isShort))              // 3
    println(data.count(!::isShort))             // 2
    println(data.count(String::isUpperCase))   // 1
    println(data.count(!String::isUpperCase)) // 4
}
```

Increments and decrements

Increment (**++**) and decrement (**--**) operators can be overloaded by providing parameterless functions **inc()** and **dec()** for the corresponding operand type. Return value of these functions must correspond to "next" and "previous" value, respectively according to some ordering. The way **inc()/dec()** are used depends on whether the operator is written in its prefix or postfix form similar to how **++/--** work for numbers. For example, suppose we have an **enum** class listing rainbow colors:

```
enum class RainbowColor {
    RED, ORANGE, YELLOW, GREEN, BLUE, INDIGO, VIOLET;
}
```

Let's define **inc()/dec()** according to the preceding ordering looping around first and last elements so that the next of **VIOLET** is **RED** and the prior of **RED** is **VIOLET**:

```
enum class RainbowColor {
    RED, ORANGE, YELLOW, GREEN, BLUE, INDIGO, VIOLET;


    operator fun inc() = values[(ordinal + 1) % values.size]


    operator fun dec() = values[(ordinal + values.size - 1) % values.size]


    companion object {
        private val values = enumValues<RainbowColor>()
    }
}
```

Now, let's consider how increment and decrement would work for this class. As we've already seen in *Chapter 2, Language Fundamentals*, the postfix form of **++/--**

operators updates a variable but returns its value before change. This is also true for overloaded operators. For example, the code:

```
var color = RainbowColor.INDIGO
println(color++)
```

Would mean:

```
var color = RainbowColor.INDIGO
val _oldColor = color
color = color.inc()
println(_oldColor) // INDIGO
```

In the case of prefix form, the result of the increment/decrement expression is equal to the updated value, so this fragment:

```
var color = RainbowColor.INDIGO
println(color++)
```

Would actually translate into:

```
var color = RainbowColor.INDIGO
color = color.inc()
println(color) // VIOLET
```

Note that the presence of assignment like `color = color.inc()` implies two things:

- `++` and `--` are only applicable to mutable variables
- The return type of **inc()/dec()** functions must be a subtype of their receiver type

Binary operations

Kotlin allows you to overload most binary operators. Similar to unary ones, you need to provide a corresponding operator function. The major difference is that binary operator functions take their left operand as the receiver while the right operand is passed as an ordinary argument.

The *Table 11.2* lists conventional names for arithmetical operators, `..` and **in/!in**:

Expression	Meaning
a + b	a.plus(b)
a - b	a.minus(b)

a * b	a.times(b)
a / b	a.div(b)
a % b	a.rem(b)
a .. b	a.rangeTo(b)
a in b	b.contains(a)
a !in b	!b.contains(a)

Table 11.2: Binary operator conventions

Initially, the **%** operation was a shorthand for the **mod()** operator function which is currently superseded by **rem()**. As of now, the **mod()** convention is still available but deprecated.

For example, let's consider a simple prototype implementation of rational numbers supporting basic arithmetic operations:

```kotlin
import kotlin.math.abs

class Rational private constructor(
    val sign: Int,
    val num: Int,
    val den: Int
) {
    operator fun unaryMinus() = Rational(-sign, num, den)

    operator fun plus(r: Rational): Rational {
        val gcd = gcd(den, r.den)
        val newDen = den/gcd*r.den
        val newNum = newDen/den*num*sign + newDen/r.den*r.num*r.sign
        val newSign = newNum.sign()
        return Rational(newSign, abs(newNum), newDen)
    }

    operator fun minus(r: Rational) = this + (-r)

    operator fun times(r: Rational): Rational {
```

```kotlin
        return of(sign*r.sign*num*r.num, den*r.den)
    }

    operator fun div(r: Rational): Rational {
        return of(sign*r.sign*num*r.den, den*r.num)
    }

    override fun toString(): String {
        return "${sign*num}" + if (den != 1) "/$den" else ""
    }

    companion object {
        private fun Int.sign() = when {
            this > 0 -> 1
            this < 0 -> -1
            else -> 0
        }

        private tailrec fun gcd(a: Int, b: Int): Int {
            return if (b == 0) a else gcd(b, a % b)
        }

        fun of(num: Int, den: Int = 1): Rational {
          if (den == 0) throw ArithmeticException("Denominator is zero")
            val sign = num.sign() * den.sign()
            val numAbs = abs(num)
            val denAbs = abs(den)
            val gcd = gcd(numAbs, denAbs)
            return Rational(sign, numAbs/gcd, denAbs/gcd)
        }
    }
}
```

Using operator conventions, we can build arithmetic operations out of the **Rational** instances:

```
fun r(num: Int, den: Int = 1) = Rational.of(num, den)


fun main() {
    // 1/2 - 1/3
    println(r(1, 2) - r(1, 3))        // 1/6


    // 2/3 + (1/3)/2
    println(r(2, 3) + r(1, 3)/r(2))  // 5/6


    // 3/4 * 8/9 / (2/3)
    println(r(3, 4)*r(8, 9)/r(2, 3)) // 1


    // (1/10)*2 - 2/6
    println(r(1, 10)*r(2) - r(2, 6)) // -2/15
}
```

We can also introduce some additional operator functions which would allow us to mix the **Rational** objects with values of other types such as **Int**. For example:

```
operator fun Rational.plus(n: Int) = this + Rational.of(n)
operator fun Int.plus(r: Rational) = r + this


operator fun Rational.minus(n: Int) = this - Rational.of(n)
operator fun Int.minus(r: Rational) = Rational.of(this) - r


fun main() {
    // -1/3 + 2
    println(r(-1, 3) + 2)          // 5/3


    // 1 - (1/4)*(1/2)
    println(1 - r(1, 4)*r(1, 2)) // 7/8
}
```

To demonstrate usage of the **..** operation, let's define the **RationalRange** class representing a closed interval between two rational numbers:

```kotlin
class RationalRange(val from: Rational, val to: Rational) {
    override fun toString() = "[$from, $to]"
}
```

Now, we can define the **rangeTo()** function which would construct an instance of **RationalRange**:

```kotlin
operator fun Rational.rangeTo(r: Rational) = RationalRange(this, r)
```

```kotlin
fun main() {
    println(r(1, 4)..r(1)) // [1/4, 1]
}
```

The **in/!in** operations are expressed by the **contains()** operator function. Note that unlike all other binary operations arguments of **contains()** are swapped as compared to its operator form. Let's enhance the RationalRange class with an ability to check whether the given number belongs to the range:

```kotlin
private fun Rational.isLessOrEqual(r: Rational): Boolean {
    return num*r.den <= r.num*den
}
```

```kotlin
class RationalRange(val from: Rational, val to: Rational) {
    override fun toString() = "[$from, $to]"

    operator fun contains(r: Rational): Boolean {
        return from.isLessOrEqual(r) && r.isLessOrEqual(to)
    }

    operator fun contains(n: Int) = contains(r(n))
}
```

```kotlin
fun main() {
    // 1/2 in [1/4, 1]
}
```

```
    println(r(1, 2) in r(1, 4)..r(1)) // true


    // 1 not in [5/4, 7/4]
    println(1 !in r(5, 4)..r(7, 4))    // true
}
```

One more group of overloadable operators deals with comparisons like **<** and **>**. These operators do not correspond to separate functions. Instead, you can use a single **compareTo()** function to implement a full set of comparisons for a given combination of operand types. This function returns an Int value which signifies the comparison result. All comparison operations are implemented on top of it according to *Table 11.3*:

Expression	Meaning
a < b	a.compareTo(b) < 0
a <= b	a.compareTo(b) <= 0
a > b	a.compareTo(b) > 0
a >= b	a.compareTo(b) >= 0

Table 11.3: Comparison operator conventions

Now, we can get rid of the **isLessThan()** function above replacing it with a more general **compareTo()** implementation:

```
operator fun Rational.compareTo(r: Rational): Int {
    val left = num * r.den
    val right = r.num * den
    return when {
        left < right -> -1
        left > right -> 1
        else -> 0
    }
}


operator fun Rational.compareTo(n: Int) = compareTo(r(n))
operator fun Int.compareTo(r: Rational) = -r.compareTo(this)
```

```
class RationalRange(val from: Rational, val to: Rational) {
    override fun toString() = "[$from, $to]"

    operator fun contains(r: Rational) = r >= from && r <= to

    operator fun contains(n: Int) = contains(r(n))
}


fun main() {
    println(1 > r(1, 3))      // false
    println(r(3/4) <= r(7/8)) // true
}
```

One more binary convention we've already used in previous chapters is concerned with equality. When you use `==` or `!=`, the compiler automatically reduces the operator to the `equals()` call. Note that the `equals()` implementation does not need an explicit operator modifier since it's inherited from the base version declared in `Any` class. For the same reason `equals()` can only be implemented as a member and even if you have the `equals()` extension, it won't be used as `==`/`!=` implementation since extensions are always shadowed by member declarations with the same signature.

Note that Kotlin doesn't allow you to overload `&&` and `||`: they are built-in operations supported only for Boolean values. The same goes for Kotlin identity equality operations `===` and `!==`.

What if you want to implement a binary operation with a custom name? Although Kotlin doesn't allow you to introduce new operators, you can use ordinary identifiers as names for infix operations. We'll see how to do it in the next section.

Infix operations

We've already seen operations like to or until which can be used as infix operations:

```
val pair1 = 1 to 2  // infix call
val pair2 = 1.to(2) // ordinary call
```

To enable such calls, you need to mark a function with the **infix** modifier. Similar to binary operators, the function of interest must be either a member or an extension and have a single parameter. For example, that's how standard to function is defined:

```kotlin
infix fun <A, B> A.to(that: B): Pair<A, B> = Pair(this, that)
```

Let's refine our earlier predicate example a bit by introducing infix operations for a predicate conjunction and disjunction:

```kotlin
infix fun <T> ((T) -> Boolean).and(other: (T) -> Boolean): (T) -> Boolean {
    return { this(it) && other(it) }
}


infix fun <T> ((T) -> Boolean).or(other: (T) -> Boolean): (T) -> Boolean {
    return { this(it) || other(it) }
}
```

Now, we can use them to combine functional literals in a more concise way:

```kotlin
fun main() {
    val data = listOf("abc", "abcde", "ABCDE", "aBcD", "ab")
    println(data.count(::isShort and String::isUpperCase))   // 0
    println(data.count(::isShort or String::isUpperCase))    // 4
    println(data.count(!::isShort or String::isUpperCase))   // 2
    println(data.count(!(::isShort and String::isUpperCase))) // 5
}
```

Keep in mind that all infix operations have the same precedence. For example, complex expressions involving **and/or** operations we've defined earlier would parse differently than similar expressions with built-in **||** and **&&** boolean operators. Say, the following expression:

```kotlin
!::isShort or String::isEmpty and String::isUpperCase
```

Would mean

```kotlin
(!::isShort or String::isEmpty) and String::isUpperCase
```

While the Boolean expression

```kotlin
!s.isShort() || s.isEmpty() && s.isUpperCase()
```

Would be equivalent to

```
!s.isShort() || (s.isEmpty() && s.isUpperCase())
```

Due to **&&** having higher precedence than **||**.

Assignments

The next group of binary operations deals with augmented assignments like +=. In *Chapter 7, Exploring Collections and I/O*, we've seen that these operations behave differently for mutable and immutable collections. Namely, applying += to a variable of an immutable collection type would create a new collection object and *assign it to the variable,* thus changing its value. The variable must be defined as mutable in this case:

```
var numbers = listOf(1, 2, 3)

numbers += 4

println(numbers) // [1, 2, 3, 4]
```

When using **+=** on a mutable collection, however, we *modify collection content* while preserving an original object identity:

```
val numbers = mutableListOf(1, 2, 3)

numbers += 4

println(numbers) // [1, 2, 3, 4]
```

Note that if we put a mutable collection into a mutable variable, then **+=** would produce an error since the compiler can't decide which convention to follow:

```
var numbers = mutableListOf(1, 2, 3)

// Should we update a variable or collection content?

numbers += 4 // Error

println(numbers)
```

Both conventions can be supported for arbitrary types thanks to their respective operator functions. The behavior of augmented assignments depends on the following factors (see *Table 11.4*):

- Presence of the corresponding binary operator function: **plus()** for **+=**, **minus()** for **-=** and so on.
- Presence of the custom assignment function: **plusAssign()** for **+=**, **minusAssign()** for **-=** and so on
- Mutability of assignment left-hand side.

Expression	Meaning	
	Simple assignment reduction	**Custom assignment function**
`a += b`	`a = a.plus(b)`	`a.plusAssign(b)`
`a -= b`	`a = a.minus(b)`	`a.minusAssign(b)`
`a *= b`	`a = a.times(b)`	`a.timesAssign(b)`
`a /= b`	`a = a.div(b)`	`a.divAssign(b)`
`a %= b`	`a = a.rem(b)`	`a.remAssign(b)`

Table 11.4: *Assignment operator conventions*

Let's consider possible cases. When the left-hand side has a corresponding binary operator (for example, **plus()**) but not a custom assignment function, the augmented assignment is reduced to a simple one. This is what happens with primitive types and immutable collections. We can also use such assignments for our **Rational** objects since they already support binary operations like **+** and **-**. For example:

```
var r = r(1, 2) // ½
// The same as r = r + r(1, 3)
r += r(1, 3)    // 1/2 + 1/3
println(r)      // 5/6
```

Note that assignment left-hand side must be a mutable variable in this case.

When a left-hand side has only a custom assignment function (for example, **plusAssign()** but not **plus()**), then an augmented assignment is reduced to its call. To illustrate this convention, let's revisit the **TreeNode** class we introduced in *Chapter 9, Generics*, and change its API a bit:

```
class TreeNode<T>(val data: T) {
    private val _children = arrayListOf<TreeNode<T>>()

    var parent: TreeNode<T>? = null
        private set

    operator fun plusAssign(data: T) {
        val node = TreeNode(data)
        _children += node
```

```
        node.parent = this
    }


    operator fun minusAssign(data: T) {
        val index = _children.indexOfFirst { it.data == data }
        if (index < 0) return
        val node = _children.removeAt(index)
        node.parent = null
    }


    override fun toString() =
        _children.joinToString(prefix = "$data {", postfix = "}")
}
```

Now, we can use **+=** and **-=** operator on instances of **TreeNode** to add and remove tree elements:

```
val tree = TreeNode("root")
tree += "child 1"
tree += "child 2"
println(tree) // root {child 1 {}, child 2 {}}
tree -= "child 2"
println(tree) // root {child 1 {}}
```

Note that custom assignment functions must have the **Unit** return type.

When the left-hand side has both a custom assignment and a simple binary operation, the result depends on the left-hand side mutability:

- It the left-hand side is immutable, then the compiler chooses the custom assignment function because a simple assignment is not applicable.

- If the left-hand side is a mutable variable, the compiler reports an error because it resolves ambiguity: whether **a += b** is supposed to mean **a = a + b or a.plusAssign(b)**.

The preceding behavior is demonstrated by Kotlin mutable collection classes such as lists or sets because they have both the **plus()/minus()** functions inherited from immutable collections and their own **plusAssign()/minusAssign()**.

Invocations and indexing

Invocation convention allows you to use values in call expressions similar to functions. To do this, you just need to define the **invoke()** function with necessary parameters. Values of functional types automatically get **invoke()** as their member, but you can also add invocation support to an arbitrary type. For example, by defining the following function:

```
operator fun <K, V> Map<K, V>.invoke(key: K) = get(key)
```

We can use any Map instance as a function which returns a value by its key:

```
val map = mapOf("I" to 1, "V" to 5, "X" to 10)
println(map("V")) // 5
println(map("L")) // null
```

A useful case is to add the **invoke()** function to a companion object turning it into a factory. For example, if we augment out the **Rational** class with an extension:

```
operator fun Rational.Companion.invoke(num: Int, den: Int = 1) =
    of(num, den)
```

We can construct the **Rational** instances by referring to its class name:

```
val r = Rational(1, 2)
```

The preceding code looks like a direct constructor call but in fact reduces to the invocation chain: **invoke()** → **of()** → private constructor of **Rational**.

A similar convention allows you to use the indexing operator **[]** similar to how it applies to strings, arrays, lists, and maps. The underlying call depends on whether the indexing expression is used as a value or a left-hand side of assignment. In the first case, the compiler assumes *reading* access and reduces the indexing operator to the call of the **get()** function with the same set of arguments.

```
val array = arrayOf(1, 2, 3)
println(array[0]) // the same as println(array.get(0))
```

When the indexing expression is used as an assignment left-hand side, however, the compiler reduces it to the call of the **set()** function which on top of indices takes the assigned value as its last argument:

```
val array = arrayOf(1, 2, 3)
array[0] = 10 // the same as array.set(0, 10)
```

Indices are not necessarily integers; in fact, they may be arbitrary values. For example, the indexing operator for maps takes the key value as its argument.

Let's for example add both **get()/set()** operators to our **TreeNode** class to access its children:

```kotlin
class TreeNode<T>(var data: T) {
    private val _children = arrayListOf<TreeNode<T>>()

    var parent: TreeNode<T>? = null
        private set

    operator fun plusAssign(data: T) {
        val node = TreeNode(data)
        _children += node
        node.parent = this
    }

    operator fun minusAssign(data: T) {
        val index = _children.indexOfFirst { it.data == data }
        if (index < 0) return
        val node = _children.removeAt(index)
        node.parent = null
    }

    operator fun get(index: Int) = _children[index]

    operator fun set(index: Int, node: TreeNode<T>) {
        node.parent?._children?.remove(node)
        node.parent = this
        _children[index].parent = null
        _children[index] = node
    }
}
```

```
fun main() {
    val root = TreeNode("Root")
    root += "Child 1"
    root += "Child 2"
    println(root[1].data) // Child 2
    root[0] = TreeNode("Child 3")
    println(root[0].data) // Child 3
}
```

A more sophisticated case is using the indexing operator in an augmented assignment. The resulting code depends on the meaning of the assignment operator for the type of left-hand side which is effectively the return type of the **get()** operator function. For example, if we consider an array of the **Rational** objects which do not have the **plusAssign()** function, the code becomes as follows:

```
val array = arrayOf(r(1, 2), r(2, 3))
array[0] += Rational(1, 3)
```

Would mean:

```
val array = arrayOf(r(1, 2), r(2, 3))
array[0] = array[0] + r(1, 3)
```

Or, reducing everything to function calls:

```
val array = arrayOf(r(1, 2), r(2, 3))
array.set(0, array.get(0) + r(1, 3))
```

If we, however, use an array of **TreeNode** objects which have the **plusAssign()** function, but no **plus()**, a similar fragment:

```
val array = arrayOf(TreeNode("Root 1"), TreeNode("Root 2"))
array[0] += TreeNode("Child 1")
```

Would translate to:

```
val array = arrayOf(TreeNode("Root 1"), TreeNode("Root 2"))

array.get(0).plusAssign(TreeNode("Child 1"))
```

Note that the **get()** function is required in both cases.

Destructuring

We've already seen how to use destructuring declarations for instances of data classes to declare multiple variables at once and initialize them to the values of corresponding data class properties. By using operator overloading, you can enable this feature for arbitrary types. All you need is to define a parameterless member/extension function **componentN()** where N is a 1-based number. Then, each entry in a destructuring declaration initialized by an instance of the corresponding receiver type is assigned a value returned by the component function with the respective index.

To demonstrate this convention, let's define component functions for the **RationalRange** class we introduced in an earlier section:

```
operator fun RationalRange.component1() = from

operator fun RationalRange.component2() = to
```

Now, we can apply destructuring to our **RationalRange** instances:

```
fun main() {
    val (from, to) = r(1, 3)..r(1, 2)
    println(from) // 1/3
    println(to)   // 1/2
}
```

Data classes are no different in this regard. It's just that their component functions are autogenerated by the compiler rather than written explicitly. The Kotlin standard library includes some extension component functions as well. That's what allows you to destructure map entries:

```
val map = mapOf("I" to 1, "V" to 5, "X" to 10)
for ((key, value) in map) {
    println("$key = $value")
}
```

Or extract the first elements of a list or an array:

```
val numbers = listOf(10, 20, 30, 40, 50)
val (a, b, c) = numbers
println("$a, $b, $c") // 10, 20, 30
```

Iteration

In Chapter 3, *Defining Functions*, we introduced the for loop statement which can be applied to various objects, including strings, ranges, and collections. Their common feature which allows us to use the for loop is a presence of the **iterator()** function which returns the corresponding Iterator instance. By defining this function as either a member or an extension, you can support iteration via for statement for any type you like.

As an example, let's support iteration for the **TreeNode** class we introduced in an earlier section:

```
operator fun <T> TreeNode<T>.iterator() = children.iterator()
```

Now, we can use the **TreeNode** instances in a **for** loop without explicit references to its children member. For example, the program:

```
fun main() {
    val content = TreeNode("Title").apply {
        addChild("Topic 1").apply {
            addChild("Topic 1.1")
            addChild("Topic 1.2")
        }
        addChild("Topic 2")
        addChild("Topic 3")
    }
    for (item in content) {
        println(item.data)
    }
}
```

```
Would print:
Topic 1
Topic 2
Topic 3
```

This concludes our discussion of operator overloading in Kotlin. In the next section, we'll talk about delegation mechanism which allows you to introduce new kinds of properties into the Kotlin code.

Delegated properties

Delegated properties give you a way to implement the custom property access logic hidden behind a simple syntactic facade. We've already seen an example of lazy delegate which defers property computation till its first access:

```
val result by lazy { 1 + 2 }
```

Conciseness of property delegates makes them a helpful tool in designing both simple-to-use APIs and domain-specific languages.

Similarly to operators we've discussed in previous sections, implementation of delegated property is based on a set of conventions which allows you to define how a property is read or written and control construction of delegate object itself. In this section, we'll talk about these conventions in more detail as well as address some ready-to-use delegates provided by the Kotlin standard library.

Standard delegates

The Kotlin standard library includes a bunch of ready-to-use delegate implementations which cover many common uses cases. In *Chapter 4*, *Working with Classes and Objects*, we've already seen an example of such a delegate representing a lazy property:

```
val text by lazy { File("data.txt").readText() }
```

In fact, the **lazy()** function has three versions which allow you to fine-tune the behavior of the lazy property in a multi-threaded environment. By default, it creates a thread-safe implementation which uses synchronization to guarantee that the lazy value is always initialized by a single thread; in this case, the delegate instance also serves as a synchronization object.

When necessary, you can also specify your own synchronization object using another **lazy()** version:

```
private val lock = Any()

val text by lazy(this) { File("data.txt").readText() }
```

You can also choose between 3 basic implementations by passing a value of the **LazyThreadSafetyMode** enum:

- **SYNCHRONIZED:** Property access is synchronized so that only one thread can initialize its value (this implementation is used by default).

- **PUBLICATION:** Property access is synchronized in such a way that the initializer function can be invoked multiple times, but only the result of its first call becomes the property value.

- **NONE:** Property access is not synchronized; in a multi-threaded environment, property behavior is effectively undefined.

The major difference between **SYNCHRONIZED** and **PUBLICATION** becomes apparent if the initializer function has side effects. For example, if we have a property like this:

```
val myValue by lazy {
    println("Initializing myValue")
    123
}
```

The message gets printed at least once because the **SYNCHRONIZED** mode (which is used by default) ensures that the initializer is not called multiple times. If we, however, change the safety mode to **PUBLICATION**:

```
val myValue by lazy(LazyThreadSafetyMode.PUBLICATION) {
    println("Initializing myValue")
    123
}
```

The property values remains the same but the message is printed as many times as there are threads trying to initialize **myValue**.

The **NONE** mode provides the fastest implementation and is useful when you can guarantee that initializer is never called by more than one thread. A common case is a lazy local variable:

```
fun main() {
    val x by lazy(LazyThreadSafetyMode.NONE) { 1 + 2 }
    println(x) // 3
}
```

Note that if the initializer throws an exception, the property remains uninitialized, so the delegate will try to reinitialize it on the next access attempt.

Some standard delegates can be constructed by members of the **kotlin.properties. Delegates** object. The **notNull()** function provides a delegate which allows you to defer property initialization:

```
import kotlin.properties.Delegates.notNull
```

```kotlin
var text: String by notNull()

fun readText() {
    text = readLine()!!
}

fun main() {
    readText()
    println(text)
}
```

The semantics of the **notNull()** delegate is basically the same as that of lateinit properties. Internally, the null value is used as a marker of the uninitialized property so if it still happens to be null when you try to read from it, the delegate throws NPE. In most situations, it's worth using lateinit properties instead of **notNull()** since lateinit has a more concise syntax and better performance. An exception is a case of primitve types which are not supported by lateinit:

```kotlin
import kotlin.properties.Delegates.notNull

var num: Int by notNull() // Can't use lateinit here

fun main() {
    num = 10
    println(num) // 10
}
```

The **observable()** function allows you to define a property which sends a notification when its value is changed. It takes an initial value a lambda which is invoked after each change:

```kotlin
import kotlin.properties.Delegates.observable

class Person(name: String, val age: Int) {
    var name: String by observable(name) { property, old, new ->
        println("Name changed: $old to $new")
```

```
        }
}


fun main() {
    val person = Person("John", 25)
    person.name = "Harry"    // Name changed: John to Harry
    person.name = "Vincent" // Name changed: Harry to Vincent
    person.name = "Vincent" // Name changed: Vincent to Vincent
}
```

Note that the notification is sent even if the new value is the same as the old one. The lambda should check this by itself if necessary.

The **vetoable()** function constructs a similar delegate but takes a lambda which returns Boolean and is called *before* actual modification. If this lambda returns false, the property value remains unchanged:

```
import kotlin.properties.Delegates.vetoable


var password: String by vetoable("password") { property, old, new ->
    if (new.length < 8) {
        println("Password should be at least 8 characters long")
        false
    } else {
        println("Password is Ok")
        true
    }
}


fun main() {
    password = "pAsSwOrD" // Password is accepted
    password = "qwerty"    // Password should be at least 8 characters long
}
```

If you want to combine both pre- and post-change notifications, you may implement your own delegate by subclassing **ObservableProperty** and overriding **beforeChange()/afterChange()** functions.

The standard library also allows you to store/retrieve the property value using a map where the property name serves as a key. You can do it by using the map instance as a delegate:

```
class CartItem(data: Map<String, Any?>) {
    val title: String by data
    val price: Double by data
    val quantity: Int by data
}


fun main() {
    val item = Cartitem(mapOf(
        "title" to "Laptop",
        "price" to 999.9,
        "quantity" to 1
    ))
    println(item.title)     // Laptop
    println(item.price)     // 999.9
    println(item.quantity) // 1
}
```

When you access a property, its value is taken from a map and cast down to the expected type. Map delegates should be used with care because they break type safety. In particular, access to a property value will fail with cast exception if it doesn't contain a value of the expected type.

Using this feature, you can also define mutable variables backed by a mutable map:

```
class CartItem(data: MutableMap<String, Any?>) {
    var title: String by data
    var price: Double by data
    var quantity: Int by data
}
```

What if standard delegates are not enough? In this case, you can implement your own by following language conventions. We'll see how to do it in the next section.

Creating custom delegates

To create your own property delegate, you need a type which defines special operator function(s) which implement reading and writing of the property value. The reader function must be named **getValue** and have two parameters:

1. **receiver:** This contains the receiver value and must be of the same type as a receiver of the delegated property (or its supertype).

2. **property:** This contains a reflection object representing a property declaration; it must be of type **KProperty<*>** or its supertype.

Parameter names are not actually important, only their types matter. The return type of the **getValue()** function must be the same as the type of the delegated property (or its subtype).

Let's, for example, create a delegate which memorizes the property value associating it with a particular receiver to create a kind of cache:

```
import kotlin.reflect.KProperty


class CachedProperty<in R, out T : Any>(val initializer: R.() -> T) {
    private val cachedValues = HashMap<R, T>()


    operator fun getValue(receiver: R, property: KProperty<*>): T {
     return cachedValues.getOrPut(receiver) { receiver.initializer()
}
    }
}


fun  <R,  T  :  Any>  cached(initializer:  R.()  ->  T)  =
CachedProperty(initializer)


class Person(val firstName: String, val familyName: String)


val Person.fullName: String by cached { "$firstName $familyName" }


fun main() {
    val johnDoe = Person("John", "Doe")
```

```
    val harrySmith = Person("Harry", "Smith")
    // First access for johnDoe receiver, computed and stored to cache
    println(johnDoe.fullName)
    // First access for harrySmith receiver, computed and stored to cache
    println(harrySmith.fullName)
    // Repeated access for johnDoe receiver, taken from cache
    println(johnDoe.fullName)
    // Repeated access for harrySmith receiver, taken from cache
    println(harrySmith.fullName)
}
```

Since **fullName** is a top-level property, its delegate becomes part of the global state, and the property value is only initialized once for a particular receiver (if we set multi-threading issues aside).

The ReadOnlyProperty interface from the **kotlin.properties** package can serve a good starting point for creating custom read-only delegates. This interface defines an abstract version of the **getValue()** operator which you'll need to implement in your own class:

```
interface ReadOnlyProperty<in R, out T> {
    operator fun getValue(thisRef: R, property: KProperty<*>): T
}
```

For a read-write delegate which can be applied to var properties, you also need to define the corresponding **setValue()** function which is invoked upon each property assignment. This function must have a Unit return type and take three parameters:

- **receiver:** This has the same meaning as **getValue()**.
- **property:** This has the same meaning as **getValue()**.
- **newValue:** This has a new value of a property which must have the same type as a property itself (or its supertype).

In the following example, we define a delegate class which implements a final version of the lateinit property which doesn't allow you to initialize it more than once:

```
import kotlin.reflect.KProperty


class FinalLateinitProperty<in R, T : Any> {
    private lateinit var value: T
```

```
    operator fun getValue(receiver: R, property: KProperty<*>): T {
        return value
    }


    operator fun setValue(receiver: R, property: KProperty<*>, newValue:
    T) {
        if (this::value.isInitialized) throw IllegalStateException(
            "Property ${property.name} is already initialized"
        )
        value = newValue
    }
}


fun <R, T : Any> finalLateInit() = FinalLateinitProperty<R, T>()


var message: String by finalLateInit()


fun main() {
    message = "Hello"
    println(message) // Hello
    message = "Bye" // Exception: Property message is already initialized
}
```

The Kotlin standard library also includes a mutable version of the **ReadOnlyProperty**
interface which is called **ReadWriteProperty**. You can similarly implement this
interface in your delegate class:

```
public interface ReadWriteProperty<in R, T> {
    operator fun getValue(thisRef: R, property: KProperty<*>): T


    operator fun setValue(thisRef: R, property: KProperty<*>, value: T)
}
```

Note that the **getVersion()/setVersion()** functions may be defined as either
members or extensions. The latter option allows you to turn virtually any object into

some kind of delegate. Delegation to `Map`/`MutableMap` instances, in particular, is implemented by the extension function from the Kotlin standard library:

```kotlin
inline operator fun <V, V1 : V> Map<in String, V>.getValue(
    thisRef: Any?,
    property: KProperty<*>
): V1 {...}
```

Since Kotlin 1.1, you can control delegate instantiation via the **provideDelegate()** function. By default, the delegate instance is defined by an expression coming after the **by** keyword in a property declaration. Alternatively, you can pass an intermediate instance which serves as a kind of delegate factory with the **provideDelegate()** function. Similar to **getValue()**, this function takes the property receiver and reflection object as parameters instead of retrieving the property value returns an actual delegate object. This can be useful when the delegate needs the property metadata for proper initialization.

Suppose that we want to introduce the `@NoCache` annotation which prevents property caching. In this case, we'd like our **CachedProperty** implementation to throw an exception early, during property initialization rather than deferring failure till the moment the property is accessed. We can achieve it by adding the delegate provider which validates the target property before creating the delegate:

```kotlin
@Target(AnnotationTarget.PROPERTY)
annotation class NoCache


class CachedPropertyProvider<in R, out T : Any>(val initializer:
R.() -> T) {
    operator fun provideDelegate(
        receiver: R,
        property: KProperty<*>
    ): CachedProperty<R, T> {
        if (property.annotations.any { it is NoCache }) {
            throw IllegalStateException("${property.name} forbids
            caching")
        }
        return CachedProperty(initializer)
    }
```

```
}
class CachedProperty<in R, out T : Any>(val initializer: R.() -> T) {
    private val cachedValues = HashMap<R, T>()


    operator fun getValue(receiver: R, property: KProperty<*>): T {
      return cachedValues.getOrPut(receiver) { receiver.initializer()
}
    }
}


fun <R, T : Any> cached(initializer: R.() -> T) =
    CachedPropertyProvider(initializer)
```

Now, when we attempt to use caching delegate on a property with the **@NoCache** annotation, the provider will fail with an error:

```
class Person(val firstName: String, val familyName: String)


@NoCache val Person.fullName: String by cached {
    if (this != null) "$firstName $familyName" else ""
}


fun main() {
    val johnDoe = Person("John", "Doe")
    println(johnDoe.fullName) // Exception
}
```

Just like delegate accessors, **provideDelegate()** may be implemented as either a member or extension function.

Delegate representation

Wrapping up our discussion of delegated properties, let's talk about how delegates are represented and can be accessed at runtime.

At runtime, the delegate is stored in a separate field while the property itself gets automatically generated accessors which invoked corresponding methods of the delegate instance. For example, the code:

```kotlin
class Person(val firstName: String, val familyName: String) {
    var age: Int by finalLateInit()
}
```

Is effectively equivalent to the following:

```kotlin
class Person(val firstName: String, val familyName: String) {
    private val `age$delegate` = finalLateInit<Person, Int>()
    var age: Int
        get() = `age$delegate`.getValue(this, this::age)
        set(value) {
            `age$delegate`.setValue(this, this::age, value)
        }
}
```

With the exception that the delegate field **age$delegate** can't be used in Kotlin code explicitly.

Reflection API allows you to access the delegate value using the corresponding property object via its **getDelegate()** member. The signature varies depending on the number of receivers. For example:

```kotlin
import kotlin.reflect.jvm.isAccessible


class Person(val firstName: String, val familyName: String) {
    val fullName by lazy { "$firstName $familyName" }
}


fun main() {
    val person = Person("John", "Doe")
    // KProperty0: all receivers are bound
    println(
        person::fullName
            .apply { isAccessible = true }
            .getDelegate()!!::class.qualifiedName
    ) // kotlin.SynchronizedLazyImpl
    // KProperty1: single receiver
```

```kotlin
    println(
        Person::fullName
            .apply { isAccessible = true }
            .getDelegate(person)!!::class.qualifiedName
    ) // kotlin.SynchronizedLazyImpl
}
```

Note the need to use **isAccessible = true** to access the private field where the delegate instance is stored.

What if our property is defined as an extension? In this case, the delegate instance is shared among all possible receivers and we can **getExtensionDelegate()** to obtain it without specifying a particular receiver instance:

```kotlin
val Person.fullName: String by cached { "$firstName $familyName" }
```

```kotlin
fun main() {
    println(
        Person::fullName
            .apply { isAccessible = true }
            .getExtensionDelegate()!!::class.qualifiedName
    ) // CachedProperty
}
```

Higher-order functions and DSLs

In this section, we'll demonstrate how to design a domain-specific language using type-safe builders. This task won't require any new knowledge and instead will just rely on what we've already learned about higher-order functions in Kotlin.

Fluent DSL with infix functions

Our first example will demonstrate how to use infix functions for creating fluent APIs. We'll create a simple DSL for querying collection data using SQL-inspired syntax.

Namely, we'd like to be able to write code like the following (readers familiar with C# would probably recognize similarity with LINQ):

```kotlin
val numbers = listOf(2, 8, 9, 1, 3, 6, 5)
```

```kotlin
val query = from(numbers) where { it > 3 } select { it*2 } orderBy { it }
println(query.items.toList())
```

So, basically we want our query to consist of the following:

1. **The from** clause which specifies an original collection.
2. Followed by an optional **where** clause which specifies the filtering condition.
3. Followed by an optional **select** clause which maps original data to output values.
4. When select is present, we can also use an optional **orderBy** clause which specifies an ordering key.

So how do we implement such an API? First, let's define some classes representing intermediate structures of a query. Since most of them represent a kind of data set be it an original collection or result of filtering, we'll introduce a common interface with an ability to return the resulting sequence of items:

```kotlin
interface ResultSet<out T> {
    val items: Sequence<T>
}
```

Now, we can define classes representing query components:

```kotlin
class From<out T>(private val source: Iterable<T>) : ResultSet<T> {
    override val items: Sequence<T>
        get() = source.asSequence()
}


class Where<out T>(
    private val from: ResultSet<T>,
    private val condition: (T) -> Boolean
) : ResultSet<T> {
    override val items: Sequence<T>
        get() = from.items.filter(condition)
}


class Select<out T, out U>(
    private val from: ResultSet<T>,
```

```
    private val output: (T) -> U
) : ResultSet<U> {
    override val items: Sequence<U>
        get() = from.items.map(output)
}


class OrderBy<out T, in K : Comparable<K>>(
    private val select: ResultSet<T>,
    private val orderKey: (T) -> K
) : ResultSet<T> {
    override val items: Sequence<T>
        get() = select.items.sortedBy(orderKey)
}
```

Now that we have our building blocks, we can define a set infix functions to link them together according to our DSL requirements:

```
// where may follow from
infix fun <T> From<T>.where(condition: (T) -> Boolean) =
    Where(this, condition)


// select may follow either from or where
infix fun <T, U> From<T>.select(output: (T) -> U) =
    Select(this, output)
infix fun <T, U> Where<T>.select(output: (T) -> U) =
    Select(this, output)


// orderBy may follow select
infix fun <T, K : Comparable<K>> Select<*, T>.orderBy(orderKey: (T) -> K) =
    OrderBy(this, orderKey)
```

The last piece is the **from()** function which starts a query:

```
fun <T> from(source: Iterable<T>) = From(source)
```

Now, the original example is as follows:

```kotlin
val numbers = listOf(2, 8, 9, 1, 3, 6, 5)
val query = from(numbers) where { it > 3 } select { it*2 } orderBy { it }
println(query.items.toList())
```

Will compile and correctly print:

```
[10, 12, 16, 18]
```

Note that type-safety ensures rejection of queries which doesn't conform to our intended syntax. For example, the code:

```kotlin
val query = from(numbers) where { it > 3 } where { it < 10 }
```

Won't compile since only one where clause is allowed. If we'd wanted to permit multiple where clauses, however, we'd just need to add one more infix function:

```kotlin
infix fun <T> Where<T>.where(condition: (T) -> Boolean) =
    Where(this, condition)
```

Now, let's look at more complex examples with nested structures.

Using type-safe builders

A common case in designing a DSL is a representation of hierarchical structures where some domain objects can be nested inside others. In Kotlin, you have a powerful solution which allows you to express such structures in a somewhat declarative way by combining builder functions with extension lambdas. Let's see how they can be implemented by an example of simple component layout DSL.

Our goal will be an API which would allow you to describe a program UI in the following manner:

```kotlin
fun main() {
    val form = dialog("Send a message") {
        borderLayout {
            south = panel {
                +button("Send")
                +button("Cancel")
            }
            center = panel {
                verticalBoxLayout {
                    +filler(0, 10)
                    +panel {
```

```
                  horizontalBoxLayout {
                      +filler(5, 0)
                      +label("Message: ")
                      +filler(10, 0)
                      +textArea("")
                      +filler(5, 0)
                  }
              }
              +filler(0, 10)
          }
        }
      }
    }
    form.size = Dimension(300, 200)
    form.isVisible = true
}
```

So basically, we want our DSL to do the following:

- Describe a hierarchical structure of UI components.
- Support standard layout managers like BorderLayout or BoxLayout.
- Provide helper functions to create and initialize common components like buttons, text fields, panels, and windows.

Figure 11.2 displays the window produced from the preceding code:

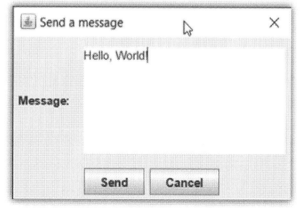

Figure 11.2: *Window generated by layout DSL*

How do we implement such a language? First, let's see which kinds of objects are involved in UI description:

- Simple components like button or text field which do not have nested structure.
- Containers like panels or windows: you may attach some layout to them or add nested components directly via the + operator.
- Layouts which allow you to specify child components of the corresponding container. The specifics depend on a particular layout; for example, border layout binds children to predetermined areas (**NORTH, SOUTH,** and so on.) while box layout allows you to add components sequentially placing them in a row or column.

Functions like **button()** are the simplest part since just wrap component constructors without any extra processing:

```kotlin
fun label(text: String) = JLabel(text)

fun button(text: String) = JButton(text)

fun textArea(text: String) = JTextArea(text)
```

The more interesting case is the **panel()** function which takes a lambda with definitions of nested components. In order to maintain a container state, we'll introduce the **ContainerBuilder** class which allows you to add nested components and define layouts:

```kotlin
class ContainerBuilder(private val container: Container) {
    operator fun Component.unaryPlus() = apply { container.add(this) }

    fun borderLayout(body: BorderLayoutBuilder.() -> Unit) {
        BorderLayoutBuilder(container).body()
    }

    fun horizontalBoxLayout(body: BoxLayoutBuilder.() -> Unit) {
        BoxLayoutBuilder(container, BoxLayout.LINE_AXIS).body()
    }

    fun verticalBoxLayout(body: BoxLayoutBuilder.() -> Unit) {
        BoxLayoutBuilder(container, BoxLayout.PAGE_AXIS).body()
    }
```

```
}
```

Now, we can define the **panel()** and **dialog()** functions:

```
fun panel(body: ContainerBuilder.() -> Unit) = JPanel().apply {
    ContainerBuilder(this).body()
}


fun dialog(
    title: String,
    body: ContainerBuilder.() -> Unit
): JDialog = JDialog().apply {
    this.title = title
    pack()
    defaultCloseOperation = JDialog.DISPOSE_ON_CLOSE
    ContainerBuilder(contentPane).body()
}
```

You can see these functions take a lambda which serves as an extension on the **ContainerBuilder** class. This allows us to directly call members of **ContainerBuilder** inside a lambda since this receiver is assumed implicitly. For example, the portion:

```
panel {
    horizontalBoxLayout {
        +filler(5, 0)
        ...
    }
}
```

Really means:

```
panel {
    this.horizontalBoxLayout {
        // dispatch receiver of BoxLayoutBuilder is implicit
        filler(5, 0).unaryPlus()
        ...
    }
```

```
}
```

What about layouts? We can define their builders in a similar way remembering an API difference between various layouts. For example:

```
class BoxLayoutBuilder(private val container: Container, direction:
Int) {

    init {
        container.layout = BoxLayout(container, direction)
    }


    operator fun Component.unaryPlus() = apply { container.add(this) }


    fun filler(width: Int, height: Int) =
        Box.createRigidArea(Dimension(width, height))
}
```

We've added **unaryPlus()** to **BoxLayoutBuilder** because we want to add its children sequentially like we do with a container like panel. In case of **BorderLayoutBuilder**, we'll need a set of properties like **north, south, west**, and so on which retain the value of the added component and add it to the container when changed. We can pack this logic into a variety of observable delegates:

```
fun constrained(
    container: Container,
    constraint: Any?
) = observable<Component?>(null) { _, _, value ->
    container.add(value, constraint)
}


class BorderLayoutBuilder(container: Container) {
    init {
        container.layout = BorderLayout()
    }
```

```
    var north by constrained(container, BorderLayout.NORTH)

    var south by constrained(container, BorderLayout.SOUTH)

    var west by constrained(container, BorderLayout.WEST)

    var east by constrained(container, BorderLayout.EAST)

    var center by constrained(container, BorderLayout.CENTER)
}
```

Many Kotlin DSLs are implemented in a similar manner. In the upcoming chapters, we'll take a closer look at some languages targeted at common tasks: test specification, description of UI in Android application, request handling rules in a web application, and type-safe generation of HTML. For now, though, we have one more topic to discuss, and that's how to control the scope of builder functions.

@DslMarker

When using a hierarchical DSL like the one we discussed in the previous section, you may find that members of outer blocks are leaking into nested scopes. For example, using our layout DSL we could've written:

```
val myPanel = panel {
    borderLayout {
        borderLayout {


        }
    }
}
```

This is certainly unintended because we didn't want the layout-introducing function to be available on layouts themselves. Still the preceding code is correct and both the **borderLayout()** calls in fact have the same receiver, namely, the instance of **ContainerBuilder** passed to the outermost lambda. The problem is that each of these receivers is available not only in its declaration scope, but in all nested scoped as well. If we'd made the receivers explicit, the out code would look like:

```
val myPanel = panel {
    this@panel.borderLayout {
        this@panel.borderLayout {
```

```
            }
        }
}
```

Now, it's clear that both receivers are the same.

So even though the leakage of implicit receivers into nested scopes do not break type safety, it certainly can be misleading and thus lead to error-prone code, especially if code in question is a DSL which usually has a lot of nested extension lambdas. For that reason, Kotlin 1.1 introduced the `@DslMarker` annotation which helps DSL designers to restrict visibility of implicit receivers.

@DslMarker is a meta-annotation which you can use to annotate your own annotation class meant to serve as a marker of particular DSL. Let's introduce **@LayoutDsl** for this purpose:

```
@DslMarker
annotation class LayoutDsl
```

Now, we use **@LayoutDsl** to annotate classes which are used as receivers in DSL blocks. In our case, that's **ContainerBuilder**, **BorderLayoutBuilder,** and **BoxLayoutBuilder**:

```
@LayoutDsl
class ContainerBuilder(private val container: Container) {...}
```

```
@LayoutDsl
class BorderLayoutBuilder(container: Container) {...}
```

```
@LayoutDsl
class BoxLayoutBuilder(private val container: Container, direction:
Int) {...}
```

If classes in question have a common supertype, you may annotate that supertype instead. DSL marker annotations automatically affect all subtypes.

Now that the compiler knows that these classes belong to the same DSL, it won't allow you to use corresponding receivers in nested scopes. For example, our original fragment now produces a compilation error:

```
val myPanel = panel {
```

```
        borderLayout {

            borderLayout { // Error: DSL scope violation


            }
        }
    }
```

Note that **@DslMarker** only forbids leakage of *implicit* receivers. But you still can use an explicit one if necessary:

```
val myPanel = panel {

        borderLayout {

            this@panel.borderLayout { // Correct


            }
        }
    }
```

Conclusion

This chapter has introduced us to the advanced features of Kotlin language which help to design internal domain-specific languages, thus combining simplicity of usage with type safety ensured by the Kotlin compiler. We learned conventions which allow a developer to define overloaded operators, explored standard implementations of delegated properties and discussed how you can create your own. Finally, we saw how functional programming together with type-safe builders can help to design hierarchical DSLs.

In the next chapter, we will discuss the issue of Java/Kotlin interoperability. We'll see how Kotlin declarations can be used from Java code and vice versa, how to fine-tune your Kotlin-based API for Java clients and how Kotlin tooling can help to automatically convert Java code into a Kotlin.

Questions

1. What operator overloading conventions are available in Kotlin?

2. Describe standard delegate implementations.

3. What conventions are used for property delegates? Given an example of custom delegate implementation.

4. How can you access a delegate value at runtime?

5. Describe how to design domain-specific language using higher-order functions.

6. Explain the meaning of @DslMarker annotation.

CHAPTER 12
Java Interoperability

In this chapter, we will introduce you to various topics concerned with interoperability between Java and Kotlin code. This aspect plays a major role in mixed projects where the Java code has to coexist with Kotlin. Thanks to good JVM interoperability, you can easily add Kotlin into existing projects or gradually convert the Java code with little to no changes in its surroundings.

We'll look at how Kotlin and Java types map into each other, how Kotlin declarations are presented from Java's point of view and vice versa, and look at language features which can help you to customize Java/Kotlin interoperability.

Structure

In this chapter, we will cover the following topics:

- Using the Java code from Kotlin
- Using the Kotlin code from Java

Objective

After reading this chapter, you will learn how Kotlin declarations and types are represented from the Java point of view (and vice versa) and how both languages can be mixed in a single codebase.

Using Java code from Kotlin

Since Kotlin is designed with JVM as one of its primary targets, using Java code in Kotlin is pretty straightforward. There are, however, some issues mainly arising from the fact some Kotlin features are not available in Java. For example, Java doesn't incorporate null-safety into its type system: while Kotlin types always explicitly specify whether they are nullable or not. Java types usually lack such information. In this section, we'll discuss how such issues can be resolved from both Java and Kotlin sides.

Java methods and fields

In most cases using Java methods, Kotlin poses no concerns as they are exposed as ordinary Kotlin functions. Fields when they are not encapsulated are similarly available like Kotlin properties with trivial accessor(s). Still it's worth bearing in mind some nuances stemming from language specifics.

Unit vs void

Kotlin has no **void** keyword representing an absence of return value, so every **void** method in Java is visible as the Unit function in Kotlin. If you call such a function and use the call result somewhere (for example, assign it to a variable) the compiler will generate a reference to the **Unit** object.

Operator conventions

Some Java methods such as **Map.get()** may satisfy Kotlin operator conventions. In Kotlin, you can use them in the operator form even though they do not have the **operator** keyword. For example, since the **Method** class from the Java Reflection API has the **invoke()** method, we can use it like a function:

```
val length = String::class.java.getDeclaredMethod("length")

println(length("abcde")) // 5
```

Infix calls, however, are not supported for Java methods.

Synthetic properties

Even though Java has no properties as such, using getters as setters is quite common. For that reason, Kotlin exposes getter/setter pairs as synthetic properties which the Kotlin code can access which are similar to ordinary Kotlin properties. An accessor must follow certain conventions, namely:

- The getter must be a parameterless method and have a name starting with "get".

- The setter must have a single argument and a name starting with "set".

For example, if you have a Java class:

```
public class Person {
    private String name;
    private int age;

    public Person(String name, int age) {
        this.name = name;
        this.age = age;
    }

    public String getName() {
        return name;
    }

    public void setName(String name) {
        this.name = name;
    }

    public int getAge() {
        return age;
    }

    public void setAge(int age) {
        this.age = age;
    }
}
```

You can use its instances as if they have a pair of mutable properties **name** and **age**:

```
fun main() {
    val person = Person("John", 25)
```

```
    person.name = "Harry"
    person.age = 30
    println("${person.name}, ${person.age}") // Harry, 30
}
```

This convention also works when there is only a getter method. In this case, a resulting property is immutable. When a Java class has a setter method, but no getter, however, no property is exposed since write-only properties are not currently supported in Kotlin.

As an alternative, a getter name may start with "is". In this case, a synthetic property will have the same name as the getter. Suppose we extend the preceding **Person** class by adding a boolean field with accessors:

```
public class Person {

    ...


    private boolean isEmployed;


    public boolean isEmployed() {
        return isEmployed;
    }


    public void setEmployed(boolean employed) {
        isEmployed = employed;
    }

}
```

Kotlin code can call these accessors using the **isEmployed** property.

IDE Tips: You can also use ordinary method calls instead of synthetic properties, but this is considered redundant. By default, the IntelliJ plugin warns about such calls suggesting you to replace them by the synthetic property access (see *Figure 12.1*):

Figure 12.1: Converting explicit setter call to property assignment

Note that the synthetic property syntax is only available for methods declared in a non-Kotlin code. You can't use them for get/set methods defined in Kotlin source files.

Platform types

Since Java doesn't distinguish between nullable and non-nullable types, the Kotlin compiler in general can't make any assumptions about nullability of objects coming from a Java code. Exposing them as nullable, however, is impractical because you'd have to deal with a lot of bogus nullability checks in the Kotlin code. For that reason, the Kotlin compiler relaxes null-safety when it comes to Java types and doesn't expose them as types with definite nullability. In Kotlin, objects originating from the Java code belong to special *platform types* which basically constitute type ranges between nullable and non-nullable versions. Null-safety guarantees provided by such types are basically the same as in Java; you can use their values in both nullable and non-nullable context, but such usage may fail at runtime with **NullPointerException**.

Suppose we have a Java class:

```java
public class Person {
    private String name;
    private int age;

    public Person(String name, int age) {
        this.name = name;
        this.age = age;
    }
    public String getName() { return name; }
    public void setName(String name) { this.name = name; }
    public int getAge() { return age; }
    public void setAge(int age) { this.age = age; }
    }
```

And use it from a Kotlin code:

```kotlin
fun main() {
    val person = Person("John", 25)
    println(person.name.length) // 4
}
```

In the preceding code, **person.name** has a platform type because the compiler doesn't know if it can be nullable. Nevertheless, the code compiles but nullability check is deferred to runtime when a program tries to access the length property. If we change it to the following:

```kotlin
fun main() {
    val person = Person(null, 25)
    println(person.name.length) // Exception
}
```

The program would still compile, but fail at runtime.

Note that platform types may not be written explicitly in a Kotlin source code. They are only constructed by a compiler. You can, however, see them in the IntelliJ IDEA plugin. For example, if you apply the "Show expression type" action (*Ctrl + Shift + P*/Cmd + Shift + P) to the **person.name** expression, you'll see that its type is **String!** (see *Figure 12.2*). This notation means that values of this type can pose as both values of String? and String:

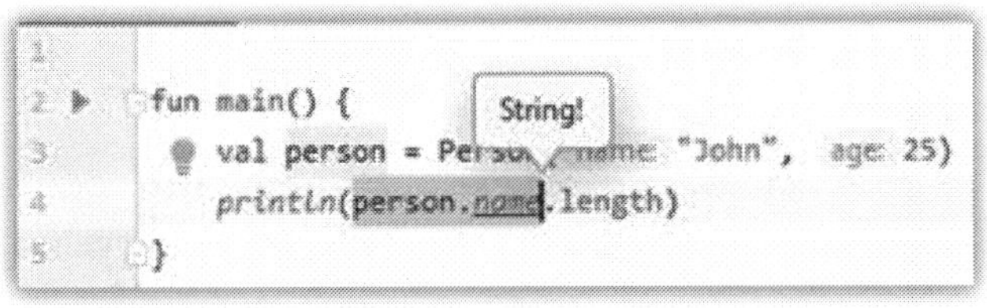

Figure 12.2: Platform type representation in IDE

If you assign an expression of a platform type to a variable or return it from a function without specifying an explicit type, it propagates. For example:

```kotlin
import java.math.BigInteger


fun Int.toBigInt() = BigInteger.valueOf(toLong()) // BigInteger!
return type


val num = 123.toBigInt() // BigInteger! type
```

If you specify a type explicitly, you might force the platform type into either nullable or non-nullable:

```kotlin
import java.math.BigInteger


// BigInteger (non-nullable) return type
```

```
fun Int.toBigInt(): BigInteger = BigInteger.valueOf(toLong())
```

```
val num = 123.toBigInt() // BigInteger (non-nullable) type
```

IDE Tips: The IntelliJ plugin can warn you about the implicit propagation of platform types and suggest either specifying the type explicitly, or adding the not-null assertion !! (as shown in *Figure 12.3*):

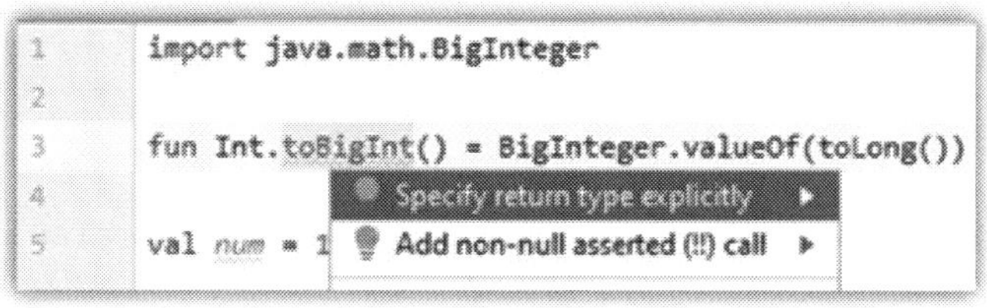

Figure 12.3: *Getting rid of platform type propagation*

If we force the platform type into a non-nullable one, the compiler will generate an assertion. This ensures that the program will fail during the assignment rather than at some later moment when the assigned value is accessed.

Kotlin also uses platform types to represent Java collection types. The reason is similar to that of nullable types. Unlike Kotlin, Java doesn't distinguish between mutable or immutable collections. So in Kotlin, each Java-originating instance of the standard collection type such as **List**, **Set,** or **Map** looks like some range between the mutable and mutable version. In IDE, such types are represented by adding a (Mutable) prefix (see, for example, *Figure 12.4*):

Figure 12.4: *Mutable platform types*

Nullability annotations

In the Java world, a common solution to a null-safety problem is using special type annotations. Modern development environments like IntelliJ IDEA can make use of such annotations reporting potential violations of nullability contracts. Some of them are supported by the Kotlin compiler as well. In this case, a respective type is exposed as either a nullable or non-nullable (depending on the annotation used) and platform type is not used. For example, if we annotate the **Person** class from our earlier example:

```java
import org.jetbrains.annotations.NotNull;

public class Person {
    @NotNull private String name;
    private int age;

    public Person(@NotNull String name, int age) {
        this.name = name;
        this.age = age;
    }


    @NotNull
    public String getName() { return name; }
    public void setName(@NotNull String name) { this.name = name; }
    public int getAge() { return age; }
    public void setAge(int age) { this.age = age; }
}
```

Types in the Kotlin code will reflect these changes as shown in *Figure 12.5*:

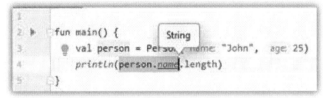

Figure 12.5: *Exposing Java type annotated with @NotNull*

Some of the nullability annotations supported by the Kotlin compiler include (you can find a more comprehensive list in the Kotlin documentation at kotlinlang.org):

- JetBrains **@Nullable** and **@NotNull** (from **org.jetbrains.annotations package**)
- Multiple varieties of **@Nullable** and **@NonNull** annotations from Android SDK
- JSR-305 nullability annotations such as **@Nonnull** (from **javax.annotation package**)

IDE Tips: The JetBrains annotations library is not added to project dependencies automatically but can be easily configured when necessary. If the **@Nullable/@ NotNull** annotation is not available, you can press *Alt + Enter* on the unresolved annotation reference and choose the **Add 'annotations' to classpath** action as shown in *Figure 12.6*:

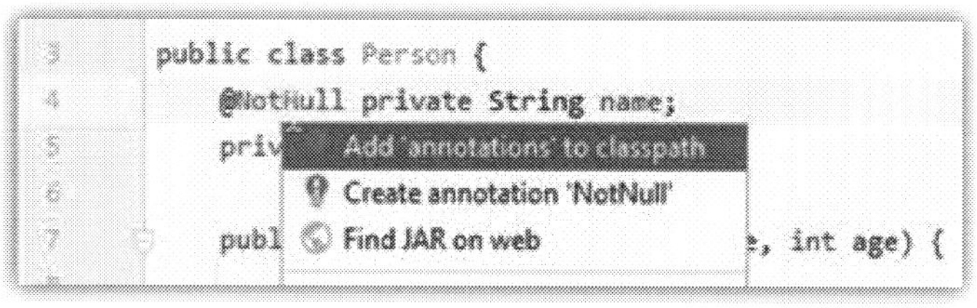

Figure 12.6: Configuring JetBrains annotations library

Note that since Java 8, you can also annotate type parameters of generic declarations provided that the nullability annotation supports the **ElementType.TYPE_USE** target. For example, JetBrains **@Nullable/@NotNull** annotations support this target starting from version 15 so we can write:

```
public class Person {

    ...


    @NotNull private Set<@NotNull Person> friends = new HashSet<>();


    public @NotNull Set<@NotNull Person> getFriends() {
        return friends;
    }
}
```

In Kotlin, the return type of the **getFriends()** method would look like **(Mutable) Set<Person>**:

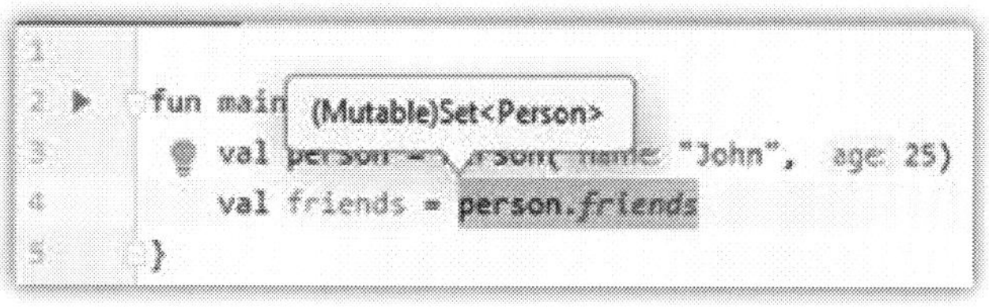

Figure 12.7: Non-nullable type parameter

When type parameters are not annotated, for example:

```java
public class Person {
    ...
    @NotNull private Set<Person> friends = new HashSet<>();
    public @NotNull Set<Person> getFriends() { return friends; }
}
```

The Kotlin compiler has to use platform types for them, so the type of **person. friends** in the preceding Kotlin sample code would be **(Mutable)Set<Person!>** instead.

Java/Kotlin type mapping

Some types have a similar meaning in Kotlin and Java. For example, Java primitive types like **int** or **boolean** correspond to built-in types of Kotlin (**Int**, **Boolean**) while **java.util.List** corresponds to a platform type **(Mutable)List**. The Kotlin compiler is able to map Java types to their Kotlin counterparts when processing usages of Java declarations in the Kotlin code and vice versa while compiling the Kotlin code for JVM. In this section, we'll discuss the basic rules of Java/Kotlin type mapping.

First, Java primitive types as well as their boxed versions map to corresponding basic types in Kotlin:

Java Type	Kotlin Type
byte/Byte	Byte
short/Short	Short
int/Integer	Int
long/Long	Long
char/Character	Char
float/Float	Float
double/Double	Double

Table 12.1: Correspondence between Java and Kotlin primitive types

This mapping also works in reverse; on JVM, values of basic Kotlin types are represented by either JVM primitive types, or corresponding boxing classes depending on how that value is used. Value of Int?, say, would be represented by an instance of **java.lang.Integer** since null may not be stored as a value of Java's **int**.

Some non-primitive built-in classes from **java.lang** packages are mapped into corresponding classes from the **kotlin** package (and vice versa). The names of classes are the same in both cases; the only exception being **Object** which is mapped into Kotlin's **Any**:

- **Object**
- **Cloneable**
- **Comparable**
- **Enum**
- **Annotation**
- **CharSequence**
- **String**
- **Number**
- **Throwable**

Note that static members of mapped Java classes (for example, **Long.valueOf()**) are not accessible directly on companions of their Kotlin counterparts. To use them, you need to mention the qualified name of the corresponding Java class:

```
val n = java.lang.Long.bitCount(1234)
```

Standard collection types in Kotlin (both mutable and immutable) are mapped into corresponding collection types from the the **java.util** package. Reverse mapping as we've discussed above produces platform types because standard Java collections use the same API for both mutable and immutable implementations. The mapped types are as follows:

- **Iterable/Iterator/List Iterator**
- **Collection**
- **Set**
- **List**
- **Map/Map.Entry**

Mapping between generic types involve some less trivial transformation due to differences in the generics syntax.

- Extends wildcards in Java correspond to covariant projections in Kotlin; for example, **TreeNode<? extends Person>** maps to **TreeNode<out Person>**.

- Super wildcards similarly map to contravariant projections: **TreeNode<? super Person>** vs. **TreeNode<in Person>**.

- Raw types in Java are represented by types with star projections; say, **TreeNode** becomes **TreeNode<*>**.

Java arrays of primitive types (like **int[ ]**) are mapped into corresponding specialized array classes (for example, **IntArray**) to avoid boxing/unboxing operations. Any other array is represented as an instance of special platform type **Array<(out) T>** (which may also be a nullably platform: for example, **Array<(out) String>!**) which combines **Array<T>** and **Array<out T>**. This, in particular, allows you to pass an array of subtypes into Java methods expecting an array of supertypes. For example, the following code passes an array of String as a value of the **Object[]** parameter:

```
import java.util.*
```

```
fun main() {
    val strings = arrayOf("a", "b", "c")
    println(Arrays.deepToString(strings))
}
```

Such behavior is consistent with Java semantics where array types are covariant. Kotlin arrays are invariant so this trick doesn't work with Kotlin methods unless you restrict the Array type to its out-projection as in **Array<out Any>**.

Single abstract method interfaces

If you have a Java interface with a single abstract method (SAM interface for short), it essentially behaves like a Kotlin functional type. Similar to Java 8+ which supports automatic conversion of lambdas into an appropriate SAM type instance, Kotlin allows you to use lambdas in context where the Java SAM interface is expected. This is called a *SAM conversion*. Consider, for example, the JDK **ExecutorService** class whose API allows you to register some tasks for asynchronous computations. Its **execute()** method takes a **Runnable** object and since **Runnable** has a form:

```
public interface Runnable {
    public void run();
}
```

It's qualified as a SAM interface in Kotlin. This allows the Kotlin code to call **execute()** methods by simply passing a lambda:

```
import java.util.concurrent.ScheduledThreadPoolExecutor
```

```kotlin
fun main() {
    val executor = ScheduledThreadPoolExecutor(5)
    executor.execute {
        println("Working on asynchronous task...")
    }
    executor.shutdown()
}
```

Instead of much more verbose:

```kotlin
import java.util.concurrent.ScheduledThreadPoolExecutor

fun main() {
    val executor = ScheduledThreadPoolExecutor(5)
    executor.execute(object : Runnable {
        override funrun() {
            println("Working on asynchronous task...")
        }
    })
    executor.shutdown()
}
```

IDE Tips: The IntelliJ plugin can warn you about unnecessary object expressions like the preceding one and automatically transform them into implicit SAM conversions (as shown in *Figure 12.8*):

Figure 12.8: Converting object expression to lambda

Sometimes a compiler doesn't have enough context information to choose a proper conversion. Say, Java **ExecutorService** has a set of **submit()** methods which take an object representing some computation to execute it in future. A computation may be an instance of either the **Runnable**, or **Callable** interface which looks like this:

```
public interface Callable<V> {
    V call() throws Exception;
}
```

Both **Runnable** and **Callable** are SAM interfaces but if we pass a lambda to one of **submit()** methods in a Kotlin code, the compiler will choose a **Runnable** version as having the most specific signature:

```
import java.util.concurrent.ScheduledThreadPoolExecutor


fun main() {
    val executor = ScheduledThreadPoolExecutor(5)
    val future = executor.submit { 1 + 2 }
                                    // implicitly converted to Runnable
    println(future.get()) // null
    executor.shutdown()
}
```

What if we want to pass a **Callable** instance instead? In this case, we have make the conversion more explicit by specifying a target type:

```
import java.util.concurrent.Callable
import java.util.concurrent.ScheduledThreadPoolExecutor


fun main() {
    val executor = ScheduledThreadPoolExecutor(5)
    val future = executor.submit(Callable { 1 + 2 })
    println(future.get()) // 3
    executor.shutdown()
}
```

Such an expression is called a *SAM constructor*.

Note that SAM conversions only work for interfaces, but not for classes even if they have a single abstract method. It also doesn't work with Kotlin interfaces: unlike Java, Kotlin has proper functional types so implicit conversion is virtually unnecessary.

Working with Java records

First introduced as a preview feature in Java 14, record classes aim to reduce the amount of boilerplate code required for simple data holder classes. As such they can be considered as Java counterparts for Kotlin data classes.

Let's consider an example. Suppose we have a Java record class:

```java
public record Person(String firstName, String familyName, int age) {
}
```

And a Kotlin file located in the same package:

```kotlin
fun main() {
    val p1 = Person("John", "Doe", 25)
    val p2 = Person("John", "Doe", 25)
    println(p1 == p2) // true
    println(p1.age()) // 25
    println(p2)// Person[firstName=John, familyName=Doe, age=25]
}
```

It's not difficult to see that all auto-generated record methods such as constructor, getters as well as **toString()/equals()/hashCode()** implementations work just as expected.

Starting from version 1.5, Kotlin will allow you to access record getters as if they were properties:

```kotlin
fun main() {
    val person = Person("John", "Doe", 25)
    println(person.firstName) // John
    println(person.familyName) // Doe
    println(person.age) // 25
}
```

Note that records currently possess some limitations as opposed to Kotlin data classes:

- They do not support the **copy()** method which allows you to create new instances based on the existing one with (possibly) different values.
- You cannot use a data class instance in a Kotlin de-structuring declaration unless the record class in question has the **componetN()** methods by itself or you've explicitly defined them as extension functions in the Kotlin code.

These constraints might be relaxed in further versions of JDK and Kotlin compilers.

Using the Java-to-Kotlin converter

The IntelliJ plugin includes an automatic tool which can convert the Java source file into an equivalent Kotlin code. Together with Java/Kotlin interoperability, this feature allows you to gradually migrate to the existing Java codebase.

To convert a file, you just need to press *Ctrl + Alt + Shift + K* or choose the "Convert Java File to Kotlin File" action from the Code menu. The IDE will then process your file, convert it into Kotlin, and update external usages when necessary.

You can also select one or several files in the Project View panel and apply the same shortcut to convert them in a single batch.

The automatic converter aims at producing idiomatic Kotlin code so although it doesn't always produce an ideal result, this tool can be used as a good starting point when migrating to the existing codebase.

Using the Kotlin code from Java

One of the Kotlin design guidelines is a smooth interoperability with an existing Java codebase. In most cases, the Kotlin code can be easily used from the Java side without much concern. Nevertheless, Kotlin possesses a number of features which don't have direct counterparts in Java. In this section, we'll talk about these nuances as well as discuss how you can fine-tune Kotlin code exposition from the Java's point of view.

Accessing properties

Since neither Java nor JVM have a concept of property, you can't access Kotlin properties directly from the Java code. In compiled JVM bytecode, however, each property is represented by accessor methods which are available to Java clients similar to ordinary methods. Accessor signatures are derived from the property definition:

- The getter is a parameterless method with a return type corresponding to the original property type; its name is computed by uppercasing the first letter of the property name and prefixing it with "get".

- The setter is a void method which takes a single parameter corresponding to a new value; its name is computed similar to the getter with "get" replaced by "set".

For example, the following Kotlin class:

```kotlin
class Person(var name: String, val age: Int)
```

Would look like the following (from Java's point of view):

```java
public class Person {
    @NotNull
    public String getName() {...}

    public void setName(@NotNull String value) {...}

    public int getAge() {...}
}
```

So a Java client code can access its properties by calling accessor methods:

```java
public class Main {
    public static void main(String[] args) {
        Person person = new Person("John", 25);
        System.out.println(person.getAge());  // 25
        person.setName("Harry");
        System.out.println(person.getName()); // Harry
    }
}
```

When a property name starts with "is", the Kotlin compiler uses another naming scheme. To be exact:

- The getter has the same name as its property.
- The setter name is computed by replacing "is" prefix with "set".

For example, if we add the isEmployed property to our Person class:

```kotlin
class Person(var name: String, val age: Int, var isEmployed: Boolean)
```

A Java code accessing a new property would look like this:

```java
public class Main {
    public static void main(String[] args) {
        Person person = new Person("John", 25, false);
        person.setEmployed(true);
```

```
        System.out.println(person.isEmployed()); // true
    }
}
```

Note that the "is" convention is purely name-based; it has nothing to do with a **Boolean** type (although, it's strongly recommended to use "is" names for the **Boolean** properties only).

If the Kotlin property requires a backing field, the compiler will generate it alongside accessor method(s). By default, however, this field is private and can't be accessed directly by the code outside property accessors. In some cases, though, you may need to expose that property to Java clients. This can be achieved by annotating the property with **@JvmField**. For example, if we modify our **Person** class by annotating its constructor parameters:

```
Class Person(@JvmField var name: String, @JvmField val age: Int)
```

We can access generated fields from the Java source code:

```
public class Main {
    public static void main(String[] args) {
        Person person = new Person("John", 25);
        System.out.println(person.age);   // 25
        person.name = "Harry";
        System.out.println(person.name); // Harry
    }
}
```

In this case, accessor methods are not generated and the backing field has the same visibility level as the property itself. Note that **@JvmField** can't be used if the property has non-trivial accessors:

```
class Person(val firstName: String, val familyName: String) {
    @JvmField // Error: property has a custom getter
    Val fullName get() = "$firstName $familyName"
}
```

@JvmField is also not applicable to open or abstract properties since their overrides may in general have custom accessors:

```
open class Person(val firstName: String, val familyName: String) {
    @JvmField // Error: property is open
```

```kotlin
    open val description: String get() = "$firstName $familyName"
}
```

When applied to a property of some named object, **@JvmField** behaves a little differently generating a static field instead of an instance one. For example, it we have a Kotlin object:

```kotlin
object Application {
    @JvmField
    val name = "My Application"
}
```

The code can access the name property by referring to the **Application.name** field directly:

```java
public class Main {
    public static void main(String[] args) {
        System.out.println(Application.name);
    }
}
```

The same also goes for properties with the **const** modifier:

```kotlin
object Application {
    const val name = "My Application"
}
```

Another way to expose the backing field is to use a **lateinit** property:

```kotlin
class Person(val firstName: String, val familyName: String) {
    lateinit var fullName: String

    fun init() {
        fullName = "$firstName $familyName"
    }
}
```

In this case, both accessors and backing field has the same visibility as the property itself:

```java
public class Main {
```

```
    public static void main(String[] args) {
        Person person = newPerson("John", "Doe");
        person.init();
        // direct field access
        System.out.println(person.fullName);        // John Doe
        // accessor call
        System.out.println(person.getFullName()); // John Doe
    }
}
```

In objects, **lateinit** generates a **static** field similar to the **@JvmField** annotation. Its accessors, however, remain instance methods, so the Java code using the object:

```
object Application {
    lateinit var name: String
}
```

would look like the following:

```
public class Main {
    public static void main(String[] args) {
        // Accessor call (non-static)
        Application.INSTANCE.setName("Application1");
        // Direct property access (static)
        Application.stdin = "Application2"
    }
}
```

Note that **@JvmField** can't be used for the **lateinit** properties.

File facades and top-level declarations

In Kotlin, you can often make use of top-level declarations which are placed directly in a package rather than inside of some other declaration. Java and JVM platform in general, however, require that methods must always belong to a particular class. To satisfy this requirement, the Kotlin compiler puts top-level functions and properties into an automatically generated class which is called a *file facade*. By default, the facade name is based on the name of the source file with extra "Kt" suffix. For example, the file:

```
// util.kt
class Person(val firstName: String, val familyName: String)


val Person.fullName
get() = "$firstName $familyName"


fun readPerson(): Person? {
    val fullName = readLine() ?: return null
    val p = fullName.indexOf(' ')
    return if (p >= 0) {
        Person(fullName.substring(0, p), fullName.substring(p + 1))
    } else {
        Person(fullName, "")
    }
}
```

Will produce the following facade class:

```
public class UtilKt {
    @NotNull
    public static String getFullName(@NotNull Person person) {...}


    @Nullable
    public static Person readPerson() {...}
}
```

Note that the facade class doesn't contain classes since they are allowed at top-level in both JVM and Java.

Since generated methods are static, you don't need to instantiate facade class when using it from the Java code:

```
public class Main {
    public static void main(String[] args) {
        Person person = UtilKt.readPerson();
        if (person == null) return;
        System.out.println(UtilKt.getFullName(person));
```

```
    }
}
```

The Kotlin compiler allows you to tune some aspects of the generated facade. First, you can change its name by adding the file-level **@JvmName** annotation:

```
@file:JvmName("MyUtils")


class Person(val firstName: String, val familyName: String)


val Person.fullName
get() = "$firstName $familyName"
```

Now, its Java usages will need to use the specified **MyUtils** name:

```
public class Main {
    public static void main(String[] args) {
        Person person = new Person("John", "Doe");
        System.out.println(MyUtils.getFullName(person));
    }
}
```

Another useful ability is to merge top-level declarations from multiple files into a single class. To do it, you need to annotate files of interest with **@JvmMultifileClass** and specify the target class name with **@JvmName**. In this case, the Kotlin compiler will automatically combine files with the same facade class name. For example, suppose that all declarations from our example are written in separate files:

```
// Person.kt

class Person(valfirstName: String, valfamilyName: String)


// utils1.kt
@file:JvmMultifileClass
@file:JvmName("MyUtils")


val Person.fullName
get() = "$firstName $familyName"


// utils2.kt
```

```
@file:JvmMultifileClass
@file:JvmName("MyUtils")


fun readPerson(): Person? {
    val fullName = readLine() ?: return null
    val p = fullName.indexOf(' ')
    return if (p >= 0) {
        Person(fullName.substring(0, p), fullName.substring(p + 1))
    } else {
        Person(fullName, "")
    }
}
```

Thanks to **@JvmMultifile** and **@JvmName,** we can still access both declarations as members of the **MyUtils** class:

```
public class Main {
    public static void main(String[] args) {
        Person person = MyUtils.readPerson();
        if (person == null) return;
        System.out.println(MyUtils.getFullName(person));
    }
}
```

Note that facade classes are not available to the Kotlin code and are only usable by other JVM clients.

Objects and static members

On JVM, Kotlin object declarations are compiled into ordinary classes with the static INSTANCE field. For example, if we have the Kotlin declaration:

```
object Application {

val name = "My Application"


fun exit() { }
```

```
}
```

The Java code can use access its members using **Application.INSTANCE**:

```
public class Main {
    public static void main(String[] args) {
        System.out.println(Application.INSTANCE.getName());
        Application.INSTANCE.exit();
    }
}
```

We've already seen that using @JvmField on an object property turns it into a static field from Java's point of view. Sometimes, it can be useful to make object functions or property accessors available as static *methods*. To do that, you can use the **@ JvmStatic** annotation:

```
Import java.io.InputStream

object Application {
    @JvmStatic
    var stdin: InputStream = System.`in`

    @JvmStatic
    Fun exit() { }
}
```

In the Java code, such functions and properties can be invoked without mentioning a particular instance:

```
import java.io.ByteArrayInputStream;

public class Main {
    public static void main(String[] args) {
        Application.setStdin(
            new ByteArrayInputStream("hello".getBytes())
        );
        Application.exit();
    }
```

}

Changing the exposed declaration name

We've already seen how **@JvmName** can be used to specify the name of the facade class for top-level declarations. In fact, this annotation is applicable not only to files, but also to functions and property accessors. It allows you to change the name of the corresponding JVM methods.

The primary use case of this feature is an ability to resolve signature clashes between declarations which are valid in Kotlin but forbidden in Java. Suppose that we have the following Kotlin code:

```
class Person(val firstName: String, val familyName: String)


val Person.fullName
get() = "$firstName $familyName"        // Error


fun getFullName(person: Person): String { // Error
    return "${person.familyName}, ${person.firstName}"
}
```

This code will produce a compilation error; even though the Kotlin client can easily distinguish between the function and property, on JVM both declarations will produce a method with a signature:

```
@NotNull

public static String getFullName(@NotNull Person person) {...}
```

Thus, leading to ambiguity. Using @JvmName, you can change the conflicting name thus resolving the problem:

```
@JvmName("getFullNameFamilyFirst")

fun getFullName(person: Person): String { // Error
    return "${person.familyName}, ${person.firstName}"
}
```

Now, the Java client will be able to call this function using the **getFullNameFamilyFirst** name, while the Kotlin code will use the original **getFullName**.

We can similarly specify the JVM name for properties by annotating either particular accessor(s):

```
Val Person.fullName
    @JvmName("getFullNameFamilyLast")
    get() = "$firstName $familyName"
```

Or to property itself (with appropriate use-site target):

```
@get:JvmName("getFullNameFamilyLast")
val Person.fullName
    get() = "$firstName $familyName"
```

@JvmName, in particular, allows you to circumvent the standard naming scheme used for property accessors:

```
class Person(@set:JvmName("changeName") var name: String, val age: Int)
```

When seen from the Java code, the class Person will now have the **changeName()** method instead of **setName()**:

```
public class Main {
    public static void main(String[] args) {
        Person person = newPerson("John", 25);
        person.changeName("Harry");
        System.out.println(person.getName());
    }
}
```

@JvmName is also useful when the Kotlin function's name coincides with the Java keyword which makes it unusable from the Java source code. For example:

```
class Person(val firstName: String, val familyName: String) {
    @JvmName("visit")
    fun goto(person: Person) {
        println("$this is visiting $person")
    }

    override fun toString() = "$firstName $familyName"
}
```

The **goto()** function is not callable in Java since **goto** is a reserved keyword. Providing custom JVM name fixes the problem.

Generating overloads

When the Kotlin function has parameters with a default value, a number of arguments in its call may vary since some of them may be skipped:

```kotlin
// util.kt
fun restrictToRange(
    what: Int,
    from: Int = Int.MIN_VALUE,
    to: Int = Int.MAX_VALUE
): Int {
    return Math.max(from, Math.min(to, what))
}


fun main() {
    println(restrictToRange(100, 1, 10)) // 10
    println(restrictToRange(100, 1))     // 100
    println(restrictToRange(100))        // 100
}
```

Java, however, has no concept of default values so the preceding function will look like this:

```java
public int restrictToRange(int what, int from, int to) {...}
```

And any Java clients would be forced to explicitly pass all arguments:

```java
public class Main {
    public static void main(String[] args) {
        System.out.println(UtilKt.restrictToRange(100, 1, 10));
        System.out.println(UtilKt.restrictToRange(100, 1)); // Error
        System.out.println(UtilKt.restrictToRange(100));    // Error
    }
}
```

Kotlin gives you a solution with the **@JvmOverloads** annotation:

```kotlin
@JvmOverloads
```

```kotlin
fun restrictToRange(
    what: Int,
    from: Int = Int.MIN_VALUE,
    to: Int = Int.MAX_VALUE
): Int {
    return Math.max(from, Math.min(to, what))
}
```

The effect of **@JvmOverloads** is to generate additional overloads for an original Kotlin function:

- The first one has all parameters of an original except the last parameter with a default value.
- The second one has all parameters of an original except the last and the second-to-last parameters with a default value and so on.
- The last overloaded version has only parameters without default values.

For example, the **restrictToRange()** function now has three overloads from Java's point of view:

```java
public int restrictToRange(int what, int from, int to) {...}
                                                // base version
public int restrictToRange(int what, int from) {…}
public int restrictToRange(int what) {...}
```

Additional overloads will call an original function providing explicit values for omitted arguments. Now, our original Java usages become valid as all three overloads are correctly resolved:

```java
public class Main {
    public static void main(String[] args) {
        System.out.println(UtilKt.restrictToRange(100, 1, 10)); // 10
        System.out.println(UtilKt.restrictToRange(100, 1));   // 100
        System.out.println(UtilKt.restrictToRange(100));      // 100
    }
}
```

Note that although overloaded versions produced by the **@JvmOverloads** annotation are added to compiled binaries, they are not available in the Kotlin code. These overloads are meant to be used for Java interoperability only.

Declaring exceptions

In *Chapter 3, Defining Functions,* we mentioned that Kotlin doesn't distinguish between checked and unchecked exceptions. Your functions and properties may throw arbitrary exceptions without any extra code. Java, on the other hand, requires to explicitly list checked exceptions which are not caught in the method body. This may lead to problems if the Java code wants to handle a checked exception which may be thrown by calling a Kotlin declaration. For example, suppose that we have a Kotlin function:

```
// util.kt

Fun loadData() = File("data.txt").readLines()
```

And use it from the Java side:

```
public class Main {
    public static void main(String[] args) {
        for (String line :UtilKt.loadData()) {
            System.out.println(line);
        }
    }
}
```

If **data.txt** can't be read, **loadData()** throws **IOException** which remains unhandled. As a result, the **main()** method will fail silently. If we try to add an exception handler to **main(),** we face another problem:

```
Import java.io.IOException;


public class Main {
    public static void main(String[] args) {
        try {
            for (String line :UtilKt.loadData()) {
                System.out.println(line);
            }
        } catch (IOException e) { // Error
            System.out.println("Can't load data");
        }
    }
```

```
}
```

Compilation fails because Java forbids handling of checked exceptions which are not declared inside the corresponding try block. The problem is that from Java's point of view, our **loadData()** function looks like this:

```
@notNull

public List<String>loadData() {...}
```

And so it doesn't provide any information about possibly thrown exceptions. The solution is to use the special **@Throws** annotation where you can specify exception classes:

```
// util.kt

@Throws(IOException::class)

fun loadData() = File("data.txt").readLines()
```

Now, we can properly handle its call within Java's try-catch block. Calling it outside the exception handler and any method with explicit throws the **IOException** clause will lead to a compilation error as expected:

```
public class Main {

    public static void main(String[] args) {

        // Error: Unhandled IOException

        for (String line :UtilKt.loadData()) {

            System.out.println(line);

        }

    }

}
```

Bear in mind that the Kotlin compiler doesn't validate the consistency of **@Throws** annotations between base and overriding members. For example, we can write:

```
import java.io.File

import java.io.IOException


abstract class Loader {

  abstract fun loadData(): List<String>

}
```

```
Class FileLoader(val path: String) : Loader() {
    @Throws(IOException::class)
    override fun loadData() = File(path).readLines()
}
```

Such a class hierarchy can't be declared in the Java source code since the language specification forbids adding extra checked exceptions in overriding methods.

Inline functions

Since Java has no notion of inline functions, Kotlin functions marked with inline modifiers are exposed as ordinary methods. You can call them in the Java code, but their bodies are not inlined in this case.

A special case is a generic inline function with reified type parameter(s). As of now, type reification can't be implemented without inlining so calling such functions from the Java code is not possible. For example, if we define a generic cast() function:

```
inline fun<reifiedT : Any>Any.cast(): T? = this as? T
```

It will be exposed as a private member of the facade class, thus forbidding any external access:

```
public class Main {
    public static void main(String[] args) {
        UtilKt.<Integer>cast(""); // Error: cast is private
    }
}
```

Type aliases

Kotlin type aliases can't be used in the Java code. Any declaration referring to type aliases will use ts underlying type when seen from the Java code. For example, from the JVM's view the following definitions would produce the **Person** class with the **Name** alias replaced by **String**

```
typealias Name = Stringclass Person(val firstName: Name, val familyName:
Name)
```
:
```
// Java code:
```

```java
public class Main {

    public static void main(String[] args) {

        Person person = new Person("John", "Doe");

        System.out.println(person.getFamilyName()); // Doe

    }

}
```

Exposing Kotlin classes as Java records

Starting from Kotlin 1.5, you make use of the special **@JvmRecord** annotation which exposes the Kotlin data class as a Java record. Consider the following code:

```kotlin
@JvmRecord

data classPerson(

  val firstName: String,

  val familyName: String,

  val age: Int

)
```

From Java's point of view, it has essentially the same effect as a similar declaration of the Java record with an extra set of Kotlin-specific methods like **copy()** and **componentN()**:

```java
public record Person(String firstName, String familyName, int age) {

}
```

This, in particular, allows the Java code to access data class properties via record-style getters.

```java
class Main {

    public static void main(String[] args) {

        var person = new Person("John", "Doe", 25);

        System.out.println(person.firstName());// John

        System.out.println(person.familyName());// Doe

        System.out.println(person.age());// 25

    }

}
```

Keep in mind that common-convention getters (for example, `getFirstName()` or `getAge()`) are not generated when using `@JvmRecord`:

System.out.println(person.getAge());// *ERROR*

Conclusion

This chapter has introduced us to the topic of how to mix Kotlin and Java code within a common codebase. We looked at how Kotlin and Java declarations are exposed to each other, which common problems can arise when you attempt to use Java declarations in the Kotlin code and vice versa and addressed their basic solutions as well as the means to tune language interoperability on the JVM platform.

In the next chapter, we will focus on the concurrent applications. We'll see how Java concurrent primitives can be used in Kotlin and discuss various aspects of coroutines, a powerful language feature which allows you to program suspendable computations.

Questions

1. What is a synthetic property? What are the rules regarding the use of Java accessor methods in Kotlin?

2. What is a platform type? What kinds of platform types are supported in Kotlin?

3. How nullability annotations in the Java code affect Kotlin types?

4. Describe how Kotlin types are mapped to Java and vice versa.

5. Explain how SAM conversions and constructors work in Kotlin.

6. How Kotlin properties can be accessed from Java code?

7. In which cases, backing fields of Kotlin properties are available to the Java code?

8. What is a file facade? Describe how Kotlin top-level functions and properties can be used in Java.

9. How do you merge multiple Kotlin files into a single facade class?

10. Describe usages of the @JvmName annotation.

11. Describe how instances of Kotlin object declarations are exposed to the Java code.

12. How do you make object members available as static methods in Java?

13. What is an effect of using @JvmOverloads?

14. How would you declare possible checked exceptions for a Kotlin function?

CHAPTER 13
Concurrency

In this chapter, we will focus on the major topic of writing concurrent code. Our main goal will be to get an understanding of coroutines, one of the distinguishing features of Kotlin, first introduced in version 1.1 and achieving the release status in Kotlin 1.3.

We'll start with the discussion of basic ideas underlying Kotlin coroutines such as suspending functions and structured complexity and gradually move to more advanced issues of concurrent control-flow: how the coroutine state can be changed throughout its lifecycle, how cancellation and exception work, and how concurrent tasks get assigned to threads.

We will also cover techniques such as channels and actors which allow your code to implement communication between concurrent tasks and to share some mutable data in a thread-safe manner.

Finally, we'll also discuss some utilities simplifying the usage of Java concurrency API in Kotlin code: creating threads, using synchronization and locks.

Structure

In this chapter, we will cover the following topics:

- Coroutines

- Concurrent communication
- Using Java concurrency

Objective

After reading this chapter, the reader will be able to use concurrency primitives provided by the Kotlin coroutines library for building scalable and responsive code.

Coroutines

Kotlin programs can easily use Java concurrent primitives to achieve thread-safety. Using them, however, still poses a certain problem because most concurrent operations are blocking; in other words, a thread which uses operations such as **Thread.sleep(), Thread.join()**, or **Object.wait()** will be blocked until it completes. Blocking and resuming thread execution requires computationally intensive context switching at the system level which may negatively impact the program performance. On top of that, each thread consumes a considerable amount of system resources so maintaining a large number of concurrent threads may be impractical or even not possible at all.

A more efficient approach involves asynchronous programming: we can supply a lambda which needs to be called back when the requested operation is completed. The original thread in the meantime can go on with some useful work (like processing client requests or handling UI events) instead of just waiting in a blocked state. The major problem of such an approach is a drastic increase of code complexity as we can't use an ordinary imperative control-flow.

In Kotlin, you can have the best of both worlds thanks to a powerful mechanism of coroutines which allows you to write code in a familiar imperative style and yet have it automatically transformed into an efficient asynchronous computation by a compiler. This mechanism is based on the concept of suspending functions which are able to preserve their context and can be suspended and resumed at certain points of their execution.

It's worth noting that most of the coroutines' power is provided by a separate library which must be explicitly configured in your project. The version used in the book is given by the following Maven coordinates: **org.jetbrains.kotlinx:kotlinx-coroutines-core:1.4.2**.

IDE Tips: If you're using IntelliJ IDEA without relying on any particular build system like Maven or Gradle, you can add the coroutines library by following the given steps:

1. Press *F4* on the root node in the **Project View** panel or right-click on it and choose **Open Module Settings**.

2. Click on the **Libraries** item on the left, then click on **+** button on the top toolbar and choose the **From Maven...** option.

3. Type Maven coordinates of the library (for example, **org.jetbrains. kotlinx:kotlinx-coroutines-core:1.4.2**) and click on **OK** (as shown in *Figure 13.1*).

4. The IDE will then download the library with the necessary dependencies and suggest you to add it to modules of your project. Confirm it by clicking on **OK**.

In the following sections, we'll talk about basic concepts introduced by the coroutines library and see how they can be used for the purpose of concurrent programming.

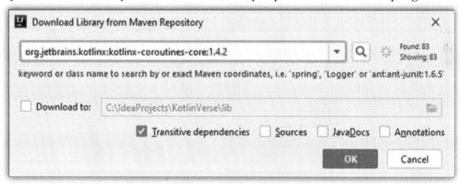

Figure 13.1: Downloading Kotlin coroutines library

Coroutines and suspending functions

The basic language primitive underlying the entire coroutines library is a suspending function. This is generalization of an ordinary function which has an ability to suspend its execution on certain points in its body retaining all the necessary context and then resuming on demand. In Kotlin, such functions are marked by the **suspend** modifier:

```
suspend fun foo() {
    println("Task started")
    delay(100)
    println("Task finished")
}
```

The preceding **delay()** function we've used is a suspending function defined in the coroutines library. Its purpose is similar to the **Thread.sleep()**; however, instead of blocking the current thread, it suspends the calling function leaving the thread free for execution of other tasks (such as switching to other suspending functions).

Suspending functions may call both suspending and ordinary functions. In the former case, such a call becomes a suspension point where the caller execution may be temporarily stopped and resumed later, while the latter proceeds just like a normal function call which returns after the invoked function has finished. Kotlin, however, forbids you to call suspending functions from an ordinary one:

```kotlin
fun foo() {
    println("Task started")
    delay(100) // Error: delay is a suspend function
    println("Task finished")
}
```

IDE Tips: When using the IntelliJ plugin, you can easily identify the suspending call by a special icon on the left-hand side of the corresponding line as shown in *Figure 13.2*:

Figure 13.2: Suspending calls in IDE

If only suspending functions are allowed to make suspending calls, how do we invoke a suspending function at all? The most obvious way to is to mark the **main()** function itself as suspend:

```kotlin
import kotlinx.coroutines.delay


suspend fun main() {
    println("Task started")
    delay(100)
    println("Task finished")
}
```

When you run the preceding code above, it prints the following:

```
Task started
```

```
Task finished
```

With a 100 ms delay in between as expected.

In more realistic cases, however, when we need some control over the lifecycle and behavior of concurrent tasks, suspending functions are executed in a specific *scope* which defines a set of concurrent tasks with a shared lifecycle and context. Various functions which are used to launch coroutines and commonly known as *coroutine builders* serve as extensions on **CoroutineScope** instances. One of its basic implementations is given by the **GlobalScope** object: it allows you to create standalone coroutines which can further spawn their own nested tasks. Now, we'll take a look at three common coroutine builders: **launch()**, **async()** and **runBlocking()**.

Coroutine builders

The **launch()** function starts a coroutine and returns a Job object which you can use to track its state and cancel the underlying task when needed. The function takes a suspending lambda of type **CoroutineScope.() -> Unit** which comprises the body of a new coroutine. Let's consider a simple example:

```
import kotlinx.coroutines.*
import java.lang.System.*

fun main() {
    val time = currentTimeMillis()
    GlobalScope.launch {
        delay(100)
        println("Task 1 finished in ${currentTimeMillis() - time} ms")
    }
    GlobalScope.launch {
        delay(100)
        println("Task 2 finished in ${currentTimeMillis() - time} ms")
    }
    Thread.sleep(200)
}
```

If you run the preceding code, you'll see something like this:

Task 2 finished in 176 ms

Task 1 finished in 176 ms

A thing worth noting is that both tasks complete at virtually the same time relative to the program start which means that they are really executed in parallel. A particular order is not guaranteed, though, so any of the two tasks may become the first depending on the circumstances. The Coroutines library also includes means for enforcing execution ordering when that's necessary: we'll discuss them in the upcoming sections devoted to concurrent communication.

The **main()** function itself uses **Thread.sleep()** to temporarily block the main thread execution: this should give coroutine threads enough time to complete since by default, they are run in the daemon mode and would be shut down early once the **main()** thread terminates.

Keep in mind that while using thread-blocking functions like **sleep()** is possible inside suspending function as well, you're strongly discouraged from doing this because such code defeats the entire purpose of coroutines. For that reason, we've used suspending **delay()** inside our concurrent tasks.

IDE Tips: The IntelliJ plugin warns you about potentially blocking function calls like **Thread.sleep()** or **Thread.join()** inside the coroutine code.

Note that coroutines are substantially more lightweight than threads. In particular, you can easily afford a huge number of concurrently running coroutines since each of them usually only has to keep a relatively compact state and do not need a full-fledged context switching when being suspended or resumed.

The **launch()** builder is suited for cases when the concurrent task is not supposed to compute some result: that's why it takes a Unit-typed lambda. If we do need a result, however, there is another builder function which is called **async()**. This function returns an instance of **Deferred**, a special **Job** subtype which provides access to the computation result through the **await()** method. When invoked, **await()** suspends until the computation is either completed (thus, producing a result), or cancelled. In the latter case, **await()** fails with an exception. You can consider them a non-blocking counterpart of Java futures. For example:

```
import kotlinx.coroutines.*


suspend fun main() {
    val message = GlobalScope.async {
```

```
        delay(100)
        "abc"
    }
    val count = GlobalScope.async {
        delay(100)
        1 + 2
    }
    delay(200)
    val result = message.await().repeat(count.await())
    println(result)
}
```

In this case, we've also marked the **main()** function with suspend to directly call the **await()** methods of both deferred tasks. The output unsurprisingly looks as follows:

abcabcabc

By default, both **launch()** and **async()** builders run coroutines in a shared pool of background threads while the calling thread itself is left unblocked. That's why we had to insert **sleep()** into our **launch()** example as the main thread had little work to do besides waiting for the completion of our tasks. The **runBlocking()** builder, on the other hand creates a coroutine which by default executes in the current thread and blocks until it completes. When coroutine returns successfully, the return value of the suspend lambda becomes the value of the entire **runBlocking()** call. When the coroutine is cancelled, **runBlocking()** throws an exception. Conversely, when a blocked thread is interrupted, the coroutine started by **runBlocking()** gets cancelled as well. For example:

```
import kotlinx.coroutines.*


fun main() {
    GlobalScope.launch {
        delay(100)
        println("Background task: ${Thread.currentThread().name}")
    }
    runBlocking {
        println("Primary task: ${Thread.currentThread().name}")
```

```
        delay(200)
    }
}
```

Running this program will produce something like this:

```
Primary task: main
```

Background task: `DefaultDispatcher-worker-2`

You can see that the coroutine inside **runBlocking()** is executed in the main thread while the one created by `launch()` gets assigned to a background thread from a shared pool.

Due to its blocking nature, the **runBlocking()** shouldn't be used inside other coroutines. It's intended as a kind of bridge between blocking and non-blocking code and can be used, for example, as a top-level builder in the main function or tests.

Coroutine scopes and structured concurrency

So far, our example coroutines were running in the global scope which effectively means that their lifetime is limited only by that of the entire application. In some cases, though, we may want to ensure that the coroutine execution is restricted to a particular operation. This is possible thanks to the parent-child relationship between concurrent tasks: when you start one coroutine in the context of another, the latter becomes a child of the former. The lifecycles of parent and child are related so that the parent coroutine may complete only after completion of all its children.

This feature is called a *structured concurrency*. It can be compared to using blocks and subroutines to constrain a scope of local variables. Let's look at some examples:

```
import kotlinx.coroutines.*

fun main() {
    runBlocking {
        println("Parent task started")
        launch {
            println("Task A started")
            delay(200)
            println("Task A finished")
```

```
        }
        launch {
            println("Task B started")
            delay(200)
            println("Task B finished")
        }
        delay(100)
        println("Parent task finished")
    }
    println("Shutting down...")
}
```

The preceding code starts a top-level coroutine which then launches a pair of children by calling launch on the current instance of CoroutineScope (which is passed as a receiver to the suspending lambda). If you run this program, you'll see the following result:

```
Parent task started
Task A started
Task B started
Parent task finished
Task A finished
Task B finished
Shutting down...
```

You can see that the main body of the parent coroutine represented by suspend lambda of the runBlocking() call finishes before its children due to having a smaller delay of 100 ms. The coroutine itself is not completed at this point and just waits in a suspended state until the completion of both the children. After that, the parent coroutine completes as well and since we're using the runBlocking() builder here, it also unblocks the main thread allowing it to print the final message.

You can also introduce a custom scope by wrapping a code block inside the coroutineScope() call. Similarly to runBlocking(), this function returns the value of its lambda and doesn't complete until its children reach completion. The main different between coroutineScope() and runBlocking() is that the former is a suspending function which doesn't block the current thread:

```kotlin
import kotlinx.coroutines.*

fun main() {
    runBlocking {
        println("Custom scope start")
        coroutineScope {
            launch {
                delay(100)
                println("Task 1 finished")
            }
            launch {
                delay(100)
                println("Task 2 finished")
            }
        }
        println("Custom scope end")
    }
}
```

Note that the **"Custom scope end"** message is printed last because the preceding **coroutineScope()** call suspends until both the children finish their execution.

In general, parent-child relationships can form complex coroutine hierarchies which define a shared scope for processing of exceptions and cancellation requests. We'll revisit this topic in the following sections when talking about coroutine jobs and cancelling.

Coroutine context

Each coroutine has an associated context which is represented by the **CoroutineContext** interface and can be accessed by the **coroutineContext** property of the enclosing scope. The context is an immutable collection of key-value pairs which contains various data available to the coroutine. Some of them have a special meaning for the coroutine machinery and affect how a coroutine gets executed at runtime. The following elements are of particular interest:

- **job** which represents the cancellable task performed by the coroutine.
- **dispatcher** which controls how coroutines are associated with threads.

In general, the context can store any data implementing **CoroutineContext.Element.** To access a particular element, you can use the **get()** method or indexing operator supplying a corresponding key:

```
GlobalScope.launch {
    // obtains current job and prints "Task is active: true"
    println("Task is active: ${coroutineContext[Job.Key]!!.isActive}")
}
```

By default, coroutines created by standard builders like **launch()** or **async()** inherit their context from the current scope. When necessary, you can supply a different one by using the context parameter of the corresponding builder function. To create a new context, you may use the **plus()** function/+ operator which merges data from two contexts together and the **minusKey()** function which removes an element with a given key:

```
import kotlinx.coroutines.*


private fun CoroutineScope.showName() {
    println("Current coroutine: ${coroutineContext[CoroutineName]?.
    name}")
}


fun main() {
    runBlocking {
        showName()      // Current coroutine: null
        launch(coroutineContext + CoroutineName("Worker")) {
            showName() // Current coroutine: Worker
        }
    }
}
```

You can also switch context during the coroutine execution using the **withContext()** function which takes a new context and a suspending lambda. This can be useful, for example, if you want to run some block of code inside a different thread. We'll take a look at an example of such thread-jumping in a section about coroutine dispatchers.

Coroutine control-flow

In this section, we'll consider the specifics of how control is transferred within the coroutine framework that covers topics such as cancellation, exception handling, and assigning coroutines to threads.

Job lifecycle

A **job** is an object which represents a lifecycle of a concurrent task. Using jobs, you can track task states and cancel them when necessary. Possible states of a job are shown in *Figure 13.3*. Let's take a closer look at what these states mean and how the job transition moves from one state into another.

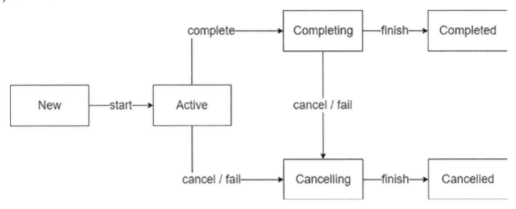

Figure 13.3: *Job states*

An *active* state means that a job has been started but hasn't yet come to completion. This state is usually used by default: in other words, job is implicitly started after it's created. Some coroutine builders like **launch()** and **async()** allow you to choose the initial state by specifying an argument of the **CoroutineStart** type:

- **CoroutineStart.DEFAULT** is the default behavior where the job is started immediately.
- **CoroutineStart.LAZY** means that the job has not started automatically; in this case, it's placed into a *new* state and awaits starting.

A job in the *new* state can be started by calling its **start()** or **join()** method after which it transitions to the active state. For example:

```
import kotlinx.coroutines.*


fun main() {
    runBlocking {
```

```
        val job = launch(start = CoroutineStart.LAZY) {
            println("Job started")
        }
        delay(100)
        println("Preparing to start...")
        job.start()
    }
}
```

The preceding program defers the child coroutine start until the root one prints its message. The output looks as follows:

```
Preparing to start...
```

```
Job startd
```

While in the active state, a job can be repeatedly suspended and resumed by the coroutines machinery. It can also start new jobs which become its children thus forming a tree-like dependency structure between concurrent computations. You can determine a list of non-completed children jobs by using the **children** property. For example:

```
import kotlinx.coroutines.*

fun main() {
    runBlocking {
        val job = coroutineContext[Job.Key]!!
        launch { println("This is task A") }
        launch { println("This is task B") }
        // 2 children running
        println("${job.children.count()} children running")
    }
}
```

When the coroutine finishes the execution of the suspending lambda block, its job changes its state to *completing* which basically means "waiting for children completion". Job retains this state until all of its children complete after which it transitions to the *completed* state.

You can use **Job's join()** method to suspend the current coroutine until the job in question is completed. The following program ensures that the root coroutine message is printed after both its children finish their execution:

```kotlin
import kotlinx.coroutines.*


fun main() {
    runBlocking {
        val job = coroutineContext[Job.Key]!!
        val jobA = launch { println("This is task A") }
        val jobB = launch { println("This is task B") }
        jobA.join()
        jobB.join()
        println("${job.children.count()} children running")
    }
}
```

The resulting output is as follows:

```
This is task A
```

```
This is task B
```

```
0 children running
```

As expected, there are no active children at the point **job.children.count()** is evaluated.

Cancelling and cancelled states reflect the status of a job whose execution is being/ was cancelled either due to unhandled exception, or an explicit call to the **cancel()** method.

The current state of a job can be tracked by its properties: **isActive, isCancelled,** and **isComplete**. Their meaning can be summarized in the following table and you can also find it in the documentation to the Job interface:

Job State	isActive	isCompleted	isCancelled
New	false	false	false
Active	true	false	false
Completing	true	false	false
Cancelling	false	false	true

Cancelled	false	true	true
Completed	false	true	false

Table 1: *Determining current state by Job properties*

Note that **isCompleted** returns true for both completed and cancelled jobs, you can distinguish between the two by checking the **isCancelled** property. Completed and completing states, on the other hand, are indistinguishable from the outside of job itself.

Cancellation

Jobs can be cancelled by calling their **cancel()** method. This provides a standard mechanism for terminating computations which are no longer necessary. The cancellation is cooperative; in other words, a cancellable coroutine itself must check whether its cancellation is requested and respond appropriately. Consider the following program:

```kotlin
import kotlinx.coroutines.*


suspend fun main() {
    val squarePrinter = GlobalScope.launch(Dispatchers.Default) {
        var i = 1
        while (true) {
            println(i++)
        }
    }
    delay(100) // let child job run for some time
    squarePrinter.cancel()
}
```

The code starts a coroutine which constantly prints integer numbers, allows it to run for about 100 milliseconds, and then tries to cancel. However, if you run the program, you'll find that **squarePrinter** continues to execute. The reason is that it doesn't cooperate in cancellation. One way to fix this is to repeatedly check whether the coroutine was cancelled before doing the next piece of work:

```kotlin
import kotlinx.coroutines.*
```

```kotlin
suspend fun main() {
    val squarePrinter = GlobalScope.launch(Dispatchers.Default) {
        var i = 1
        while (isActive) {
            println(i++)
        }
    }
    delay(100) // let child job run for some time
    squarePrinter.cancel()
}
```

The **isActive** extension property checks whether the current job is in the active state. On **CoroutineScope** (which is passed as a receiver to the coroutine suspend lambda), it simply delegates it to the **isActive** property of the current job. Now, when the parent coroutine calls the **cancel()** method, the **squarePrinter** state is changed to *cancelling* and the next check of the **isActive** condition forces loop termination. When the coroutine finishes its execution, the state is changed to *cancelled*. If you run the preceding code, you'll see that it terminates after running approximately 100 milliseconds.

Another solution is to replace the state check with a call to some suspending function which can respond to cancellation by throwing **CancellationException**. This exception is used internally by the coroutine library as a control-flow token signalling that job cancelling is in progress. This is true for all suspending functions defined in the coroutines library such as **delay()** or **join()**. One more example is **yield()** which suspends a given job freeing its thread for other coroutines (similarly to how **Thread.yield()** may suspend the current thread by giving other threads an extra chance to run):

```kotlin
import kotlinx.coroutines.*

suspend fun main() {
    val squarePrinter = GlobalScope.launch(Dispatchers.Default) {
        var i = 1
        while (true) {
            yield()
            println(i++)
        }
```

```
    }
    delay(100) // let child job run for some time
    squarePrinter.cancel()
}
```

When a parent coroutine is cancelled, it automatically cancels the execution of all its children and the process continues until all hierarchy is cancelled. Consider the following example:

```kotlin
import kotlinx.coroutines.*

fun main() {
    runBlocking {
        val parentJob = launch {
            println("Parent started")
            launch {
                println("Child 1 started")
                delay(500)
                println("Child 1 completed")
            }
            launch {
                println("Child 2 started")
                delay(500)
                println("Child 2 completed")
            }
            delay(500)
            println("Parent completed")
        }
        delay(100)
        parentJob.cancel()
    }
}
```

The program launches a coroutine which then starts a pair of children. All three tasks are supposed to be delayed for 500 ms before printing the completion message. The parent job, however, is cancelled after 100 ms. As a result, neither it nor its children reach completion and the program output looks as follows:

```
Parent started
Child 1 started
Child 2 started
```

Timeouts

In some cases, we can't wait for completion of a task indefinitely and need to set up some timeout. The coroutines library has a special **withTimeout()** function exactly for this purpose. For example, the following code starts a coroutine which suspends while the file is being read:

```kotlin
import kotlinx.coroutines.*
import java.io.File


fun main() {
    runBlocking {
        val asyncData = async { File(«data.txt»).readText() }
        try {
            val text = withTimeout(50) { asyncData.await() }
            println("Data loaded: $text")
        } catch (e: Exception) {
            println("Timeout exceeded")
        }
    }
}
```

If the file gets read within 50 milliseconds, **withTimeout()** just returns the result if its block. Otherwise, it throws **TimeoutCancellationException** (which is a subclass of **CancellationException**) and the reading coroutine is cancelled.

There is also a similar function **withTimeoutOrNull()** which doesn't throw an exception when the timeout is exceeded and simply returns null instead.

Coroutine dispatching

While coroutines give you a thread-independent way to implement suspendable computations, they still need to be associated with some thread(s) when run. The coroutine library includes a special component whose task is to control which thread is used to execute a particular coroutine. This component is called a *coroutine dispatcher*.

Dispatcher is a part of coroutine context so you can specify it in coroutine builder functions like **launch()** and **runBlocking()**. Since dispatcher is also a singleton context by itself, you can simply pass it as a context parameter:

```kotlin
import kotlinx.coroutines.*


fun main() {
    runBlocking {
        // running coroutine using global thread pool dispatcher
        launch(Dispatchers.Default) {
            println(Thread.currentThread().name)

                                        // DefaultDispatcher-worker-1

        }
    }
}
```

Coroutine dispatchers are somewhat similar to Java executors which distribute threads between a set of parallel tasks. In fact, you can easily convert the existing implementation of the Executor into a respective coroutine dispatcher by using the **asCoroutineDispatcher()** extension function. In the following example, we create a pool-based executor service with the custom thread factory which assigns names like **WorkerThread1, WorkerThread2, …** to executor threads. Then, we convert it into a dispatcher and use it to start several coroutines in parallel. Note that we explicitly set up worker threads as daemons so that they won't prevent the program termination after all coroutines complete:

```kotlin
import kotlinx.coroutines.*
import java.util.concurrent.ScheduledThreadPoolExecutor
import java.util.concurrent.atomic.AtomicInteger


fun main() {
    val id = AtomicInteger(0)
    val executor = ScheduledThreadPoolExecutor(5) { runnable ->
        Thread(
```

```
            runnable,
            "WorkerThread-${id.incrementAndGet()}"
        ).also { it.isDaemon = true }
    }
    executor.asCoroutineDispatcher().use { dispatcher ->
        runBlocking {
            for (i in 1..3) {
                launch(dispatcher) {
                    println(Thread.currentThread().name)
                    delay(1000)
                }
            }
        }
    }
}
```

The delay forces the executor to create separate threads so the preceding code would print the following:

```
WorkerThread-1
```

```
WorkerThread-2
```

```
WorkerThread-3
```

Although the specific thread order may vary.

Note that when invoked on an instance of **ExecutorService**, **asCoroutine Dispatcher()** returns **ExecutorCoroutineDispatcher** which also implements the **Closeable** interface. You need to use the **close()** method to shut down the underlying executor service and free system resources allocated to maintain its threads or wrap dispatcher usages inside the **use()** function block like we did in the preceding example.

The coroutines library also comes with a set of out-of-the box dispatcher implementations. Some of them can be accessed via the **Dispatchers** object:

- **Dispatchers.Default:** This is a shared tread pool whose size is by default equal to the number of available CPU cores or 2 (whatever is greater). This implementation is generally suited for CPU-bound computations where the task performance is limited primarily by the CPU speed.

- **Dispatchers.IO:** This is a similar implementation based on a thread pool which is optimized for running potentially blocking I/O-intensive tasks such as reading/writing files. This dispatcher shares the thread pool with the default implementation adding or terminating extra threads when necessary.

- **Dispatchers.Main:** This is a dispatcher which operates exclusively in the UI event thread where the user input is processed.

It's also possible to create a dispatcher based on a private thread pool or even a single thread by using either the **newFixedThreadPoolContext()**, or **newSingleThreadPoolContext()** function. For example, we can rewrite our Executor-based sample as follows:

```
import kotlinx.coroutines.*


@Suppress(«EXPERIMENTAL_API_USAGE»)
fun main() {
    newFixedThreadPoolContext(5, "WorkerThread").use { dispatcher ->
        runBlocking {
            for (i in 1..3) {
                launch(dispatcher) {
                    println(Thread.currentThread().name)
                    delay(1000)
                }
            }
        }
    }
}
```

Note that we've used the **@Suppress** annotation because **newFixedThreadPool Context()** and **newSingleThreadPoolContext()** are currently marked as obsolete API and are expected to be replaced by newer functions based on a shared thread pool.

When the dispatcher is not specified explicitly (like we did in earlier examples), it's automatically inherited from the scope you use to start a coroutine. Consider the following example:

```kotlin
import kotlinx.coroutines.*

fun main() {
    runBlocking {
        println("Root: ${Thread.currentThread().name}")
        launch {
            println("Nested, inherited: ${Thread.currentThread().
            name}")
        }
        launch(Dispatchers.Default) {
            println("Nested, explicit: ${Thread.currentThread().
            name}")
        }
    }
}
```

We start a top-level coroutine which runs in the main thread and launches two nested coroutines: one whose context (and coroutine dispatcher as a result) is inherited from the parent coroutine and another where the dispatcher is specified explicitly. Thus, the preceding code would print the following:

```
Root: main

Nested, explicit: DefaultDispatcher-worker-1

Nested, inherited: main
```

In the absence of a parent coroutine, the dispatcher is implicitly assumed to be **Dispatchers.Default** except for the **runBlocking()** builder which is confined to the current thread.

The coroutine does not need to have the same dispatcher throughout its entire lifetime. Since the dispatcher is a part of coroutine context, it can be overridden by using the **withContext()** function:

```kotlin
import kotlinx.coroutines.*

@Suppress(«EXPERIMENTAL_API_USAGE»)
fun main() {
    newSingleThreadContext("Worker").use { worker ->
```

```
    runBlocking {
        println(Thread.currentThread().name)      // main
        withContext(worker) {
            println(Thread.currentThread().name) // Worker
        }
        println(Thread.currentThread().name)      // main
    }
  }
}
```

This technique comes in handy when we want to confine an execution of a particular routine fragment to a single thread.

Exception handling

When it comes to exception handling, various coroutine builders follow one of the two basic strategies. The first one implemented by builders like **launch()** is to propagate exception to the parent coroutine. In this case, the execution proceeds as follows:

1. The parent coroutine is cancelled with the same exception as a cause. This causes it to cancel all the remaining children.

2. When the children are cancelled, the parent passes an exception to further up the coroutine tree.

The process continues until it reaches a coroutine with a global scope. After that, it's handled by **CoroutineExceptionHandler**. Consider, for example, the following program:

```
import kotlinx.coroutines.*

fun main() {
    runBlocking {
        launch {
            throw Exception("Error in task A")
            println("Task A completed")
        }
        launch {
```

```
            delay(1000)
            println("Task B completed")
        }
        println("Root")
    }
}
```

The top-level coroutine starts a pair of nested tasks with the first one throwing an exception. This causes cancellation of the root task and both of its children and since no custom handler is provided, the program falls back to the default behavior represented by **Thread.uncaughtExceptionHandler**. As a result it would print the following:

Root

Exception in thread "main" java.lang.Exception: Error in task A

Followed by the exception stack trace.

CoroutineExceptionHandler defines a single method which takes the current coroutine context and a thrown exception:

```
fun handleException(context: CoroutineContext, exception: Throwable)
```

The simplest way to construct a handler is to use the **CoroutineExceptionHandler()** function which takes a two-argument lambda:

```
val handler = CoroutineExceptionHandler { _, exception ->
    println("Caught $exception")
}
```

To configure its instance for processing exceptions, you can put it into coroutine context. Since the handler is a trivial context by itself, you can just pass it as a context argument into the coroutine builder:

```
import kotlinx.coroutines.*


suspend fun main() {
    val handler = CoroutineExceptionHandler { _, exception ->
        println("Caught $exception")
    }
    GlobalScope.launch(handler) {
```

```
        launch {
            throw Exception("Error in task A")
            println("Task A completed")
        }
        launch {
            delay(1000)
            println("Task B completed")
        }
        println("Root")
    }.join()
}
```

Now, the program prints the following:

```
Root
```

```
Caught java.lang.Exception: Error in task A
```

Thus, overriding the default behavior.

When no handler instance is defined in context, the coroutines library will invoke *all* global handlers configured via the JVM **ServiceLoader** mechanism as well as **uncaughtExceptionHandler** for the current thread.

Note that **CoroutineExceptionHandler** can only be specified for a coroutine launched in the global scope and is used only for its children. That's why we had to replace **runBlocking()** with **GlobalScope.launch()** and mark the **main()** function with **suspend** to make use of suspending **join()** call. If we've retained **runBlocking()** from our original example, but supplied it with a handler:

```
import kotlinx.coroutines.*


fun main() {
    val handler = ...
    runBlocking(handler) {

        ...

    }
}
```

The program would still use the default exception handler since our coroutines wouldn't be run in the global scope.

Another way to handle exception, used by the **async()** builder, is to preserve the thrown exception and rethrow it later when the corresponding **await()** is called. Let's modify our example slightly:

```
import kotlinx.coroutines.*


fun main() {
    runBlocking {
        val deferredA = async {
            throw Exception("Error in task A")
            println("Task A completed")
        }
        val deferredB = async {
            println("Task B completed")
        }
        deferredA.await()
        deferredB.await()
        println("Root")
    }
}
```

Now, the output looks as follows:

```
Exception in thread "main" java.lang.Exception: Error in task A
```

The reason is that the exception is re-thrown by **deferredA.await()** so the program fails to reach the **println("Root")** statement.

Note async-like builders which rethrow an exception when you access coroutine data do not rely on **CoroutineExceptionHandler**. So even if you have its instance preconfigured in the coroutine context, it has no effect (just as we've seen in the **runBlocking()** example); the program will still fall back to the default handler.

What if we want to process exceptions thrown by the nested coroutines at the level of their parent without relying on global handlers? Let's see what happens if we attempt to process an rethrown exception using the try-catch block:

```kotlin
import kotlinx.coroutines.*

fun main() {
    runBlocking {
        val deferredA = async {
            throw Exception("Error in task A")
            println("Task A completed")
        }
        val deferredB = async {
            println("Task B completed")
        }
        try {
            deferredA.await()
            deferredB.await()
        } catch (e: Exception) {
            println("Caught $e")
        }
        println("Root")
    }
}
```

If you run this code, you'll see that the handle is indeed activated, but the program still fails with an exception:

```
Caught java.lang.Exception: Error in task A
Root
Exception in thread "main" java.lang.Exception: Error in task A
```

The reason is that the exception is rethrown automatically to cancel the parent coroutine when its child (task A in this case) fails. To override this behavior, we can use a so called *supervisor* job.

With supervisor jobs, the cancellation propagates only in the downward direction; if you cancel a supervisor, it automatically cancels all its children, but if a child is cancelled instead, the supervisor and its remaining children remain active.

To turn the parent coroutine into a supervisor, we define a new scope using the **supervisorScope()** function instead of **coroutineScope()**. Let's modify the previous example:

```
import kotlinx.coroutines.*
```

```
fun main() {
    runBlocking {
        supervisorScope {
            val deferredA = async {
                throw Exception("Error in task A")
                println("Task A completed")
            }
            val deferredB = async {
                println("Task B completed")
            }
            try {
                deferredA.await()
            } catch (e: Exception) {
                println("Caught $e")
            }
            deferredB.await()
            println("Root")
        }
    }
}
```

Now, the exception is not rethrown after processing and both task B and root coroutine reach completion:

```
Task B completed
Caught java.lang.Exception: Error in task A
Root
```

Note that the supervisor behavior extends to normal cancellations as well: calling **cancel()** on one of its children jobs doesn't cause cancellation of its siblings or supervisor itself.

Concurrent communication

In this section, we'll talk about more advanced features of the coroutines library which allow you to efficiently share data between multiple concurrent tasks while retaining thread-safety. To be exact, we'll focus on channels which provide a mechanism for passing data streams between coroutines and actors which allow you to safely share the mutable state without any synchronizations and locks.

Channels

Channels offer you a convenient way to share an arbitrary data stream between coroutines. The basic operations on any channel represented by the **Channel** interface is sending data elements by the **send()** method and receiving them by the **receive()** method, respectively. When these methods can't complete their work – for example, when the channel's internal buffer is full and you try to send data to it – they suspend the current coroutine and resume them later when it's possible. That's the major difference between channels and blocking queues which play a similar role in Java's concurrency API but work by *blocking* calling the thread.

Channels can be constructed by the generic **Channel()** function which takes an integer value describing the channel capacity. One of the basic implementations is a channel with an internal buffer of a limited size. When the buffer is full, a call to **send()** is suspended until at least one element is received. Similarly, a call to **receiver()** suspends when the buffer is empty until at least one element gets sent. Let's consider a small example:

```
import kotlinx.coroutines.channels.Channel

import kotlinx.coroutines.*

import kotlin.random.Random


fun main() {
    runBlocking {
        val streamSize = 5
        val channel = Channel<Int>(3)
        launch {
            for (n in 1..streamSize) {
                delay(Random.nextLong(100))
                val square = n*n
```

```
            println("Sending: $square")
            channel.send(square)
        }
    }
    launch {
        for (i in 1..streamSize) {
            delay(Random.nextLong(100))
            val n = channel.receive()
            println("Receiving: $n")
        }
    }
}
}
```

The first coroutine produces a stream of integer squares and sends them to the channel which can hold up to 3 elements while the second one concurrently receives generated numbers. We've inserted random delays to provoke occasional suspension when either of coroutines don't catch up with its counterpart leading to an empty/full channel buffer. A possible result may look like this:

```
Sending: 1
Receiving: 1
Sending: 4
Receiving: 4
Sending: 9
Sending: 16
Receiving: 9
Sending: 25
Receiving: 16
Receiving: 25
```

Although, the output may vary depending on actual delays and other circumstances, channels ensure that all values are received in the same order as they are being sent.

The **Channel()** function can also take some special values which produce channels with different behavior. These values are represented by constants in the companion object of the Channel interface:

- **Channel.UNLIMITED (= Int.MAX_VALUE):** This is a channel with unlimited capacity whose internal buffer grows on demand. Such channels never suspend on **send()**, but can suspend on **receiver()** when the buffer is empty.

- **Channel.RENDEZVOUS (= 0):** This is a *rendezvous* channel which has no internal buffer. Any call to **send()** suspends until some other coroutine invokes **receive()**. Similarly, the **receive()** call is suspended until someone invokes **send()**. This channel is created by default when you omit capacity argument.

- **Channel.CONFLATED (= -1):** This is a *conflated* channel which stores at most one element which is overwritten by **send()** so that any unread sent values are lost. In this case, the **send()** method never suspends.

Any positive value less than **UNLIMITED** produces a channel with a limited-size buffer.

The Rendezvous channel ensures that producer and consumer coroutines are activated in turns. For example, if we change our earlier example by setting the channel capacity to zero, we'll always get a stable operation order regardless of delays:

Sending: 1

Receiving: 1

Sending: 4

Receiving: 4

Sending: 9

Receiving: 9

Sending: 16

Receiving: 16

Sending: 25

Receiving: 25

Conflated channels can be used if you don't need *every* element in a stream and can afford *discarding* some of them if the consume routine doesn't catch up with the producer. Let's modify our first example by setting the consumer delay to be twice as much as producer's:

```kotlin
import kotlinx.coroutines.channels.Channel
import kotlinx.coroutines.*

fun main() {
    runBlocking {
        val streamSize = 5
        val channel = Channel<Int>(Channel.CONFLATED)
        launch {
            for (n in 1..streamSize) {
                delay(100)
                val square = n*n
                println("Sending: $square")
                channel.send(square)
            }
        }
        launch {
            for (i in 1..streamSize) {
                delay(200)
                val n = channel.receive()7
                println("Receiving: $n")
            }
        }
    }
}
```

As a result, only about half of produced values are received and processed. A possible output may look as follows:

```
Sending: 1
Receiving: 1
Sending: 4
Sending: 9
Receiving: 9
Sending: 16
```

Sending: 25

Receiving: 25

If you run the preceding program, you'll also see that it doesn't terminate after printing the last line. The reason is that our receiver expects to get at least 5 values since we're iterating from 1 to **streamSize**. But since only about **streamSize/2** values are actually received, this condition can never be satisfied. What we need in this situation is some kind of signal which would mean that the channel is closed and won't send any further data. The Channel API allows you to do that by calling the **close()** method on the producer side. On the consumer side, we can replace the fixed-number loop with an iteration over the channel data:

```kotlin
import kotlinx.coroutines.channels.Channel

import kotlinx.coroutines.*


fun main() {
    runBlocking {
        val streamSize = 5
        val channel = Channel<Int>(Channel.CONFLATED)
        launch {
            for (n in 1..streamSize) {
                delay(100)
                val square = n*n
                println("Sending: $square")
                channel.send(square)
            }
            channel.close()
        }
        launch {
            for (n in channel) {
                println("Receiving: $n")
                delay(200)
            }
        }
    }
}
```

Now, the program terminates after the data exchange is complete.

On the consumer side, you can also use the **consumeEach()** function to read all channel content instead of explicit iteration:

```
channel.consumeEach {
    println("Receiving: $n")
    delay(200)
}
```

After the channel is closed, any attempt to call **send()** will fail with **ClosedSendChannel Exception**. Calls to **receive()** will return unread elements until the channel is exhausted after which they will throw **ClosedSendChannelException** as well.

Channel communication does not necessarily involve just a single producer and a single consumer. For example, the same channel can be concurrently read by multiple coroutines. This is called *fanning out*:

```
import kotlinx.coroutines.channels.Channel
import kotlinx.coroutines.*
import kotlin.random.Random

fun main() {
    runBlocking {
        val streamSize = 5
        val channel = Channel<Int>(2)
        launch {
            for (n in 1..streamSize) {
                val square = n*n
                println("Sending: $square")
                channel.send(square)
            }
            channel.close()
        }
        for (i in 1..3) {
            launch {
                for (n in channel) {
```

```
                    println("Receiving by consumer #$i: $n")
                    delay(Random.nextLong(100))
                }
            }
        }
    }
}
```

Data stream generated by a producer coroutine is split between 3 consumers. A possible output can look like as follows:

```
Sending: 1

Sending: 4

Sending: 9

Receiving by consumer #1: 1

Receiving by consumer #2: 4

Receiving by consumer #3: 9

Sending: 16

Sending: 25

Receiving by consumer #3: 16

Receiving by consumer #1: 25
```

Similarly, we can *fan in* by collecting the output of multiple producers in the same channel and feeding it into a single consumer coroutine. In a more general case, any number of producers and consumers can communicate via multiple channels. In general, the channel behavior is *fair* with respect to multiple coroutines in a sense that a coroutine which gets to invoke **receive()** first, gets the next element.

Producers

There is a special **producer()** coroutine builder which allows you to construct concurrent data stream similar to the **sequence()** function we've discussed earlier when talking about the Collection API. This builder introduces **ProducerScope** which provides the **send()** method similar to a channel:

```kotlin
import kotlinx.coroutines.channels.*
import kotlinx.coroutines.*

fun main() {
    runBlocking {
        val channel = produce {
            for (n in 1..3) {
                val square = n*n
                println("Sending: $square")
                send(square)
            }
        }
        launch {
            channel.consumeEach { println("Receiving: $it") }
        }
    }
}
```

Note that you do not need to explicitly close a channel in this case; the **producer()** builder will do it automatically on coroutine termination.

In terms of exception handling, **produce()** follows the policy of **async()/await()**: an exception thrown inside **produce()** is preserved and rethrown in the first coroutine which invokes the channel's **receive()**.

Tickers

The coroutines library has a special variety of a rendezvous channel which is called a *ticker*. This channel produces a stream of Unit values with a given delay between subsequent elements. To construct it, you can use the **ticker()** function which allows you to specify the following:

- **delayMillis:** Delay in milliseconds between ticker elements
- **initialDelayMillis:** Delay before producing the first element; by default, it's the same as **delayMillis**
- **context:** Coroutine context in which the ticker is supposed to run (empty by default)

- **mode:** A value of **TickerMode** enum which determines a mode of ticker behavior:

  - **TickerMode.FIXED_PERIOD:** This ticker will choose a delay to maintain a constant period between element generations as much as possible.

  - **TickerMode.FIXED_RATE:** This ticker will simply make a specified delay before sending each element regardless of how much time has passed since the last receive.

To see the difference between ticker modes, let's consider the following code:

```
import kotlinx.coroutines.*
import kotlinx.coroutines.channels.*


fun main() = runBlocking {
    val ticker = ticker(100)
    println(withTimeoutOrNull(50) { ticker.receive() })
    println(withTimeoutOrNull(60) { ticker.receive() })
    delay(250)
    println(withTimeoutOrNull(1) { ticker.receive() })
    println(withTimeoutOrNull(60) { ticker.receive() })
    println(withTimeoutOrNull(60) { ticker.receive() })
}
```

When run, it produces the following output:

```
null
kotlin.Unit
kotlin.Unit
kotlin.Unit
null
```

Let's see how its execution proceeds step-by-step:

1. We try to receive the ticker signal within 50 ms timeout. Since the ticker delay is 100 ms, **withTimeOutOrNull()** returns null as no signal was sent yet.

2. Then, we try receiving the signal within the next 60 ms. This time we'll almost certainly get a non-null result because at least 100 ms will pass since the ticker starts. Once the **receive()** is called the ticker will resume.

3. Then, the consumer coroutine is suspended for about 250 ms. 100 ms later the ticker sends another signal and suspends waiting for it to be received. After that, both coroutines remain in a suspended state for 150 ms.

4. The consumer coroutine resumes and tries to request the signal. Since the signal was already sent, `receive()` returns immediately (thus, we can set a small timeout of 1 ms) allowing the ticker coroutine to resume. Now, the ticker will measure the time elapsed since the last signal was sent and find that it's about 250 ms. This interval contains two whole delays (200 ms) and a remainder of about 50 ms. The ticker then adjusts its own waiting time before the next signal to be 100 – 50 = 50 ms so that the signal is sent when the whole delay (100 ms) is passed.

5. The consumer tries to receive the single within 60 ms timeout and most certainly succeed since the next signal should be sent in less than 50 ms.

6. The last attempt to receive the signal happens almost immediately so the ticker will wait for the whole delay (100 ms) again. As a result, the last call to `receive()` returns null because the signal won't be received within 60 ms timeout.

If we set the ticker mode to **FIXED_RATE**, however, the result will change:

```
null
kotlin.Unit
kotlin.Unit
null
kotlin.Unit
```

At first, the execution proceeds in almost the same way. The difference comes after the consumer coroutine resumes after making a long delay of 250 ms. The third `receive()` also returns immediately since the ticker has already sent its signal within that 250 ms period but now, it won't take the elapsed time into account and simply wait for another 100 ms. As a result, the fourth call to `receive()` returns null because the signal is not sent yet after 60 ms. At the moment of the fifth call, however, this interval rises above 100 ms and the signal is received.

Note that the ticker-related API is currently considered experimental and may be replaced in future versions of the coroutines library.

Flows

Similar to producers, **flows** provide a way to share a sequence of data among different coroutines allowing the data itself to be both generated and consumed asynchronously. Let's consider our Producer example with square generation and represent it in terms of flows:

```kotlin
import kotlinx.coroutines.flow.*
import kotlinx.coroutines.*

fun main() {
    runBlocking {
        val flow = flow {
            for (n in 1..3) {
                val square = n*n
                println("Sending: $square")
                emit(square)
            }
        }
        launch {
            flow.collect { println("Receiving: $it") }
        }
    }
}
```

So both concepts are pretty much equivalent in terms of their basic API:

- You can use the **flow()** builder instead of **produce()** to construct a concurrent flow instance.
- You can use the **emit()** method of an implicit **FlowCollector** to generate individual flow items instead of sending them to a channel via **send()**.
- You can use the **collect()** function to consume flow items inside another coroutine instead of the channel's **consumeEach()**.

However, there is not much point adding a separate framework concept if it only differs from the existing one by the names of classes and methods involved in its API. In fact, introduction of flows enriches the coroutines library with a new asynchronous computation pattern somewhat erasing the boundaries between coroutines and Kotlin sequences. So let's look at how flow features can be used in various use cases.

First, unlike producers, flows are multi-use which means that they are started anew for each **collect()** call. This can be compared to behavior of sequences generated

by the **sequence()** builder (which also makes use of the coroutines machinery). If
we modify the example by adding one more collector coroutine, both the collectors
will see an entire sequence of items:

```kotlin
import kotlinx.coroutines.flow.*

import kotlinx.coroutines.*


fun main() {
    runBlocking {
        val flow = flow {
            for (n in 1..3) {
                val square = n*n
                println("Sending: $square")
                emit(square)
            }
        }
        launch {
            flow.collect { println("Receiving #1: $it") }
        }
        launch {
            flow.collect { println("Receiving #2: $it") }
        }
    }
}
```

The result will look like this (with a possible change in order between collectors #1
and #2):

```
Sending: 1
#1 Receiving: 1
Sending: 4
#1 Receiving: 4
Sending: 9
#1 Receiving: 9
Sending: 1
```

```
#2 Receiving: 1
Sending: 4
#2 Receiving: 4
Sending: 9
#2 Receiving: 9
```

In the case of our channel/producer example, an asynchronous data generation is launched by the coroutine builder itself and is shared between all consumers. So adding a second consumer coroutine would produce something as follows:

```
Sending: 1
#1 Receiving: 1
Sending: 4
Sending: 9
#1 Receiving: 4
#2 Receiving: 9
```

In other words, each value would be sent and received exactly once.

Besides creating flows by a builder function, you can also transform a fixed set of values or a collection into a flow using the **flowOf()** or **asFlow()** function, respectively:

```
// 3-value flow
val fixedFlow = flowOf("abc", "def", "ghi")
// sequence emitted as flow
val seqFlow = generateSequence(1) { 2*it }.take(10).asFlow()
```

Another useful feature of flows is the ability to transform them using the API similar to that of Kotlin collections. In particular, flows can be filtered and transformed by the familiar pair of the **flowOf()/filter()** functions:

```
runBlocking {
    val flow = (1..10).asFlow().filter { it % 2 == 0 }.map { it*it }
    launch {
        flow.collect { println("Collected: $it") }
    }
}
```

Note that lambdas passed into these functions are suspendable just like a flow body so filtering and mapping do not block the coroutine thread as collection operators do.

More complex transformations can be implemented with the **transform()** function that replaces each item of an original flow with an arbitrary sub-flow generated by the **emit()** calls. In the following example, **transform()** produces a flow where even numbers are filtered out while odd ones are emitted twice:

```kotlin
runBlocking {
    val flow = (1..5).asFlow().transform {
        if (it % 2 == 0) return@transform
        emit(it)
        emit(it)
    }
    launch {
        flow.collect { println("Collected: $it") }
    }
}
```

Running the preceding code, we get the following:

```
Collected: 1

Collected: 1

Collected: 3

Collected: 3

Collected: 5

Collected: 5
```

It's possible to truncate the flow data to a given number of items using **take()**. The special feature of this operation as opposed to ordinary collection is forced cancellation of the flow coroutine on reaching the maximum size. You can also explicitly cancel a flow by calling **cancel()** inside a collector coroutine:

```kotlin
runBlocking {
    val flow = (1..5).asFlow()
    launch {
        flow.collect {
```

```
            if (it > 3) cancel() // stop flow after collecting 3
            println("Collected: $it")
        }
    }
}
```

Similar to collections whose elements might be collections themselves, it's possible to create a flow of flows. This can happen, if values from some asynchronous sequence trigger new computation which results in its own flow. Consider an example:

```
import kotlinx.coroutines.flow.*
import kotlinx.coroutines.*


fun main() {
    runBlocking {
        val flow = (1..4).asFlow().map { den ->
            (1 until den).asFlow().map { num ->
                delay(50) // imitate delays
                "$num/$den"
            }
        }
        launch {
            val startTime = System.currentTimeMillis()
            flow.collect { subFlow ->
                subFlow.collect { println(it) }
            }
            val endTime = System.currentTimeMillis()
            println("Collection time: ${endTime - startTime} ms")
        }
    }
}
```

The program result (with a possible variation in its running time) will look like this:

```
1/2

1/3
```

2/3

1/4

2/4

3/4

```
Collection time: 392 ms
```

It often comes in handy to replace such a nested flow with its flattened version. In case of ordinary collections, we have functions like **flatten()** and **flatMap()** to do the job so it seems reasonable to have an equivalent functionality for flows as well. Indeed, the coroutines library not only supports flow flattening but also allows you to choose different modes of combining nested items into a resulting flow.

The most straightforward mode which parallels ordinary collection concatenation is implemented by **flattenConcat()**. In this case, the collector processes each nested flow entirely before switching to the next one effectively duplicating the effect of a nested loop shown in the previous example:

```
launch {

    flow.flattenConcat().collect { println(it) }

}
```

The second option is given by **flattenMerge()** which takes items from multiple nested flows emitting them as soon as possible. In general, this leads to original flows being mixed. For example, if we replace our previous collector with:

```
launch {

    flow.flattenMerge().collect { println(it) }

}
```

The print trace might look like this (note the smaller running time as compared with the concatenation mode):

1/2

1/3

1/4

2/3

2/4

3/4

```
Collection time: 236 ms
```

The merge mode decreases the collection time and so might be preferable when you don't need to preserve an original ordering of nested flows.

The number of simultaneously collected flows can be specified by the optional argument which by default equals to the **DEFAULT_CONCURRENCY** constant.

Both versions of **flattenXXX()** have corresponding **flatMapXXX()** functions which combines the effects of map() and flattenXXX(). For example:

```
val flow = (1..4).asFlow().flatMapMerge { den ->
    (1 until den).asFlow().map { num ->
        delay(50)
        "$num/$den"
    }
}
```

One more flattening mode implemented by the **flatMapLatest()** function (it has no **flatten()** counterpart) cancels each nested flow as soon as the next one is started. In our example, the most likely result will look as follows:

```
1/4
```

```
2/4
```

```
3/4
```

```
Collection time: 240 ms
```

Since all four nested flows are started almost simultaneously (assumed a system with at least 4 CPU cores) and only the last one is retained by the collector.

Note that the **flatten()** and **flatMap()** functions are available as well but are explicitly declared as error-deprecated. This enforces the explicit naming of the flattening mode in the code and improves its readability.

A related task is combining two separate flows by applying some transformation to the element pairs. One of its possible implementation is given by the **zip()** function that pairs corresponding elements of both flows and transforms them with a given lambda. The resulting flow collection suspends until both elements are emitted so if original flows are generated with different rates, the collector is forced to always wait for the slower one. Consider the following code:

```
import kotlinx.coroutines.*
import kotlinx.coroutines.flow.*
```

```
fun main() {
    runBlocking {
        val fast = ('a'..'c').asFlow().transform {
            delay(50)
            emit(it)
        }
        val slow = (1..3).asFlow().transform {
            delay(100)
            emit(it)
        }
        launch {
            (fast.zip(slow) { i, j -> "$i/$j" }).collect { println(it)
}
        }
    }
}
```

When run, it prints each pair of corresponding elements only once:

a/1

b/2

c/3

An alternative mode is implemented by the **combine()** function which pairs most recent items of both flows. It doesn't need to wait for the slower flow but in return breaks the strict correspondence between original elements. If we replace **zip()** with **combine()** in our previous example, the likely result could look like this:

a/1

b/1

c/1

c/2

c/3

Note that some elements in the **combine()** output may be missing or duplicated while retaining the individual orderings of original flows (a, b, c and 1, 2, 3).

All in all, the Kotlin flows provide you with a rich declarative-style API that greatly simplifies manipulation of asynchronous data sequences.

Actors

A common way to implement a thread-safe access to a shared mutable state is given by the actor model. An **actor** is an object which comprises some internal state and means to concurrently communicate with other actor by sending messages. Actors listen for incoming messages and can respond to them by modifying their own state, sending more messages and starting new actors. The actor's state is private so other actors can't use it directly – it can only be accessed by sending a message thus relieving you from the need to use lock-based synchronization.

Keep in mind that the actor API is currently is subject to change and will be replaced with a new one in the future versions of the coroutines library.

In Kotlin, the coroutines library actors can be created by using the **actor()** coroutine builder. It introduces a special scope (**ActorScope**) which combines the basic coroutine scope with a receiver channel you can to access incoming messages. This builder is somewhat similar to **launch()** since it also starts a job which isn't meant to produce the result by itself and follows the same exception handling policy as **launch()** coroutine builders similarly relying on **CoroutineExceptionHandler**.

To demonstrate the basic usage of the actor API, let's consider a simple example of the actor which maintains a bank account and can withdraw/deposit a given amount of money. First, we need to define a set of classes which represent incoming messages:

```kotlin
sealed class AccountMessage

class GetBalance(val amount: CompletableDeferred<Long>) :
AccountMessage()

class Deposit(val amount: Long) : AccountMessage()

class Withdraw(
    val amount: Long,
    val isPermitted: CompletableDeferred<Boolean>
) : AccountMessage()
```

Using sealed class, hierarchy will allow us to employ exhaustive when expressions for instances of the **AccountMessage** class.

Note that the **GetBalance** instance has a property of the **CompletableDeferred** type. Our actor will use this property to send the current account balance back to the coroutine which requests it using the **GetBalance** message. Similarly, the Withdraw class has the **isPermitted** property which will receive true if withdraw is successful and false otherwise.

Now, we can implement the actor responsible for maintaining the account balance. The basic logic is simple: we continuously poll the incoming channel and perform one of the possible actions depending on the received message:

```kotlin
fun CoroutineScope.accountManager(
    initialBalance: Long
) = actor<AccountMessage> {
    var balance = initialBalance
    for (message in channel) {
        when (message) {
            is GetBalance -> message.amount.complete(balance)
            is Deposit -> {
                balance += message.amount
                println("Deposited ${message.amount}")
            }
            is Withdraw -> {
                val canWithdraw = balance >= message.amount
                if (canWithdraw) {
                    balance -= message.amount
                    println("Withdrawn ${message.amount}")
                }
                message.isPermitted.complete(canWithdraw)
            }
        }
    }
}
```

The **actor()** builder can be thought of as a counterpart of **produce()**; both rely on channels for communication but while actors use them for *receiving* data, producers create channels for *sending* data to their consumers. By default, actors use rendezvous channels, but you can change it by specifying the capacity argument in the **actor()** function call.

Note the use of the **complete()** method on **CompletableDeferred**; that's how we send the request result back to the actor client.

Now, let's add a pair of coroutines which communicate without the actor:

```
private suspend fun SendChannel<AccountMessage>.deposit(
    name: String,
    amount: Long
) {
    send(Deposit(amount))
    println("$name: deposit $amount")
}


private suspend fun SendChannel<AccountMessage>.tryWithdraw(
    name: String,
    amount: Long
) {
    val status = CompletableDeferred<Boolean>().let {
        send(Withdraw(amount, it))
        if (it.await()) "OK" else "DENIED"
    }
    println("$name: withdraw $amount ($status)")
}


private suspend fun SendChannel<AccountMessage>.printBalance(name:
String) {
    val balance = CompletableDeferred<Long>().let {
        send(GetBalance(it))
        it.await()
    }
```

```
        println("$name: balance is $balance")
}


fun main() {
    runBlocking {
        val manager = accountManager(100)
        withContext(Dispatchers.Default) {
            launch {
                manager.deposit("Client #1", 50)
                manager.printBalance("Client #1")
            }
            launch {
                manager.tryWithdraw("Client #2", 100)
                manager.printBalance("Client #2")

            }
        }
        manager.tryWithdraw("Client #0", 1000)
        manager.printBalance("Client #0")
        manager.close()
    }
}
```

To send the actor a message, we use the **send()** method provided by the corresponding channel. Here is an example of the possible output:

```
Client #1: deposit 50
Deposited 50
Withdrawn 100
Client #2: withdraw 100 (OK)
Client #2: balance is 50
Client #1: balance is 50
Client #0: withdraw 1000 (DENIED)
Client #0: balance is 50
```

Although the operation order may vary (especially when it comes to parallel execution), the results remain consistent. We don't need any synchronization primitives like locks or critical sections since there is no publicly accessible mutable state.

One more thing worth noting is that actor **builders()** are currently considered an experimental API which is subject to possible changes in future.

Using Java concurrency

Besides Kotlin-specific coroutines library, you can also make use of JDK concurrency API when targeting the JVM platform. In this section, we'll discuss some helper functions provided by the Kotlin standard library to simplify common concurrency-related tasks such as creating threads and synchronization.

Starting a thread

To start a general-purpose thread, you can use the **thread()** function which allows you to specify both a thread runnable in the form of Kotlin lambda as well as a set of basic thread properties:

- **start:** Whether thread should be started immediately after creation (true by default)

- **isDaemon:** Whether thread should be started in daemon mode (false by default). Daemon threads do not prevent JVM termination and thus are shut down automatically on termination of the main thread.

- **contextClassLoader:** Custom class loader which is used by thread code to load classes and resources (null by default).

- **name:** Custom thread name. By default, it's null which means that the name is chosen automatically (in a form of "Thread-1", "Thread-2", etc.).

- **priority:** Thread priority which ranges from **Thread.MIN_PRIORITY (= 1)** to **Thread.MAX_PRIORITY (= 10)** and affects how much CPU time the thread will get as compared to others. By default, it's equal to -1 which means that priority is chosen automatically.

- **block:** A function value of **type () -> Unit** which is run in the new thread.

For example, the following program starts a thread which prints a message every 150 milliseconds:

```kotlin
import kotlin.concurrent.thread

fun main() {
    println("Starting a thread...")
    thread(name = "Worker", isDaemon = true) {
        for (i in 1..5) {
            println("${Thread.currentThread().name}: $i")
            Thread.sleep(150)
        }
    }
    Thread.sleep(500)
    println("Shutting down...")
}
```

Since a new thread is started as a daemon, however, it only manages to print its message four times because JVM terminates once the main thread finishes execution after 500 ms of sleep. As a result, the program output looks as follows:

```
Starting a thread...

Worker: 1

Worker: 2

Worker: 3

Worker: 4

Shutting down...
```

Another group of functions is related to Java timers which allow you to concurrently execute some periodic action at the specific time. The **timer()** function schedules a timer which runs some tasks with a fixed delay relative to the time of its last execution. As a result, when some execution takes more time, all subsequent runs are postponed. In this sense, it can be compared to a Kotlin ticker working in the **FIXED_RATE** mode. When configuring a timer with a **timer()** call, you can specify the following options:

- **name:** Name of the timer thread (null by default)
- **daemon:** Whether the time thread is executed in daemon mode (false by default)

- **startAt:** The Date object describing when the first time event should happen.
- **period:** Desired number of milliseconds between successive timer executions.
- **action: TimeTask.() -> Unit** lambda which is run on each timer's execution.

Alternatively, you can use another **timer()** overload with the **initialDelay** parameter which specifies the moment of the first event as delay from the current time (defaulting to zero).

Let's rewrite our previous example using timers:

```
import kotlin.concurrent.timer

fun main() {
    println("Starting a thread...")
    var counter = 0
    timer(period = 150, name = "Worker", daemon = true) {
        println("${Thread.currentThread().name}: ${++counter}")
    }
    Thread.sleep(500)
    println("Shutting down...")
}
```

There is also a similar pair of **fixedRateTimer()** functions which sets up a timer with a fixed delay between starts of subsequent executions. It can be compared to a ticker in the **FIXED_PERIOD** mode which tries to compensate additional delays to ensure a constant period of timer events in the long run.

Synchronization and locks

Synchronization is a common primitive which ensures that a specific code fragment is executed in a single thread. When such a fragment is already being executed in some threads, any other threads trying to enter it are forced to wait. In Java, there are two ways of introducing synchronization into your code. First, you can wrap it inside a special synchronized block specifying some object which acts as a lock. In Kotlin, the syntax is quite similar, although you use a standard library function with a lambda rather than the built-in language structure:

```kotlin
import kotlin.concurrent.thread

fun main() {
    var counter = 0
    val lock = Any()
    for (i in 1..5) {
        thread(isDaemon = false) {
            synchronized(lock) {
                counter += i
                println(counter)
            }
        }
    }
}
```

Although the order of individual additions may vary, thus giving different intermediate results, synchronization ensures that the total sum is always equal to 15. A possible output may look like this:

1

4

8

13

15

In general, the **synchronized()** function returns the value of its lambda. For example, we can use it to retrieve one of intermediate counter values at the moment of call:

```kotlin
import kotlin.concurrent.thread

fun main() {
    var counter = 0
    val lock = Any()
    for (i in 1..5) {...}
```

```
    val currentCounter = synchronized(lock) { counter }
    println("Current counter: $currentCounter")
}
```

While the result may vary, it is always equal to some intermediate values produced by one of the five adder threads.

Another way you can use in Java is to mark a method with the synchronized modifier; in this case, the entire method body is considered synchronized with respect to the current instance of the containing class or **Class** instance itself (if the method in question is static). In Kotlin, you can use the **@Synchronized** annotation for the same purpose:

```
import kotlin.concurrent.thread


class Counter {
    private var value = 0

    @Synchronized fun addAndPrint(value: Int) {
        value += value
        println(value)
    }
}


fun main() {
    val counter = Counter()
    for (i in 1..5) {
        thread(isDaemon = false) { counter.addAndPrint(i) }
    }
}
```

The standard library also includes the **withLock()** function which allows you to execute some lambda under a given Lock object (from the **java.util.concurrent.locks** package) similar to the synchronized block. In this case, you don't need to worry about releasing your lock on exception because this is handled **withLock()**. As an example, let's apply it to our Counter class:

```kotlin
class Counter {
    private var value = 0
    private val lock = ReentrantLock()

    fun addAndPrint(value: Int) {
        lock.withLock {
            value += value
            println(value)
        }
    }
}
```

On top of it, there are **read()** and **write()** functions which execute the given action under the read/write locks of the **ReentrantReadWriteLock** object. The **write()** function also extends on the **ReentrantReadWriteLock** semantics by supporting the automatic upgrade of the existing read lock to write one.

Java vs. Kotlin: Note that **wait()**, **notify()**, and **notifyAll()** methods defined by Java's **Object** class are not available for Kotlin's Any. If necessary you can, however, use them by explicitly casting a value to **java.lang.Object:**

```kotlin
(obj as Object).wait()
```

Keep in mind that **wait()**, like any other blocking method, shouldn't be used inside suspending functions.

Coroutine debugger

Starting from Kotlin 1.4, the IntelliJ IDEA plugin comes with a built-in coroutine debugging support which greatly simplifies an otherwise tedious task of tracking the execution of coroutine-powered asynchronous code. Now, the *Debug* tool window has an additional *Coroutines* tab which lists all currently running and suspended coroutines grouped by their context dispatchers as shown in *Figure 13.4*. This tree also gives you basic information about each coroutine such as its name, thread, and current state:

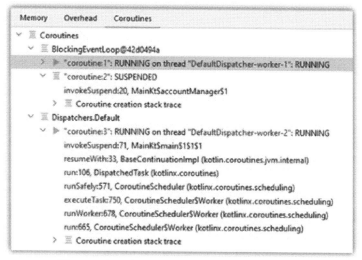

Figure 13.4: Coroutine tree in IntelliJ debugger

By expanding a particular coroutine in the tree, you get access to its full stack trace, including variables stored in all intermediate frames. Just like with synchronous code debugging, you can use the coroutine stack trace to find corresponding places in your code, and local variables can be watched and changed in the usual way (see *Figure 13.5*). Besides that each coroutine node contains a separate creation stack trace that you can use to track the code where your respective coroutine is started:

Coroutine debugging is currently available in Kotlin/JVM IntelliJ IDEA projects with a coroutines library of version 1.3.8 or newer.

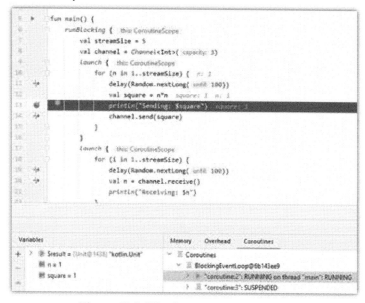

Figure 13.5: Viewing coroutine variables

Conclusion

In this chapter, we learned the fundamentals of coroutine-based concurrency in Kotlin. We looked at how concurrent code can be made of suspending functions and coroutine builders and how to manage coroutine lifetime using contexts and scopes. We also discussed the cooperative cancellation and exception handling mechanisms and examined the lifecycle of concurrent tasks. We learned how to use channel- and actor-based communication for efficient sharing of data between multiple concurrent tasks.

As an extra topic, we looked at some helpful functions the Kotlin standard library provides to utilize concurrency API available on the JVM platform in a better way.

In the next chapter, we'll focus on the subject of testing. We'll discuss several Kotlin-aware frameworks and see how Kotlin features and DSLs can help us in writing various kinds of test cases.

Questions

1. What is a suspending function? How does its behavior differ from that of an ordinary function?

1. How do you create coroutines with **launch()** and **async()** builders? What's their difference?

2. Explain the purpose of the **runBlocking()** builder.

3. What is a structured concurrency?

4. Describe the lifecycle of a coroutine job. How job cancellation is propagated in a coroutine tree?

5. What is a coroutine dispatcher? Describe common dispatcher implementations provided by coroutines library.

6. How can you change a dispatcher from inside the coroutine?

7. Describe exception handling mechanisms used by the coroutines library. What is a purpose of **CoroutineExceptionHandler?**

8. What is a supervisor job? How can you use it to handle exceptions thrown by nested coroutines?

9. What is a channel? What kinds of channels are supported by coroutines library?

10. How can you build a channel with the **produce()** function?

11. Describe the behavior of ticker channels.

12. Give an overview of the Flow API and its concurrent computation patterns.

13. Describe an idea of the actor model. How can you use actors in Kotlin coroutines library?

14. Which utilities do the Kotlin standard library provides for creating threads?

15. How can you use thread synchronization and locks in Kotlin code?

CHAPTER 14
Testing with Kotlin

Testing frameworks constitutes a major part of the software development ecosystem. They help creating of reusable test code which helps to maintain the software quality throughout the development lifecycle. Thanks to a well-designed Java interoperability, Kotlin developers can benefit from numerous testing tools targeting the JVM platform such as JUnit, TestNG, Mockito, and others.

The Kotlin ecosystem, however, has given rise to some frameworks which specifically targets Kotlin developers by utilizing powerful features of the language to create concise and expressive test code. In this chapter, we'll focus on the KotlinTest, a powerful open-source testing framework developed at http://github.com/kotlintest/kotlintest. We'll take a look at the following three main topics:

- How to use organize test code using KotlinTest specification styles?

- How to express various test assertions using matchers, inspectors, and autogenerated data sets for property-based testing, and so on?

- How to ensure correct initialization and finalization of a test environment as well as provide a test configuration?

We'll start with explaining how to configure KotlinTest for use in IntelliJ IDEA projects.

Structure

The following topics will be covered in this chapter:

- KotlinTest specifications
- Assertions
- Fixtures and configurations

Objective

After reading this chapter, the reader will learn to write test specifications using features provided by the KotlinTest framework.

KotlinTest specifications

In this section, we'll talk about how to configure KotlinTest for use in IntelliJ IDEA projects and different test layouts provided by this testing framework. All examples presented in the chapter will use KotlinTest 3.3.

Getting started with KotlinTest

In order to use KotlinTest, we need to add the project dependencies. We've already seen how to add an external dependency to the IntelliJ IDEA project in *Chapter 13, Concurrency,* when discussing the Kotlin coroutines library. Adding the test framework is basically similar. First, we need to add a library in the Project Structure dialog using its Maven coordinates **io.kotlintest:kotlintest-runner-junit5:3.3.0** (see *Figure 14.1*).

If you're using a build automation system like Maven or Gradle, you can configure KotlinTest by adding its dependency to the corresponding buildfile.

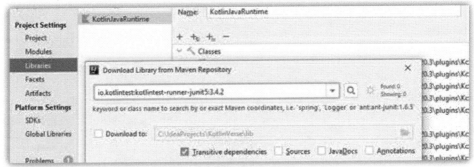

Figure 14.1: Adding KotlinTest library

After that, the IDE will suggest you to add a new library to the modules of your project. The next step is to set a dependency scope. Switch to the **Modules** view on the left-hand side, select a module of interest, and open the **Dependencies** tab. You'll see the newly added library added to dependencies with its scope set to **Compile**. It means that the library will be included in the classpath of both production and test sources during their compilation and running in the IDE. Since we need KotlinTest only for testing purposes, the scope should be changed to **Test** (*Figure 14.2*):

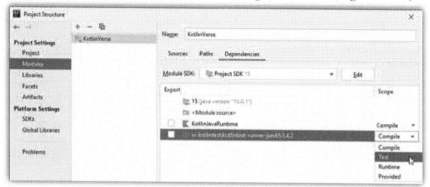

Figure 14.2: *Choosing test dependency scope*

The final preparation step is to configure a directory to contain our test source code. If you don't have it already, create a new directory (say, **test**) right next to **src,** which holds production sources by right clicking on the module root in the **Project** view and choosing **New | Directory**. Now, we need to tell IDE that it will be our test source root. To do this, right click on the newly added directory and choose **Mark Directory as | Test Sources Root**. The test directory will change its color to green showing that IDEA will now treat its content as source files for our tests.

It's also worth installing a special plugin which improves the IntelliJ integration with KotlinTest. You can do it via the **Plugins** tab in the **Settings** dialog (**File | Settings**) by searching for **kotlintest** (*Figure 14.3*). After clicking on **Install** and downloading and installing, you'll need to restart the IDE:

Figure 14.3: *Installing KotlinTest plugin for IntelliJ IDEA*

Now, we can start writing a code just like we did earlier. Let's create a new file in the **test** directory and write a simple test specification:

```
import io.kotlintest.shouldBe

import io.kotlintest.specs.StringSpec


class NumbersTest : StringSpec({
  "2 + 2 should be 4" { (2 + 2) shouldBe 4 }
  "2 * 2 should be 4" { (2 * 2) shouldBe 4 }
})
```

We'll explain the meaning behind this definition in a moment, but even now you'll surely be able to recognize a pair of simple tests named **2 + 2 should be 4** and **2 * 2 should be 4** after checking some arithmetic identities. To run the test, notice the triangular markers on the left. By clicking on one of them, you can execute either the corresponding test or a whole specification (*Figure 14.4*):

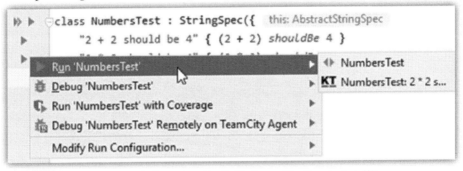

Figure 14.4: *Running KotlinTest specification in IntelliJ*

Now, we are ready to begin our discussion of the KotlinTest feature. Our first topic will be related to various specification styles you can use to organize your test cases.

Specification styles

KotlinTest supports multiple specification styles; each of them affects how your test code is organized. You can easily mix different styles in your project and even define your own by creating an implementation of the **AbstractSpec** class or one of its more specific subclasses like **AbstractStringSpec**. In this section, we'll take a look at the styles which are available right out of the box once you add KotlinTest to your project.

To define a test case, you need to inherit from one of the specification classes. Then, you can add tests either in a class initializer, or in a lambda which is passed to the superclass constructor. The way you define tests themselves is style-specific and in most cases, involve some DSL-like API. Let's consider a simple example using the **StringSpec** class:

```
import io.kotlintest.shouldBe
import io.kotlintest.specs.StringSpec


class NumbersTest :StringSpec({
  "2 + 2 should be 4" { (2 + 2) shouldBe 4 }
  "2 * 2 should be 4" { (2 * 2) shouldBe 4 }

})
```

With **StringSpec,** individual tests are defined by suspending lambdas placed after a string with a test description. As you might've guessed, this is just an operator form for the **String.invoke()** function defined by **StringSpec**. In this example, the actual verification code uses the **shouldBe** infix function which throws an exception when its arguments are not equal. This function is a part of matchers DSL which we'll cover in the next section.

Note that **StringSpec** imposes a flat test case structure where all tests in a particular class are defined on the same level. If you try to place one test block inside another, the framework will fail with an exception at runtime.

A more complex layout is given by the **WordSpec** class. In the simplest form, it allows you to define a two-level hierarchy where tests are defined, which are similar to **StringSpec,** are grouped by the calls of the **should()** function:

```
import io.kotlintest.shouldBe
import io.kotlintest.specs.WordSpec


class NumbersTest2 : WordSpec({
  "1 + 2" should {
    "be equal to 3" { (1 + 2) shouldBe 3 }
    "be equal to 2 + 1" { (1 + 2) shouldBe (2 + 1) }
  }

})
```

Additionally, you can define one more level of grouping by wrapping **should()** calls inside **When()** or `when`():

```kotlin
import io.kotlintest.shouldBe
import io.kotlintest.specs.WordSpec


class NumbersTest2 :WordSpec({
  "Addition" When {
    "1 + 2" should {
      "be equal to 3" { (1 + 2) shouldBe 3 }
      "be equal to 2 + 1" { (1 + 2) shouldBe (2 + 1) }
    }
  }
})
```

What if we want a hierarchy with an arbitrary number of levels? The **FunSpec** class wraps the test code inside the **test()** function calls which take a test description and a suspending lambda to run. Unlike **StringSpec,** this style supports grouping of tests by context blocks:

```kotlin
import io.kotlintest.shouldBe
import io.kotlintest.specs.FunSpec


class NumbersTest :FunSpec({
test("0 should be equal to 0") { 0 shouldBe 0 }
  context("Arithmetic") {
    context("Addition") {
      test("2 + 2 should be 4") { (2 + 2) shouldBe 4 }
    }
    context("Multiplication") {
      test("2 * 2 should be 4") { (2 * 2) shouldBe 4 }
    }
  }
})
```

Both test and context blocks may be used at any level except inside test block themselves.

IDE Tips: When they run in the IDE, the results of such multi-level tests are also presented in a hierarchical view corresponding to the specification blocks. *Figure 14.5* shows the result of running the preceding test code in IntelliJ IDEA:

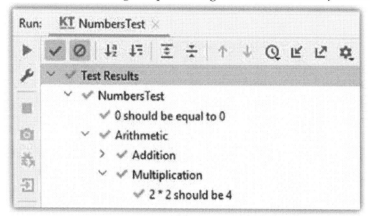

Figure 14.5: Multi-level test results in IntelliJ IDEA

The **ExpectSpec** is basically the same but uses **expect()** instead of **test()** and additionally, forbids placing tests at the top level (that is, all tests must be put within some **context()** block).

The **DescribeSpec** uses the **describe()/context()** blocks for the purpose of grouping with actual tests placed inside it():

```
import io.kotlintest.shouldBe
import io.kotlintest.specs.DescribeSpec

class NumbersTest : DescribeSpec({
  describe("Addition") {
    context("1 + 2") {
      it("should give 3") { (1 + 2) shouldBe 3 }
    }
  }
})
```

The **ShouldSpec** produces a layout similar to **FunSpec** with context blocks used for grouping and test blocks placed at the leaf level. The differences are purely syntactic. To define a context block, you will use the **invoke()** calls on the description string (similar to test blocks of **StringSpec**), while test blocks themselves are defined by the **should()** function calls:

```
import io.kotlintest.shouldBe
import io.kotlintest.specs.ShouldSpec


class NumbersTest : ShouldSpec({
should("be equal to 0") { 0 shouldBe 0 }
  "Addition" {
    "1 + 2" {
      should("be equal to 3") { (1 + 2) shouldBe 3 }
      should("be equal to 2 + 1") { (1 + 2) shouldBe (2 + 1) }
    }
  }
})
```

One more specification of a similar kind can be constructed via the **FreeSpec** class. Like **StringSpec**, it uses **invoke()** on strings to define tests while contexts are introduced by the minus operator:

```
import io.kotlintest.shouldBe
import io.kotlintest.specs.FreeSpec


class NumbersTest : FreeSpec({
  "0 should be equal to 0" { 0shouldBe 0 }
  "Addition" - {
    "1 + 2" - {
      "1 + 2 should be equal to 3" { (1 + 2) shouldBe 3 }
      "1 + 2 should be equal to 2 + 1" { (1 + 2) shouldBe (2 + 1) }
    }
  }
})
```

KotlinTest also supports BDD (behavior-driven-development) specification styles inspired by the Gherkin language. In the **FeatureSpec,** hierarchy roots are introduced by feature blocks which in turn contain scenario blocks implementing a particular test. The **and()** calls may be used to group scenarios (and other groups) within a particular feature:

```
import io.kotlintest.shouldBe
```

```
import io.kotlintest.specs.FeatureSpec

class NumbersTest : FeatureSpec({
  feature("Arithmetic") {
    val x = 1
    scenario("x is 1 at first") { x shouldBe 1 }
    and("increasing by") {
      scenario("1 gives 2") { (x + 1) shouldBe 2 }
      scenario("2 gives 3") { (x + 2) shouldBe 3 }
    }
  }
})
```

A similar style is implemented by **BehaviorSpec** which introduces three basic levels denoted by functions **given()/Given(), when()/When(),** and **then()/Then()**. Additional levels of grouping may be introduced by **and()/And()** calls which can combine several when/then blocks:

```
import io.kotlintest.shouldBe
```

```
import io.kotlintest.specs.BehaviorSpec

class NumbersTest : BehaviorSpec({
  Given("Arithmetic") {
    When("x is 1") {
      val x = 1
      And("increased by 1") {
        Then("result is 2") { (x + 1) shouldBe 2 }
      }
    }
  }
})
```

Note how using of these blocks can produce a test description which is very close to natural language ("when x is 1 and increased by 1 then result is 2").

The final spec style we will consider is **AnnotationSpec**. This style doesn't use DSL-like test specification but instead relies on **@Test** annotations you need to apply to test class methods, which are similar to test frameworks like JUnit or TestNG:

```
import io.kotlintest.shouldBe

import io.kotlintest.specs.AnnotationSpec


class NumbersTest : AnnotationSpec() {
  @Test fun `2 + 2 should be 4`() { (2 + 2) shouldBe 4 }
  @Test fun `2 * 2 should be 4`() { (2 * 2) shouldBe 4 }
}
```

You can also disable a particular test by annotating it with **@Ignore**.

Assertions

Matchers

In the previous samples of code demonstrating the use of various specification styles, we've used the **shouldBe** function which asserts simple equality of its arguments. This is just one example of numerous matchers provided by the **KotlinTest** library.

Matchers are defined as extension functions which can be invoked either in a form of an ordinary call or as an infix operator. All matcher names start with **shouldBe**. This convention facilitates readable names like **shouldBeGreaterThanOrEqual** in the test code. A full list of built-in matchers can be found in the KotlinTest documentation; we won't focus on particular examples here because most of the matcher functions have self-explanatory names and can be used in an intuitive way. In this section, we'll be interested in more advanced issues such as extending testing frameworks with your own matchers.

To define a custom matcher, you need to implement the **Matcher** interface and override its **test()** method:

abstract fun test(value: T): Result

The **Result** object describes the outcome of matching. It's a data class which contains the following properties:

- **passed:** Checks whether the assertion is satisfied (true) or not (false).
- **failureMessage:** A message which is shown when the assertion fails and tells what should happen in order to make it pass.

- **negatedFailureMessage:** This is used when you invoke the negated version of the matcher and it fails.

Let's, for example, create a matcher which checks whether a given number is odd:

```kotlin
import io.kotlintest.Matcher
import io.kotlintest.Result


fun beOdd() = object : Matcher<Int> {
  override fun test(value: Int): Result {
    return Result(
      value % 2 != 0,
      "$value should be odd",
      "$value should not be odd"
    )
  }
}
```

Now, we can use this matcher for our assertions by passing it to a built-in extension function **should()/shouldNot()**:

```kotlin
import io.kotlintest.*

import io.kotlintest.specs.StringSpec


class NumberTest :StringSpec({
  "5 is odd" { 5 should beOdd() }
  "4 is not odd" { 4 shouldNot beOdd() }
})
```

Note that we've chosen the **beOdd** name with an intention to get a human-readable name for the resulting assertion (should be odd / should not be odd).

Any implementation of the Matcher interface automatically supports and/or/invert operations which combine matchers following the logic of boolean operations. We can use them to build assertions based on complex predicates such as in the following example which combines **beOdd()** with a built-in **positive()** matcher:

```kotlin
"5 is positive odd" { 5 should (beOdd() and positive()) }
```

One more operation supported by matchers is **combine()** which allows you to generalize the existing matcher to a new type by providing the conversion function. The following function reuses the **beOdd()** matcher to assert that a given collection has odd length:

```
fun beOddLength() = beOdd().compose<Collection<*>> { it.size }
```

Note that while all matchers can be called via the **should()/shouldNot()** function, many built-in ones are also accompanied by specialized functions whose names start with should. For example, the following assertions are equivalent:

```
5 should beLessThan(10)
```

```
5 shouldBeLessThan(10)
```

Inspectors

Apart from matchers, KotlinTest also supports a related concept of inspectors. Inspector is an extension function for some collection class which allows you to verify that a given assertion holds for some group of its elements:

- **forAll()/forNone():** Checks whether all/none elements satisfy an assertion.
- **forExactly(n):** Checks whether exactly n elements satisfy an assertion; there is also a special **forOne()** function which handles the case **n = 1**.
- **forAtLeast(n)/forAtMost(n):** Checks whether at least/at most n elements satisfy an assertion; when **n = 1** you can also use specialized inspectors **forAtLeastOne()/forAtMostOne()** or **forAny()** which is the same as **forAtLeastOne()**.
- **forSome():** Checks whether some but not all elements satisfy an assertion.

Let's consider an example of using these inspectors:

```
import io.kotlintest.inspectors.*

import io.kotlintest.matchers.numerics.shouldBeGreaterThanOrEqual

import io.kotlintest.shouldBe

import io.kotlintest.specs.StringSpec


class NumberTest : StringSpec({
  val numbers = Array(10) { it + 1 }
```

```
"all are non-negative" {
  numbers.forAll { it shouldBeGreaterThanOrEqual 0 }
}
"none is zero" { numbers.forNone { it shouldBe 0 } }
"a single 10" { numbers.forOne { it shouldBe 10 } }
"at most one 0" { numbers.forAtMostOne { it shouldBe 0 } }
"at least one odd number" {
  numbers.forAtLeastOne { it % 2 shouldBe 1 }
}
"at most five odd numbers" {
  numbers.forAtMost(5) { it % 2 shouldBe 1 }
}
"at least three even numbers" {
  numbers.forAtLeast(3) { it % 2 shouldBe 0 }
}
"some numbers are odd" { numbers.forAny { it % 2 shouldBe 1 } }
"some but not all numbers are even" {
  numbers.forSome { it % 2 shouldBe 0 }
}
"exactly five numbers are even" {
  numbers.forExactly(5) { it % 2 shouldBe 0 }
}
})
```

Handling exceptions

KotlinTest has a special **shouldThrow()** assertion which checks whether some code fails due to a specific exception. This is a convenient alternative of catching exceptions with an explicit try/catch block. On being successful, **shouldThrow()** returns caught exception which you can inspect afterwards:

```
import io.kotlintest.matchers.string.shouldEndWith
import io.kotlintest.shouldThrow
```

```
import io.kotlintest.specs.StringSpec

class ParseTest : StringSpec({
  "invalid string" {
    val e = shouldThrow<NumberFormatException>{ "abc".toInt() }
    e.messageshouldEndWith "\"abc\""
  }
})
```

A useful exception-related feature of the KotlinTest is its ability to temporarily suppress exceptions thrown by failed assertions. This is called soft assertion and may be useful if your test consists of several assertions and you want to see all that failed. Normally, this doesn't happen because tests terminate after the first thrown exception. KotlinTest allows you to work around this behavior using the **assertSoftly** blocks. **AssertionError** exceptions are automatically caught inside the block and accumulated allowing all assertions to run (unless they fail with some other exception). When the block is finished, **assertSoftly** packs all accumulated exceptions (if there are any) into a single **AssertionError** and throws it back to the caller. Let's consider an example:

```
import io.kotlintest.assertSoftly
import io.kotlintest.inspectors.forAll
import io.kotlintest.specs.StringSpec

class NumberTest : StringSpec({
  val numbers = Array(10) { it + 1 }

  "invalid numbers" {
    assertSoftly {
      numbers.forAll { it shouldBeLessThan 5 }
      numbers.forAll { it shouldBeGreaterThan 3 }
    }
  }
})
```

Without **assertSoftly()**, the second **forAll()** assertion won't even be checked after the first one fails. Now, both assertions are executed and the test fails with an exception:

```
io.kotlintest.tables.MultiAssertionError:
```

```
The following 9 assertions failed
```

```
...
```

As you can see the resulting message lists all individual failures.

Testing non-deterministic code

When having to deal with a non-deterministic code, which sometimes passes only after several attempts, you can use a convenient alternative to timeouts and multiple invocations. The **eventually()** function verifies that the given assertion is satisfied at least once within a specified period of time:

```
import io.kotlintest.*
```

```
import io.kotlintest.specs.StringSpec
```

```
import java.io.File
```

```
class StringSpecWithConfig : StringSpec({

  eventually(10.seconds) {

    // Check that file eventually contains a single line

    // (within 10 seconds)

    File("data.txt").readLines().size shouldBe 1

  }

})
```

The **continually()** function similarly verifies that nested assertions are satisfied upon its call and remains within a specified interval:

```
import io.kotlintest.*
import io.kotlintest.specs.StringSpec
import java.io.File

class StringSpecWithConfig : StringSpec({
  // Check that file contains a single line
  // and line count doesn't change for at least 10 seconds
```

```
continually(10.seconds) {
    File("data.txt").readLines().size shouldBe 1
}
})
```

Property-based testing

KotlinTest is capable of property-based testing where you specify some predicates and have KotlinTest verify them against automatically generated random test data. This technique is useful when we want to check whether some condition holds over a large set of values which is hard to prepare and maintain manually.

For example, suppose that we define a function which computes the minimum of two numbers:

```
infix fun Int.min(n: Int) = if (this < n) this else n
```

You want to ensure that its result is always less or equal to each argument. To do this, we wrap the respective assertion inside the **assertAll()** call:

```
import io.kotlintest.matchers.beLessThanOrEqualTo

import io.kotlintest.properties.assertAll

import io.kotlintest.should

import io.kotlintest.specs.StringSpec


class NumbersTest: StringSpec({
    «min» {
        assertAll{ a: Int, b: Int ->
            (a min b).let {
                it should (beLessThanOrEqualTo(a) and beLessThanOrEqualTo(b))
            }
        }
    }
})
```

When you run this code, KotlinTest will generate a stream of Int pairs and test all of them against our assertion. By default, the test dataset consists of 1000 items, but you can specify its size explicitly as an argument of **assertAll()**.

There is also the **assertNone()** function which checks whether none of the generated items satisfy the given assertion.

As an alternative, we can use the **forAll()/forNone()** function which take a lambda with the Boolean return type and verifies that all/none generated items have corresponding predicates that evaluate to true:

```
import io.kotlintest.properties.forAll
import io.kotlintest.specs.StringSpec


class NumbersTest: StringSpec({
  "min" {
    forAll{ a: Int, b: Int ->
      (a min b).let { it <= a && it <= b }
    }
  }
})
```

KotlinTest have default generators for many common types such as **Int, Boolean,** and **String**. By default, it uses the runtime information of lambda parameter types to choose the generator automatically. Sometimes, though, this may be unwanted or even not possible if a type in question is simply not supported. In this case, we need to specify the generator explicitly as an instance of the Gen interface. Its companion object contains a bunch of helpful methods you can use to construct various implementations of generators. In particular (the rest can be as usually found in the documentation):

- **choose(min, max):** Generate random integers in the range from min to max (excluding max).
- **positiveIntegers()/negativeIntegers()/nats():** Generate stream of random positive/negative/non-negative integers.
- **from(collection):** Take random elements of a given list or array.

You may also define your own generator. One way to do it is to use the **Gen.create()** function which builds a generator based on a specified lambda. In *Chapter 11, Domain-Specific Languages,* we've defined a class for representation of rational numbers. Let's now check whether subtracting any rational from itself produces a zero. To do this, we need to implement a custom generator:

```
import io.kotlintest.properties.*
```

```kotlin
import io.kotlintest.specs.StringSpec
import kotlin.random.Random


class NumbersTest: StringSpec({
  "Subtraction" {
    forAll(genRationals()) { a: Rational ->
      (a - a).num == 0
    }
  }
}) {
  companion object {
    private fun genRationals(): Gen<Rational> {
      return Gen.create {
        val num = Random.nextInt()
        val den = Random.nextInt()
        Rational.of(num, if (den != 0) den else 1)
      }
    }
  }
}
```

An alternative way is to inherit from the **Gen<T>** interface directly. In this case, you need to provide an implementation of two methods:

- **constants():** Returns a collection of **T** value which are always included into the generated stream; these values are meant for various corner cases (say, default generator for integers uses **Int.MIN_VALUE, 0** and **Int.MAX_VALUE** for this purpose).

- **random()**: Returns a sequence of random elements of type **T**.

For example, we can rewrite our **Rational** generator to the following object:

```kotlin
object RationalGen : Gen<Rational> {
  override fun constants(): Iterable<Rational> {
    return listOf(Rational.of(0), Rational.of(1), Rational.of(-1))
  }
```

```
override fun random(): Sequence<Rational> {
  return generateSequence {
    val num = Random.nextInt()
    val den = Random.nextInt()
    Rational.of(num, if (den != 0) den else 1)
  }
 }
}
```

It's also possible to use a fixed test data set rather than using random values provided by the framework or custom generator. For this, you need to use the **forall()** function which takes a **vararg** of row objects:

```
import io.kotlintest.data.forall
import io.kotlintest.specs.StringSpec
import io.kotlintest.tables.row


class NumbersTest: StringSpec({
  "Minimum" {
    forall(
      row(1, 1),
      row(1, 2),
      row(2, 1)
    ) { a: Int, b: Int ->
      (a min b).let { it <= a && it <= b }
    }
  }
})
```

Note the difference in naming: **forall** vs. **forAll**.

On top of this, you can pack multiple rows into a single table object which also has a specific set of headers. The headers are then used to provide context information when the test fails. For example:

```
import io.kotlintest.matchers.numerics.shouldBeGreaterThanOrEqual
import io.kotlintest.specs.StringSpec
```

```
import io.kotlintest.tables.*

class NumbersTest : StringSpec({
  "Minimum" {
    forAll(
      table(
        headers("name", "age"),
        row("John", 20),
        row("Harry", 25),
        row("Bob", 16)
      )
    ) { name, age ->
      age shouldBeGreaterThanOrEqual 18
    }
  }
})
```

Running the preceding test will produce an error with the following message:

```
Test failed for (name, Bob), (age, 16) with error 16 should be >= 18
```

This option is supported by both **forAll()** and **forNone()** overloads. Note, however, that unlike **forAll()/forNone()** used for generator-based testing, these functions take a lambda with the **Unit** return type. That's why we've used matcher functions instead of simply returning a **Boolean** value.

Fixtures and configurations

Providing a fixture

It's often the case that tests need some kind of code which initializes the necessary environment and resources (also known as test fixture) before actual test invocation and finalizes them afterwards. In KotlinTest, you can use the **TestListener** interface to embed your code into various stages of the test case lifecycle. Let's see what methods it has:

- **beforeProject()/afterProject()**: Invoked upon test engine start/ finish.

- **beforeSpecClass():** Invoked once (regardless of how many times a given specification class is instantiated) before any tests corresponding to a given specification class are started.

- **afterSpecClass():** Invoked after all such tests are finished.

- **beforeSpec():** Invoked after instantiating a specification but before running its tests; **afterSpec()** is invoked after all tests for a given specification instance are finished.

- **beforeTest()/afterTest():** Invoked before/after running a particular test block.

In order to have some effect, a listener instance must be registered in a particular specification class by overriding its **listener()** method:

```kotlin
import io.kotlintest.*

import io.kotlintest.extensions.*

import io.kotlintest.specs.FunSpec


object MyListener :TestListener {
  override fun beforeSpecClass(spec: Spec, tests: List<TopLevelTest>)
{
    println("Before spec class: ${spec.description()}")
  }


  override fun beforeSpec(spec: Spec) {
    println("Before spec: ${spec.description()}")
  }


  override fun beforeTest(estcase: TestCase) {
    println("Before test: ${estcase.name}")
  }


  override fun afterTest(estcase: TestCase, result: TestResult) {
    println("After test: ${estcase.name}")
  }
```

```
  override fun afterSpec(spec: Spec) {
    println("After spec: ${spec.description()}")
  }

  override fun afterSpecClass(spec: Spec,
                              results: Map<TestCase, TestResult>) {
    println("After spec class: ${spec.description()}")
  }
}

class NumbersTest :FunSpec() {
  init {
    context("Increment") {
      test("2+2") {
        2 + 2 shouldBe 4
      }
      test("2 * 2") {
        2 * 2 shouldBe 4
      }
    }
  }

  override fun listeners() = listOf(MyListener)
}
```

Running the preceding code will produce the following output:

```
Before spec class: Description(parents=[], name=NamesTest)
Before spec: Description(parents=[], name=NamesTest)
Before test: IncrementBefore test: 2+2
After test: 2+2
Before test: 2 * 2
After test: 2 * 2
After test: Increment
```

```
After spec: Description(parents=[], name=NamesTest)
```

```
After spec class: Description(parents=[], name=NamesTest)
```

Note that in our example, **beforeSpec()/afterSpec()** are invoked only once just like **beforeSpecClass()/afterSpecClass()** because only one instance of **NumbersTest** is created. This is not always the case as you can configure the framework to create a new specification per each test (see isolation mode discussion in the *Test configuration* section).

The key difference between **beforeSpec()** and **beforeTest()** (as well as between **afterSpec()** and **afterTest()**) is that **beforeSpec()** is invoked only if the test in question is enabled. In the following section, we'll see how you can switch off individual tests using configurations.

If you want to provide an implementation of the **beforeProject()/afterProject()** methods, you need to register a global listener using the **ProjectConfig** singleton. This singleton must inherit from the **AbstractProjectConfig** class and be placed in the **io.kotlintest.provided** package:

```
package io.kotlintest.provided
```

```
import io.kotlintest.*
```

```
import io.kotlintest.extensions.*
```

```
object ProjectListener : TestListener {
  override fun beforeProject() { println("Before project") }
  override fun afterProject() { println("After project") }
}
```

```
object ProjectConfig : AbstractProjectConfig() {
  override fun listeners(): List<TestListener> {
    return listOf(ProjectListener)
  }
}
```

One more useful feature of KotlinTest is its ability to automatically close resources which implement the **AutoCloseable** interface. For this to work, you need to register a resource on its allocation with the **autoClose()** call:

```
import io.kotlintest.shouldBe
import io.kotlintest.specs.FunSpec
import java.io.FileReader

class FileTest : FunSpec() {
  val reader = autoClose(FileReader(“data.txt”))

  init {
    test(“Line count”) {
      reader.readLines().isNotEmpty() shouldBe true
    }
  }
}
```

Test configuration

KotlinTest gives you a set of options to configure a testing environment. In particular, specification classes provide the **config()** function which can be used to set various test execution parameters. Its usage depends on a chosen specification style but in general, it replaces an ordinary test block. Let's consider some examples:

```
import io.kotlintest.shouldBe
import io.kotlintest.specs.*
import java.time.Duration

class StringSpecWithConfig : StringSpec({
  “2 + 2 should be 4”.config(invocations = 10) { (2 + 2) shouldBe 4 }
})

class ShouldSpecWithConfig : ShouldSpec({
  “Addition” {
    “1 + 2” {
      should(“be equal to 3”).config(threads = 2, invocations = 100) {
```

Testing with Kotlin ▓ 561

```kotlin
    (1 + 2) shouldBe 3
  }
  should("be equal to 2 + 1").config(timeout = 1.minutes) {
    (1 + 2) shouldBe (2 + 1)
  }
  }
 }
})


class BehaviorSpecWithConfig : BehaviorSpec({
  Given("Arithmetic") {
    When("x is 1") {
      val x = 1
      And("increased by 1") {
        then("result is 2").config(invocations = 100) {
          (x + 1) shouldBe 2
        }
      }
    }
  }
})
```

You can find more detailed information in the documentation on a particular specification style.

Let's see what parameters we can control using the **config()** function:

- **invocations:** This is the number of times to execute a test; a test is considered passed only if all invocations succeed. This option may be useful for non-deterministic tests which may fail only occasionally.

- **threads:** This is the number of threads to use when running a test. This parameter is only meaningful when invocations are greater than 1 otherwise there is nothing to parallelize.

- **enabled:** Whether a test should be run; setting to false disables test execution.

- **timeout:** A duration object representing maximum time for test to run. If the test execution time exceeds this timeout, it's terminated and considered failed. Like the invocation count, this option is useful for non-deterministic tests.

Note that the threads option affects only parallelizing of individual tests within a test case. If you want to run multiple test cases in parallel as well, you need to use the **AbstractProjectConfig** which we discussed earlier. Just override its **parallelism()** method and return a desired number of concurrent threads:

```
package io.kotlin.provided


import io.kotlintest.AbstractProjectConfig


object ProjectConfig : AbstractProjectConfig() {
  override fun parallelism(): Int = 4
}
```

Apart from configuring each test individually, you may also specify a common configuration for all tests of a particular test case by overriding the **defaultTestCaseConfig** property:

```
import io.kotlintest.TestCaseConfig

import io.kotlintest.shouldBe

import io.kotlintest.specs.StringSpec


class StringSpecWithConfig : StringSpec({
  "2 + 2 should be 4" { (2 + 2) shouldBe 4 }
}) {
  override valdefaultTestCaseConfig: TestCaseConfig
  get() = TestCaseConfig(invocations = 10, threads = 2)
}
```

Default configuration options are inherited by tests unless you specify their own configuration explicitly.

One more feature of KotlinTest we'd like to point out in conclusion is the ability to choose how a test case instance is shared between its tests. This is called an isolation mode. By default, the test case is instantiated only once and its instance is used to run all its tests. Although this is good from the performance point of view, there are some scenarios when such a policy is undesired; if the test case has a mutable state which is read and modified by individual tests. In such cases, you may want to instantiate the test each time you start a test or test group. To achieve this, you just need to override the **isolationMode()** method of your test case class. This method returns a value of **IsolationMode** enum which defines three options:

- **SingleInstance:** A single instance of the test case is created; this is the default behavior.

- **InstancePerTest:** A new instance of the test case is created each time a context or test block is executed.

- **InstancePerLeaf:** The test is instantiated before executing an individual test block.

Let's consider an example. Suppose we have the following **FunSpec-style** test case:

```
import io.kotlintest.shouldBe
import io.kotlintest.specs.FunSpec


class IncTest :FunSpec() {
  var x = 0


  init {
    context(« Increment ») {
      println(« Increment »)
      test("prefix") {
        println("prefix)
        ++x shouldBe 1
      }
      test("postfix") {
        println("postfix)
        x++ shouldBe 0
      }
    }
  }
}
```

If you run it, you'll see that the second test fails. This happens because the **x** variable retains a value assigned in the prefix block. If we change the isolation mode to **InstancePerTest** by adding the following code:

```
override fun isolationMode() = IsolationMode.InstancePerTest
```

Both tests will pass since each of them will get its own **IncTest** instance. The messages printed to the standard output will look like the following:

```
Running context
Running context
prefix
Running context
postfix
```

This happens because **IncTest** is instantiated three times. First time to execute the context block itself, second to execute the prefix test which also runs the context block the second time, and the third for the postfix text (which again requires to run context block first). As a result, the context block is also executed three times.

If we change the isolation mode to **InstancePerLeaf,** the context blocks won't be executed by themselves but only as a part of running individual tests. As a result, **IncTest** will be instantiated only two times (once for prefix and once for postfix) and the output will look like the following:

```
Running context
prefix
Running context
postfix
```

This concludes our overview of the KotlinTest framework. For more detailed information about the features we've mentioned (as well as those we haven't), the reader is advised to follow the documentation available at https://github.com/kotlintest/kotlintest.

Conclusion

In this chapter, we learned about the basics of writing test specifications in KotlinTest, a popular open-source testing framework designed specifically for Kotlin-powered applications. We discussed how to organize our test code using out-of-the-box specification style, how to write expressive and easy-to-read tests with matchers and inspectors, how to describe test data sets and make use of automatic property testing. We also explained the use of KotlinTest set up/tear down facilities and basic test configurations. Now, you have all the necessary knowledge to write your own test specifications and to learn more advanced features of KotlinTest and other testing frameworks.

In the next chapter, we'll talk about using Kotlin to build applications for the Android platform. We'll explain how to configure a project in Android Studio, discuss basic UI and activity lifecycle, and introduce you to various useful features provided by Android extensions and Anko frameworks.

Questions

1. Give an overview of popular testing frameworks with Kotlin support.
2. Describe specification styles supported by KotlinTest.
3. What is a matcher? How can you combine and transform matchers for writing complex assertions?
4. Explain how to implement custom KotlinTest matcher.
5. Describe the **shouldThrow()** function. What is a soft assertion?
6. Describe collection inspectors available in KotlinTest.
7. Explain the meaning of **eventually()** and **continually()** functions.
8. How can you implement initialization and finalization of test resources using listeners?
9. How to specify a configuration for individual tests and specifications? How to define a global configuration?
10. Explain the difference between test case isolation modes.

CHAPTER 15

Android Applications

In this chapter, we'll talk about using Kotlin in the development of applications targeting the Android platform. Thanks to the excellent programming experience given by the language and official support from Google, this niche of Kotlin has become one of the most flourishing in its entire ecosystem. A comprehensive discussion of the Android platform fundamentals, however, does beyond doubt deserve a separate book, so our task here will be quite modest: to serve as a kind of introduction to the Android world provoking further investigation and learning.

The topic is divided into two parts. In the first half, we'll talk about the basic features of Android Studio: how to set up a new project, how Gradle is used for project configuration and build, what is an Android activity, and how to run applications using the Android device emulator. The second half will be centered on the development of a sample calculator application and discussion of more advanced issues such as using Android view binding and preserving the activity state.

Structure

The following topics will be covered in this chapter:

- Getting started with Android
- Activities

Objective

After reading this chapter, the reader will get a basic understanding of using Android Studio and Kotlin for development of applications for the Android platform.

Getting started with Android

In this section, we'll introduce the reader to Android Studio IDE and demonstrate a basic project structure using the example of a simple «Hello, World»-like application.

Setting up an Android Studio project

We'll start with the basic steps required to configure a project in Android Studio, the official Android IDE developed by Google. Android Studio is based on the JetBrains IntelliJ platform and thus is very similar to the IntelliJ IDEA we've referred to in the previous chapters. Unlike IDEA itself, it comes with a set of features specifically targeting at the development of Android applications. Like IntelliJ IDEA, Android Studio has out-of-the-box support of the Kotlin language.

If you don't have an Android Studio installed yet, you can download the latest version from https://developer.android.com/studio and follow installer instructions from https://developer.android.com/studio/install.html. In this chapter, we will use Android Studio 4.1.1.

After starting, Android Studio will present you a welcome screen where you can click on a **Start a new Android Studio project** link to start a project wizard. If you've already opened a project before, Android Studio won't show you a welcome screen and load that project instead. In this case, you can use the **File | New | New Project…** command from the IDE menu.

The first step of the wizard will ask you to choose a template for the first activity in your project (*Figure 15.1*). An activity is basically a representation of a single thing a user will be able to do using your application such as editing notes, showing the current time or in the case of our first application, simply presenting a welcome message to the user. Let's choose **Empty Activity** for now to get Android Studio generate a stub activity for us and click on **Next**.

Figure 15.1: Choosing activity for a new Android project

The next step of the project wizard requires you to enter basic project information such as its name, common package for project classes, root directory, and default language (see *Figure 15.2* for example). You may also choose a minimal version of Android SDK your application will support. The higher the version, the more powerful API you get at your disposal, but at the same time, the less fraction of devices your application can run on. You can see a comparison chart of different API versions by clicking on the "Help me choose" link. For our simple example, we can just leave an option suggested by default:

Figure 15.2: Choosing basic project configuration

After you click on **Finish**, Android Studio will automatically generate the necessary project files, including activity class and a basic set of application resources such as the UI layout and configuration files. It will then proceed with configuring the new project (notice the Building Gradle project info progress bar).

Figure 15.3 shows the structure of a new project as shown by the IDE Project view. Note that by default this view is presented in the Android mode which displays project source files grouping them by corresponding modules and source roots (such as ordinary sources files, generated files, and resources):

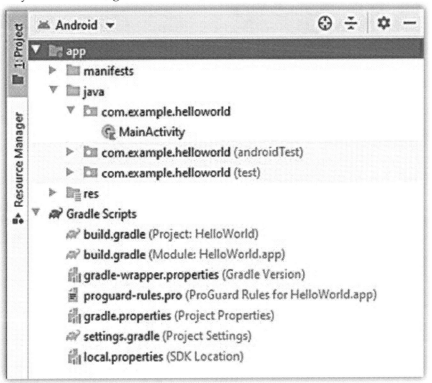

Figure 15.3: A sample project structure

A separate node in the Android view, **Gradle Scripts** contains files describing project configuration. Let's look at them in more detail.

Gradle build scripts

Android Studio relies on Gradle, a popular build system which automates tasks such as managing project dependencies, compilation, testing, and packaging. Project configuration is described in the **build.gradle** files using a domain-specific language and is written in Groovy which is reminiscent of both Java and Kotlin code (in fact, Groovy is one of the languages that had inspired the Kotlin design). We won't delve into the details of Groovy or Gradle here and instead just highlight some important points related to using Kotlin in Android applications. The project template used by the Android Studio wizard automatically generates the following files:

- The project-level **build.gradle** located in the project root directory: This file contains the common configuration of the entire project.

- **settings.gradle** (also in the project root) that specifies which modules are included in the project and may optionally contain some additional configuration commands.

- **local.properties** and **gradle.properties** contain a set of key-value pairs which define properties used in the Gradle scripts such as the path to the Android SDK directory or JVM arguments passed when starting the Gradle process.

- module-level **build.gradle** located in the root directory of the app module: This contains module-specific configuration.

Let's take a look at the root **build.gradle** file:

```
buildscript {
    ext.kotlin_version = '1.4.21'
    repositories {
        google()
        jcenter()


    }
    dependencies {
        classpath 'com.android.tools.build:gradle:4.1.2'
        classpath "org.jetbrains.kotlin:kotlin-gradle-plugin:$kotlin_
version"
        // NOTE: Do not place your application dependencies here; they belong
        // in the individual module build.gradle files
    }
}


allprojects {
```

```
repositories {
    google()
    jcenter()


}
}


task clean(type: Delete) {
    delete rootProject.buildDir
}
```

This script basically does the following:

- Defines the **kotlin_version** property which contains a version of the Kotlin standard library and can be referred to by other scripts.
- Tells Gradle to use the **com.android.tools.build:gradle** and **org. jetbrains.kotlin:kotlin-gradle-plugin** plugins when building projects. The first one adds support of Android modules while the second allows you to build projects with the Kotlin source code.
- Configures a default list of repositories to download dependency artifacts such as binaries and sources of libraries.
- Adds the **clean** task which is used to delete previous compilation results before project rebuild.

The **settings.gradle** file is quite simple and by default contains a single include command which tells Gradle which modules make up our project:

```
include ':app'
```

Let's now look at **build.gradle** which defines the configuration of our Android module:

```
plugins {
    id 'com.android.application'
    id 'kotlin-android'
}


android {
    compileSdkVersion 29
```

```
    buildToolsVersion "30.0.3"
    defaultConfig {
        applicationId "com.example.helloworld"
        minSdkVersion 27
        targetSdkVersion 29
        versionCode 1
        versionName "1.0"
        testInstrumentationRunner "androidx.test.runner.
        AndroidJUnitRunner"
    }

    buildTypes {
        release {
            minifyEnabled false
            proguardFiles
             getDefaultProguardFile('proguard-android-optimize.txt'),
                'proguard-rules.pro'
        }
    }

    compileOptions {
        sourceCompatibility JavaVersion.VERSION_1_8
        targetCompatibility JavaVersion.VERSION_1_8
    }

    kotlinOptions {
        jvmTarget = '1.8'
    }
}

dependencies {
    implementation "org.jetbrains.kotlin:kotlin-stdlib:$kotlin_version"
```

```
    implementation 'androidx.core:core-ktx:1.2.0'

    implementation 'androidx.appcompat:appcompat:1.1.0'

    implementation 'com.google.android.material:material:1.1.0'

    implementation 'androidx.constraintlayout:constraintlayout:1.1.3'

    testImplementation 'junit:junit:4.+'

    androidTestImplementation 'androidx.test.ext:junit:1.1.1'

  androidTestImplementation 'androidx.test.espresso:espresso-core:3.2.0'

}
```

The first thing it does is to enable Android and Kotlin-specific plugins which are added in the root build file. Then, comes the `android` block that contains various Android-specific configuration parameters such as application ID, version number, minimal supported version of Android SDK, and so on.

Finally, the dependencies block lists all external dependencies of our module. Each dependency has a definite *configuration* which is specified first and followed by the dependency description (usually in the form of Maven coordinates like **androidx. core:core-ktx:1.0.2**). A configuration determines when and where this dependency is used; for example, **implementation** dependencies are added to the compilation classpath and packaged to the build output, but not available during compilation of dependent modules, while **testImplementation** dependencies are added to the compilation classpath of modules tests and used during test execution. As shown in the preceding code, the Kotlin standard library gets automatically added to new module dependencies.

Activity

Let's now look at source files under the **java** root. Despite the somewhat misleading name, this directory can contain both Java and Kotlin files. Find **MainActivity.kt** and open it in the editor window. You'll see something like the following code:

```kotlin
package com.example.helloworld

import androidx.appcompat.app.AppCompatActivity
import android.os.Bundle

class MainActivity : AppCompatActivity() {
    override fun onCreate(savedInstanceState: Bundle?) {
        super.onCreate(savedInstanceState)
```

```
        setContentView(R.layout.activity_main)

    }

}
```

This is the activity class which Android Studio has generated based on the template you've chosen in the project wizard. All activity classes are derived from the **Activity** class which is a part of Android SDK. The generated class inherits from a more specific **AppCompatActivity** which adds support of a toolbar where you can show the application name and various interactive UI components.

The **onCreate()** method is invoked by the Android OS on creating the activity instance so it's a common place for an initialization code. In particular, this method sets up an activity view:

setContentView(R.layout.activity_main)

The **R** class is automatically generated during the compilation of the Android project. It contains identifiers of all **resources** put in the **res** directory. **R.layout. activity_main,** in particular, corresponds to the **activity_main.xml** file in the **res/layout**. This is called the *layout XML* file which contains the description of UI components making up an activity view. If you open it in the editor, Android Studio will present you a UI designer tool you can use to edit the UI by dragging-and-dropping components and changing their properties in the Attributes window. For example, let's choose a TextView in the center and change its text size to 36. You can see the result in *Figure 15.4*:

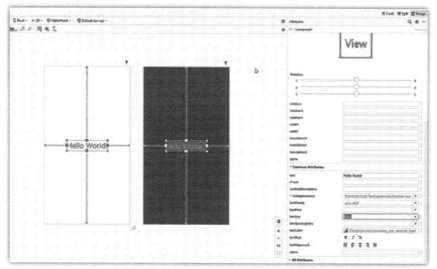

Figure 15.4: UI Designer

If you click on the **Text** tab at the bottom of the designer window, the editor will turn to a textual view where you can edit the layout like any other XML file. After changing the text size, the XML file will look like this:

```xml
<?xml version="1.0" encoding="utf-8"?>
<androidx.constraintlayout.widget.ConstraintLayout
        xmlns:android="http://schemas.android.com/apk/res/android"
        xmlns:tools="http://schemas.android.com/tools"
        xmlns:app="http://schemas.android.com/apk/res-auto"
        android:layout_width="match_parent"
        android:layout_height="match_parent"
        tools:context=".MainActivity">


    <TextView
            android:layout_width="wrap_content"
            android:layout_height="wrap_content"
            android:text="Hello World!"
            app:layout_constraintBottom_toBottomOf="parent"
            app:layout_constraintLeft_toLeftOf="parent"
            app:layout_constraintRight_toRightOf="parent"
            app:layout_constraintTop_toTopOf="parent"
            android:textSize="36sp"/>
</androidx.constraintlayout.widget.ConstraintLayout>
```

In the following sections, we'll see an example of a more complex UI layout of a calculator application. For now, let's see how this **"Hello, World"** sample may look like on an Android device.

Using an emulator

Now, we can try to run our simple application using the Android device emulator. If you haven't used an emulator yet, the first step is to configure a virtual device. To do that, choose the **Tools | AVD Manager** command from the Android Studio menu and click on the **Create Virtual Device...** button in the **Android Virtual Device Manager** dialog box.

In the dialog box that follows (see *Figure 15.5*), you can choose a phone model. For our example, the default choice should be **OK** so you can just click on **Next**:

The **System Image** dialog box allows you to choose an Android OS image to be used with an emulator. You need to download a chosen image before its first use by clicking on a corresponding Download link (*Figure 15.6*). When the download is complete, click on **Next:** In the final **Verify Configuration** dialog box of the virtual device configuration wizard, you can specify a new device name and choose its default orientation. Clicking on **Finish** will bring you back to the virtual device manager. Notice the newly added device in the list and close the AVD window.

Figure 15.5: Choosing virtual device configuration

Figure 15.6: Choosing Android OS image for a virtual device

Let's use our new emulator to run the main activity. To do that, choose the **Run | Run 'app'** command or click on the **Run** tool button (see *Figure 15.7* for an example):

Figure 15.7: Using Run command

The Android Studio will bring up a dialog box to choose a virtual device. Choose the one you've just configured and click on **OK**. The IDE will then launch an emulator, boot its operating system, and start the main activity of our application. Although the emulator appearance may vary, the result will be similar to the one you see in *Figure 15.8*:

Figure 15.8: Running application on Android emulator

You can interact with the emulator similarly with how you do it with a physical smartphone or tablet. The side panel gives you an access to some basic functions like device rotation, volume control, taking screenshots, and so on. It's also possible to debug applications deployed on an emulator; for that you need to start the application in the debug mode using the **Debug** command instead of **Run**.

Now that we've got a basic understanding of our project structure, let's see how to make our application a bit more interactive.

Activities

The remaining part of the chapter will be centered on an example of a calculator application. In the course of this section, we'll see how to define the UI activity using the XML layout, how view binding can help you simplify UI-related code as well as take a glimpse at the activity lifecycle and get to know how and you can preserve its state and when you may need to do it.

Designing an application UI

We'll take our **"Hello, World"** example as a starting point for out calculator application. First, let's change application title in the **strings.xml** resource file:

```
<resources>
    <string name="app_name">Calculator</string>
</resources>
```

Now, let's open **activity_main.xml** which contains the UI definition of the main activity. Click on the **Text** tab below to bring up a text representation of the underlying file and edit it to match the following:

```
<?xml version="1.0" encoding="utf-8"?>
<RelativeLayout  xmlns:android="http://schemas.android.com/apk/res/
android"
                xmlns:tools="http://schemas.android.com/tools"
                android:id="@+id/relative1"
                android:layout_width="match_parent"
                android:layout_height="match_parent"
                tools:context=".MainActivity">
    <TableLayout android:layout_width="match_parent"
                android:layout_height="match_parent"
                android:stretchColumns="3">
        <TextView android:id="@+id/txtResult"
                android:layout_width="match_parent"
                android:layout_height="wrap_content"
                android:textSize="40sp"/>
        <TableRow android:layout_width="match_parent"
```

```xml
        android:layout_height="match_parent">
    <Button android:id="@+id/btn7"
            android:text="7"
            android:layout_width="wrap_content"
            android:layout_height="wrap_content"/>
    <Button android:id="@+id/btn8"
            android:text="8"
            android:layout_width="wrap_content"
            android:layout_height="wrap_content"/>
    <Button android:id="@+id/btn9"
            android:text="9"
            android:layout_width="wrap_content"
            android:layout_height="wrap_content"/>
    <Button android:id="@+id/btnPlus"
            android:text="+"
            android:layout_width="wrap_content"
            android:layout_height="wrap_content"
            android:layout_gravity="end|center_vertical"/>
</TableRow>
<TableRow android:layout_width="match_parent"
            android:layout_height="match_parent">
    <Button android:id="@+id/btn4"
            android:text="4"
            android:layout_width="wrap_content"
            android:layout_height="wrap_content"/>
    <Button android:id="@+id/btn5"
            android:text="5"
            android:layout_width="wrap_content"
            android:layout_height="wrap_content"/>
    <Button android:id="@+id/btn6"
            android:text="6"
            android:layout_width="wrap_content"
```

```
                            android:layout_height="wrap_content"/>
        <Button android:id="@+id/btnMinus"
                android:text="-"
                android:layout_width="wrap_content"
                android:layout_height="wrap_content"
                android:layout_gravity="end|center_vertical"/>
    </TableRow>
    <TableRow android:layout_width="match_parent"
              android:layout_height="match_parent">
        <Button android:id="@+id/btn1"
                android:text="1"
                android:layout_width="wrap_content"
                android:layout_height="wrap_content"/>
        <Button android:id="@+id/btn2"
                android:text="2"
                android:layout_width="wrap_content"
                android:layout_height="wrap_content"/>
        <Button android:id="@+id/btn3"
                android:text="3"
                android:layout_width="wrap_content"
                android:layout_height="wrap_content"/>
        <Button android:id="@+id/btnTimes"
                android:text="*"
                android:layout_width="wrap_content"
                android:layout_height="wrap_content"
                android:layout_gravity="end|center_vertical"/>
    </TableRow>
    <TableRow android:layout_width="match_parent"
              android:layout_height="match_parent">
        <Button android:id="@+id/btn0"
                android:text="0"
                android:layout_width="wrap_content"
```

```
                android:layout_height="wrap_content"/>
        <Button android:id="@+id/btnPoint"
                android:text="."
                android:layout_width="wrap_content"
                android:layout_height="wrap_content"/>
        <Button android:id="@+id/btnSign"
                android:text="+/-"
                android:layout_width="wrap_content"
                android:layout_height="wrap_content"/>
        <Button android:id="@+id/btnDivide"
                android:text="/"
                android:layout_width="wrap_content"
                android:layout_height="wrap_content"
                android:layout_gravity="end|center_vertical"/>
    </TableRow>
    <TableRow android:layout_width="match_parent"
                android:layout_height="match_parent">
        <Button android:id="@+id/btnBackspace"
                android:text="&lt;-"
                android:layout_width="wrap_content"
                android:layout_height="wrap_content"/>
        <Button android:id="@+id/btnClear"
                android:text="C"
                android:layout_width="wrap_content"
                android:layout_height="wrap_content"/>
        <Space android:layout_width="wrap_content"
                android:layout_height="wrap_content"/>
        <Button android:id="@+id/btnCalc"
                android:text="="
                android:layout_width="wrap_content"
                android:layout_height="wrap_content"
                android:layout_gravity="end|center_vertical"/>
```

```
        </TableRow>
    </TableLayout>
</RelativeLayout>
```

Figure 15.9 shows a preview of the calculator UI:

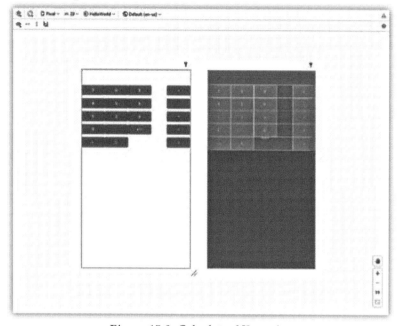

Figure 15.9: *Calculator UI preview*

Discussing the format of the XML layout is out of the scope of this book, so we won't delve into details here, but just point out some basics. The layouts are basically containers which arrange nested views in a certain way (you can compare them to Swing containers with a specific **LayoutManager**). Since the calculator UI assumes largely regular positioning of elements, we use the table layout which assigns nested components to rows and columns. The components themselves are defined by such tags as **Button** (a simple button with a text) and **TextView** (a component which displays read-only text similar to Swing's **JLabel**).

Note the **android:id** attributes: they are assigned to each view element that presents or takes some data from the user. This attribute allows you to reference the corresponding element in Java or Kotlin code. We'll see how to do it in the next section where we'll discuss the activity class.

Implementing an activity class

Let's get to the implementation of the activity class which adds some behavior to the UI. We won't go into the details of calculator business logic allowing the readers to explore it by themselves and instead highlight some Android-specific points.

Among other things, we want to access the current value typed into the calculator's display: the **txtResult** component. To do that, we use the **findViewById()** function passing a text view ID. We don't need to put an actual string from the XML layout, though, because such IDs can be referred to using the R class we've already seen in the **"Hello, World"** example:

private **val** txtResult by lazy { findViewById<TextView>(R.id.txtResult) }

Using the view reference, we can then access its members; for example, the **setOnClickListener()** method allows us to specify an action invoked when a user clicks a button:

findViewById<Button>(R.id.btn0).setOnClickListener { appendText("0") }

While reading/writing the **text** property of a **TextView** component gives access to its text content:

private **fun** clearText() {
    txtResult.text = "0"
}

Here is the full source code of the calculator's **MainActivity** class:

package com.example.helloworld

import androidx.appcompat.app.AppCompatActivity

import android.os.Bundle

import android.widget.Button

import android.widget.TextView

import android.widget.Toast

import java.lang.ArithmeticException

import java.math.BigDecimal

import java.math.RoundingMode

class MainActivity : AppCompatActivity() {
    enum class OpKind {
        ADD, SUBTRACT, MULTIPLY, DIVIDE
    }

```kotlin
companion object {
    fun OpKind.compute(a: BigDecimal, b: BigDecimal) = when (this) {
        OpKind.ADD -> a + b
        OpKind.SUBTRACT -> a - b
        OpKind.MULTIPLY -> a * b
        OpKind.DIVIDE -> a.divide(b, 10, RoundingMode.HALF_EVEN)
    }
}


private val txtResult by lazy { findViewById<TextView>(R.id.txtResult)}

    private var lastResult: BigDecimal = BigDecimal.ZERO
    private var lastOp: OpKind? = null
    private var waitingNextOperand: Boolean = false

    override fun onCreate(savedInstanceState: Bundle?) {
        super.onCreate(savedInstanceState)
        setContentView(R.layout.activity_main)


findViewById<Button>(R.id.btn0).setOnClickListener { appendText("0")}
findViewById<Button>(R.id.btn1).setOnClickListener { appendText("1")}
findViewById<Button>(R.id.btn2).setOnClickListener { appendText("2")}
findViewById<Button>(R.id.btn3).setOnClickListener { appendText("3")}
findViewById<Button>(R.id.btn4).setOnClickListener { appendText("4")}
findViewById<Button>(R.id.btn5).setOnClickListener { appendText("5")}
findViewById<Button>(R.id.btn6).setOnClickListener { appendText("6")}
findViewById<Button>(R.id.btn7).setOnClickListener { appendText("7")}
findViewById<Button>(R.id.btn8).setOnClickListener { appendText("8")}
findViewById<Button>(R.id.btn9).setOnClickListener { appendText("9")}
    findViewById<Button>(R.id.btnPoint).setOnClickListener {
        appendText(".")
```

```
}


findViewById<Button>(R.id.btnSign).setOnClickListener {
    val currentText = txtResult.text.toString()
    txtResult.text = when {
        currentText.startsWith("-") ->
            currentText.substring(1, currentText.length)
        currentText != "0" ->
            "-$currentText"
        else ->
            return @setOnClickListener
    }
}


findViewById<Button>(R.id.btnBackspace).setOnClickListener {
    val currentText = txtResult.text.toString()
  val newText = currentText.substring(0, currentText.length - 1)
    txtResult.text =
    if (newText.isEmpty() || newText == "-") "0" else newText
}


findViewById<Button>(R.id.btnClear).setOnClickListener {
clearText() }


findViewById<Button>(R.id.btnPlus).setOnClickListener {
    calc(OpKind.ADD)
}
findViewById<Button>(R.id.btnMinus).setOnClickListener {
    calc(OpKind.SUBTRACT)
}
findViewById<Button>(R.id.btnTimes).setOnClickListener {
    calc(OpKind.MULTIPLY)
}
```

```kotlin
        findViewById<Button>(R.id.btnDivide).setOnClickListener {
            calc(OpKind.DIVIDE)
        }
        findViewById<Button>(R.id.btnCalc).setOnClickListener {
            calc(null)
        }

        clearText()
    }

    private fun clearText() {
        txtResult.text = "0"
    }

    private fun appendText(text: String) {
        if (waitingNextOperand) {
            clearText()
            waitingNextOperand = false
        }
        val currentText = txtResult.text.toString()
        txtResult.text = if (currentText == "0") text else currentText
        + text
    }

    private fun calc(nextOp: OpKind?) {
        if (waitingNextOperand) {
            lastOp = nextOp
            return
        }

        val currentValue = BigDecimal(txtResult.text.toString())
        val newValue = try {
```

```kotlin
        lastOp?.compute(lastResult, currentValue) ?: currentValue
    } catch (e: ArithmeticException) {
        lastOp = null
        waitingNextOperand = true
        Toast.makeText(
            applicationContext,
            "Invalid operation!",
            Toast.LENGTH_SHORT
        ).show()
        return
    }
    if (nextOp != null) {
        lastResult = newValue
    }
    if (lastOp != null) {
        txtResult.text = newValue.toPlainString()
    }
    lastOp = nextOp
    waitingNextOperand = nextOp != null
    }
}
```

Now, we can try to run the calculator and see it in action. *Figure 15.10* shows an example of using our application in the Android emulator:

Figure 15.10: Calculator application in action

View binding

A frequent use of **findViewById()** can clatter your code, especially if you want to keep references to view components in class properties like we've done with **txtResult**. In the Java world, some libraries like Butterknife or Android Data Binding are able to work around this problem by automatically injecting view references into given class fields, but require you to manually annotate each field of interest by specifying the corresponding ID. The more concise solution is given by a newer *view binding* mechanism that we'll consider in this section.

Basically, view binding allows a compiler to automatically generate special classes which correspond to layout files and contain references to all views with an explicit ID. By using such classes in the activity code, you can get access to the required components and their properties without boilerplate calls of **findViewById()**. Let's see now how they can be applied to our calculator application.

First, we need to enable view binding in our project. To do that, we add the corresponding option to the **build.gradle** file of our main module:

android {

   ...

  buildFeatures {

     ...

    viewBinding **true** // *enable view binding*

  }

}

When you make changes in one of the Gradle build files, the IDE will detect them and present you a warning at the top of the file editor (as shown in *Figure 15.11*):

> Gradle files have changed since last project sync. A project sync may be necessary for the IDE to work properly.   Sync Now

Figure 15.11: Android Studio suggesting Gradle synchronization

After you click on the **Sync Now** link, Android Studio will synchronize its internal project model with a new Gradle-provided configuration turning on the binding class generation and also make them available in various code insight features such as automatic completion and code navigation.

Next, we add a property to hold the binding instance to our activity class:

```
private lateinit var binding: ActivityMainBinding
```

And initialize it in the **onCreate()** method:

```
override fun onCreate(savedInstanceState: Bundle?) {
    super.onCreate(savedInstanceState)
    // Initialize binding instance based on layout file
    binding = ActivityMainBinding.inflate(layoutInflater)
    setContentView(binding.root)

    ...
}
```

The **root** property refers to the root component of the layout file (in our case, it's **RelativeLayout**) while any other component can be accessed by the property with the same name as its ID. For example, now we can simplify the line:

```
findViewById<Button>(R.id.btn0).setOnClickListener { appendText("0") }
```

to:

```
binding.btn0.setOnClickListener { appendText("0") }
```

Note that those properties already have proper types (such as **Button** for **btn0**) which also makes your code more type-safe as compared with the **findViewById()** version.

As a result, the **onCreate()** method of our calculator activity transforms into:

```
override fun onCreate(savedInstanceState: Bundle?) {
    super.onCreate(savedInstanceState)
    binding = ActivityMainBinding.inflate(layoutInflater)
    setContentView(binding.root)
```

```
binding.btn0.setOnClickListener { appendText("0") }
binding.btn1.setOnClickListener { appendText("1") }
binding.btn2.setOnClickListener { appendText("2") }
binding.btn3.setOnClickListener { appendText("3") }
binding.btn4.setOnClickListener { appendText("4") }
binding.btn5.setOnClickListener { appendText("5") }
binding.btn6.setOnClickListener { appendText("6") }
binding.btn7.setOnClickListener { appendText("7") }
binding.btn8.setOnClickListener { appendText("8") }
binding.btn9.setOnClickListener { appendText("9") }
binding.btnPoint.setOnClickListener { appendText(".") }

binding.btnSign.setOnClickListener { ... }

binding.btnBackspace.setOnClickListener { … }

binding.btnClear.setOnClickListener { clearText() }

binding.btnPlus.setOnClickListener { calc(OpKind.ADD) }
binding.btnMinus.setOnClickListener { calc(OpKind.SUBTRACT) }
binding.btnTimes.setOnClickListener { calc(OpKind.MULTIPLY) }
binding.btnDivide.setOnClickListener { calc(OpKind.DIVIDE) }
binding.btnCalc.setOnClickListener { calc(null) }
clearText()
}
```

While the following explicit txtResult property:

```
private val txtResult by lazy { findViewById<TextView>(R.id.txtResult)
}
```

Becomes just a synonym for the corresponding binding property:

```
private val txtResult get() = binding.txtResult
```

Properties lacking the explicit ID in the layout file are not exposed via the binding class. On top of that, you can suppress autogeneration of bindings for a particular layout by adding **tools:viewBindingIgnore=true** to the root XML element:

```
<RelativeLayout  xmlns:android="http://schemas.android.com/apk/res/
android"

    xmlns:tools="http://schemas.android.com/tools"

    android:id="@+id/relative1"

    android:layout_width="match_parent"

    android:layout_height="match_parent"

    tools:context=".MainActivity"

    tools:viewBindingIgnore="true">

...

</RelativeLayout>
```

In earlier versions of Android Studio and Kotlin plugin, the preferred approach to access view components was provided by the Kotlin Android Extensions library. Rather than generating binding classes, this library served as a compiler plugin adding synthetic extension properties for each view component with an explicit ID and transforming references to such properties into the **findViewById()** calls. Currently, this library can still be used in Android projects but is considered deprecated in favor of view binding.

Preserving the activity state

If you experiment a bit with a calculator we created in the previous sections, you may find out a visible flaw in its behavior. Let's type some number and then imitate the device rotation. To do that, you can just click on one of the **Rotate left/Rotate right** buttons on the emulator side panel. The result is shown in *Figure 15.12*:

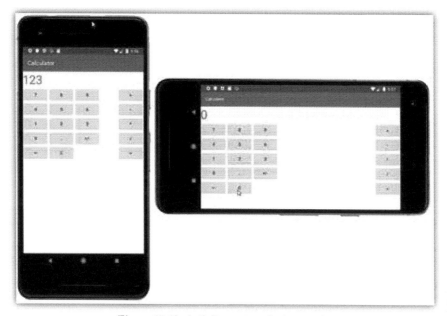

Figure 15.12: *Activity reset on device rotation*

You can see that an original number has changed to zero. In fact, the entire state of our activity has reset to the one we've provided in the initialization code. The reason of such a behavior is the change of device configuration (such as rotating its screen) forces the system to destroy our activity and recreate it from scratch. A similar case is when an activity is not visible to the user and the system runs out of resources necessary to execute the application with higher priority; as a result, Android may shut down the lesser-priority process together with its activities.

But what if we need to retain some state between different instantiations of the same activity regardless of whether it was forcibly destroyed/recreated by the system? Android provides a solution in the form of a so called *bundle* which is basically a set of key/value pairs you can use to store any serializable data. As you must've noticed, the **onCreate()** method takes a Bundle parameter which contains data preserved from the previous activity run. To fill the bundle, we need to override another Activity method, **onSaveInstanceState()**.

For example, to fix the calculator behavior, we need to preserve the activity state which in our case is composed of a text shown on the calculator display and values of instance variables **lastResult, lastOp** and **waitingNextOperand**. The first step is to override the **onSaveInstanceState()** method where we write relevant values into a **Bundle** object:

```
override fun onSaveInstanceState(outState: Bundle) {
```

```kotlin
    super.onSaveInstanceState(outState)
    outState.putString("currentText", txtResult.text.toString())
    outState.putSerializable(::lastResult.name, lastResult)
    outState.putSerializable(::lastOp.name, lastOp)
  outState.putBoolean(::waitingNextOperand.name, waitingNextOperand)
}
```

Now, even if the activity is temporarily destroyed due to a configuration change or the need to free device resources for other processes and recreated at some later time, the system preserves the bundle and passes it to the **onCreate()** method for initialization. The second step is to add a code which reads from a bundle into our **onCreate()** implementation:

```kotlin
override fun onCreate(savedInstanceState: Bundle?) {

    ...

    clearText()
    savedInstanceState?.let {
        txtResult.text = it.getString("currentText")
      lastResult = it.getSerializable(::lastResult.name) as BigDecimal
        lastOp = it.getSerializable(::lastOp.name) as OpKind?
        waitingNextOperand = it.getBoolean(::waitingNextOperand.name)
    }
}
```

An argument passed to **onCreate()** may be null. This happens when the bundle is absent; for example, if the activity has started for the first time.

Note that only serializable values may be stored in a bundle. If you need to preserve some non-serializable object, you need to either make it implement the Serializable interface, or refrain from writing it to bundle directly and take an alternative approach such as converting it to some serializable data holder or preserving the original object by parts.

One more thing worth mentioning is that bundles are only suited for preserving relatively small amounts of transient data because their serialization occupies the main thread and consumes the memory of the system process. For other cases, it's recommended that you use the local storage such as user preferences or the SQLite database.

The **onCreate()** and **onSaveInstanceState()** methods are special cases of the so-called *lifecycle callbacks* which are invoked by the Android OS when an activity transitions to a new state from the lifecycle's view. For example, the Resumed state is associated with an activity running in the foreground, the Paused corresponds to an activity which is moved to the background but remains visible to the user, while the Stopped state means that an activity becomes completely invisible.

The overridden versions of lifecycle callbacks *must* invoke inherited implementations as well because they contain a common code necessary for the proper functioning of the activity.

IDE Tips: Android Studio includes an inspection which reports an error if you override the lifecycle callback without calling the inherited method (as shown in *Figure 15.13*):

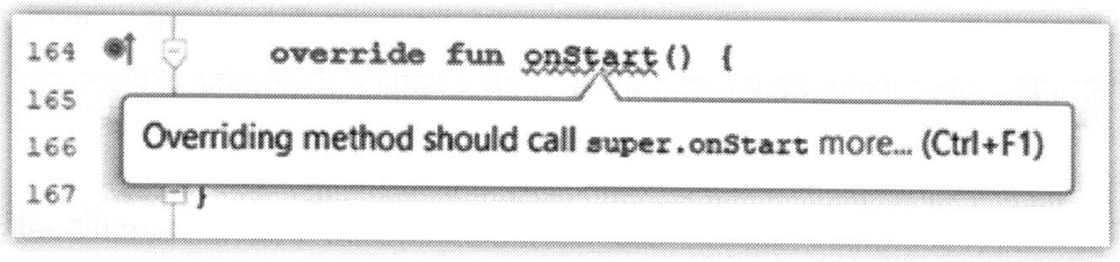

```
164    override fun onStart() {
165
166         Overriding method should call super.onStart more... (Ctrl+F1)
167    }
```

Figure 15.13: Error on absent super call

Conclusion

In this chapter, you learned how to use basic features of the Android Studio IDE and created your first Android application using Kotlin language. We introduced you to a concept of Android activity, got a taste of the UI layout description, and demonstrated how view binding can help you in writing UI-related Kotlin code.

In the next chapter, we will touch upon the topic of developing Web applications using the Ktor framework. We'll talk about basic Ktor features, project setup, and using a routing mechanism for handling client requests. We will also take a look at DSL aimed at generation of HTML content.

Questions

1. Describe the project setup in Android Studio.

2. Describe the use of Gradle for project configuration in Android Studio. How do you add a new dependency?

3. How do you configure a virtual device for running applications?

4. What is an activity? How do you describe an UI of an Android application?

5. Explain the view binding mechanism. What are the advantages of view binding as compared to accessing view components using findViewById()?

7. How do you save/restore an activity state when it gets temporarily destroyed?

CHAPTER 16

Web Development with Ktor

In this chapter, we'll take a look at basic possibilities of Ktor, a Kotlin framework with a purpose to simplify the development of connected systems composed of various client and server applications such as browsers, mobile clients, web applications, and services. Being an extension of the Coroutines library, Ktor offers you powerful and easy-to use facilities for asynchronous communication. This is certainly not meant to be an exhaustive treatment of Ktor capabilities, so in the scope of our book, we'll limit this discussion to a small set of features related to web applications, especially their server-side part: dispatching client requests, obtaining request data, and composing various kinds of responses. The readers are encouraged to continue their acquaintance with Ktor from its official website https://ktor.io and other resources.

Structure

In this chapter, we will cover the following topics:

- Setting up a Ktor project
- Server features
- Client features

Objective

After reading this chapter, the reader will learn the basic features of using Ktor for client- and server-side development of web applications.

Introducing Ktor

In this section, we'll take a quick glance at Ktor and walk through the basic steps required for setting up a project in IntelliJ IDEA. To simplify the process, you can make use of a special IntelliJ plugin which adds Ktor support to the project wizard, as shown in *Figure 16.1*:

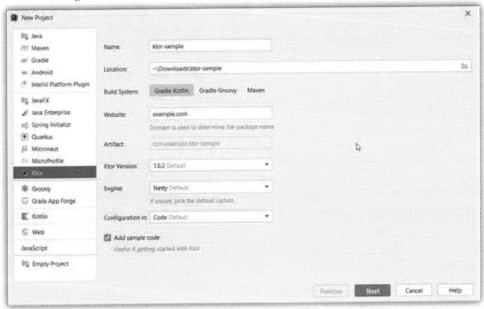

Figure 16.1: Installing the Ktor plugin for IntelliJ IDEA

Note that unlike most plugins for Web/J2EE-development, Ktor doesn't require the Ultimate edition and can be used in the IDEA Community as well. After installing the plugin and restarting the IDE, choose **File | New | Project...** and select the Ktor option in the **New Project** dialog box. Besides the basic client/server functionality, Ktor provides a set of pluggable *features* which require dependencies on additional artifacts and/or some configuration code. The Ktor project wizard allows you to choose features to be included to generate code for both client- and server-side applications (see *Figure 16.2*):

Figure 16.2: Ktor project wizard

For our example, we'll choose the HTML DSL option in the **Server** column which gives us the ability to generate the HTML markup using a simple Kotlin DSL.

Besides specific features, Ktor also allows you to choose a project build system (such as Gradle or Maven), type of an HTTP server engine (Netty/Jetty/Tomcat/ Coroutine-based) and a framework version. Our project will be Gradle-based and use Ktor 1.2.3 with Netty engine. After making sure that all options are set correctly, click on Next.

In the dialog box that follows, the IDE will ask you to fill basic information necessary for building project artifacts (group/artifact ID and version). You can leave these values as is and click on **Next**.

In the last step, choose a project name and location and click on **Finish**. The IDE will then proceed with the generation of project sources and open a new project on completion. After that, you'll be presented with the **Import Module from Gradle** dialog where you can set up basic options for Gradle/IntelliJ interoperability. For now, let's choose the **Use default gradle wrapper** option and leave all other settings as is. After you click on **OK,** the IDE will start the process of synchronization with the Gradle project model. Once it completes, you'll be able to see the following files in the IDE Project View (*Figure 16.3*):

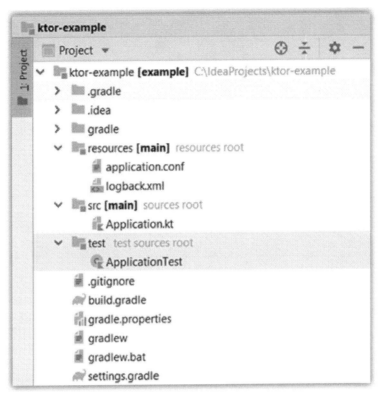

Figure 16.3: *Structure of a sample Ktor project*

Note the **application.conf** file in the resources folder. This file contains the configuration of your server application in a HOCON (Human-Optimized Config Object Notation) format. In our case, it specifies the server port number and a list of modules composing our application:

```
ktor {
    deployment {
        port = 8080
        port = ${?PORT}
    }
    application {
        modules = [ ch16.demo.ApplicationKt.module ]
    }
}
```

Detailed information about HOCON and supported configuration options can be found on the Ktor site at https://ktor.io/servers/configuration.html.

The Ktor *module* is basically an extension function of the **Application** class which is responsible for configuring features, handling client requests, and other server tasks. Modules to load must be specified by their qualified names in the server configuration file. Our sample project contains a single module implemented in the **Application.kt**:

```
package ch16.demo


import io.ktor.application.*

import io.ktor.client.HttpClient

import io.ktor.client.engine.apache.Apache

import io.ktor.html.respondHtml

import io.ktor.http.ContentType

import io.ktor.response.respondText

import io.ktor.routing.*

import kotlinx.html.*


fun main(args: Array<String>): Unit =
    io.ktor.server.netty.EngineMain.main(args)


@Suppress("unused") // Referenced in application.conf
@kotlin.jvm.JvmOverloads
fun Application.module(testing: Boolean = false) {
    routing {
        get("/") {
            call.respondText(
                "HELLO WORLD!",
                contentType = ContentType.Text.Plain
            )
        }

        get("/html-dsl") {
            call.respondHtml {
                body {
```

```
                    h1 { +"HTML" }
                    ul {
                        for (n in 1..10) {
                            li { +"$n" }
                        }
                    }
                }
            }
        }
    }
}
```

The **main()** function which is also defined in this file simply starts the chosen HTTP server engine (in our case, it's **Netty**) which then reads **application.conf** and loads the server module represented by the **Application.module()** function.

The module body contains the routing block which sets up rules for handling client requests based on their URL path. In particular, when a client application (for example, web browser) accesses the root path of our server, Ktor invokes the following handler:

```
call.respondText(
    "HELLO WORLD!",
    contentType = ContentType.Text.Plain
)
```

This code generates the HTTP response with a plain-text message for the body. If you compile and start the server application and then open **localhost:8080** in some browser, you'll see something similar to *Figure 16.4*:

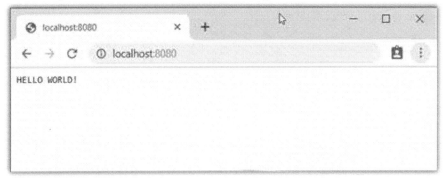

Figure 16.4: *Accessing root path of "Hello, World" application in browser*

Similarly, the **/html-dsl** path shows an example of generating a server response using the HTML DSL library. This DSL allows you to present the HTML markup in the form of nested blocks corresponding to different HTML tags. As you've probably guessed, the following handler generates the HTML page with level-1 heading and a bullet list of numbers:

```
call.respondHtml {
    body {
        h1 { +"HTML" }
        ul {
            for (n in 1..10) {
                li { +"$n" }
            }
        }
    }
}
```

Figure 16.5 shows the result of rendering the DSL code into an HTML page:

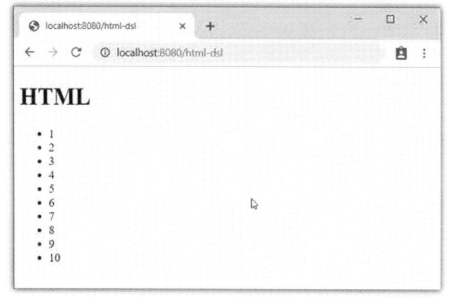

Figure 16.5: *HTML response associated with /html-dsl path*

In the upcoming section, we'll take a closer look at both HTML DSL and routing rules as well as some other server features of Ktor.

The IDE-generated project also includes a sample server test. Let's open the **ApplicationTest** class:

```
package ch16.demo

import io.ktor.http.*
import io.ktor.server.testing.*
import kotlin.test.*

class ApplicationTest {
    @Test
    fun testRoot() {
        withTestApplication({ module(testing = true) }) {
            handleRequest(HttpMethod.Get, "/").apply {
                assertEquals(HttpStatusCode.OK, response.status())
                assertEquals("HELLO WORLD!", response.content)
            }
        }
    }
}
```

This code configures the test application for running with a given set of modules (note the use testing = true argument which allows the module code to distinguish test and production environments) and then checks the results of handling the simple HTTP request to the root path. You can use this class as a starting point for writing your own tests covering various aspects of the server behavior.

As an alternative to an IntelliJ plugin, you can make use of the online project generator available at https://start.ktor.io. The generator UI allows you to specify the same basic options, including a set of client/server features you'd like to use in your application. After you click on the **Build** button, the backend will suggest you to download an archive file containing a generated project. *Figure 16.6* shows an example:

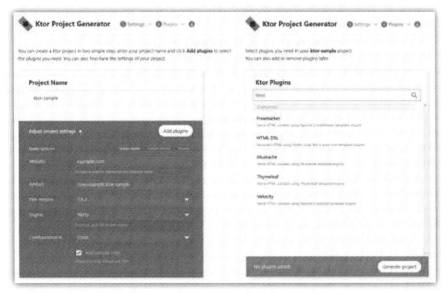

Figure 16.6: Ktor project wizard at start.ktor.io

This concludes our introduction to the basic project setup. In the upcoming sections, we'll focus on specific features provided by both client- and server-sides of the Ktor framework.

Server features

In this section, we'll consider a few topics regarding the development of web server applications. Most of the Ktor functionalities are organized as a set of pluggable features which can be configured by the call of the **install()** method which takes a feature object and an optional configuration block. For example, to enable compression of the outgoing content, you can add the following code to the module function:

```
install(Compression)
```

If you want to specify additional (feature-specific) options such as choose a compression method, you may do so in the configuration block:

```
install(Compression) {
    gzip()
}
```

The examples in this chapter use an embedded HTTP server which allows them to run as a standalone program. In many cases, though, you may need to deploy the Ktor application in the context of some web/application container such as Apache Tomcat, Docker, or Google App Engine. To install your application, you'll need to assemble an archive which contains application classes together with all its dependencies and prepare container-specific configuration files. A discussion on container-specific details is beyond the scope of this book, but you can find detailed instructions on the official Ktor site at https://ktor.io/servers/deploy.html.

Routing DSL

The routing feature allows you to implement a structured handling of HTTP requests based on the hierarchical system of pattern matchers. The routing configuration is expressed by a special DSL inside the feature installation block:

```
fun Application.module() {
    install(Routing) {
        // routine description
        get("/") { call.respondText("This is root page") }
    }
}
```

Or a **routing()** block which serves as a shorthand for the corresponding **install()** call:

```
fun Application.module() {
    routing {
        get("/") { call.respondText("This is root page") }
    }
}
```

The simplest routing scenario is given by the **get()** function which tells the server to execute a given handler for any HTTP GET request with a given URL path prefix. For example, the preceding code responds with a plain text string to the GET request at the site root while requests to any other path on the same site or with any other HTTP verb will result in 404 (see an example in *Figure 16.7*):

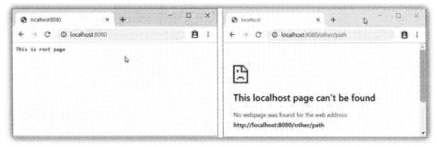

Figure 16.7: Results of get("/") routing

Ktor supports similar routing functions for all HTTP verbs, including **post()**, **put()**, **delete()**, **patch()**, **head()**, and **options()**.

Paths mentioned in routing functions may use *parameters* which match the specific segment of the request path and can be retrieved later from the application call. To introduce a parameter, you just need to enclose its name in braces. For example, consider the following:

```
routing {
    get("/hello/{userName}") {
        call.respondHtml {
            body {
                h1 { +"Hello, ${call.parameters["userName"]}" }
            }
        }
    }
}
```

The routing will match any URL which starts with **/hello/** and contains exactly two segments. Note that the parameter by itself can match just one segment so paths like **/hello** or **/hello/John/Doe** will remain unmatched (as shown in *Figure 16.8*):

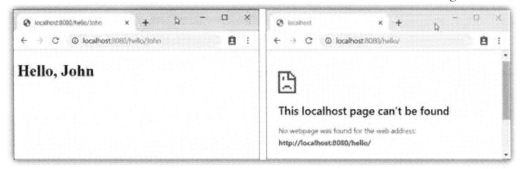

Figure 16.8: Matching by a single-segment path parameter

If the parameter value is not really used, you can replace it by a * character (wildcard):

```kotlin
routing {
    get("/hello/*") {
        call.respondHtml {
            body {
                h1 { +"Hello, World" }
            }
        }
    }
}
```

The preceding routing accepts the same set of paths as the previous one without capturing any parameters.

If you want to introduce an optional parameter which may match an empty path segment, just add **?** to its name, as shown here:

```kotlin
routing {
    get("/hello/{userName?}") {
        val userName = call.parameters["userName"] ?: "Unknown"
        call.respondHtml {
            body {
                h1 { +"Hello, $userName" }
            }
        }
    }
}
```

Figure 16.9: Optional matching

The routing will accept both **/hello/John** and **/hello** URLs as shown in *Figure 16.9*:

The tailcard... placed after the parameter name will match all URL segments at the path end. In this case, you can make use of **getAll()** methods of the the Parameters class to obtain all captured segments split into a List. Let's for example create a simple service which performs basic arithmetic operations on integer numbers and accepts input data in the form of URL paths such as **/calc/+/123/456**:

```kotlin
routing {
    get("/calc/{data...}") {
        val data = call.parameters.getAll("data") ?: emptyList()
        call.respondHtml {
            body {
                h1 {
                    if (data.size != 3) {
                        +"Invalid data"
                        return @h1
                    }
                    val (op, argStr1, argStr2) = data
                    val arg1 = argStr1.toBigIntegerOrNull()
                    val arg2 = argStr2.toBigIntegerOrNull()
                    if (arg1 == null || arg2 == null) {
                        +"Integer numbers expected"
                        return @h1
                    }
                    val result = when (op) {
                        "+" -> arg1 + arg2
                        "-" -> arg1 - arg2
                        "*" -> arg1 * arg2
                        "/" -> arg1 / arg2
                        else -> null
                    }
                    +(result?.toString() ?: "Invalid operation")
                }
            }
        }
    }
}
```

```
        }

}
```

You can see some of its results in *Figure 16.10*. Note that tailcard accepts zero-length path tails so **/calc** is handled as well. The special {...} tailcard accepts the path tail but similarly to * doesn't capture any parameters.

Figure 16.10: Tailcard matching

Note that tailcards must be placed at the end of the routing path, since it'll remain unmatched otherwise.

Besides **get()**-like functions which match the entire URL path, Ktor allows you to define a routing tree matching subsequent portions of the URL and/or various request data. Consider the following example:

```
routing {
    method(HttpMethod.Get) {
        route("user/{name}") {
            route("sayHello") {
                handle {
                call.respondText("Hello, ${call.parameters["name"]}")
                }
            }
            route("sayBye") {
                handle {
                call.respondText("Bye, ${call.parameters["name"]}")
                }
            }
        }
```

```
    }
}
```

When the server receives an HTTP request, it starts looking for a matching routing rule starting from the tree root. In our case, the root node is **method(HttpMethod. Get)** which matches any request with the GET verb. If the client request satisfies this condition, the server goes down the tree and checks the **route("user/{name}")** rule which accepts URLs with a given path prefix. If the path fits, the server goes deeper and checks one of the **route("sayHello")** and **route("sayBye")** rules which check the remaining portion of the URL path. At the lowest level, we have the **handle()** blocks which generate the response provided that all rules on the corresponding branch are matched.

Note that the HTTP verb can be specified in the **route()** call without the explicit use of the **method()** function. The **get()** function we've seen earlier is basically a shorthand for the top-level **route()** block with a handler. For example, the code:

```
routing {
    get("/hello/{userName}") {
        call.respondText("Hello, ${call.parameters["userName"]}")
    }
}
```

Is equivalent to:

```
routing {
    route("/hello/{userName}", HttpMethod.Get) {
        handle {
            call.respondText("Hello, ${call.parameters["userName"]}")
        }
    }
}
```

The **route()** and **method()** are not the only matchers at your disposal. There are additional builders as well:

- **header(name, value):** This accepts requests with a specific header.
- **param(name, value):** This accepts requests with a specific parameter value.
- **param(name):** This accepts requests which have a parameter with a specific name and captures its value.

- **optionalParam(name):** This accepts an optional parameter with a given name.

In the following example, we choose a response based on the value of the **action** parameter:

```
routing {
    route("/user/{name}", HttpMethod.Get) {
        param("action", "sayHello") {
            handle {
                call.respondHtml {
                    body { h2 { +"Hello, ${call.parameters["name"]}" } }
                }
            }
        }
        param("action", "sayBye") {
            handle {
                call.respondHtml {
                    body { h2 { +"Bye, ${call.parameters["name"]}" } }
                }
            }
        }
    }
}
```

Figure 16.11 demonstrates the results:

Figure 16.11 Matching by request parameter

The Ktor API allows you to create your own matchers, thus extending routing DSL. To do this, you need to provide an implementation of the **RouteSelector** class and add the corresponding builder function.

Handling calls

In this and the next sections, we'll demonstrate basic capabilities of request/response processing in Ktor. We've already seen various examples of a simple response generation via **responseText()** or **respondHtml()** inside a routing handler. Consider, for example, the following code:

```
routing {
    get("/") { call.respondText("This is root page") }
}
```

The call property available inside this handler is an instance of **ApplicationCall** which basically combines an incoming request with a response to be composed. A common case is building a response based on a text which is handled by the **responseText()** function. In the preceding example, we're sending a simple plain-text body, but you can also specify the body MIME type by using the **contentType** parameter as in the following code:

```
call.respondText("<h2>HTML Text</h2>", ContentType.Text.Html
```

Which sends an HTML-based response. As an alternative, the response text can be provided by a suspending lambda:

```
call.respondText(ContentType.Text.CSS) { "p { color: red; }" }
```

You can also compose the body text using **PrintWriter**:

```
call.respondTextWriter(ContentType.Text.Html) {
    write("<head><title>Sample page</title><title>")
    write("<body><h2>Sample page</h2></body>")
}
```

To send an arbitrary binary data, you can use the **respondBytes()** function which takes **ByteArray** instead of a String:

```
get("/") {
    val data = "<h2>HTML Text</h2>".toByteArray()
    call.respondBytes(data, ContentType.Text.Html)
}
```

The **respondFile()** function can be used to transfer a file from the server to a client:

```
get("/{fileName}") {
    val rootDir = File("contentDir")
    val fileName = call.parameters["fileName"]!!
    call.respondFile(rootDir, fileName)
}
```

In addition to the body, you can set a response header data by using the call.response property:

- **status(code: HttpStatusCode):** This sets the HTTP response status.
- **header(name: String, value: String):** This appends the given header to the HTTP response.

Ktor supports automatic redirection responses with status **301** ("**moved permanently**") or **302** ("**moved temporarily**"):

```
routing {
    get("/") {
        call.respondRedirect("index")
    }
    get("index") {
        call.respondText("Main page")
    }
}
```

To access a request parameter, you can use the **request.queryParameters** object which serves as a kind of map from parameter names to their values:

```
routing {
    // e.g. /sum?left=2&right=3 responds with 5
    get("/sum") {
      val left = call.request.queryParameters["left"]?.toIntOrNull()
      val right = call.request.queryParameters["right"]?.toIntOrNull()
        if (left != null && right != null) {
            call.respondText("${left + right}")
        } else {
            call.respondText("Invalid arguments")
        }
```

```
        }
}
```

When a parameter is used more than one time, the **get()** function only returns its first value. The **getAll()** function, on the contrary, returns a complete list of parameter values in the form of **List<String>**:

```
routing {
    // e.g. /sum?arg=1&arg=2&arg=3 responds with 6
    get("/sum") {
        val args = call.request.queryParameters.getAll("arg")
        if (args == null) {
            call.respondText("No data")
            return @get
        }
        var sum = 0
        for (arg in args) {
            val num = arg.toIntOrNull()
            if (num == null) {
                call.respondText("Invalid arguments")
                return @get
            }
            sum += num
        }
        call.respondText("$sum")
    }
}
```

Similarly, you can use **request.headers.get()** and **reqiest.headers.getAll()** to obtain values of the request header data.

HTML DSL

The HTML DSL library together with the Ktor HTML builder allow you to generate a response based on the HTML content. This gives an alternative to techniques like JSP which embed executable code into the UI markup. With HTML DSL, you have both a concise syntax and all the benefits of a Kotlin code, including type safety and powerful IDE code insight. In this section, we won't discuss any details of the DSL library and simply focus on an example using it to compose HTML forms. For more information, we relegate the reader to the HTML DSL website at https://github. com/Kotlin/kotlinx.html.

Let's create a simple web application for generating random numbers. Our server will present a page with a form where a user can enter the desired range and a number of values to generate as shown on the Figure 16.12. The server will also perform a basic validation of input data ensuring that:

- all values are valid integers
- "From" bound is less than or equal to "To" bound
- the "How many" field contains a positive number

When some of the preceding requirements are violated on the form submission, the server will return the form back to the client with error message(s) beside the corresponding text field(s).

Here is the complete text of our server application:

```kotlin
package com.example


import io.ktor.application.*
import io.ktor.html.respondHtml
import io.ktor.routing.*
import kotlinx.html.*
import kotlin.random.Random


fun main(args: Array<String>): Unit =
    io.ktor.server.netty.EngineMain.main(args)


private const val FROM_KEY = "from"
private const val TO_KEY = "to"
private const val COUNT_KEY = "count"
private const val GENERATE_KEY = "generate"


private suspend fun ApplicationCall.randomGeneratorForm() {
    respondHtml {
```

```kotlin
val parameters = request.queryParameters

val isGenerate = parameters.contains(GENERATE_KEY)
var from: Int? = null
var to: Int? = null
var count: Int? = null

val errors = HashMap<String, String>()

if (isGenerate) {
    from = parameters[FROM_KEY]?.toIntOrNull()
    to = parameters[TO_KEY]?.toIntOrNull()
    count = parameters[COUNT_KEY]?.toIntOrNull()

    if (from == null) {
        errors[FROM_KEY] = "An integer is expected"
    }
    if (to == null) {
        errors[TO_KEY] = "An integer is expected"
    } else if (from != null && from > to) {
        errors[TO_KEY] = "'To' may not be less than 'From'"
    }
    if (count == null || count <= 0) {
        errors[COUNT_KEY] = "A positive integer is expected"
    }
}

fun FlowContent.appendError(key: String) {
    if (!isGenerate) return
    errors[key]?.let { strong { +" $it" } }
}
```

```
head { title("Random number generator") }
body {
    h1 { +"Generate random numbers" }
    form(action = "/", method = FormMethod.get) {
        p { +"From: " }
        p {
            numberInput(name = FROM_KEY) {
                value = from?.toString() ?: "1"
            }
            appendError(FROM_KEY)
        }
        p { +"To: " }
        p {
            numberInput(name = TO_KEY) {
                value = to?.toString() ?: "100"
            }
            appendError(TO_KEY)
        }
        p { +"How many: " }
        p {
            numberInput(name = COUNT_KEY) {
                value = count?.toString() ?: "10"
            }
            appendError(COUNT_KEY)
        }
        p { hiddenInput(name = GENERATE_KEY) { value = "" } }
        p { submitInput { value = "Generate" } }
    }
    if (isGenerate && errors.isEmpty()) {
        h2 { +"Results:" }
        p {
            repeat(count!!) {
```

```
                                +"${Random.nextInt(from!!, to!! + 1)} "
                            }
                        }
                    }
                }
            }
        }
```

```
@Suppress("unused") // Referenced in application.conf
fun Application.module() {
    routing {
        get("/") { call.randomGeneratorForm() }
    }
}
```

Note the **form()** block inside the **body()**: this call defines an HTML form and introduces a scope where you can add input components such as text fields and buttons. The `action` argument specifies the target URL where the form data is sent to.

HTML DSL provides a whole set of functions for creating all basic kinds of input components such as:

- **input():** A general-purpose text field.
- **passwordInput():** A text field for entering passwords.
- **numberInput():** A text field for numeric values with next/prior buttons.
- **dateInput()/timeInput()/dateTimeInput():** Specialized text fields for entering date and time.

fileInput(): A text field with the browse button for uploading a local file.

The **submitInput()** call creates a Submit button which packs the form data into an HTTP request and sends it to the server.

If you look at the source of the page rendered in a browser, you'll be presented a markup similar to the following code:

```
<!DOCTYPE html>
<html>
  <head>
```

```
    <title>Random number generator</title>
  </head>
  <body>
    <h1>Generate random numbers</h1>
    <form action="/" method="get">
      <p>From: </p>
      <p><input type="number" name="from" value="200"></p>
      <p>To: </p>
      <p>
        <input type="number" name="to" value="100">
        <strong> 'To' may not be less than 'From'</strong>
      </p>
      <p>How many: </p>
      <p>
        <input type="number" name="count" value="-10">
        <strong> A positive integer is expected</strong>
      </p>
      <p><input type="hidden" name="generate" value=""></p>
      <p><input type="submit" value="Generate"></p>
    </form>
  </body>
</html>
```

It's not hard to see a direct correspondence between HTML tags and DSL blocks in the server code. Just like with the Anko layout, we can easily refactor and reuse this UI code which would've been noticeable harder if we'd decided to keep it as a HTML file resorting to JSP or some template engine like Velocity to provide dynamic content.

Figure 16.12: Showing error messages

Error: Reference source not found shows generation results after submitting the form in a browser:

Figure 16.13: Form with generation results

The HTML DSL can also be used separately from the Ktor HTML builder library. In this case, you'll need to include a dependency on the DSL artifact itself. In Gradle, for example, this amounts to adding into the corresponding **dependencies** block:

```
compile "org.jetbrains.kotlinx:kotlinx-html-jvm:0.6.12"
```

If your project doesn't use an external build system like Gradle or Maven, you can add HTML DSL support by configuring a new library in the Project Structure dialog box (similar to how we've done it with the Coroutines library in *Chapter 13, Concurrency*).

Besides HTML, Ktor supports some popular template engines such as Velocity, Thymeleaf, and Mustache. You can find detailed information and examples on the Ktor website.

Sessions support

Ktor comes with a built-in support of the *session* mechanism which allows a web application to persist some data between different HTTP requests and identify a particular client or user. User preferences, shopping cart items, and authorization data are common cases of information which can be kept in a session.

To use a session, you need to install a corresponding feature and specify how you want to store its data. For example, to keep a session inside a client cookie you can write:

```
install(Sessions) {
    cookie<MyData>("my_data")
}
```

The MyData here is a class which represents a session data: its instances can be accessed on the server side using **ApplicationCall** and automatically serialized/deserialized when communicating with the client. The default serializer can handle classes with properties of simple types like Int or String but you can override it by creating your own implementation of SessionSerializer and providing it in the **install()** block. The **my_data** value serves as a cookie key which distinguishes **MyData** instances from other sessions installed in the server.

Let's consider an example which renders a simple HTML page and can track the number of times it's been visited by a particular client:

```
package ch16.sessionDemo

import io.ktor.application.*
import io.ktor.html.*
import io.ktor.response.*
import io.ktor.routing.*
import io.ktor.sessions.*
```

```kotlin
import kotlinx.html.*

fun main(args: Array<String>): Unit =
    io.ktor.server.netty.EngineMain.main(args)

data class Stat(val viewCount: Int)

private const val STAT_KEY = "STAT"

private suspend fun ApplicationCall.rootPage() {
    val stat = sessions.getOrSet { Stat(0) }
    sessions.set(stat.copy(viewCount = stat.viewCount + 1))
    respondHtml {
        body {
            h2 { +"You have viewed this page ${stat.viewCount} time(s)" }
                a("/clearStat") { +"Clear statistics" }
        }
    }
}

@Suppress("unused") // Referenced in application.conf
fun Application.module() {
    install(Sessions) {
        cookie<Stat>(STAT_KEY)
    }

    routing {
        get("/") {
            call.rootPage()
        }
        get("/clearStat") {
            call.sessions.clear(STAT_KEY)
```

```
            call.respondRedirect("/")
        }
    }
}
```

It's reasonable to keep session instances immutable because the server usually runs in a multi-threaded environment so keeping session states in mutable objects can lead to error-prone code. Instead you can read and replace the session as a whole by using the **get()/set()** functions. The **getOrSet()** allows you to initialize the session it doesn't yet exist.

If you run the application and open **localhost:8080** in your browser, you'll see that the view count increases each time a page is refreshed. *Figure 16.11* shows results of four updates in a row:

Figure 16.14: Using session data to track page view count

Clicking on the **Clear statistics** link forces the server to remove the session data, thus resetting the count back to zero. Note the **responseRedirect()** call at the end of **/clearStat** handler; it's needed to render the page again after the session is cleared.

As an alternative to cookies, you may also store sessions in the header of HTTP requests and responses:

```
install(Sessions) {
    header<MyData>("my_data")
}
```

Ktor sessions can be stored at either the client or server side. By default, all session data is transferred to the client who keeps them and sends it back with a next request. This may pose a security issue since the built-in serializer represents the session data as a plain text. To overcome this problem, Ktor provides a *session transformer* mechanism which implements additional encoding/decoding of the transferred data.

One of the built-in transformers, **SessionTransportTransformerMessage Authentication** accompanies the session data with their hash computed according to a specific algorithm (SHA256 by default). In a simplest case, you just need to provide a secret key:

```
install(Sessions) {
    cookie<Stat>(STAT_KEY, SessionStorageMemory()) {
        val key = Random.Default.nextBytes(16)
    transform(SessionTransportTransformerMessageAuthentication(key))
    }
}
```

The original session data remains unchanged so the third party can still view them on the client-side. They, however, won't be able to change the session data without the server's consent because that would invalidate the digest and computing a new one relies on the knowledge of a secret key.

A stronger security guarantee is given by **SessionTransportTransformerEncrypt** which encrypts the session data preventing their read by a third party. To configure this transformer, you'll need to provide both an encryption and authentication key (the latter is used to create a digital signature of the session data):

```
install(Sessions) {
    cookie<Stat>(STAT_KEY) {
        val encryptionKey = Random.Default.nextBytes(16)
        val signKey = Random.Default.nextBytes(16)
        transform(SessionTransportTransformerEncrypt(encryptionKey,
        signKey))
    }
}
```

It's also possible to add your own transformer by the implementing **Session TransportTransformer** interface.

By default, both the **cookie()** and **header()** blocks configure client-side sessions. In this case, all session data is stored on the client-side and transferred to/from the server with each request/response. Alternatively, you can configure a session storage which tells Ktor to store the session body on the server side and transfer only session IDs:

```
install(Sessions) {

    cookie<Stat>(STAT_KEY, SessionStorageMemory())

}
```

SessionStorageMemory is a built-in implementation which keeps the session data in a server memory. Note that memory consumption grows with a number of active clients so server-side sessions are worth being kept as compact as possible.

This concludes an overview of basic features available to server applications of Ktor. In the next section, we'll focus on the other side of communication and look at using Ktor for programming HTTP clients.

Client features

Ktor is not limited to writing server applications and can be used to greatly simplify the development of asynchronous clients communicating with various services. In this section, we'll focus on a small subset of its features centered on the **HttpClient** class which allows you to communicate with web servers using the HTTP protocol.

Requests and responses

The simplest way to issue an HTTP request via **HttpClient** is to use its generic **get()** method and pass a target URL. The method type arguments determine what kind of object is returned by the client to represent the server response. For example, to obtain a response body as a single piece of text you may use **get<String>()**:

```
import io.ktor.client.HttpClient

import io.ktor.client.request.get

import kotlinx.coroutines.runBlocking


enum class DayOfWeek {
    SUNDAY,
    MONDAY,
    TUESDAY,
```

```
        WEDNESDAY,
        THURSDAY,
        FRIDAY,
        SATURDAY
}


fun main() {
    runBlocking {
        HttpClient().use {
          val url = "http://worldtimeapi.org/api/timezone/Europe/
          London.txt"
            val result = it.get<String>(url)
            val prefix = "day_of_week:"
            val from = result.indexOf(prefix)
            if (from < 0) return @runBlocking
            val to = result.indexOf('\n', from + 1)
            if (to < 0) return @runBlocking
            val dow =
                result.substring(from + prefix.length, to).trim().
                toInt()
            println("It's ${DayOfWeek.values().getOrNull(dow)} in
            London!")
        }
    }
}
```

Besides string representation, we can access the response body using the binary form by converting it to a byte array:

```
val bytes = client.get<ByteArray>(url)
```

Or obtaining an asynchronous **ByteReadChannel**:

```
val channel = client.get<ByteReadChannel>(url)
```

Request-making methods of **HttpClient** are suspending functions and thus must be called in some coroutine context. That's why we've used the **runBlocking()** in the preceding examples. In general, you're free to use any of asynchronous computation primitives offered by the Kotlin coroutines.

Note also that `HttpClient` requires explicit finalization via the **close()** method. When its scope is limited, though, we can hide its call behind the **use()** block which is similar to how we do it with any other instance of the **Closeable** type.

As you've probably guessed the **get()** method directly corresponds to the HTTP GET. The Ktor client provides similar shorthands for all methods supported by the HTTP 1.x/2.x standard: **post()**, **put()**, **delete()**, **patch()**, **head()**, **options()**.

These methods accept an optional lambda of **HttpRequestBuilder.() -> Unit** type where you can configure additional request parameters such as adding headers or body. To add a header, you can use the headers method defined in **HttpRequestBuilder**:

```
client.get<ByteArray>(url) {

    header("Cache-Control", "no-cache")

}
```

Or the methods of **HeadersBuilder** available via the headers property or its namesake block:

```
client.get<ByteArray>(url) {

    headers {

        clear()
        append("Cache-Control", "no-cache")
        append("My-Header", "My-Value")

    }

}
```

HttpClient provides a simplified way to supply the User-Agent header which allows the server to identify the client software (such as a web browser and its particular version). To do that, you just need to install the **UserAgent** feature and specify the header value using the agent property:

```
val client = HttpClient(Apache) {

    install(UserAgent) {

        agent = "Test Browser"

    }

}
```

You can also use one of the predefined User-Agent settings:

- **BrowserUserAgent():** This includes popular browsers like Chrome or Safari.
- **CurlUserAgent():** This corresponds to the Curl agent.

The preceding functions replace the entire feature installation block. For example:

```
val client = HttpClient() {
    BrowserUserAgent()
}
```

To supply a request body, (for example, for a POST request) you can use the body property of **HttpRequestBuilder**. The simplest case is writing a String representation:

```
client.get<String>(url) {
    body = "my_key1=my_value1&my_key2=my_value2"
}
```

Alternatively, you can supply any implementation of **OutgoingContent** such as **TextContent** which is similar to writing a String but additionally allows you to specify a MIME type, **ByteArrayContent** which is useful to pass binary data, **LocalFileContent** which allows you to transfer a file, and so on. Additionally, by installing the **JsonFeature,** you can enable automatic serialization of arbitrary objects in a JSON form.

The **submitForm()** function implements a common scenario by imitating the behavior of HTML forms. For example, the following code submits the form data for the server application we've demonstrated in the "HTML DSL" section:

```
val result = client.submitForm<String>(
    url = "http://localhost:8080",
    encodeInQuery = true,
    formParameters = parametersOf(
        "from" to listOf("0"),
        "to" to listOf("100"),
        "count" to listOf("10"),
        "generate" to emptyList()
    )
)
```

The parameters are passed as a set of key-value pairs while the **encodeInQuery** argument determines their representation as a part of request data:

- **true:** HTTP GET with parameters encoded in the request URL

- **false:** HTTP POST where parameters passed in the request body

The Ktor client comes with an out-of-the-box support of HTTP redirects. This feature is installed by default so whenever server sends back a response with a redirect status, the client automatically follows a new location.

Cookies

If the HTTP server uses cookies to preserve some data between client calls – in particular to maintain a user session – the client has to arrange proper storage of such data and provide them with HTTP requests. Ktor simplifies this task by providing the ready-to-use cookies feature. To demonstrate its usage, let's write a simple client for the view counter application we discussed in the server section (see *Figure 16.14*):

```
package com.example


import io.ktor.client.HttpClient
import io.ktor.client.engine.apache.Apache
import io.ktor.client.features.cookies.HttpCookies
import io.ktor.client.request.get
import kotlinx.coroutines.*


fun main() {
    HttpClient(Apache) {
        install(HttpCookies)
    }.use { client ->
        runBlocking {
            repeat (5) {
                val htmlText = client.get<String>("http://localhost:8080")
                val from = htmlText.indexOf("<h2>")
                val to = htmlText.indexOf("</h2>")
                if (from < 0 || to < 0) return @runBlocking
```

```
        val message = htmlText.substring(from + "<h2>".length, to)
            println(message)
            delay(500)
        }
    }
  }
}
```

As you can see our client retrieves the root-path (**/**) response, finds a header enclosed inside a **<h2>** tag, and prints it to the standard output. Note the **install(HttpCookies)** call which configures **HttpClient** to handle cookies. Since the request/response cycle is repeated five times (each time with an updated cookie), the output will look as follows:

```
You have viewed this page 0 time(s)
You have viewed this page 1 time(s)
You have viewed this page 2 time(s)
You have viewed this page 3 time(s)
You have viewed this page 4 time(s)
```

By default, the HTTP client starts with empty cookies and uses data provided by the server passing them together with a next request. This corresponds to a typical browser behavior. Sometimes, though, you may need to send a request with a preconfigured set of cookies without getting them from the server – say, to use them in a test case which verifies a server response. In this case, you may change a cookies storage policy by changing the storage property to **ConstantCookiesStorage** and supplying a set of Cookie objects. The client will then ignore any new cookies sent back by the server and add the same data to each request. To see this feature in action, we'll need to run a plain-text version of our server without any cookies transformations. Now, change **client** definition to the following:

```
val client = HttpClient(Apache) {
    install(HttpCookies) {
        storage = ConstantCookiesStorage(Cookie("STAT",
        "viewCount=%23i2"))
    }
}
```

It's not hard to see that this cookie forces the `viewCount` variable to take the value of 2. As a result, when we rebuild and run the client application the server will simply repeat the same response five times:

```
You have viewed this page 2 time(s)

You have viewed this page 2 time(s)

You have viewed this page 2 time(s)

You have viewed this page 2 time(s)

You have viewed this page 2 time(s)
```

The default behavior where cookies are automatically taken from the server is given by the `AcceptAllCookiesStorage` class. You can add your own storage policy by implementing the `CookiesStorage` interface.

Conclusion

This chapter has introduced us to the basic features of the Ktor framework aimed at creating of connected client/server applications. We got an understanding of the basic Ktor project structure and its common features provided for both server- and client-side applications such as handling requests and responses, describing routing rules, and using sessions. The material in this chapter will help you to get a grip on basic ideas in preparation for a more thorough investigation what Ktor can offer to Java/Kotlin developers. We recommend you to start with an official Ktor site (https://ktor.io) and give a special consideration to the "Samples" section at https://ktor.io/samples.

In the next chapter, we'll continue with the connectivity topic and talk about using Kotlin for development of microservices. We'll discuss the basics of the microservice architecture and look at how Kotlin can help us in creating them on the platform of Ktor and Spring Boot.

Questions

1. Describe the basic steps of Ktor project configuration.
2. How do you generate an HTML-based content in Ktor? Explain the basic features of the HTML domain-specific language.
3. How do you extract client-supplied data from HTTP requests?
4. Explain basic ways to generate an HTTP response in Ktor.
5. Describe Ktor routing DSL.

6. How can you add a session support to your web application? Explain differences between client and server sessions.

7. Describe how to build and send an HTTP request using Ktor.

8. How can you access the body and headers of HTTP response using the Ktor client?

9. Describe the client-side use of cookies in Ktor.

CHAPTER 17

Building Microservices

The microservice architecture provides you with a way of building applications which consists of multiple interconnected components aimed at performing fine-grained domain-specific tasks. This architecture contrasts with a more traditional technique of creating a monolithic application which is deployed as a whole. Microservices facilitate modular development by allowing you to physically separate pieces of functionality and ease development, testing, and deployment/update of individual application parts.

In this chapter, we'll explain the basics of microservice architecture as well as its defining principles and look at how Kotlin can help you in the microservice implementation using the example of Spring Boot and Ktor frameworks. The Spring framework is a commonly used tool in the Java world which has a special focus on the Kotlin support in its recent versions while Ktor, we've already discussed in the previous chapter, is specifically targeted at the development of various types of connected applications and makes heavy use of Kotlin features. Having worked through the chapter, you will be able to compose simple services and have the necessary foundation for further learning of more specific microservice frameworks.

Structure

In this chapter, we will cover the following topics:

- The microservice architecture
- Introducing Spring Boot
- Microservices with Ktor

Objectives

After reading this chapter, the reader will be able to understand the fundamental principles of the microservice architecture and learn the basics of creating microservices with Spring Boot and Ktor frameworks.

The microservice architecture

The big idea of the microservice architecture is to replace a monolithic application – deployed and delivered as a whole – by a set of lightweight loosely-coupled services; each having a specific task and communicating with other services using well-defined protocols.

To give a more specific example, suppose that we want to build an online store-like application which provides users with basic set of features like browsing goods catalog and making orders. By following a monolithic application approach, we might come up with a design similar to the one shown in *Figure 17.1*:

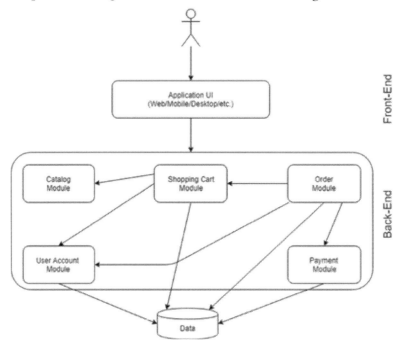

Figure 17.1: A monolithic application example

This is a common three-level architecture which includes separate layers for the application UI (be it a desktop, web, or mobile client), business logic, and data storage/retrieval. The back-end part of the application which is responsible for implementing its domain-specific workflows can be decomposed into more specific modules such as providing access to the catalog, maintaining user's shopping cart, placement/tracking/cancellation of orders, payments as well as authentication, and user profile management. Note that although modules themselves might be loosely-coupled, they are not usually distributed or deployed independently making the server application a monolith.

This approach, however, can pose certain problems as the application grows. Any change in the codebase be it an implementation of some new feature or a bug fix requires you to update/redeploy the entire application which increases its startup time and introduces an opportunity for new bugs. This also hinders the application scalability. With a monolithic approach, you have to deal with scaling the entire application which is significantly more complicated than scaling specific modules or functions. One more issue to consider is reliability since running all back-end modules under the same process makes your application more vulnerable to possible memory leaks and other kinds of bugs.

A Service-oriented architecture (SOA) mitigates these problems by means of decomposing a monolithic application into a set of self-contained services which can be developed, updated, and deployed largely independently. Microservices can be considered a step in the SOA evolution with the focus on making services as small and simple as possible; although in practice, both terms are often used as synonyms.

If we try to break down our original monolithic application design, we might end up with something resembling *Figure 17.2*:

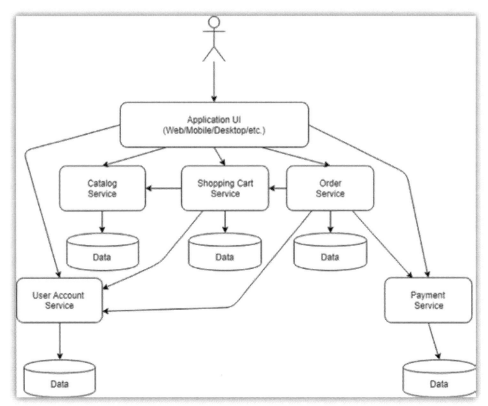

Figure 17.2: A microservice architecture

You can see that the original modules are replaced with services which perform the same functions and communicate with each other using some kind of network protocol like HTTP. Now, individual services can be developed, updated, and configured more or less independently from each other. They may also use separate databases which might even be managed by a different DBMS.

Although microservices lack a rigorous definition, all their practical implementations are based on a common set of principles:

- Each microservice is focused on performing some domain-specific task such as managing goods catalog or user's shopping cart in our e-commerce application example.

- Microservices communicate using some well-defined protocol which effectively establishes their API. A common case involves using HTTP combined with XML and JSON formats for transferring complex data as well as **RPC (remote procedure call)**-based protocols.

- Microservices can be independently versioned, deployed, and updated.

- Microservices are language-and framework-agnostic, which means that, in general, you can implement them in any programming language you deem fit for the purpose and use any development framework of your choice. All that matters is a communication protocol your service will use for interacting with others.

This should give you a basic understanding of what a microservice architecture is and in what cases you might want to employ it in your application. Later, we'll demonstrate how a microservice programming may look in the context of the Kotlin language. It will provide a foundation for your own investigation of more specific technological stacks and frameworks such as Spring, Netflix, or Ktor.

Introducing Spring Boot

Spring is one of the most frequently used Java framework which provides a rich set of facilities for building various applications with a primary focus on the J2EE platform. In this chapter, we'll talk about using a powerful Spring/Kotlin combination for development of microservices using the example of a Spring Boot project. In general, Spring Boot is a collection of utilities simplifying the setting up of various Spring project types and the framework configuration. Similarly, we'll start with guiding you through basic steps required for creating a Spring Boot microservice.

Setting up a project

One of the easiest ways of starting a Spring application is to use a special web tool called Spring Initializr to automatically generate a project skeleton based on the chosen application type. To make use of this tool, open https://start.spring.io in your browser (see *Figure 17.3*):

Figure 17.3: Using Spring Initializr to generate a new project

This page allows us to choose a set of basic options which determine the type of project the Initializr will generate:

- A build system type (Maven/Gradle) that will be used to configure and build a project from sources; for example, we'll use Gradle as it gives you a more flexible and concise way to adjust the project configuration.

- The primary language of a new project which initializer will use to generate a sample source code (Kotlin in our case). This will also affect the project configuration as using Kotlin, for example, will require some additional dependencies in Maven/Gradle build files.

- Version of Spring Boot to use: We'll choose the latest release version of Spring at the time of writing the book, which is 2.1.8.

- Project group and artifact ID which define its Maven coordinates for artifact publication.

Additionally, you may use the `Dependencies` field to specify some common packages to be included into our project. Since our services will use HTTP, we'll need the web support. Type `Web` in the field and choose the **Spring Web** option in the suggestion list.

After choosing all the necessary options, click on the **`Generate the project`** button and download a ZIP file containing an initializer-created project. To open the project in an IntelliJ IDEA, you need to do the following:

1. Unpack the archive to some local directory.

2. Call the **`File | New | Project`** from **`Existing Source...`** menu command and specify the path to the unpacked project root as well as a build system kind (Gradle).

3. Wait until the IDE finishes its synchronization with the Gradle build model after which you'll see a project structure similar to the one in *Figure 17.4*:

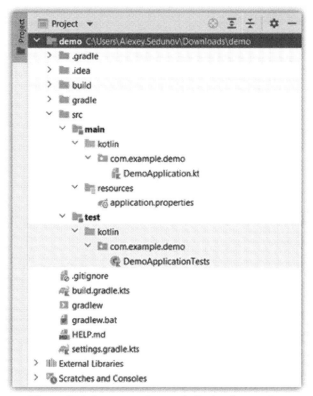

Figure 17.4: *Structure of a sample Spring Boot project*

Similarly, in a project generated by the Ktor wizard, the **build.gradle.kts** file will contain the definition of project dependencies. Note down the **.kts** extension. It means that the buildfile is written in Kotlin rather than Groovy. For this reason, the script follows a slightly different syntax than the ones we've seen in Ktor and Android examples:

```
import org.jetbrains.kotlin.gradle.tasks.KotlinCompile

plugins {
    id("org.springframework.boot") version "2.1.7.RELEASE"
    id("io.spring.dependency-management") version "1.0.8.RELEASE"
    kotlin("jvm") version "1.3.41"
    kotlin("plugin.spring") version "1.3.41"
}

group = "com.example"
```

```
version = "0.0.1-SNAPSHOT"
java.sourceCompatibility = JavaVersion.VERSION_1_8

repositories {
  mavenCentral()
}


dependencies {
  implementation("org.springframework.boot:spring-boot-starter-web")
  implementation("com.fasterxml.jackson.module:jackson-module-kotlin")
  implementation("org.jetbrains.kotlin:kotlin-reflect")
  implementation("org.jetbrains.kotlin:kotlin-stdlib-jdk8")
                                              testImplementation(
            "org.springframework.boot:spring-boot-starter-test"
  )
}


tasks.withType<KotlinCompile> {
  kotlinOptions {
    freeCompilerArgs = listOf("-Xjsr305=strict")
    jvmTarget = "1.8"
  }
}
```

You might want to make some adjustments such as upgrading the Kotlin version to a more recent one before proceeding. Just like with any other Gradle project, IDEA will suggest you to resynchronize a project model on any change in the **build. gradle** file (unless you have auto import switched on, in which case synchronization starts up automatically).

The **application.properties** file contains various properties (in a simple **key=value** format) affecting the Spring behavior. By default, it's empty but later, we'll use it to change the port our service will listen.

The entry point of our project is defined in the **DemoApplication.kt** file which contains the definition of the **DemoApplication** class and the **main()** function delegating the application start-up to the framework:

```
package com.example.demo

import org.springframework.boot.autoconfigure.SpringBootApplication
import org.springframework.boot.runApplication

@SpringBootApplication
class DemoApplication

fun main(args: Array<String>) {
  runApplication<DemoApplication>(*args)
}
```

The **runApplication()** function will create the **DemoApplication** instance as well as automatically instantiate and wire all services required for our application. For a web application with a default configuration like ours, it also starts a bundled Tomcat server which is going to handle client requests dispatching them to the Spring-supplied servlet. The **DemoApplication** instance will serve as a global context which can be injected into other application components when necessary. Note the **@SpringBootApplication** annotation; this is handy shortcut which allows you to configure a given class as a Spring application context.

After the application is started (you use the **Run** command from IDEA main menu to do this), we can access it using an HTTP client such as a web browser. Since our application doesn't contain the actual request processing code yet, the Spring servlet will response with a standard error page on every request we make. *Figure 17.5* shows you an example:

Figure 17.5: Default response page provided by the Spring framework

Note that Spring uses the **8080** port to listen to the client requests unless it's explicitly changed in the `application.properties` file.

IDE Tips: There are plugins which add the Spring support to IntelliJ IDEA and, in particular, allow one to generate various Spring-powered projects similar to the Initializr tool. Note, however, that these plugins are not available in the IDEA Community Edition. IDEA Ultimate, on the other hand, has them bundled out of the box.

In the upcoming sections, we'll use this project stub as a base for creating sample microservices. But the first thing we have to do before getting to the actual coding is to define what our services will do and how they will communicate with their clients. To demonstrate a common practice of implement microservices as small web applications, we'll use HTTP as a base of our example communication protocol.

Deciding on the Services API

In this chapter, we'll walk you through a simple example of designing a pair of communicating services. The first service will be similar to a random number generator we've demonstrated in *Chapter 16, Web Development with Ktor,* but will have a more formalized input and output to be usable in the form of API. When given a request with the URL of the form:

`/random/int/from/X/to/Y/quantity/N`

It will produce a list of N random numbers in the range between X and Y (both inclusive). The result will be given as a JSON object with a pair of fields:

- **status:** A string which contains an error message or null in case of successful completion.
- **values:** An array of generated integers (empty when the status signifies an error).

Possible cases of error status:

- Non-integer values for X, Y or N
- Non-positive N
- $Y<X$

Let's give some examples of the expected service output for a given URL:

URL example	Service response
/random/int/from/10/to/20/ quantity/5	{"status":null, "values":[16,17,18,17,12]}
/random/int/from/20/to/10/ quantity/5	{"status":"Range may not be empty", "values":[]}
/random/int/from/10/to/20/ quantity/-1	{"status":"Quantity must be positive", "values":[]}
/random/int/from/1X/to/20/ quantity/5	{"status":"Range start must be an integer", "values":[]}

Table 17.1: Examples of number generator output

Another function of our service will be generation of floating-point numbers. We'll use a URL of the following form:

/random/float/quantity/N

This URL will get the service to produce N double precision numbers in the range between 0 and 1 (excluding 1).

The second service will provide a similar API for generating random passwords. Given a URL of the form:

/password/length/L/quantity/N

It will produce N alphanumeric strings each having length L. The password generator will use the same output format; the only difference being that the values field will be an array of strings rather than numbers.

URL example	Service response
/password/length/8/ quantity/5	{"status":null, "values":["B0zDWtvG","JrSkXl7X", "oDwR7cp2","X8sRfzDW","nUcRXzn1"]}
/password/length/bbb/ quantity/5	{"status": "Length must be an integer", "values":[]}
/password/length/-1/ quantity/ccc	{"status": "Length must be positive", "values":[]}
/password/length/8/ quantity/-5	{"status": "Quantity must be positive","values":[]}

Table 17.2: Examples of password generator output

To demonstrate service communication, we'll make a password generator which depends on the numeric one. When requested for a new password(s), it will call the number generator first to produce a series of random indices which are then turned to characters and joined together to produce strings.

Now that it's clear how our service API will look, we can get to the actual implementation. We'll start with the random number generator since it's going to be used by another service.

Implementing a random generator service

Let's set up a new Spring Boot project for our generator service following the steps from the *Setting up a project* section. The service entry point will become largely unchanged. In our case, it'll be enough to rename the application class and package:

```
package com.example.randomGen


import org.springframework.boot.autoconfigure.SpringBootApplication
import org.springframework.boot.runApplication


@SpringBootApplication
class RandomGenerator


fun main(args: Array<String>) {
  runApplication<RandomGenerator>(*args)
}
```

Before writing the actual business logic of the service itself, we need to define classes which hold up the data we're going to pass around in a JSON form. Since our service input consists of primitive values passed in the URL path, the only structured data is its output. That's exactly the job for a Kotlin data class:

```
package com.example.randomGen


data class GeneratorResult<T>(
  val status: String?,
  val values: List<T>
)
```

```
fun <T> errorResult(status: String) =
  GeneratorResult<T>(status, emptyList())
fun <T> successResult(values: List<T>) =
  GeneratorResult<T>(null, values)
```

The pair of utility functions, **errorResult()** and **successResult()**, will come in handy to simplify the construction of **GeneratorResult** in the service code.

The core logic of service is implemented in the so-called controller class which handles processing of client requests. To convert a given class into the Spring controller, you just need to annotate it with **@RestController**. Spring will automatically load the class and create its instance during component scanning. We won't discuss the scan process in detail here, but you can find them in the Spring framework documentation (see, for example, the **@ComponentScan** annotation).

The stub of our controller class will therefore look like this:

```
package com.example.randomGen


import org.springframework.web.bind.annotation.*


@RestController
class RandomGeneratorController
```

To define a request handler, we mark the controller's methods with special annotation which associate them with specific request attributes. For example, the **@RequestMapping** annotation allows you to bind a method to requests with a particular URL:

```
@RequestMapping("/hello")
fun hello() = "Hello, World"
```

Similarly, in Ktor, you can use wildcards like ***** and parameter names to define path templates. In the following example, the last portion of the URL path gets automatically bound to the method parameter marked with the **@PathVariable** annotation:

```
@RequestMapping("/hello/{user}")
fun hello(@PathVariable user: String) = "Hello, $user"
```

Method parameter names may differ from variables you use in the path template; in this case, you need to specify the path parameter as the **@PathVariable** argument:

```kotlin
@RequestMapping("/sum/{op1}/{op2}")
fun hello(
  @PathVariable("op1") op1Str: String,
  @PathVariable("op2") op2Str: String
): Any {
val op1 = op1Str.toIntOrNull() ?: return "Invalid input"
val op2 = op2Str.toIntOrNull() ?: return "Invalid input"
  return op1 + op2
}
```

Apart from the URL path, the **@RequestMapping** annotation allows you to associate handlers based on various request data such as the HTTP method (GET, POST, and so on), content of headers and request parameters. Similarly, there are some alternatives to **@PathVariable** you can use to bind method parameters to request parameters (**@RequestParam**), request headers (**@RequestHeader**), session data (**@SessionAttributes**), and so on. The mapping options are quite similar to the routing mechanism of the Ktor; although in the case of Ktor, it's specified as a piece of ordinary Kotlin code rather than some metadata in an annotation form. We won't delve into the details here but interested readers can find relevant documentation on the Spring site at **docs.spring.io**.

When several methods of the controller share a common path prefix, it may be convenient to add **@RequestMapping** to the controller class as well. In this case, paths mentioned in the method-level annotations are defined relative to the class one. For example, instead of writing:

```kotlin
@RestController
class SampleController {
  @RequestMapping("/say/hello/{user}")
  fun hello(@PathVariable user: String) = "Hello, $user"


  @RequestMapping("/say/goodbye/{user}")
  fun goodbye(@PathVariable user: String) = "Goodbye, $user"
}
```

We can extract the common /say part into the SampleConroller's annotation:

```kotlin
@RestController
```

```kotlin
@RequestMapping("/say")
class RandomGeneratorController {
  @RequestMapping("hello/{user}")
  fun hello(@PathVariable user: String) = "Hello, $user"


  @RequestMapping("goodbye/{user}")
  fun goodbye(@PathVariable user: String) = "Goodbye, $user"
}
```

Keeping this in mind, let's implement the controller method which will take care of **/random/int** paths according to our service API:

```kotlin
@RequestMapping("/int/from/{from}/to/{to}/quantity/{quantity}")
fun genIntegers(
  @PathVariable("from") fromStr: String,
  @PathVariable("to") toStr: String,
  @PathVariable("quantity") quantityStr: String
): GeneratorResult<Int> {
  val from = fromStr.toIntOrNull()
    ?: return errorResult("Range start must be an integer")
  val to = toStr.toIntOrNull()
    ?: return errorResult("Range end must be an integer")
  val quantity = quantityStr.toIntOrNull()
    ?: return errorResult("Quantity must be an integer")
  if (quantity <= 0) return errorResult("Quantity must be positive")
  if (from > to) return errorResult("Range may not be empty")
  val values = (1..quantity).map { Random.nextInt(from, to + 1) }
  return successResult(values)
}
```

Handling of floating-point numbers corresponding to the **/random/float** paths can be done in a similar way. The full source text of this service can be found at **https://github.com/bpbpublications/Kotlin-In-Depth/ch17/number-gen-service**.

If we start our application and try to access the service via a browser, we'll get an expected response. You can see an example of getting a list of random numbers in

Figure 17.6:

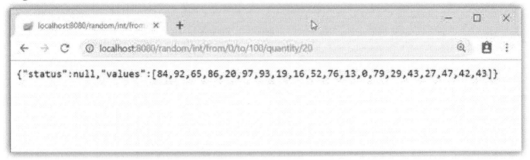

Figure 17.6: *An example of success response*

You can also make sure that our service can correctly handle common errors in client requests. For example, *Figure 17.7* shows the result you get when requesting numbers in the range from 50 to 20:

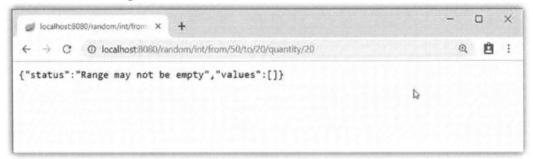

Figure 17.7: *Generator responding with an error*

As expected, the service responds with an error indicating that the specified interval is empty since its upper bound is less than the lower one.

Implementing a password generator service

Now, we can easily implement a second password-generating service using the first as the starting point. Let's create a similar Spring Boot project placing our code into the **com.example.passwordGen** package.

The crucial difference from the random number generator is that the second service will have to communicate with the first one. Spring comes with out-of-the-box **RestTemplate** class which simplifies making requests to other web applications and retrieves their responses. For example, the code:

```
val url = "http://localhost:8080/random/int/from/0/to/10/quantity/5"

val restTemplate = RestTemplate()

val result = restTemplate.getForObject(url, GeneratorResult::class.
```

java) as GeneratorResult<Int>

Will return a result containing a list of five random integers in the range between 0 and 10.

Let's now use this idea to transform numbers into password characters. Here is the full text of a password generator controller class:

```
package com.example.passwordGen


import org.springframework.web.bind.annotation.*
import org.springframework.web.client.RestTemplate


private val chars = ('a'..'z') + ('A'..'Z') + ('0'..'9')


@Suppress("unused")
@RestController
@RequestMapping("/password")
class PasswordGeneratorController {
  @RequestMapping("/length/{length}/quantity/{quantity}")
  fun genPasswords(
    @PathVariable("length") lengthStr: String,
    @PathVariable("quantity") quantityStr: String
  ): GeneratorResult<String> {
    val length = lengthStr.toIntOrNull()
      ?: return errorResult("Length must be an integer")
    val quantity = quantityStr.toIntOrNull()
      ?: return errorResult("Quantity must be an integer")
    if (quantity <= 0) return errorResult("Quantity must be positive")
    val prefix = "http://localhost:8080/random/int"
    val url = "$prefix/from/0/to/${chars.lastIndex}/quantity/$length"
    val restTemplate = RestTemplate()
    val passwords = (1..quantity).map {
      val result = restTemplate.getForObject(
        url, GeneratorResult::class.java
```

```
    ) as GeneratorResult<Int>
    String(result.values.map { chars[it] }.toCharArray())
  }
  return successResult(passwords)
 }
}
```

Note that the password generator service will need the definition of the **GeneratorResult** class to represent both its own response and the number generator. For a simple case like this, we can just copy this definition to our second project. In more complex scenarios with a multitude of classes to represent the request/response data, it may be worth using some code sharing; we could've, for example, set up a multi-module project which includes both services and a separate module for the shared classes or extracted shared code into a separate project whose output is published into some artifact repository and then used as a dependency in both services.

Since both our services are running as standalone applications, they'll have to listen on different ports. So, before running the password generator service, make sure that its port doesn't conflict with the first one. For this example, we'll set it to **8081** by changing **application.properties** to:

```
server.port=8081
```

Now, we can start the second service and try to make use of its functionality by querying a URL of the form **localhost:8081/password/length/12/quantity/10**. When processing such a URL, our password service will make multiple requests to the random number generator and use its response to compose a list of passwords. *Figure 17.8* shows an example result of accessing the password service via a browser:

Figure 17.8: An example of a password generator response

Note that the password service makes a sequence of requests which are then processed synchronously:

```
val passwords = (1..quantity).map {
  val result = restTemplate.getForObject(
    url, GeneratorResult::class.java
  ) as GeneratorResult<Int>
  String(result.values.map { chars[it] }.toCharArray())
}
```

In other words, the service thread becomes blocked each time you call the **getForObject()** methods and is unable to do any useful work until it gets all expected responses. This may hinder the service scalability when a number of simultaneous requests grow, so in general we might need to use some asynchronous programming technique such as the Kotlin Coroutines library or reactive frameworks like RxJava or Akka.

With Ktor, as we'll see in the following section, this problem is largely mitigated by the fact that the framework is already built on top of the Coroutines library and provides out-of-the-box support of asynchronous computations via suspending functions. Let's see how our password generator service might look like when implemented using Ktor facilities.

Microservices with Ktor

In the previous chapter, we introduced you to the Ktor framework which simplifies the development of connected client/server applications. In the remaining sections, we will extend our knowledge by showing you how Ktor can be used to easily implement a microservice.

The section is composed of two parts. In the first one, we'll introduce one more Ktor feature which deals with JSON-based object serialization both on the client and server sides. This feature allows you to automatically convert Kotlin objects into the corresponding JSON description on sending as well as restore them from JSON on receiving, which is similar to how the Spring framework does that in our earlier example.

In the second part, we'll re-implement the password generator service using the Ktor API. This will allow you to compare Ktor features with their Spring counterparts (for example, routing DSL vs request mapping annotations) and also serve as a demonstration of how microservices powered by different frameworks are able to seamlessly communicate with each other.

Using the JSON serialization feature

In the previous chapter, we saw examples of sending plain text responses using Ktor's **respondText()** function. Although, we certainly can use it for composing JSON, Ktor provides an easier solution with the **ContentNegotiation** feature which allows you to configure converters for serializing arbitrary objects. In general, to use it for a particular MIME type, you need to register the corresponding implementation of the **ContentConverter** interface which handles send/receive operations. Ktor comes with an out-of-the-box support of three basic serialization mechanisms:

- `Jackson library (https://github.com/FasterXML/jackson)`

- `google-gson library (https://github.com/google/gson)`

- `kotlinx.serialization (https://github.com/Kotlin/kotlinx.`
  `serialization)`

In our example, we'll use the Jackson-based implementation. Since the corresponding converter belongs to a separate **io.ktor:ktor-jackson** artifact, make sure you include the necessary dependency in the **build.gradle** file:

```
compile "io.ktor:ktor-jackson:$ktor_version"
```

After that, you can configure the JSON serialization using the **ContentNegotiation** installation block:

```
fun Application.module() {
  ...
  install(ContentNegotiation) {
  jackson()
  }
  ...
}
```

The preceding **jackson()** function associates **JacksonConverter** with the application/json content type and sets the default behavior of output formatting. Serialization covers both request and response data. For example, we can send some objects into the response and they are automatically converted into the JSON text format:

```
call.respond(successResult(listOf("12345678")))
```

Similarly, we can deserialize JSON objects received with a client's request turning them into ordinary Kotlin objects:

```
data class PasswordSpec(val length: Int, val quantity: Int)

...

val spec = call.receive<PasswordSpec>()
```

In our case, though, we'll be receiving JSON data as a response from another service after making the corresponding request; we also have to configure serialization for our **HttpClient** instance. Ktor supports the same three serializer implementations for client applications as well. We just need to add respective dependencies to the service **build.gradle**:

```
compile "io.ktor:ktor-client-json:$ktor_version"
```

```
compile "io.ktor:ktor-client-jackson:$ktor_version"
```

To enable serialization on the client-side, we then install the JsonFeature:

```
val client = HttpClient(Apache) {

  ...

  install(JsonFeature)

  ...

}
```

By default, the particular serializer implementation is chosen automatically based on the included artifact. When necessary, we can also specify it explicitly by assigning an instance of **JsonSerializer** to the serializer property:

```
val client = HttpClient(Apache) {

  ...

  install(JsonFeature) {
    serializer = JacksonSerializer()
  }

  ...

}
```

Having configured **JsonFeature,** we can automatically read our objects from HTTP responses using the **get()** function:

```
val url = "http://localhost:8080/random/int/from/0/to/10/quantity/5"
```

```
val result = client.get<GeneratorResult<Int>>(url)
```

Now that we have automatic serialization at our disposal, let's see how we can use it together with other Ktor features for the actual microservice implementation.

Implementing a password generator service

To demonstrate the difference between the Ktor and Spring approach, we'll re-implement the password generator service. Most of the code will expectedly remain the same as both the implementations will follow the same business logic.

To access our first service, we'll use **HttpClient** instead of **RestTemplate:**

```
val prefix = "http://localhost:8080/random/int"

val url = "$prefix/from/0/to/${chars.lastIndex}/quantity/$length"

val passwords = (1..quantity).map {

  val result = client.get<GeneratorResult<Int>>(url)

  String(result.values.map { chars[it] }.toCharArray())

}
```

Note that unlike our Spring-based example, this code is asynchronous; the **HttpClient.get()** is a suspending function invoked in a Ktor-supplied coroutine context. As a result, the service threads are not blocked and our server can process further requests while waiting for a response from the random number generator.

The Ktor routing DSL will replace the request dispatching based on the Spring's **@RestController/@RequestMapping** annotations:

```
route("/password") {

  get("/length/{length}/quantity/{quantity}") { ... }

}
```

As you can see, the path syntax is basically the same but the use of the DSL allows one to largely eliminate a boilerplate code.

To put our Ktor version of password generator, here is the complete text of the server application module:

```
package com.example


import com.fasterxml.jackson.databind.SerializationFeature

import io.ktor.application.*

import io.ktor.client.HttpClient

import io.ktor.client.engine.apache.Apache

import io.ktor.client.features.json.*
```

```kotlin
import io.ktor.client.request.get
import io.ktor.features.ContentNegotiation
import io.ktor.jackson.jackson
import io.ktor.response.respond
import io.ktor.routing.*

fun main(args: Array<String>): Unit =
  io.ktor.server.netty.EngineMain.main(args)

private val chars = ('a'..'z') + ('A'..'Z') + ('0'..'9')

@Suppress("unused") // Referenced in application.conf
fun Application.module() {
  install(ContentNegotiation) {
    jackson {
      enable(SerializationFeature.INDENT_OUTPUT)
    }
  }

  val client = HttpClient(Apache) {
    install(JsonFeature) {
      serializer = JacksonSerializer()
    }
  }

  suspend fun ApplicationCall.genPasswords(): GeneratorResult<String>
{
    val length = parameters["length"]?.toIntOrNull()
      ?: return errorResult("Length must be an integer")
    val quantity = parameters["quantity"]?.toIntOrNull()
      ?: return errorResult("Quantity must be an integer")
  if (quantity <= 0) return errorResult("Quantity must be positive")
```

```
    val prefix = "http://localhost:8080/random/int"
  val url = "$prefix/from/0/to/${chars.lastIndex}/quantity/$length"
  val passwords = (1..quantity).map {
    val result = client.get<GeneratorResult<Int>>(url)
    String(result.values.map { chars[it] }.toCharArray())
  }
  return successResult(passwords)
}


routing {
  route("/password") {
    get("/length/{length}/quantity/{quantity}") {
      call.respond(call.genPasswords())
    }
  }
}
}
```

Since our original Spring Boot implementation was listening to the port **8081,** we need to make necessary changes in the Ktor version as well by adjusting its **application.conf** file:

```
ktor {
  deployment {
    port = 8081
    port = ${?PORT}
  }
  application {
    modules = [ com.example.ApplicationKt.module ]
  }
}
```

Now, if you start both the number and password generator services and open your browser at **localhost:8081/password/length/12/quantity/10,** you'll see a very similar result to the one shown in *Figure 17.8* (albeit with a different list of passwords). Note that even though the number generator is based on Spring, the password generator now uses Ktor; both services are easily communicating regardless of their implementational differences.

Conclusion

In this chapter, we got a basic understanding of how you can implement a microservice-based application in Kotlin using either Spring or Ktor frameworks. We explained the key ideas of the microservice architecture, walked you through the setup steps of a simple Spring Boot project, and discussed the usage of Spring REST controllers and templates for the purpose of microservice implementation. We also described how to configure and use JSON serialization in Ktor, a feature which is especially useful for web applications providing some formalized API. Starting from these basics, you can now refine your knowledge by referring to additional resources. We recommend you to begin with guides from the spring.io (**https://spring.io/guides**) as well as Ktor samples we've already mentioned in the previous chapter at **https://ktor.io/samples**.

Questions

1. Explain basic principles of the microservice model.
2. Describe basic steps for setting up a Spring Boot project.
3. What is a Spring controller class? Explain how request data are mapped to controller methods.
4. Compare Spring request mapping with Ktor routing.
5. How do you configure JSON serialization in Ktor?
6. Give an example of microservice implementation using both Spring Boot and Ktor.

Index

Made in United States
Troutdale, OR
02/12/2024

17607353R10381